# *The Advanced Measurement Approach to Operational Risk*

# *The Advanced Measurement Approach to Operational Risk*

**Edited by Ellen Davis**

Risk*books*

Published by Risk Books, a Division of Incisive Financial Publishing Ltd

Haymarket House
28–29 Haymarket
London SW1Y 4RX
Tel: +44 (0)20 7484 9700
Fax: +44 (0)20 7484 9800
E-mail: books@incisivemedia.com
Sites: www.riskbooks.com
www.incisivemedia.com



ISBN 1 904339 88 3

British Library Cataloguing in Publication Data
A catalogue record for this book is available from the British Library

Publisher: Laurie Donaldson
Assistant Editor: Lisa Reading
Designer: Rebecca Bramwell

Typeset by Mizpah Publishing Services Private Limited, Chennai, India

Printed and bound in Spain by Espacegrafic, Pamplona, Navarra

# Contents

# About the Editor

**Ellen Davis** is the editor of *OpRisk & Compliance* magazine, based in London. Previously, she was an editor on *Risk* magazine, and the editor of *AsiaRisk* magazine and based in Hong Kong. She originally hails from New York City, where she had a long freelance career during which her work appeared in *Treasury & Risk Management*, *Global Finance*, *BusinessWeek*, *CFO* magazine, and a number of other financial publications. She holds a BA from Wellesley College and an MBA from New York University. Her first book as editor, "Operational Risk: Practical Approaches to Implementation", was published in March 2005 by Risk Books.

# List of Contributors

**Gene Álvarez** is the director for treasury management and controls at Fannie Mae. His responsibilities include span operational risk management, SOX compliance, and anti-fraud management.

With nearly a decade of experience in the financial services industry, he began his career at Bankers Trust, managing the bank's on-line front office trading system and back office reconciliation. Joining Operational Risk Inc. (ORI), Gene built and managed a data information team to research and code historical operational risk loss events found in the public domain. He went onto work at The Bank of Tokyo-Mitsubishi, where he was one of the primary architects of an innovative operational risk management framework that was implemented at BTM.

He has developed models for market, credit and operational risk, as well as an historical market risk VaR Monte Carlo engine, a bond spread Monte Carlo VaR model, an operational risk capital allocation Monte Carlo engine, an alternative investment value-at-risk model, and stress tests for market and operational risks.

Gene holds a PhD in experimental physics from Indiana University.

**Marco Bee** is assistant professor in economic statistics at the University of Trento (Italy). After spending one year as a visiting scholar at the department of mathematics of the Indiana University and receiving a PhD in mathematical statistics from the University of Trento in 1998, from 1999 to 2005 he has held positions at the risk management department of Banca Intesa in Milan, where he has been developing quantitative models in the areas of operational and credit risk. His current research interests focus on quantitative risk management and applied statistics, with particular emphasis on the analysis of the computational aspects of the models.

**Patrik Buchmüller** has a degree in economics from Tübingen University. He has published several papers on Basel II and operational risk during his PhD studies. Patrik has gained practical insight into AMA implementation and operational risk management when working for Bayerische Landesbank between 2002 and 2003. Since then he has been working for Germany's Federal Financial Supervisory Authoriy (BaFin), where he is responsible for the implementation of the OpRisk rules of Basel II. Patrik is member of AIGOR, a subgroup of the Basel Committee.

**Anna Chernobai** is currently completing her PhD thesis on operational risk management at the University of California, Santa Barbara, in the department of statistics and applied probability. Her research interests include risk management, stochastic processes, financial modeling, and heavy-tailed distributions in finance. She is the author of several articles on operational risk and has been a speaker at various conferences and professional meetings. Anna holds her MSc in finance from Warwick Business School, University of Warwick, and BA in economics from Sophia University in Japan.

**Jonathan Davies** is the managing director of the Americas divisions of Risk*Business*. Previously the head of operational risk control for UBS Warburg (UBSW), Jonathan was responsible for the development of the UBSW operational risk management, risk measurement and risk education process. Jonathan was also responsible for the production of cost and efficiency measures including the design and implementation of the UBSW activity-based costing process. He actively represented UBSW to regulators and the industry on the revisions to the regulatory capital framework. He chaired the ISDA working group on operational risk and was a member of the ITWG and the IIF and RMA working groups.

**Ashish Dev** is an executive vice president at KeyCorp. As a member of ALCO and other high-level risk committees of KeyCorp, he is involved in decision making in all areas of risk (enterprise risk) in the bank. Ashish has been an active contributor to deliberations at all levels relating to Basel II. Under his direction, the efforts in operational risk AMA in KeyCorp won an international *Operational Risk Achievement Award in 2005.* Ashish is listed as one of the most published authors amongst cutting-edge papers in *Risk* magazine during the period 1994-2003. Prior to joining KeyCorp, he was head of quantitative research and analysis in Bank One. Ashish has a PhD in economics and holds the CFA professional designation.

**Ana Fernández Laviada** BA (Hons) in management & business administration and BA in economics, is part of the financial accounting and auditing group of the University of Cantabria (UC) in Spain. She received her doctorate in 2003 and her doctoral thesis was awarded by the UC Social Council. Fernández-Laviada is assistant professor at the faculty of business and economics where she teaches on courses in financial accounting and auditing. She has also held several visiting appointments including London School of Economics and Political Sciences, University of Toronto, University of Technology Sydney, University of Berkeley and Harvard University. Ana has received external research grants from the Spanish government, the Marcelino Botín Foundation and the Banco Herrero Foundation. Her research interests include risk management, operational risk, internal and external auditing, internal control and derivatives. She presents her work regularly at conferences in Europe and the

United States. She is currently involved in researching the impact of the latest developments in the area of operational risk management. She is also editing a book on this topic in collaboration with some leading Spanish financial firms.

**Mike Finlay** is the managing director of the Europe, Middle East, Africa and Asia-pacific divisions of Risk*Business*. He has many years experience in banking and finance, having started out pricing equity derivatives on the Johannesburg Stock Exchange. He has been responsible for establishing new business departments in the derivatives area, restructuring international payments businesses, developing regulatory banking law and implementing risk management frameworks in both international banking firms and in large corporates. He also developed the risk management framework for the Bond Market Exchange of South Africa.

**Marcus Haas** has studied mathematics and finance at the University of Darmstadt, Germany. He is currently working as a banking supervisor at Deutsche Bundesbank, where he is involved in the OpRisk rules implementation of Basel II in Germany. Marcus is the author of numerous articles on operational risk and has been an invited speaker to international conferences and expert group meetings.

**Dee Harris** is an operational risk consultant in Wachovia Securities Risk Management Department. In this capacity, she provides operational risk management oversight for Wachovia Securities. Prior to her current position, Dee was part of the Institutional Risk Group and worked to create the operational loss process for the corporation. Her educational background includes a BA from the University of South Carolina and a BS in computer information systems from High Point University.

**Michael Haubenstock** has joined SunTrust Mortgage in Richmond, Virginia, a division of SunTrust Bank, as senior vice president of operational risk management. He is responsible for building and implementing the operational risk framework at the mortgage company and coordinating compliance activities. Previously Michael was director of enterprise risk management at Capital One, where he led the operational risk team and led development of the approach for enterprise risk management. In this role he was responsible for the firm-wide efforts of operational risk self assessment and supporting technologies, the event data base, building key risk indicators and operational risk economic capital. In 2001, he was a partner in the financial risk management practice at Pricewaterhouse-Coopers where he led the practice for operational risk management for financial institutions. He led the global benchmarking study, Operational Risk – The Next Frontier, sponsored by the RMA, BBA and ISDA, and was a driver behind the development of operational risk frameworks and capital models.

**Jeff Hause** is director of operational risk management at Capital One, responsible for the corporate level analysis and reporting of operational risk and operational risk economic capital modelling. In 2005 he led Capital One's global initiative to build an operational loss data collection process. In this role he was responsible for the firm-wide efforts of operational risk loss collection and supporting technologies, consulting with internal divisions on the development of event collection processes. He was part of Internal Audit at Capital One from 1999 to 2002

Jeff previously worked at Wachovia Bank, TransAmerica Insurance, and Springs Industries. He holds a BS from The University of Georgia and a MBA from The College of William and Mary.

**Eric Holmquist** is vice president, director of operational risk management for Advanta Bank Corp. In this capacity, Eric has responsibility for design and oversight of the bank's operational risk management program as a component of the bank's independent Risk Management function. In addition, he serves as the bank's information security officer as well as chair of the bank's MIS Council, its MIS governance body. He also chairs the Operational Risk Management for Information Technology committee through the Risk Management Association based in Philadelphia.

Eric has over 25 years of experience working within the financial services industry in management roles and a prominent industry consultant, author and speaker.

**Rudi De Koker** is managing director and head of global risk analysis within Citigroup Risk Architecture. He leads a team of 25 risk professionals whose responsibilities include the measurement, reporting and analysis of Citigroup's consolidated risk profile across all businesses and regions, as well as the development of operational risk analytics and risk capital allocation methodologies. Rudi is a regular speaker at leading industry conferences and regulatory Basel II forums. Before joining Citigroup, Rudi was a management consultant at McKinsey and Company, specialising in strategy projects for financial institutions, commodity businesses and private equity. Rudi holds a PhD in biophysics from Stanford University, and is located in London.

**Tom Longstroth** is an operational risk consultant in Wachovia's Institutional Risk Group. In this capacity, he provides operational risk management support for the Finance Division, Risk Management Group, and other parent/institutional areas. Prior to his current position, Tom worked at Zions Bancorporation where he helped develop and deploy their operational risk framework and management tools. His educational background includes a BA in accounting and a BS in computer information systems from the University of Utah.

**Tara McLenaghen** is an executive director at Risk*Business*, responsible for North America. Tara has 20 years of experience in financial services, including a variety of roles in business banking, and in operational risk. She was vice president, operational risk at RBC Financial Group from 1999 to 2003, responsible for creating a Basel II compliant operational risk function. Previous industry experience in the field of operational risk also includes work as chair of the Operational Risk Committee of the Canadian Bankers Association, chair of the RMA Operational Risk Council, a founding member of the Working Group on Operational Risk (WGOR), as well as a member of the Institute of International Finance (IIF) Operational Risk Taskforce.

**Francisco Javier Martínez García** is full professor in accounting, head of the Financial Accounting and Auditing Group and vice-rector of personnel at the University of Cantabria (UC) in Spain. Since January 2006, he is the director of the new UC Foundation for the study and research of the Financial System (UCEIF). Francisco has extensive teaching experience in accounting and auditing. At present, he teaches primarily at the postgraduate level, specialising in research in the areas of auditing and banking. Francisco pioneered and established a leading postgraduate program in financial markets and banking sponsored by the Santander Group at UC. He has also established strategic alliances with universities in Mexico and Dominican Republic. He lead the establishment of a master in financial markets and banking in Mexico (he is the director) and he is currently negotiating a similar program in Dominican Republic. His publications cover a wide range of auditing, financial and management accounting issues. He has published 10 books and numerous articles in prestigious accounting journals. In these fields he has presented seminars throughout Spain and South America.

**Christian Menn** is currently a visiting assistant professor in the School of Operations Research and Industrial Engineering at Cornell University. Christian holds a degree in mathematics from the University J. Fourier in Grenoble, France and from the University of Karlsruhe, Germany. In 2004, he earned his doctorate in economics from the school of business engineering at University of Karlsruhe. Christian's research interests include mathematical and empirical finance, applied probability, and risk management.

**Giulio Mignola** has been the group operational risk manager for Sanpaolo IMI Spa since 2004. He joined the operational risk team in 2000 and since then he has been very active in the international community participating in the IIF Working Group for Operational Risk and in the Forum for European Discussion on Operational Risk, of which he was president from 2003 to 2005. He participated actively in the foundation of the Operational Riskdata eXchange Association, in which he represents Sanpaolo IMI in the executive committee. He has a physics education and a PhD in theoretical physics. He also worked in Geneva at CERN from 1994 to 1996.

**Marco Moscadelli** is head of the operational risk team at the Bank of Italy, where he has the responsibility for the implementation of the operational risk legislation and for the validation of the Italian banks' internal models. Inside the Committee of European Banking Supervision (CEBS), he leads the Operational Risk Workstream established at the end-2004. Marco is also member of the AIG Operational Risk subgroup of the Basel Committee. His research focuses on the sensitivity analysis of conventional actuarial distributions and models stemming from the Extreme Value Theory in computing suitable capital figures for operational risk.

**Jeremy Quick** is head of operational risk framework at LloydsTSB. He previously worked at the Bank of England, the IMF and UK FSA.

**Svetlozar T. Rachev** is chair-professor at the University of Karlsruhe in the School of Economics and Business Engineering and professor emeritus at the University of California, Santa Barbara in the department of statistics and applied probability. He has published eight monographs and more than 250 research articles. His research areas include mathematical and empirical finance, econometrics, probability, and statistics. Svetlozar is co-founder of Bravo Risk Management Group specialising in financial risk-management software. Bravo Group was recently acquired by FinAnalytica for which he currently serves as chief-scientist.

**Vandana Rao** is associate professor of economics in the business & economics division of Indiana University East. She is also the coordinator of the online program in business. Her research interests range from applied econometrics to local area business development strategies to corporate finance and financial institutions. She teaches courses in economics, finance and statistics at the undergraduate and graduate levels. Vandana has published several academic papers in reputed journals in economics and higher education pedagogy. She has also won awards for excellence in teaching. Vandana has a PhD in economics.

**Bernd Rummel** has studied business administration at the University of Applied Sciences of the Deutsche Bundesbank. He works as a banking supervisor at Germany's Federal Financial Supervisory Authority (BaFin), where he is responsible for the implementation of the OpRisk rules of Basel II and the corresponding EU-Directives. Bernd is a member of a subgroup of the Committee of European Banking Supervisors.

**Sergio Scandizzo** is head of the operational risk unit at the European Investment Bank in Luxembourg. Prior to his position at the EIB he was senior manager in the London office of PricewaterhouseCoopers and, prior to that, a senior manager in the operational risk group at the Canadian Imperial Bank of Commerce in Toronto. He holds degrees in computer science and finance and is author of several publications on the subjects of fuzzy logic, genetic algorithms and risk management.

**Karsten Stickelmann** has studied mathematics and finance at the University of Marburg, Germany and worked for two public banks before joining the supervision department of Deutsche Bundesbank in 1999. As head of section "Market Risk Models, Operational Risk and IT" he is involved in international and national supervisory and industry working groups, regular meetings with banks and on-site audits. Moreover he is a lecturer in the Bundesbank training program and has been an invited speaker at international and national conferences and seminars.

**Stefan Trück** is a postdoctoral research fellow at the School of Economics and Finance of Queensland University of Technology. He holds a PhD in statistics from the School of Economics and Business Engineering, University of Karlsruhe, Germany. His research areas include mathematical and empirical finance, econometrics and risk management. He has published various articles on credit risk management, operational risk and power markets in leading academic journals. Stefan also has several years of experience as consultant for financial institutions.

**Roberto Ugoccioni** has been a member of the group operational risk management unit at Sanpaolo IMI since March 2005. He is working on the development of the statistical model for the group's operational risks. Prior to his current position, he worked in particle physics phenomenology, acquiring interest and expertise in the statistical analysis of fluctuations and rare events with high severity. He holds a PhD in physics from the University of Torino.

**Duncan Wilson** is an executive director at Risk*Business* responsible for Europe. Duncan has over 20 years finance and risk management experience, starting his career with Touche Ross & Co, where he qualified as a chartered accountant in 1988. Amongst other roles, Duncan headed up the risk management consulting practice in Europe, Middle East and Africa for IBM and was a partner at Ernst and Young in the financial risk management practice, specialising in market and credit risk management. In 2001, he became global head of operational risk management at BNP Paribas, where he implemented the risk management and measurement processes for the Advanced Measurement Approach. Duncan actively participated in the lobbying of supervisors and regulators at the global level through membership of the Institute of International Finance's Working Group on Operational Risk and the Accord Implementation Group.

# Introduction

In the US, there used to be an advertising campaign for an ultra-thin cigarette that was being marketed primarily to women, called Virginia Slims. The ads had what my grandmother would call a "women's lib" theme – usually a woman dealing with a difficult situation involving humorous sexism. But the tagline was so memorable that it became a kind of slang expression in the 1980s – "You've come a long way, baby." Indeed, its cultural cachet was such that Fatboy Slim made an album of that title in the late 1990s.

When I was asked to edit a book on operational risk (OR) modelling, and started asking industry experts to contribute chapters, I was excited by the diversity of subjects and the depth of discussion that the discipline's experts were willing to write about. It was a far cry from three years ago, when I started editing a small newsletter called *Operational Risk*, which focused primarily on the ins and outs of Basel II negotiations. As a discipline, OR has very much arrived.

In short, well, you've come a long way, baby.

For this, I think operational risk executives would be justified in taking some pride. The chapters in this book reflect the practical approach that firms are now taking to tackling the challenge of OR modelling. Gone are the days of fantasies written in the Greek alphabet. What people want to know about is how they are meant to model OR within their firms, in such a way that they are delivering the numbers they need for regulatory approval, and they are also delivering value to their business lines.

As a result, this book is focused firmly on practical solutions to modelling issues. The first section, "The AMA Framework", contains two chapters that outline a general approach to constructing an advanced measurement approach framework within a firm – the basis upon which any op risk model is built. The second section, "Modelling Basics", dives right into the fundamentals of OR modelling with two chapters – one provides some discussion of general concepts as well as a bit of advanced modelling, while the second outlines the mathematical models regularly used to analyse loss data.

The third section – "Modelling Challenges" – contains four chapters that grapple with the way models can be adjusted to overcome limitations in the underlying data. The fourth section "Alternative Modelling Approaches", looks at related qualitative modelling issues such as scenario analysis, key risk indicators (KRIs) and the modelling of less tangible risks, such as technology risk.

The last section, "Comparative Views of Implementation", contains an overview of an OR framework at a US bank, plus two studies on implementation – one in Germany and the other in Spain. These are included to help readers get to grips with how OR frameworks and models are being fashioned in the "real world".

But what this book is *not* is the last word on operational risk modelling. This discipline is far too dynamic, and I think that, although we've come a long way from the dark days when some prominent critics insisted OR couldn't be modelled, we've still got a long road ahead. The lack of data – and the incomplete or damaged nature of the existing data – will provide much grist for quantitative mills over the coming years as firms seek a way around these flaws in their modelling approaches. And at the same time, there is growing interest in incorporating qualitative information in OR models because of the recognition that some operational risks are difficult to quantify. In short, there is much to look forward to from the continued development of this discipline.

Briefly, I'd like to thank all of the authors who contributed – you have all given something important to the development of the discipline and the spreading of the operational risk gospel. I'd also like to thank the Risk Books team, who have been ever so patient with my regular requests for deadline extensions, and provided much-needed support and advice. And, lastly, I'd like to thank my husband, Colin, for making cups of tea, walking the dog and placating the cat while I read chapters.

*Ellen Davis*

# Section One

# The AMA Framework

Although this book is principally about the modelling of operational risk, there is no doubt that, before we rev up the computer software and break out the distribution curves, it's important to consider what kind of advanced measurement approach (AMA) framework your firm will have.

Indeed, after speaking with several executives whose firms were at the forefront of the development of the OR discipline, I realised that this really was the place to start any robust discussion of the modelling of op risk. They all insisted that implementing the Basel II op risk AMA framework should never be a mere compliance exercise for a company – what would be the point of that? Instead, OR executives should look at implementing the AMA within the context of the businesses their firms are in, their management structure and their firms' goals, as well as its challenges to profitability.

Jeremy Quick, in his chapter "The Advanced Measurement Approach – Getting It Started", addresses the fundamental importance of considering OR alongside a firm's business strategy. He talks about the basic infrastructure a firm needs to qualify for the AMA, outside of a robust modelling tool, including business continuity plans, strong internal and external corporate governance frameworks and a robust commitment from senior management and the board of directors to OR measurement and management.

He also gives some general guidelines and advice for constructing an AMA framework, including do's and don'ts.

In the second of the pair of chapters in this section, Michael Haubenstock and Jeff Hause take a more detailed approach to just what an OR manger should consider when thinking about what approaches they want to take to actually model OR. Titled "Practical Decisions to Successfully Model Operational Risk Capital", their chapter provides step-by-step guidance on such important issues as how to select the data to be incorporated into the model, granularity, correlation, and diversification.

Hopefully these two chapters will provide some guidance to the basic questions OR managers should be asking themselves, their senior management and their business partners about the goals of their OR programme and how best to formulate a strategy to achieve them.

# 1

# *The Advanced Measurement Approach – Getting It Started*

**Jeremy Quick***

LloydsTSB

This chapter is about some of the challenges and solutions around starting an Advanced Measurement Approach (AMA) project. Outlined are the general prerequisites of an AMA programme, the reasons why a firm might want to adopt the AMA, and early deliverables. Also discussed are the need to identify benefits and customers, to scope the AMA, and to run it as a project.

## PRELIMINARIES TO THE FRAMEWORK

The AMA needs to be based on a general operational framework. However, although the framework is important, it will only work if (a) it is part of a bigger commitment to effective operational management and (b) if senior management change behaviour on the basis of the new data and opportunities that the framework will supply. Before considering the framework, it is useful to spend some time on (a) and (b).

### (a) The wider context

An AMA programme has to be part of a wider commitment to the good functional management of operational risk (OR). For

*Although I work for LloydsTSB, a UK banking/insurance group, none of this chapter should be taken to reflect the activities or views of the group.

example, any firm looking to qualify for the AMA will need the following:

- tested business continuity and disaster recovery plans;
- an event escalation process and reaction strategy;
- a coherent approach to external fraud;
- appropriate expertise in internal fraud investigation;
- IT security and risk functions;
- a compliance function that understands the risk/reward principle;
- proven engagement with key legal, political and regulatory developments;
- a basic understanding of risk metrics by business owners;
- an informed and supportive senior management;
- joined-up governance, to include the many different owners of OR; and
- linkage to other risk types, for example, many default characteristics are determined by operational risk issues.

The AMA is about more than getting the methodology right. The above need to be in place as prerequisites.

### (b) The need for managerial action

Senior management should be attracted to the AMA because of the commercial benefits it offers. These are as follows:

- better pricing, as the risk of periodic large losses will have been priced into the product or business line;
- less net income volatility, in so far as the risk of large losses has been closed off;
- greater efficiency on the basis that the expected loss level would not be reduced beyond what is cost-efficient;
- fewer losses by taking account of leading indicators;
- a cost-efficient but still effective control framework, thus either reducing the everyday costs of the control framework and increasing business opportunities or, in cases where the current control framework is ineffective, creating a safer operating environment;
- lower costs on the basis that a single business unit can take greater risk at less cost through diversification benefits offered through the group;

- some regulatory capital relief; and
- a better profile with bond and shareholder interests.

In order to achieve these benefits, senior management must be committed to act. It is one thing to create an appropriate framework for OR. It is another to act on it. Management need to be prepared:

- to create an appropriate corporate culture that eschews, for instance, blaming front-line staff for operational errors rather than focusing on likely design and managerial questions;
- to define the business strategy on the basis of long-term profitability, and taking account of OR;
- to shift mitigation resources to be more in line with the risk profile;
- to set tolerance levels around frequent losses appropriate to net profit – that is, less loss is not necessarily the right answer;
- to use the information provided by leading indicators – that is, reducing business volumes or adjusting the control framework;
- to allocate managerial accountability for OR;
- to take action when a manager has agreed controls are adequate when they are in fact either deficient or excessive;
- to close down big risks through mitigation;
- to empower management to see and deal with risk even when it crosses business silos;
- to ensure that operational risk responsibilities are set both horizontally for each business unit and vertically across the group as a whole – this will ensure linkage between group and business unit governance; and
- to secure business transformation such that the level of control is appropriate for the amount of risk that a firm is willing to accept.

It is only through the above means that the benefits of an AMA can be delivered.

## IDENTIFYING THE CUSTOMER

The AMA programme needs to identify its main customers. There are two. The first is the head of a business unit (the MD), together with the various risk owners within the business. The second is group senior management.

The head of a business unit should, if correctly incentivised, want to aim to have an effective control structure on which he can rely. He will also be supportive of setting tolerance levels and key risk indicators. He will therefore welcome an AMA programme, subject to cost, on the basis that the AMA delivers the essential tools for that purpose.

Group senior management will support local business management for the above purposes. However, it has additional aims. It will want to set group-wide tolerance levels and take an aggregate view. For example, it may wish to set tolerance levels for expected and unexpected loss around external fraud. In order for this to be achieved, business units will have to achieve the targets set at group level, to be measured as systemically as the AMA will allow. There are significant challenges here, being:

- ❑ the ability of the methodology to present comparable metrics across business lines and risk types, so as to enable senior management to compare apples with apples;
- ❑ the ability of the IT framework to track these aggregate metrics; and
- ❑ the willingness of senior management to appoint owners of aggregate risk types with the authority to overrule local heads who may be content with the amount of risk in their particular area – this is a real challenge in big firms that pride themselves on delegating authority to local heads or to product line heads.

It is important to recognise that any AMA framework needs both to serve and to link both the above constituencies.

## SCOPING THE AMA

Although the AMA has many common elements, it is advisable to establish some general principles that will shape the AMA in any particular firm. To this end a series of questions need to be posed and answered. These might be as follows:

- ❑ *Is the aim to arrive at a capital calculation alone or should you be more ambitious?* For example, the aim could be to assess such factors as reputation risk or customer service. This will necessitate some kind of soft scoring in the methodology. This is covered in more detail below.
- ❑ *Do you wish to extend the AMA remit?* For example, many of the AMA tools can be applied to non-OR areas – for example credit

controls. Similarly, an AMA programme can be closely linked to the Sarbanes-Oxley programme. A view here is that an Enterprise-Wide Risk Management approach is cost-efficient as it may be able to remove the need to have yet another self-assessment approach for Turnbull requirements. In contrast, linkage with Sarbox at this stage may simply be too challenging.

- *To what extent do you wish to limit the AMA project to a risk assessment or, in addition, specifically extend it to business and process transformation?*
- *How interested are you in covering expected loss?* This will affect the choice of the loss-data base threshold and the granularity of the control self-assessment system. A view here is that it is impossible to limit the AMA to looking at rare but large losses. The reasons for this are that (a) in practice you can engage the firm on a daily basis around the small losses and (b) the same control failures can lead to both small and large losses.
- *Do many people in your firm have a reasonable knowledge of quantitative techniques?* If not, you will need a methodology that keeps the quantitative side at a minimum.
- *Does your firm already have certain aspects of the AMA embedded?* For example, in a firm that already uses economic capital for credit decisions, it should not be too difficult adjusting to the use of the same technique for OR.
- *How closely should the AMA programme be linked with internal audit?* One option here is to keep internal audit at a distance at first in order to encourage business units to be open about control failings; and then bring in internal audit later.
- *How does your firm handle change?* Some firms are hierarchical in decision making but consensus-driven in implementation. Others have different characteristics. This will affect whether you drive the methodology through high-level policies and assurance or through more democratic workshops.

It is only after questions of this nature have been answered that implementation can be planned.

## THE AMA PROJECT

An AMA programme needs to be run just like any other project. It should entail all that a formal project requires in a financial group – a formal mandate (ideally from a board committee), a budget, a timeline, pilots, qualified project managers, a steering committee and so on. An advantage of the project formula is that it takes the AMA outside everyday business. A new infrastructure needs some time to be able to develop without the constraints of everyday business demands. This still allows staged delivery into the business environment.

An inevitable part of an AMA programme is the IT element. In a perfect if imaginary world, every head of OR would want to avoid the problems that every major IT programme brings – for instance, possible misalignment between business requirements and IT design, the length of time it takes to build an IT solution, the cost. However, it is impossible in a big firm to run a sustainable and usable AMA programme through the traditional mixture of Excel and Access spreadsheets. An intranet solution is required not least for immediacy, security and aggregation. The challenge is increased in the AMA world in that there is currently no off-the-shelf vendor solution, although there are increasingly good solutions for different parts of the AMA. Given that very few firms would self-build, the result is the need to customise a vendor offering.

The frustrating element of an AMA project is the length of time it takes. For example consider the number of modules needed, such as the loss-data base, the KRIs, the self-assessment system, the capital calculation. It also has to be closely allied to a detailed training process for those who are going to use the tools, as well as the creation of a training process for those who follow. The main way of shortening the wait is to launch each module as soon as possible after design, if only through an interim solution. Getting the tools quickly and then improving them is better than waiting until their design is perfect.

The relationship with the business units is another challenge. On the one hand, the business units are of course the main customer and their involvement in the design process is key. They alone have the business knowledge to ensure that the design meets business needs. On other hand, they will have their own agenda. In addition, they are unlikely to have the requisite expertise for the AMA – and can therefore slow the programme down while all this is explained.

## SOME AMA OPTIONS

The details of the construction of the AMA framework will differ from firm to firm. However, there are areas where either some firms have created difficulties for themselves or such difficulties are waiting to arise. So, things not to do are the following.

- ❑ Do not adopt the classic audit-driven process mapping solution. This will submerge your firm under a sea of paper as each function tries to map its key processes. This may work for Sarbox and it may in some cases have a roll to play – but do you really want to subject all your operational risks to the "Sarbox treatment"?
- ❑ Do not produce lots of tail estimates for the model via scenarios but at the price of business buy-in. Quality is better than quantity.
- ❑ Do not approach the challenge of "qualitative assessment" by arbitrarily shifting the model curve to the right or left. This lacks credibility.
- ❑ Do not make too much use of the famous traffic-light approach. This has its place but you are supposed to be producing specific loss estimates.

No doubt, as the industry develops, we will learn more about the don'ts of the AMA.

## TOOLS

In order to build an AMA framework, four elements have to be put in place. These are *qualitative adjustment, internal data, external data,* and *scenarios*. Although each of these was established in order to facilitate the capital measurement of operational risk, each has a very immediate business benefit. Some of the more general tools will also be covered – soft scores, capital and management information.

### Qualitative adjustment

In practice, this term means control self-assessment. This has generally won a poor reputation among financial firms. The reason is that it has often been executed at a high level and as a tick-box exercise so as to secure some sort of regulatory compliance – in the UK, for instance, Turnbull.

For the AMA, it is impossible to produce credible numbers around scenarios or expected loss, let alone make some sort of capital adjustment around controls, without a clear and honest understanding of the overall control environment. Although this is not easy, the basis of success is to possess a business-friendly self-assessment mechanism that can be completed without fear but that is assured effectively. There will be a real business demand for such a tool from risk owners and from business heads. Such owners want to able to have an effective tool by which they can examine the effectiveness and efficiency of their controls. It may be that control self-assessment will at last come of age through the AMA. It will not be possible to both fudge control self-assessment and retain AMA status, since the former is the basis for the numbers in the latter.

### Internal data

Internal data compromises many characteristics, but for our current purposes let's restrict it to internal loss data. The collection of internal loss data is a key AMA requirement. The output is also of considerable interest to the firm. In most firms the general ledger will not, for various reasons, be able to supply data on internal losses to the degree of either accuracy or granularity required by the AMA. It is also the case that in most firms, due to the absence of a taxonomy around operational risk, operational losses have been conflated with both credit and business losses. Outside certain well-defined categories such as external fraud, few firms know with a degree of certainty how much they lose on an expected basis due to operational risk. A loss-data base changes that.

The process of collecting loss data by itself has benefits. It forces business to admit process and control failures, rather than hide losses in general cost lines. Only in this way can repeat losses be avoided. Without going into specifics, the AMA also requires a loss-data point to be linked to cause and control failure. Again, this can help ensure non-repetition. Loss data must also be categorised according to an event-driven taxonomy. This will ensure that the firm will be able to develop a risk profile for each event. This will help ensure that the various very different risk profiles of the components of operational risk are treated as appropriate for each. Finally, loss-data collection requires an accurate understanding of the nature of the OR taxonomy and the distinction between direct loss (for which capital has to be held) and other types of loss – for instance, indirect loss. It is only on this basis that the business can produce accurate scenario estimates.

### External data

This AMA component is vital for modelling. However, it too has a qualitative business benefit. Financial firms, especially in the middle-management ranks, have a habit of thinking that they are better than the opposition and that their business and way of doing business is unique. This means that they do not learn enough from the mistakes of their competitors. A well-designed, international, external database can mitigate this in a few minutes. It is especially useful for a UK firm in tracking loss experiences in the US that are likely to migrate in due course to the UK. External data are also a useful starting point for scenarios.

### Scenarios

The main qualitative purpose of scenarios is to give risk owners the opportunity to think outside the box. If properly conducted, they also give risk owners the opportunity to key into expert help outside their area – for example, HR, IT or legal experts. This sort of joined-up thinking continues to be rare, and an annual process to ensure it takes place is no bad thing. Scenarios are important in that they can demonstrate the extent of loss where expected losses are low or negligible. They can therefore provide management with an insight as to where best to place mitigation resources. The key here, of course, is to resolve the tension between the business requirement of scenarios, where the emphasis will be on bad things happening in a lifetime at the most, and the modelling requirements, which aspire to a longer timeframe. The modellers, however, will be able to square this circle. Finally the scenario should be set by the risk owners for their specific circumstances, rather than group-wide, although one refinement is to set group-wide scenario themes (eg, money laundering).

### Soft scores

*Soft scores* means a mechanism whereby the non-capital impact of operational risk is captured. This is not part of the AMA.

However, it is important. Firms will want to allocate resources other than on a strict consideration of capital loss. Indirect loss – that is to say, time wasted – and reputation impact are both relevant considerations. The AMA requires that, in the first instance, we construct a capital estimate that is better than the simplified approaches used so far. If this is difficult, estimating indirect loss is even more difficult. We should therefore start by getting the capital impact nailed down before considering in great detail the non-capital side. However, we still need, on an ongoing basis and using the tools available, to consider indirect loss. Consequently, it is a good idea to introduce, as part of an AMA programme, soft scores that estimate non-capital risk as far as possible. The result will be far less accurate than the direct-loss estimate but it is perfectly possible to envisage an event that will lead to zero direct loss but considerable indirect loss.

### Capital and management information

This chapter is not about the capital estimate of operational risk. However, from the point of view of embedding capital as an incentive of better operational risk management, a few points can be made.

- It helps if the groundwork for business management on capital is already laid by the market or credit experts. Operational risk capital can then just be "slotted in".
- As far as possible, therefore, the methodology for capital estimation should be the same across all risk types.
- The capital number for operational risk for each business or risk type has to be able to be clearly explained to a non-quant. And it has to move in relation to the nature of the business and control environment of each business and risk type.
- It will take a while to arrive at credible capital numbers for operational risk. However, this should not prevent management from acting on them as soon as possible. They may not be perfect first or second time round – but they will be much better than the current information available.

On management information, it is important to distinguish between two types. On the one hand there is the analytical type, which will be of interest to middle management. This can be as extensive as you like. There is then the high-level type, which will be of interest to senior management. This should be very sparse and should move to an exception basis only as quickly as possible.

### Beyond roll-out

All projects face the problem of converting themselves into business-as-usual at some point. This is no different for an AMA programme.

Some of the other major issues not covered here, but are prominent and should be highlighted are:

- how to maintain momentum;
- managing the transition to business-as-usual;
- how to link business practice to the model; and
- how to run a permanent AMA structure.

## CONCLUSION

This chapter has been about starting an AMA programme. The main theme has been about the need to keep in mind and prove the business benefits for the AMA, and to treat it like any other big project. Having started the project, you are, at least and at last, halfway there.

2

# *Practical Decisions to Successfully Model Operational Risk Capital*

**Michael Haubenstock; Jeff Hause***

SunTrust Mortgage; Capital One

When taking on the challenge of quantifying operational risk (OR) capital, there is bad news and good news. The bad news is that there is no "correct" methodology for modelling economic capital. Whatever methodology is chosen, someone will raise issues with the methodology and/or results. For example, they might say the approach does not represent changes in the business or control environment, it does not reflect past loss experience, it may not apportion capital in the ideal manner to business units or products, or the results are too low/high. The good news is that it is hard to prove the results are wrong as long as some basic principles are followed, and in most cases there is not necessarily a better alternative methodology.

The reason for this paradox is that the theory of capital calculation is still advancing, and practices vary widely, even across leading institutions. Putting the theory into practice requires many assumptions and decisions on the theory's application for a given institution at a certain point in time. The purpose of this chapter is to define most of those assumptions and decisions, and provide many of the alternatives to consider. This should prove helpful in either planning a quantification exercise, or to validate a current approach. There is no right answer. Most decisions that each

*The authors would like to acknowledge the following individuals for their review and comment: Vi Johnson of Washington Mutual, Richard Cambell of Wachovia and Tim Elliott of Comerica Bank.

company will make are subjective, based on individual preferences, resources and the data that are available. The decisions reached by any institution regarding its approach must be well documented. The objective here is to help define these decisions, to better enable planning and raise awareness of the range of alternatives and issues that will arise.

## MODEL APPROACHES

Determining capital held to protect against operational losses can be accomplished through several methodologies, or combinations thereof. There is ample literature that defines the details of these methodologies, and describing these details is beyond our scope here. The first decision, however, is to select a methodology. Therefore, the relative pros and cons of each are outlined below to provide the considerations for the selection.

- *Basic indicator and standardised approaches*: Both approaches, defined in Basel II, take a simple formulaic approach to operational risk capital. The key advantage is simplicity and low cost. The downside is that results may not reflect the true risk profile and there is lost potential for a lower regulatory capital charge. For purposes of this chapter we will assume the decision has been made to use an *advanced measurement approach* (AMA) that meets Basel II qualifying criteria.
- *Loss distribution approach (LDA)*: This approach primarily relies on a history of internal loss event data as a basis for the capital calculation. The institution's loss history is used to construct frequency and severity distributions that are then used in Monte Carlo simulations. This approach has the appeal of being the most objective and, with adequate data, potentially the most accurate. It suffers from the high dependency on loss data that are often not available, either due to the organisation's ability to capture the data, the number of years of data required or that the organisation simply has had few significant losses. This is particularly problematic for representing extreme risks, also known as *tail events*. The LDA approach also requires the institution to have the most quantitative expertise and it is often criticised as backward-looking, as a data history may not reflect the current business and internal control environment.

- *Structured scenario analysis (SSA)*: This approach utilises the opinion of experts across the company to develop frequency and severity distributions. This approach is appealing in its forward-looking nature and lower data requirements but is often criticised for its qualitative inputs, sensitivity to assumptions and potential for higher year-over-year volatility. It may also be difficult to get consistent and credible estimates across business areas. The resource requirements for obtaining scenario data are often very high, as it requires the participation of a broad range of senior managers to understand the scope of scenarios that could impact the institution. SSA data are typically expressed as frequencies in five to eight impact ranges within severity distributions. This small number of data points can make modelling difficult due to the need to fit a severity distribution to few data points.
- *Scorecard*: Scorecard approaches utilise various measures to assess the OR at a corporate or business-unit level. These measures typically include volume, cost, complexity of operations, geographic spread and some key risk indicators (KRIs) such as employee turnover and number of servers, to name just two. Scorecard approaches are appealing due to the relative simplicity of their implementation and their ability to define explicitly the criteria to modify capital/create incentives, but they are fairly qualitative in nature because of the subjectivity inherent in the selection and weighting of scoring factors. Some questionnaire-based approaches can be time-consuming. Scorecards are not that useful for calculating total capital for an institution, and it is difficult to consider explicitly tail events within these approaches. They have been most effectively used to allocate risk to lower levels of the organisation in a top-down quantification approach.
- *Hybrid*: Most leading institutions actually utilise some combination of these approaches. A combination can offset the weaknesses of a given approach by combining it with another. It also leaves the door open to a wider variety of approaches as experience is gained and the risk profile is better understood. There are many different combinations that can be constructed. For example, with limited data availability, an institution can perform an LDA analysis at the top of the house or major business line and

then use scorecards to allocate capital to lower levels of the organisation. It is possible to use an LDA for business areas or risks where there are sufficient data and use scenarios as a basis where there are not sufficient data. One can also use an LDA for the body of a distribution and scenarios for the tails, or even take weighted averages of the two approaches depending on the quality of the data. Combination models often produce more holistic results but can be much more data- and effort-intensive than any single approach.

## FACTORS TO CONSIDER IN DETERMINING APPROACH

Keep in mind that there is no right approach. Each institution's approach must be tailored to meet its unique circumstances, including needs, abilities and preferences. Inherent in each of the approaches noted above are several factors that may support or limit an institution's probability of success. Each of the factors outlined below should be considered in determining the approach to modelling capital.

### Availability of inputs

One of the first steps is to determine the availability of data inputs, primarily the history of loss event data. Data availability will have a direct impact on selection of the modelling approach and the granularity of model implementation. For example, if there is not a robust data-collection process and a sufficient history of events, the LDA approach is not a practical alternative. It is also important to investigate the number of internal loss data available for each business area and risk category. Even with a robust process, there still might not be sufficient data to model with. Understanding the availability of these data, the sufficiency or quality of them and the institution's willingness to gather the data or implement new processes is key to selecting an appropriate modelling approach.

### Resource availability and effort

The level of effort and skills both within the department performing the capital calculations and within the business units also warrants consideration. LDA approaches can be executed with minimal involvement of senior management and business resources, assuming the processes and data already exist. If they do not exist, the effort to create and obtain these data can be monumental. In any case, event-collection processes can be time-consuming, regardless of the capital approach.

Structured scenario approaches can be more resource-intensive in terms of both the number of hours required to complete and the seniority/expertise of the staff necessary to participate. Participants must understand the breadth of risks facing the institution (or business areas within the institution) and the environment in which it operates, have the historical perspective to know what has and could happen and be appropriately conservative in their outlook.

There is also a consideration for quantitative analysis skills. LDA approaches tend to be more quantitatively extensive. Having the internal skills in actuarial techniques, statistics and modelling is necessary to establish ownership of the models and build understanding of the implications regarding modelling choices.

## Incentives to manage risk

Capital is quantified for a variety of reasons, including better measurement of risk, adherence to Basel II requirements, market expectations and management incentives for managing risk. Creating incentives is a key change management tool and important consideration. Capital is an excellent tool for linking the management of OR into financial performance and overall incentive schemes.

Individual managers can influence their capital charge in the short term through qualitative factors, and in the long term through improving controls and resulting loss rates. While incentives are typically considered in the qualitative adjustments to any model, they are also implicit in loss experience, as, over time, a lower loss rate should ultimately be reflected in lower capital. However, changes from lower loss rates tend to appear over a number of years, while the impact of qualitative adjustments can be immediate. Incentives are also immediate and explicit in scorecard approaches

## Cost considerations

The approaches to capital can be completed with varying levels of cost. Several companies offer software and consulting solutions tailored to OR capital that can relieve the need for significant investments in data analysis and quant resources. However, they might not be as flexible as one might desire. Others choose to invest in the quantitative expertise and either build or rely upon more generic modelling software that might be more flexible, but more expensive to implement. Whether or not to purchase a public database and/or participate in a loss consortium is another direct cost. Either way, the implementation costs of an AMA approach can be significant, depending upon the gaps in existing processes and the methodology chosen.

### Organisational culture

What will be culturally accepted is an important consideration when selecting an approach to modelling. The more quantifiable approaches are good for data-driven organisations but may not fare as well in more qualitative cultures. The approach to other financial decisions within the organisation may provide clues as to how best to approach this in your institution. The best capital processes do not guarantee success if not embraced at both the corporate and business-line levels. Regardless of approach, the more transparent the process and risk-sensitive the result, the better the acceptance rate. A communications strategy for the methodology and results is important for success.

## MODELLING DECISIONS

### Model inputs

Regulatory guidance indicates that methodologies should utilise a combination of internal loss data, external data, scenarios and assessments of the control environment. However, upon observation of the data available, there are always gaps and data quality issues. Institutions can work to improve data quality, but gaps are an inherent problem. While there may always be an opportunity to improve data collection, looking for more data or waiting for more data to be available is not always the right answer. It is the goal of risk managers to reduce, ultimately, the frequency and severity of events. Therefore it can be viewed as a good thing *never* to have enough events to create full distributions and easily model risk. Any methodology must be able to combine weak data, with gaps, and end in a result with integrity.

*Internal loss data.* At some level, this is the basis for most capital calculations. The loss history represents the inherent operational risks and the state of the controls at a point in time. The key decision is whether modelling should be performed directly off the data (as is typical in an LDA approach) and at what level of granularity (top of house, business line, product, process, risk subcategory). Where data are too sparse to create reliable distributions they can instead be used to inform scenarios or other scorecard approaches.

*External public data.* Loss data extracted from public sources can be readily purchased from several vendors or collected internally. The key decision is how to use the data. There is no statistically sound basis for combining them with internal data, yet internal and external data must be used in the methodology. Public databases have reporting biases in that only larger events (typically over US$1 million) are captured and only certain types of events are ever made public, leaving many risk exposures underrepresented. Alternative approaches to the use of external public data include using the data to inform scenario analysis, using them in setting the maximum loss in simulations, using them to perform modelling on select data when it is viewed as comprehensive, using them in extreme value analysis to quantify the tails, using them as a reasonableness check on internal data, using them to inform the risk-assessment process and using them on a relative relation basis to help complete missing internal data.

*Consortium data.* Consortiums are becoming more popular as a means to obtain more data and overcome the biases in public data. They are still in the early stages, and in most cases the databases are valuable in some areas but lack sufficient data for effective modelling of some types of risk or business areas. Where there are ample data, consortium data, in theory, provide a sound basis for creation of a severity distribution. The assumption is that the average data from diverse participants provide meaningful information. The key decisions are determining where the consortium data are better than internal data, the cost and legal risk of potential disclosure, and whether and how to combine the internal and consortium information.

*Legal provisions.* Event data related to litigation usually consist of closed cases with final amounts. Earlier inclusion in loss databases is typically forbidden by legal departments for risk of discovery, as any amount could be an admission of guilt or set a floor for negotiation. Consequently, recording the event often occurs years after the litigation started, and the data are a very lagging indicator of risk and the control environment. Yet legal departments do set aside provisions for the expected losses of future litigation. Should these values be included in capital calculations? Where there is large litigation pending, beyond the historical level of expected loss, inclusion could be warranted. The simplest approach is to treat the amount as a current-year loss along with other internal loss data. An aggregate estimate can overcome the risk of discovery related to an individual case. One is then faced with the issue of how to modify historical data once the litigation issues are settled.

*Expected loss reserves.* For some types of risk, typically high-frequency, low-severity events, there may be sufficient information to reasonably estimate expected loss. Examples are fraud, processing errors, insurance claims, cash-drawer errors and NSF checks. Basel guidance permits capital calculations to be offset by these reserves when the institution can demonstrate that it has measured and accounted for its expected-loss exposures. Therefore the key decisions are:

- ❑ For what types of events do these data exist?
- ❑ How should one calculate expected loss for the sake of this adjustment?
- ❑ Is the expected loss adequately represented in the budgeting and accounting process?

In the United States, Financial Accounting Standards (FAS 5) defines the criteria to set accounting reserves for expected losses and this is the standard the regulators might apply.

*Scenarios.* There are two basic types of scenarios. The first is an estimate of a specific occurrence (such as a business continuity event) and represents one data point in a severity distribution. The second is an estimate of an entire distribution informed by historical event data, the business-and-control environment and judgement. The first must be combined with internal data to create a severity distribution. This leads to questions about how many scenarios to use, whether they are they consistent and how they correlate. The second type of scenario can be modelled directly. These scenarios can be built with structured examples that business experts work through, or conducted in a more unstructured process, relying upon experts to identify the what if scenarios. Some approaches model scenarios and internal data separately and then take weighted averages of the two, depending on the perceived validity and completeness of the internal data. Others use internal data for the body of the distribution and scenario analysis for the tail of the distribution.

*Scorecards.* Scorecards can be used as a capital methodology in themselves. However, they are frequently used in conjunction with LDA/scenario approaches to allocate capital further down the institution. The key decisions are what measures to use for each type of risk and the relative weights to put on these measures. There is also the question of whether measures have a linear or other relationship to risk. After various allocations, it is possible that large risks in small business units could be underrepresented. Some institutions use quantitative metrics/KRIs; others use questionnaires and aggregate scores around the quality of controls; and another approach is to score qualitatively the level of risk or control.

**Top-down *versus* bottom-up**

Capital is typically calculated either at a top-of-house level and then allocated down to lower-level business areas, or at lower levels and aggregated up to a top-of-house number. Both approaches have their relative benefits that must be weighed against the effort and other implications.

A top-of-house approach simplifies the overall modelling, allows for an earlier adoption of an LDA approach and, if the data exist, is typically less resource-intensive. However, it requires the development of risk-based scorecards or the identification of other methodologies to allocate capital to business areas. Legal entity and home host considerations may make top-down approaches unacceptable to many regulators unless the process starts at the entity level.

A bottom-up approach focuses on determining capital for major business units, which is aggregated up to an institutional total. This requires more corporate resources to execute but does provide greater potential for improved business-area accuracy and for business units to manage their capital, and it can be useful in building business unit buy into the process (top-of-house calculations can be perceived as a corporate tax on units, rather than the amount of capital they need for their OpRisk). Bottom-up approaches require the calculation of capital at multiple points (typically major business lines, but potentially many more units if capital is desired at a lower level) and potentially against multiple Basel risk types.

### Level of granularity

A related decision concerns the level of granularity to assign or to calculate capital. The further down the organisation, the more business lines, and the more effort involved. By the same token, being more granular would imply a greater level of accuracy and buy-in by the business areas. There are several questions to consider:

- At what level can behaviour be influenced?
- At what level is capital assigned for credit and market risk?
- At what level are the risks so substantially different that separate calculations are necessary to understand the risk profile?
- What legal entities or countries require stand-alone capital calculations to meet regulatory expectations?
- At what level are there sufficient event data to build distributions (assuming LDA)?
- What level of resources (risk management and business) is available to expend to achieve capital calculations?
- At what point would results be too small as to be immaterial and not worth the effort?

One observed phenomenon is that using many assessable units can potentially overstate the frequencies of rare events, especially in structured-scenario or scorecard approaches. For example, many structured-scenario approaches consider a minimum frequency the model will accept (say 1 in 100 years, or 0.01). Experts in each of 10 assessable units may consider a 0.01% chance of a US$100 million event occurring, indicating a 10% probability. However, if assessed at the corporate level, the true likelihood is probably much less.

### Model parameters

Once a modelling approach and inputs have been selected, the data are typically modelled using Monte Carlo simulations to determine the final initial capital amounts for each entity and Basel category.

The Monte Carlo simulations are filled with options that may have a significant impact on overall capital levels. Let us look at some of these options.

*Severity distributions.* Selection of a severity distribution is a key decision. Various statistical techniques can be used to determine or evaluate the fit of various distributions to event data. For example, transformed beta, gamma normal, Pareto and lognormal are some of the common severity distributions. It is beneficial to use as few different distributions as possible, or aggregation of results becomes more difficult. Lognormal distributions underrepresent the fat tails commonly found in operational loss data. Transformed beta, while extremely flexible, can produce unstable results when used with few data points (such as provided by structured scenario approaches). Institutions should develop a preferred methodology for fitting these distributions but have alternatives to compare results against and to replace the existing methodology in situations where the fit is not appropriate.

*Frequency distributions.* Poisson and negative binomial are the two most common distribution types used in frequency modelling. Poisson is the more common of the two, but probably not as theoretically pure. In the end, the two do not produce materially different results.

*Maximum loss amounts.* Due to the unlimited tail of distributions and the nature of Monte Carlo simulations, not capping the severity distributions can lead to unrealistically high capital results. The best approach is to model the loss profile both with alternate levels of maximum losses, and without maximum loss amounts, and assess the impact on capital amounts. Regulators will expect a rigorous explanation of the selection of maximum loss amounts and a sensitivity analysis of the effect of alternate maximums on capital estimates.

Maximum losses can be established at the corporate level, or they can vary based upon business area, Basel event type or a combination of the two. One must balance the desire to minimise capital, yet be conservative enough to cover true worst cases and not be open to criticism of unduly influencing the results. In setting the maximum loss, there are a variety of sources that should be considered:

- *Worst-case historical losses*: It is human nature to look at the worst loss in your history and assume that is the maximum loss amount. Given the limited histories of most companies' loss tracking, this is not a conservative assumption. The worst-case historical losses should serve as a minimum, with investigation into how much worse it could be given today's environment, changes in business size, and the effects any mitigating controls may have had on the loss.

- *External loss data*: Public or consortium datasets are useful to help determine what industry worst-case losses have been. These can serve as a starting point to help an institution determine its individual exposure. Rarely will an external event be a perfect fit for your entity's profile. Consideration must be given to the need to scale the data for difference in the size of companies (either up or down, and be aware that some event types do not scale well), the environments in which they happened and difference in time at which the events occurred. External fraud is an example loss type that may not scale well. A branch robbery at a small community bank may produce very comparable losses to the same event at a multinational institution.
- *Expert opinion*: All institutions have a talented staff of experts who can be leveraged to help determine what the maximum loss amounts may be for any given scenario. These estimates should be viewed with a healthy level of scepticism to ensure that unintentional biases ("that could not happen here") do not enter into the assessments.

The best approach is often a blend of the three, resulting in expert opinions that are grounded in internal and external datasets.

*Body versus tail estimates.* Many approaches focus on fitting the severity curve to the entire distribution of losses, while others, such as the extreme-value theory (EVT), focus solely on fitting the tail of the distribution, where capital is most applicable. Both methods are widely used in the industry, but a decision must be made as to how best to assess the fit of your models. Fitting to the overall curve or the tail is a specific decision. In any case, understand both approaches. When other assumptions are necessary, such as the selection of thresholds for an EVT calculation, document the sensitivity analysis of capital levels for various assumptions.

*Confidence intervals.* The level of confidence selected in the model will have an impact on the overall result and stability of models. Stability influences the number of simulations required and the time it takes individual models to run. Basel II specifies a 99.9% confidence interval over a one-year time horizon, which should be seen as the minimum. Many institutions have adopted other, more stringent intervals to correspond with their credit ratings (A is 99.95%). The choice is based primarily on internal factors and will vary from institution to institution.

## Qualitative adjustments

A common principle of capital calculations is that capital should reflect the control environment and create incentives to improve that environment. Given that risk and controls are not directly measurable, the challenge becomes determining which measures best reflect the control environment and how they should be applied. Assuming that the initial calculation of capital was based on losses (that reflect the business and control environment), any qualitative adjustment for controls introduces some level of double counting. This is usually accepted to create incentives and reflect factors that do not result in direct losses. Also, existing measures may not align well with the granularity of the capital model. While the decisions in any one company are largely dependent on the availability of information and consistency of its application, common measures of the control environment include the following:

- *Audit scores*: Audit ratings can easily adjust capital levels, potentially providing incentives for strong control environments and penalties for weak ones. Audit scores are a consistent and independent measure of controls and can provide objective incentives for a business unit.
- *Self-assessments*: Control and/or risk self-assessments often rate the controls and risks for each business unit. These can be leveraged to reward business areas based upon the quality of the assessments or the relative risk indicated.
- *KRIs*: Indicators can theoretically monitor the quality of controls and be used as a reflection of the control environment. Typically the most valuable KRIs are very process/risk-specific, and very few can be used consistently across business lines. This makes the creation of a comprehensive framework based on KRIs, measuring the changes in controls across all business units, difficult.

In addition, the KRIs that reflect risk in one year might prove stable and uninformative in future years if the control environment has improved.

- *Quality of risk management*: Scorecards can be used to assess the quality of the risk-management process. These may be complemented by metrics indicating how well the process is operating (eg, time to record events, length of time open, late mitigation plans).
- *Open issues (number and time to remediation)*: Issues can include mitigation plans, open audit or regulatory exam issues, or other items awaiting action. The number of open issues and late issues can be combined into an adjustment. This is often seen as more real-time than audit opinions, but it is also a very point-in-time measure and may not provide an accurate reflection of the consistent actions taken by business areas to control risk.

With any of these factors, one can adjust capital levels. But practical decisions are yet to be made. By how much can each measure change capital? Up or down 5%, 10%, 25%? Can capital levels be decreased or only increased by each measure? Is the adjustment linear, or somehow exponential with a more severe penalty for poor results? How frequently are adjustments applied? Is there a maximum adjustment for the combination of measures? What happens in the second and future years? If percentage changes are applied in subsequent years, there is an unintended compounding effect (eg, a 5% reduction in two consecutive years results in a slightly different result from 10% applied in one year). The answers to these questions are completely subjective. Common practice indicates adjustments would range from −10% to +25%, individually and aggregate, with an increasing penalty for poor controls.

### Year-over-year stability

Capital calculations are updated periodically, typically annually, though changes in qualitative adjustments might be applied more frequently. Updates include reflecting new data inputs, recalibrating distributions and testing sensitivities, and updating the capital results. In addition, enhancements to the methodology may be introduced. The OR capital process is filled with variables that can differ each year. Changes in the basic scenarios and in qualitative adjustments (such as audit ratings) can have a material impact on capital levels.

Institutions must make a conscious decision either to allow these swings in capital or to create caps on the amount of year-over-year change in capital levels. In systems that rely heavily upon loss data, these swings tend to be muted, due to the averaging effect of using years of loss history (AMA requires a minimum of five years). Some concerns with unstable models (year-over-year) include the following:

- *Eroding business support due to the appearance of instability in the numbers*: These drastic swings and the difficulty the business has in controlling the results can reduce their confidence in the results, especially if they are used in incentive schemes.
- *Difficulty in the annual planning process*: Typically, these processes anticipate some changes in the underlying cost of funds and capital burdens, but dramatic swings can make the planning for future years difficult.
- *The changes themselves may provide a sense of false precision*: All capital calculations are by their nature estimates, and care needs to be taken to ensure too much precision is not implied in the annual changes.
- *Implied perception on the potential to manipulate the results*: If volatile, business areas may try to influence the assumptions.

## DIVERSIFICATION/CORRELATION ASSUMPTIONS

A key component of any capital methodology is the approach to correlation of risk and diversification benefits. This is less of an issue with top-down approaches. With a top-of-the-house risk calculation and allocation, correlation and diversification are either implicitly assumed or considered in the calculation methodology. When capital is calculated for each business area (or other level of granularity) the issue is apparent.

For example, let's say there are three business units with capital levels of US$10, 20, and 30 million. Portfolio theory would indicate that the risk level for the combined entity is less than the sum of the three units, US$60 million. For example, a simultaneous simulation could indicate a total risk level of US$45 million, assuming independence of risk events, or a diversification benefit of US$15 million.

A conservative approach would just add together the business areas and use US$60 million for capital. A more theoretically pure approach would use the US$45 million. The decision about which figure to use is often based on the result. If US$45 million is determined to be material and sufficient, and, if capital is scarce, one can rationalise using this result. If the results are coming out low, and there is ample capital that needs to be allocated to business areas, and a higher capital allocation is desired to create material incentives, then the undiversified US$60 million might be used. If there is a benefit (say US$15 million), is it kept at the corporate level, or pro-rated and shared with the business areas?

There is a common argument that there is some positive correlation between operational events. Examples include the following:

- If a business has a weak control environment and an event occurs, isn't there a higher probability that another similar event would occur?
- If systems are weak, shouldn't probability of a process error increase?
- If a company is being targeted by litigants, multiple lawsuits – and presumably settlements – will occur together.
- If events are recorded separately by cause or business line, positive correlation may also be evident. Examples are single events with multiple effects, one system outage that affects multiple business lines and a litigation event that crosses multiple years.

Unfortunately, the data to quantify the impact of this correlation does not exist. Therefore, one must decide whether there is correlation, and what assumptions and methodology to use to quantify it. Basel demands a sound process, integrated with integrity, that takes into account extreme events and is properly validated. This is a high bar, and, at this time, this may be limited to the clear articulation of the assumptions and a sensitivity analysis of the results. Common practice is to assume positive correlation resulting in an additional 10–20% more capital than the result if perfectly uncorrelated. More substantiation will be required for ultimate AMA approval by regulators.

Another question is the same diversification/correlation question, but across risk categories. Is OR correlated with market, credit or strategic risks? The same questions need to be answered, as well as the issue of whether to apply the methodology within a business line or at the corporate level.

## INSURANCE

Most insurance policies mitigate some element of OR. In theory, insurance should reduce capital requirements; however, the limits, deductibles and coverages must be carefully analysed to understand this benefit.

Perhaps the first key decision is whether the core loss data or risk-assessment methodology considers exposures before or after insurance coverage. If insurance has already been considered, there is nothing more to do. If the data are pre-insurance, then the insurance benefits can be measured. An important consideration for designing loss databases is to capture losses pre-insurance so that this data can be used as input to the capital models.

The first step in insurance analysis is to identify all the coverages and map them against the standard OR categories. Unfortunately, insurance contracts are structured differently, so a subjective process is required. The goal is to determine the deductible, cap and percentage coverage of any risk category. The percentage coverage is important, since it indicates that there are certain risks that are not insured, that there are exclusions in the insurance contracts and also that there is always a risk of negotiation/dispute with the carrier that could cause the loss to be incurred without recovery. Sampling the history of loss-event data to determine what would be covered and what would not be covered can provide input to this assumption. Note that under the new Basel guidelines there is a cap of the maximum reduction that can be calculated from insurance.

The actual structure of insurance contracts is often much more complicated than can be represented by the three inputs of deductible, caps and coverage. However, accurate quantification would require much more advanced modelling, and the result might not be materially different. Assuming this simplified approach, an insurance benefit can be calculated. Assuming this benefit is at the corporate level, the resulting benefit needs to be allocated back to the business areas.

## MODEL VALIDATION

It should now be apparent that, regardless of the approach used to quantify capital, there are many subjective inputs and related assumptions. These inputs and assumptions all have some related sensitivity and impact on the final result. Any one decision can have a major impact on the end result. Therefore, validating the results is perhaps the most important step in the capital process. One can follow any methodology, but the compound effect of various decisions could render the output meaningless. A comprehensive validation process provides the checks and balances over the quantitative methodology. The goal is that total capital levels be appropriate at both the business-line and aggregate levels, as well as that year-over-year changes be logical.

There are many techniques to validate the results. Some work top-down; others are more bottom-up. If alternate approaches can be applied that provide similar answers, there will be increased confidence in the results. If not, the underlying assumptions can be re-examined and changed if necessary.

The independence of the validation must be considered as well. Most practitioners will choose to run these validations themselves, to ensure the results are valid and supportable; and then have independent parties revalidate the results. This revalidation can be performed by external firms, internal audit or other independent analytical functions within the company.

### Top-down

Top-down validation approaches attempt to validate the total capital level calculated for the institution. By providing several independent calculations, one can evaluate whether the methodology provides an aggressive, conservative or more average result. Here are some suggested approaches.

*Basel formulas.* The Basel methodologies (standardised and basic indicator approaches) afford a simple formula to calculate capital. Most companies pursue an advanced-measurement approach under the premise that regulatory capital can be reduced. Therefore, barring a history of large events or a very weak control environment, the Basel approaches provide a benchmark on capital levels.

*Alternate approaches.* Depending on the choice of core methodology, an alternate methodology may be followed to validate the core one. It can be simplified and performed with less granularity to minimise the effort. For example, one can take the largest events in the database and follow an extreme-value theory methodology to calculate capital levels separately. Or, if one used some type of bottom-up LDA approach, a top-down scorecard can validate business-level results.

*Coverage for largest losses.* Assemble the largest internal and external losses and compare them with capital levels. Most of the time, external losses are larger than internal ones. Assuming that they could happen here, can capital cover the largest applicable industry loss? More conservatively, can capital cover the largest two or three losses if they occurred in any one year?

*Industry benchmarks.* While there are few, if any, public benchmarks with the results of capital calculations, this information may become available. Some of the largest banks are beginning to disclose their economic capital results in annual reports. OR benchmarking and Qualitative Impact Study surveys by the US banking agencies provide the regulators with a basis for benchmarking. This information may become public at some point in time. Consultants often have client data from engagements that may be shared on an anonymous basis. There is also the opportunity to reach out to industry peers. Many would be willing to share sufficient information to permit benchmarking.

**Bottom-up**

The second strategy is more bottom-up, focused on business-area results. Depending on the methodology, this could be performed before or after the top-down analysis. Some strategies are the following.

*Compare with risk perceptions.* If we asked a number of senior executives to rank the businesses from high to low in terms of riskiness, what would they say? This question could be asked either in the context of total capital or in terms of relative risk per dollar of assets or other measure. In either case, how does perception compare with the methodology results? Executives can be amazingly intuitive in this area but also can have blind spots. Differences should be rationalised and perhaps trigger analysis of related assumptions.

*Alternative approaches.* Similar to the top-down validation, alternate approaches can be applied at the business level. For example, if an LDA or scenario-based approach forms the underlying methodology, one could develop a top-down scorecard allocation method as an alternate approach. It doesn't need the level of detail or buy-in that a core methodology might need, just enough to understand the major risk factors and provide insight to the drivers of capital. Once again, rationalise the differences or analyse the assumptions.

*Pure play comparisons.* Sometimes there are public mono-line companies where their capital can be directly measured and compared against capital levels for a business area of a larger bank.

*Internal peer comparisons.* Often there are multiple business lines or products that can have results compared on a capital/asset or capital/account basis. To illustrate, take consumer financial products. Capital levels can be compared for credit cards, home equity, mortgages, deposit accounts, instalment loans and car loans. Since operational errors are probably more proportional to the number of accounts than asset size, calculate capital per account and compare across products. Results can be normalised for average account balances. The results then are compared with the fundamental understanding of risk: which businesses are riskier and why, and do the capital calculations confirm or contradict this understanding?

## SUMMARY

While the financial-services industry seems to be migrating towards hybrid approaches for capital quantification, commonly based on event history as the anchor point for analysis, the actual implementations differ widely. Data are being combined in different ways, at different levels of granularity, with different types of adjustment. As a result, for a similar business and size, capital levels can vary materially across institutions.

The various decisions and alternatives institutions face in the quantification of OR capital have been highlighted. There is no definition of best practice at this time, only preferences based on data availability, cultural acceptance and individual opinions. Over time, continued sharing of experience, additional data availability and benchmarking of methodologies and results may make practices more aligned. In the meantime, conservative assumptions and extensive validation are recommended to arrive at the best possible result.

# Section Two

# Modelling Basics

It is encouraging that the debate about op risk modelling has – for the most part – moved on from a discussion of "is it possible?" into being considered a discipline in its own right. But that is not to say modelling operational risk isn't full of challenges and pitfalls. In my more contemplative moments I like to think of it as being as difficult as modelling a Shakespeare play: how do you capture humanity's fallibility in a simple curve on two axes?

To help readers navigate the challenges, the two chapters that make up this section are designed to provide an introduction to the discipline of operational risk modelling, but they are written so that both beginners and those with a more advanced understanding of the subject will find them of interest.

In the first chapter, Rudi De Koker asks the question "Operational Risk Modelling: Where Do We Go From Here?" In a conversational way, De Koker discusses the evolution of OR modelling and the challenges and shortcomings inherent in the discipline at the moment. The chapter is an invaluable guide to some of the hottest topics in OR modelling today.

The second part of the section is authored by Gene Álvarez. This more comprehensive and technical exploration of OR modelling covers most of the main methodologies for modelling operational risk, and includes a thorough discussion of both the frequency and severity distributions, performing economic capital calculations and dealing with diversification issues, scenario analysis, event classification, and mixing internal and external data.

# 3

# *Operational Risk Modelling: Where Do We Go From Here?*

**Rudi De Koker***

Citigroup

Any review of the current state of the art in operational risk analytics needs to acknowledge two basic facts: the modelling of operational risk is still a very young discipline, certainly in comparison with market and credit risk modelling; and much progress has been made in the last few years, despite – or perhaps because of – the novelty of the enterprise. The chapters in this book, as well as recent industry conferences, provide ample evidence of both progress and ongoing challenges.[1] Individual researchers may differ in their views on the speed of progress, and the degree of convergence in industry practices. But it is clear that, in a number of institutions, operational risk analytics is no longer a purely theoretical exercise, and the models are beginning to shed light on historical loss experience, as well as on the likely levers for improved senior management decision making.

As operational risk analytics moves out of the laboratory and into the boardroom, there is a need to translate the complexities of a very technical discipline into a handful of clear and convincing messages. What does the CEO of a financial institution need to know about operational-loss behaviour and operational risk measurement? This chapter aims to outline the beginnings of an answer to that question. Three tentative but broad conclusions present themselves, and are supported by growing evidence gathered by

*The views expressed here are those of the author and not necessarily those of Citigroup.

industry researchers, regulators and academics. First, operational losses appear to follow a few basic laws, which allow us to extrapolate the remote likelihood of large future losses from the body of historical loss experience. Second, these laws can be translated into simple calculation rules for economic and regulatory capital – rules that are similar both in spirit and in application to the Basel II advanced IRB (internal ratings-based) approach for corporate credit risk. Third, while operational-loss behaviour is naturally segmented into frequency analysis and severity analysis, practical management attention should be focused on understanding (and reducing) the frequency of large loss events. In contrast, severity estimates for various operational risk types are hard to measure precisely, but appear to be fairly constant from firm to firm and across the business cycle. If this is true, the most productive research for banks going forward will be focused on identifying, testing and improving the key drivers of large loss frequency. The rest of this chapter outlines the evidence and conceptual background for these conclusions, and reviews some of the mathematics required in a more technical appendix.

## STATISTICAL MODELLING OF OPERATIONAL RISK: TWO CHALLENGES

The loss distribution or actuarial approach to operational risk measurement starts from a very simple premise: that operational losses can be modelled statistically by means of (independent) frequency and severity distributions, each derived from a careful analysis of historical data. Frequency analysis is little more than counting: how many operational-loss events are likely to occur in a given time period (typically, the following year)? Severity analysis adds dollar numbers: when an operational loss occurs, how likely is it to exceed a given dollar amount (ranging from a few thousand to a few billion dollars)? Once these two questions have been answered – through the specification of statistical frequency and severity distributions that best fit the available historical data – future losses can be simulated using standard Monte Carlo techniques.

Anyone with a credit risk background may recognise in the preceding paragraph an almost exact analogy with credit defaults: simply substitute default frequency for operational event frequency, and loss given default for event severity. Why then is operational risk modelling a novel discipline with multiple challenges? Two complications make operational risk harder to quantify than credit risk. First, there is no simple operational risk equivalent to the concept of credit exposure (balance-sheet exposure for straight lending, loan-equivalent exposure for off-balance-sheet positions). Unlike credit risk, where in most circumstances it is hard to lose much more than 100% of your balance sheet, operational losses are notoriously unrelated to any simple measure of dollars-at-risk – not assets, not income, not even revenues. The Basel II language for the advanced measurement approach for operational risk reflects this: while it introduces the term *operational risk exposure*, this term refers to the output of the risk model, that is, to the risk measure more commonly called *risk capital* or *economic capital*. In other words, risk exposure and risk capital have the same meaning in Basel II – presumably because nobody has been able to identify a more fundamental, more directly observable measure of exposure.

As a second complication, operational risk appears to be very fat-tailed. While most operational events lead to small dollar losses, every institution occasionally observes very large loss events. And, while these are rare, they are more prevalent than would be the case if operational losses were normally distributed. Practically, this means that any realistic model of operational risk will be very sensitive to the assumptions made about the tail of the loss distribution. This is again quite different from credit risk, where the loss severity of any one single default event does not have a large impact on portfolio behaviour – at least for reasonably well-diversified portfolios. Thus, severity is typically expressed as a portfolio average for credit portfolios – an average loss-given default of say 10% or 20% or 50% for a particular type of credit exposure. While more advanced credit portfolio models introduce severity *distributions*, it is still generally the case that portfolio risk capital is not very sensitive to assumptions about the tail of the loss distribution (except for extremely concentrated portfolios).

Models that are sensitive to precise assumptions about the loss tail are inconvenient for practical reasons. Tail events are rare by definition, and it is therefore hard to collect sufficient data for a precise estimate across different product lines, risk types and business models.

## SYMPTOMS OF POWER-LAW BEHAVIOUR

The two issues discussed in the preceding section are often presented as annoying but temporary constraints on operational risk modelling. Basel II implicitly assumes that more comprehensive data collection, and ongoing research, will be sufficient to either remove or at least mitigate both perceived impediments before the switchover date to the new Capital Accord. But what if, rather than representing temporary annoyances to be overcome through cleverness or brute force, these two issues are fundamental to the real-world behaviour of operational risk? As it turns out, much can be learned from taking these obstacles seriously. Indeed, rather than annoyances, the lack of exposure indicators and prevalence of fat tails are key features that help motivate a compelling, elegant and surprisingly simple framework to explain, predict and quantify operational losses. Both issues are indications of scale-independence and power-law behaviour – something that has been studied by physicists, statisticians and (yes) social scientists in a wide variety of fields. And, as we will see, at least some of the mathematics for dealing with fat tails is surprisingly elegant and simple.

Let us begin by looking at a few facts, illustrated in a pseudo-empirical distribution of operational losses. The histogram in Figure 1 represents the typical frequency of losses as a function of size. Although the underlying dataset was artificially generated, it captures the typical features of real-world operational-loss data. The sample of losses is truncated from below, and contains only loss events that were each over US$10,000 individually. A simple pattern is readily apparent: whichever loss size is chosen, roughly half of the losses exceeding the chosen loss amount also exceed twice the amount. Specifically, of about 1,500 events over US$10,000, roughly half were over US$20,000, one quarter were over US$40,000, one eighth over US$80,000 and so on. The factor of two in this example is incidental – it might as well be (and in some instances indeed appears to be the case) that doubling the loss size reduces the frequency by a factor of 3 or 4. But what characterises power-law behaviour is that the frequency reduces by the same, constant factor whenever the loss size is doubled – independent of loss size, and over a wide range of magnitudes. In simple notation,

$$p(loss > X) \sim X^{-\alpha} \tag{1}$$

**Figure 1** Histogram of loss sizes for a typical operational loss dataset. Each column shows the number of events in the dataset exceeding the loss size noted at the bottom of the column

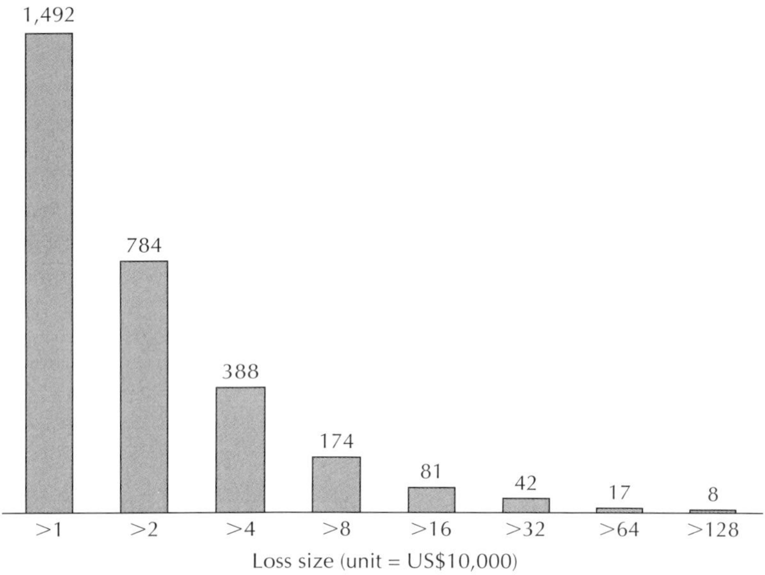


where $p(loss>X)$ represents the probability that a loss event exceeds $X$, $\alpha$ is the so-called tail exponent, and the squiggle represents proportionality. For typical operational-loss data, the tail exponent appears to be somewhere between 1 and 2 – it is slightly above 1 in the example shown in Figure 1. When the size distribution of losses follows a power law, this one parameter $\alpha$ is sufficient to fully characterise severity. Often, severity is expressed in the so-called tail parameter $p = 1/\alpha$, which is the inverse of the exponent in the power law. Typical tail exponents between 1 and 2 translate into tail parameters between 0.5 and 1, with the higher tail parameters characterising loss distributions of higher severity.

A very simple way to highlight power-law behaviour is to show frequency as a function of loss size in a double-logarithmic plot. Figure 2 shows the same data underlying Figure 1. Each data point in this plot depicts an individual loss event, and shows the number of events in the sample exceeding each loss size. The graph demonstrates that logarithmic losses are (approximately) linearly related to

**Figure 2** Number of exceedances (events in excess of a given loss size) as a function of loss size.
In a double-logarithmic plot, the frequency-size relationship is almost perfectly linear, except for small sample noise in the tail. This behaviour is typical for operational loss data from a wide variety of sources

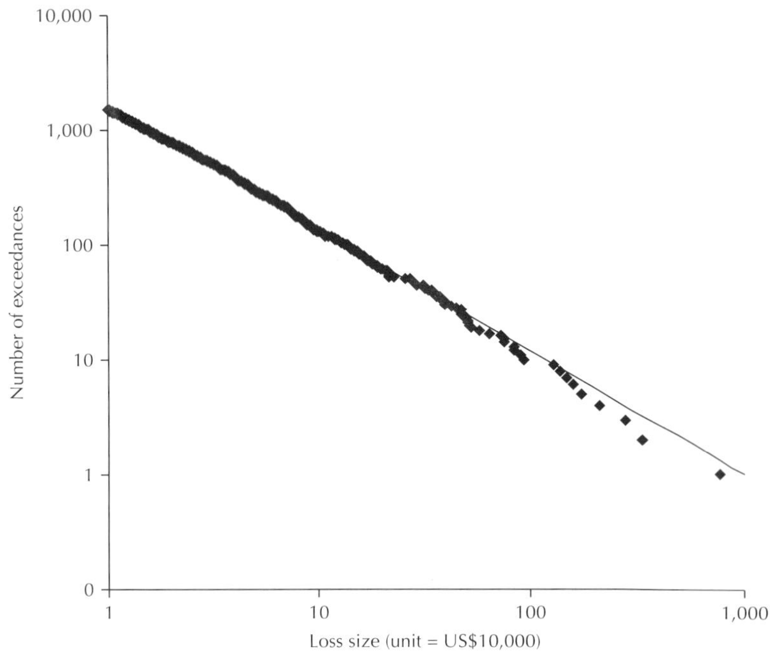


logarithmic frequency, with a remarkably good statistical fit (an $R^2$ of over 90% in the example), and over several orders of magnitude.

The simplest phenomenological explanation for power-law behaviour is the lack of a natural scale to measure losses. In the natural world, power-law behaviour occurs when natural phenomena have no single, dominant scale. For example, the magnitude of earthquakes is power-law-distributed, in part because the geophysical forces at work do not have a fundamental scale – unlike, say, molecular forces or the size of manmade structure. Similarly, some social scientists may remember Zipf's Law: the surprising observation that the number of cities exceeding a given population size decreases in inverse proportion to the population. For every city with more than 10 million people, there are 10 cities with a population over

1 million. While several possible explanations for Zipf's Law have been developed, they all have in common that there is no single, natural scale dominating city growth or decline. Presumably, cities below a certain size lack critical mass, and either decline or remain stagnant, while cities that are too large or too densely populated become unmanageable, or simply haven't had enough time to grow into such a large size. In other words – the power law breaks down for very large and very small cities. But, in between those two extremes, cities of various sizes are possible, and follow a power law almost exactly.

Other phenomena that appear to follow simple power laws are such diverse things as hurricanes, flood waves, traffic jams, stampedes, the market capitalisation of listed firms, the size of companies measured in employees and the settlement amounts in class-action lawsuits. The intuitive connection of these phenomena to operational risk is clear. More fundamental explanations than the scale-independence heuristic given above can be developed in many cases, but a review of those is beyond the scope of this chapter.

Instead, we take the empirical observations on fat tails and power laws at face value, and incorporate them into a fundamental, heuristic framework for operational risk measurement. Almost any operational-loss dataset – whether taken from publicly disclosed financials, derived from a single firm's internal loss data, or collected across firms by regulators or industry consortiums – appears to exhibit simple power-law behaviour. Frequency of large losses is inversely proportional to loss size – or to a power of loss size. If this is true, it means that the remote likelihood of multibillion-dollar losses can be extrapolated from the observed frequency of smaller, more frequent losses. For example, if a bank experiences 10 loss events per year that are over US$1 million each, simple power-law behaviour with a tail exponent of 1 would predict that a loss event over US$100 million will be observed (on average) once every 10 years. So this is one simple consequence of power-law behaviour. As we will now discuss, the power-law heuristic leads to a number of important and far-reaching conclusions about operational risk measurement and capital requirements. While power-law behaviour may be inconvenient for the data collector, it makes the mathematics of operational risk capital incredibly straightforward.

## THE CAPITAL CONSEQUENCES OF POWER-LAW BEHAVIOUR

Before reviewing the consequences of fat tails and power laws, let me establish somewhat more precisely the assumptions required to derive the conclusions that follow. While extreme-value theory offers a potential explanation for power-law behaviour, and provides an elegant framework for the statistics of (some types of) operational risk, it is not assumed and need not be assumed in the following derivations. Also, while it has been conveniently stated above that operational losses follow a power law, any fat-tailed distribution will do – generalised Pareto, Burr, lognormal gamma. In particular, it is not required that loss distributions follow an exact power law over all loss sizes. All we need assume is that logarithmic losses over a relevant range of sizes for operational risk capital measurement – say, from a few million to a few billion dollars in individual event sizes – fall roughly on a straight line *vs* log frequency, as in Figure 2. Perhaps the "real" underlying distribution is normal or lognormal, and it only looks like a power law over a limited range of loss sizes. No objection – the following will hold as long as there is no reason to assume that the observed, approximate power law breaks down at loss levels around the capital amount to be calculated. In other words, if the capital resulting from the calculation is US$1 billion, all that is required for the calculation to be consistent is that log frequency and log size be roughly linearly related for losses up to a few billion dollars in magnitude.

Under these broad assumptions, the following properties of operational risk losses can be derived mathematically, and/or verified through Monte Carlo simulation:

- ❑ The aggregate operational losses over a one-year period follow an approximate power law, with the same tail behaviour as the underlying severity distribution of single losses.
- ❑ The tail of this aggregate loss distribution and therefore any tail measure of operational risk (including economic capital) is completely dominated by the likelihood of a single, catastrophic loss event. See the next section and Figure 3 for a more complete discussion of this property.
- ❑ operational risk capital, defined at a high confidence level, is fully determined by two parameters: the tail exponent (or tail

parameter) of the loss distribution, and the expected frequency of losses. In particular, it makes no appreciable difference whether the frequency of future losses is deterministic (ie, a single, known number) or itself the random outcome of a stochastic process. (In technical terms, it does not matter whether the frequency follows a Poisson distribution, positive or negative binomial distribution, to pick just a few of the usual suspects.)

- The joint operational risk capital for two or more business units, geographies or operational event types does not depend on the frequency correlations between those units. One can assume frequencies to be 100% correlated, or uncorrelated, and it makes no appreciable difference.
- Simulations are unnecessary to determine operational risk capital with a high degree of precision – it is approximately given by

$$RC \approx X_L \left( \frac{f_L}{1-CL} \right)^p \tag{2}$$

where $X_L$ is a suitable large loss size (say, US\$1 million), $f_L$ is the annual frequency of loss events over this size, $CL$ is the confidence level (eg, 99.9% for Basel II calculations), and $p$ is the tail parameter. In other words, operational risk capital at a 99.9% confidence level can be calculated in a tedious, time-consuming computer simulation using a few million simulation runs, or it can be calculated by means of this simple formula. The results are very nearly equal (apart from simulation noise, which tends to make the simple formula much more precise for very fat-tailed risks).

- The joint distribution of operational losses of two or more event types or product lines, each with a different tail parameter, is dominated by the loss type (or product line) with the highest tail parameter (fattest tail). Adding a thin-tailed loss type (eg, high-frequency, low-severity processing errors that may be normally distributed in aggregate) does not increase capital appreciably as long as at least one fat-tailed risk is present with significant probability. In other words, all that matters is that the most fat-tailed risks are properly captured – the rest is practically irrelevant for capital estimation.
- The accuracy of operational risk capital estimates is fundamentally limited by the available data on individual large loss

events, and at least a few dozen such events are required in order to reduce the estimation errors to acceptable levels (say, 20–30% of the total operational risk capital estimate). This means that there are fundamental limits to the amount of "granularity" that can be achieved (ie, the ability to distinguish different event types, product lines or geographies). It also makes operational-loss severity intrinsically an over-the-cycle, industry concept: insufficient data exist to differentiate periods of high or low severity, or to differentiate loss severity (for a given activity or risk type) in one firm from that in another.

All of these assertions can be derived with mathematical rigour, but that is beyond the intent of this chapter (the first few steps of the necessary derivations are outlined in a brief technical appendix). The key property of power laws that explains all is captured in the first and second bullet points above: the fact that the worst-case operational losses are driven by single outlier events. This may sound like the motherhood and apple pie of operational risk, and indeed it is. It is generally acknowledged that operational risk capital is determined by infrequent, large events – as opposed to the vastly more frequent, small events that are predictable in aggregate and contribute a steady cost of doing business. However, saying that risk capital is driven by the need to cover infrequent, large losses is not going far enough. Risk capital is driven by the *single* largest loss likely to be experienced at a high confidence level. In order to survive the worst annual operational losses with 99.9% confidence, an institution needs to hold just enough capital to cover the worst single loss event with 99.9% confidence – plus a few dollars. The likelihood that two very bad events hit in one year is much, much smaller than the chance of experiencing one ruinously bad event. In order to calculate capital, therefore, all we need to do is estimate the likelihood of that one super-sized event. No small task, perhaps – but surely easier than simulating thousands or millions of variations of several events (or scenarios) playing out together.

## AN IRB APPROACH FOR OPERATIONAL RISK?

The heading of this section is meant in a metaphorical sense, and is somewhat tongue-in-cheek. Obviously there are many differences between credit risk and operational risk, and there is no operational risk equivalent as yet of the rating models used in credit risk assessments, and assumed in the internal ratings-based approach in Basel II. But the IRB approach has other features, some of which are eminently applicable to operational risk measurement. The IRB approach derives approximate capital formulas from a very simple single-factor model applied to a well-diversified credit portfolio. These formulas then take as firm-specific inputs a handful of parameters derived from internal firm loss statistics – PD (probability of default) to measure frequency, LGD (loss-given default) to measure severity. Firms can choose how to segment their portfolio into a sufficient number of sub-portfolios, each quantified by a PD/LGD combination. And firms are free to develop a range of statistical techniques to establish and validate PD/LGD parameters. Capital, however, is derived from standardised and approximate formulas. The reason this works in credit risk is that most banks' portfolios are fairly well diversified, and the approximations behind the Basel formulas capture most of the relevant tail behaviour in the portfolio loss distribution. Firms' internal portfolio models offer further refinements and greater precision, but Basel II IRB captures most of what matters, and represents a suitable trade-off between cross-firm consistency, and risk-sensitivity to each firm's specific portfolio mix.

In a sense, operational risk behaves like a very highly concentrated credit portfolio. Rather than capital requirements being the result of correlated default behaviour across a large number of exposures, they are driven by the losses resulting from single, very large events – as if a very high proportion of the balance sheet were exposed to a single, low-PD obligor. Because the aggregate operational-loss behaviour is dominated by those single events, operational risk capital can be derived from simple mathematical approximations. Thus, while the approximations behind the formulas are very different from those used in IRB, the principle is the same: capital is derived from simple, universal calculation rules, which are then populated with firm-specific estimates of frequency and severity. If a firm observes 10 events per year over US$1 million each, and estimates its overall loss severity to be described by a tail parameter of 0.75, capital at a 99.9% confidence level is simply given by

**Figure 3** Contribution of the largest event to operational risk capital obtained in a simulation of 30 annual events (triangles) or 60 annual events (squares).
The two lines near the top of the chart correspond to 99.9% capital; the lower lines correspond to 99% capital. Additional lines for higher confidence levels (for example, 99.95% or 99.97%) could be added, but their large event contribution would be nearly indistinguishable from 100%

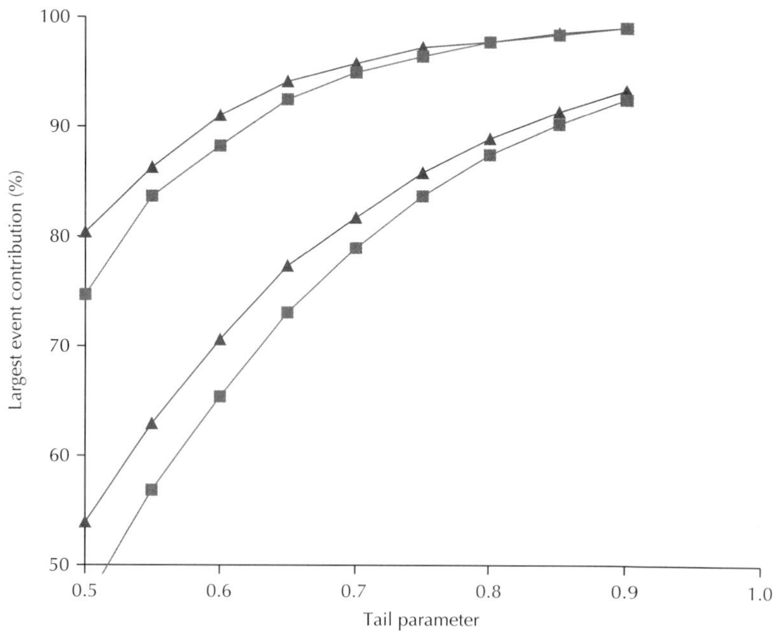


$$RC \approx X_L\left(\frac{f_L}{1-CL}\right)^p = \left(\frac{10}{0.1\%}\right)^{0.75} = \text{US\$1 billion} \tag{3}$$

In order to illustrate the approximations involved, Figure 3 shows just how much of the total risk capital is contributed by the single, worst event. For tail parameters between 0.7 and 1, and 30 to 60 large events annually, the largest single event contributes more than 95% of risk capital at the 99.9% confidence level. The higher the tail parameter (the more fat-tailed the distribution), the more closely the single worst loss approximates the total risk capital needed. The approximations get slightly worse as the number of annual events increases. This is not surprising – as the number of events increases, the likelihood of two large events hitting together increases quadratically. But the point is this: for realistic event frequencies and tail parameters, single event-loss estimates provide an exceedingly good and simple approximation to the total risk capital needed, and capital can be calculated using a very simple closed formula.

## A SHIFT IN FOCUS: FROM SEVERITY TO FREQUENCY

While it would be premature to suggest that regulators should develop an IRB-like framework for operational risk capital requirements, basing capital estimates on simple, transparent calculation rules has distinct advantages – even for internal risk measurement within a single firm. For risk capital to be easily integrated into a firm's decision-making processes, it needs to meet a number of requirements: be transparently calculated, easily explained, broadly understood, easily aggregated across the firm, and easily budgeted/forecast in the financial planning cycle. All of this is difficult to do when capital is the outcome of a complex simulation process, particularly if the simulation results change unpredictably when input parameters are updated.

The instability of operational risk capital estimates is a topic that has attracted a fair amount of attention in the industry literature, and represents yet another clue to the fundamental nature of operational risk, and to the likely avenues for more productive future research. Some of this instability is the result of sampling noise in risk-capital simulations. As the preceding discussion and the appendix indicate, this source of measurement instability can be easily avoided by using analytical approximations based on rank statistics, rather than simulation results directly. However, a more fundamental source of potential capital instability needs to be looked for elsewhere.

One advantage of the approximate capital formula, Equation 2, is that it shows very clearly how capital depends on frequency and severity (or tail parameter). A small change in frequency estimates has a proportionately small impact on capital. In the example of Equation 3, if the annual frequency of events over US$1 million increases from 10 to 11 events, capital at 99.9% confidence level increases from US$1 billion to US$1.074 billion. For typical severities, a 5–10% increase in frequency has a 4–8% impact on capital – and this is independent of confidence level or business size. However, capital is much more sensitive to severity assumptions. In the same example, if the tail parameter were increased from 0.75 to 0.8, capital goes up to US$1.585 billion – that is, a capital increase of nearly 60% for a 6% increase in the tail parameter. Even a much more modest increase in severity, from 0.75 to 0.76, adds US$96 million (or nearly 10%) of capital in the same example. This parameter sensitivity gets worse for larger businesses (higher event frequency) and higher confidence levels, and is fundamental to the assumed fat-tailed behaviour of operational losses. It is not due to estimation techniques or simulation methodologies, but ultimately originates from the key underlying feature of operational risk capital: that large aggregate losses are driven by single outsized events. Even a modest change in the assumed likelihood of those large events therefore has a significant impact on the capital estimate.

Very large events are rare in any one institution, the only way to directly observe the frequency of those events with any degree of precision is to pool data across institutions and over a long time period. It is fairly straightforward to show that at least a few dozen events in the range of US$100 million to US$1 billion are needed to estimate tail severity with an estimation error below 5–10%. This is of the same order of magnitude as the number of events in large business lines (such as trading and sales) that have been observed across the entire industry in the last 15 years. Given this data availability, it is hard to imagine that any plausible, fact-based mechanism can make severity estimates much more granular – that is, specific to one firm, specific to one time period, or specific to one control environment. Indeed tail parameters appear to be, essentially, over-the-cycle estimates of industry severity. Different statistical techniques may lead to somewhat different estimates of severity – but only because each technique picks a different point estimate out of the same plausible statistical estimation range. For example, maximum-likelihood estimation methods will identify a single severity estimate that provides a "best fit"; but the goodness-of-fit surface is extraordinarily flat for severity estimates within 5–10% of the best-fit number, and any estimate within this range can be made "best fit" through slight tweaks in the estimation routines or underlying assumptions. It does not appear to me, therefore, that these firm-to-firm differences in specific estimation routines – and the resulting differences in severity estimates – are particularly useful, or even contain real information about operational risk severity.

There is a silver lining in this cloud. First, some empirical observations. While it is difficult to establish a precise severity estimate for any one business line or event type (for the reasons discussed above), statistical analysis of industry data does establish a fairly robust relative ranking of severity across business lines. Thus, almost any dataset, and almost any statistical fitting routine, will establish corporate finance as relatively high-severity and processing businesses as relatively low-severity activities. This is apparent in publicly disclosed industry loss data collected over the last 15 years; but it also emerges from analysis of proprietary firm data collected by regulators over the last few years[2] (see de Fontnouvelle, Jordan and Rosengren, 2006). Moreover, the resulting relative severity rankings appear to be more or less in line with the intuition of experienced risk and business professionals. And, in the few instances where results are counterintuitive, further investigation of those risk types or business lines is likely to be instructive.

Why is this a silver lining? Because, if we are rapidly approaching the point of diminishing returns in exactly that area of research that is the most difficult mathematically, it frees up resources and management attention for more productive avenues of investigation. While most PhD-carrying operational risk researchers are currently deployed in devising more sophisticated estimation routines or simulation algorithms, this chapter has argued that those areas are unlikely to lead to breakthrough discoveries in the near future. Moreover, few if any business managers are likely to be able to contribute productively to these technical discussions. In contrast, frequency analysis is an area that is so far little explored, and where business and risk professionals have both relevant experience and a direct interest in the outcome. What drives the frequency of medium-to-large loss events? Why do some businesses see ten million-dollar events each year, and others only one or two? How much difference in loss frequency is there across similar-sized banks in similar markets? Focusing on the frequency of million dollar events is a practical compromise. Those events are large enough to matter – they cause real pain – but, unlike the billion dollar losses that attract most headline news, they are also frequent enough that some statistical analysis, and some back-testing of models, is possible even within a single institution and with a few years' worth of carefully collected internal data.

Frequency driver analysis can offer tools for identifying and mitigating the most common sources of large losses; for predicting how frequencies may change in the future – for example, when transaction volumes increase or headcount is reduced; for benchmarking businesses against each other; for tracking the results of corrective action plans and other control efforts; and in a variety of other ways that have so far remained mostly unexplored. Through capital formulas like Equation 2, a systematic reduction in event frequency has a beneficial impact on risk capital. But, in addition, every million-dollar event avoided has a direct impact on the bottom line. Thus, operational risk management focused on large event frequency aims to influence the most reliable drivers of the capital calculation – but it also leads to observable results that impact shorter-term profitability. While few business managers have strong opinions on tail parameter estimation techniques, all of them appreciate the value of an operational risk programme that adds significantly to the bottom line, and most should be supportive of the development of tools and tracking devices that accomplish this goal (as well as making the capital estimates more robust, as a side benefit).

## CONCLUSION

If operational losses in the real world are (effectively) power-law-distributed, the key issues in operational risk management and capital estimation can be captured in an elegant conceptual framework as outlined above, and in simple analytical capital calculation rules. Complex simulations are unnecessary, and many finesses such as the exact shape of loss distributions (Pareto, Burr, Cauchy. . .) or assumptions about frequency volatility and frequency correlations have little impact on the capital results. Precise measurement of severity, by business line or risk type, is difficult and unlikely to improve much beyond current industry best practice. Most institutions that follow a loss distribution approach (LDA) already assume, implicitly or explicitly, that losses are fat-tailed, and that tail estimation requires the analysis of large industry datasets. Almost any LDA model can be replaced with a few simple formulas such as Equation 2 above (and Equation A12 in the appendix for multiple business lines or event types), with the right frequency and severity parameters, and the capital results will be the same.

While the precise parameter values for loss severity will differ from firm to firm, the relative severity rankings for different activities and event types are fairly consistent across the industry. Much more productive is the analysis and discussion of large loss event frequency. Why do some business lines experience large losses routinely, while others almost never see losses over a million dollars? How much variation is there from bank to bank for similar businesses, and how much of that variation depends on the business or control environment? What is the cost-benefit trade-off of reducing loss event frequency of a certain type by 20%? How does event frequency correlate, if at all, with market or credit cycle downturns? And does that mean operational risk practices should be tightened during certain stages of the business cycle? Finally, which event types are routine and unlikely to contribute to headline risk or capital requirements, and which event types should be the focus of discussions in the boardroom or the CEO's office?

There are no definitive answers to any of these questions today, and few firms have investigated these issues systematically. It is therefore to be expected that much valuable information remains hidden in the data, and in the collective knowledge of experienced business managers. The simpler we make the mathematics, and the more we focus on observable frequencies and underlying frequency drivers – the more likely this work will pay off in better controls, better risk measures and more efficient capital allocation.

## APPENDIX: MATHEMATICAL DERIVATION OF KEY RESULTS

For the reader who is interested in pursuing the finesses of power-law approximations with greater rigour, this appendix outlines the mathematical steps required to derive key results. The starting point is the power-law approximation to the cumulative severity distribution of operational losses for a given business or event type. Let us assume that this cumulative distribution is given by

$$p(loss > X) = f(X), \quad f(X_c) = 1 \tag{A1}$$

where $X_c$ is the collection threshold – for example, US$10,000. Fat-tailed distributions can be defined as those distributions that approximate a power law for large enough losses, that is losses greater than $X_L$:

$$p(loss > X) = f(X) \approx bX^{-\alpha} \text{ for } X \geq X_L \tag{A2}$$

$\alpha$ is the tail exponent or power law exponent, $p = 1/\alpha$ is the tail parameter, and $b$ is a normalisation constant. The severity distribution of large losses $X > X_L$ thus becomes approximately

$$p(loss > X/X > X_L) = \frac{f(X)}{f(X_L)} \approx \left(\frac{X}{X_L}\right)^{-\alpha} \tag{A3}$$

For specificity, large losses can be assumed to be those losses greater than US\$1 million – but this is an empirical question: how large do losses have to be before their severity distribution is approximately equal to a power law? In practice, losses in excess of a few hundred thousand to a few million dollars appear to fit power laws well for most operational event types. For example, take a generalised Pareto distribution (GPD) given by

$$f(X) = (1 + \xi x/\beta)^{-1/\xi} \tag{A4}$$

where $\xi$ is the shape parameter and $\beta$ the scale parameter. In a typical fit of operational loss data, $\xi$ might equal 0.8, and $\beta$ might be US\$25,000. Then large losses over US\$1 million fall within 2.5% of a pure power law, and losses over US\$10 million within 0.25%.

Assume now that a given business experiences on average $N$ large loss events over $X_L$ each year. The statistical mean aggregate loss contributed by those large events is easily computed to be $N \cdot X_L \cdot \alpha/(\alpha - 1)$. For example, if a large business experiences 10 events over US\$1 million each year, and the severity distribution of those events follows a power law with tail parameter 0.8 as above, then the expected aggregate loss due to these large events is US\$50 million. Note that this may be a small fraction of the total expected aggregate loss in the business – most of the expected losses are likely to be contributed by much more frequent loss events that are under US\$1 million each.

How do we approximate the risk capital required to cover those $N$ large events? It has become standard to define risk capital or economic capital as the worst total loss at a 99.9% confidence level (Basel) or worst unexpected loss at a 99.95–99.97% confidence level (most firms' internal definitions). We saw in Figure 3 and the corresponding discussion that most – nearly all – of these worst-case losses derive from the single largest event observed. We therefore approximate risk capital by the 99.9% (or higher) quantile of the severity distribution of this largest loss. This distribution can be derived easily using rank statistics. When $N$ losses are drawn at random from a severity distribution $f(X)$, it can be verified that the largest loss (out of $N$) follows a severity distribution $f_N(X)$ given by

$$f_N(X) = 1 - (1 - f(X))^N \tag{A5}$$

The easiest way to derive this is to note that, if the largest loss does not exceed $X$, then none of the $N$ losses do. With the power law approximations discussed above, the severity distribution of the largest loss is then approximately given by

$$f_N(X) = 1 - (1 - f(X))^N \approx Nf(X) \approx N\left(\frac{X}{X_L}\right)^{-\alpha} \tag{A6}$$

and risk capital is approximated by the 99.9% (or higher) quantile of this severity distribution,

$$RC \approx \left(\frac{N}{1 - 99.9\%}\right)^{1/\alpha} = \left(\frac{f_L}{1 - 99.9\%}\right)^{p} \tag{A7}$$

In the example used so far, $f_L = 10$, $X_L =$ US\$1 MM and $p = 0.8$; 99.9% risk capital therefore equals US\$1,585 million as can be verified with a pocket calculator.

While we have assumed so far that the number of large events observed each year is constant, essentially the same results hold when $N$ is a stochastic variable. The simplest case to derive is when $N$ is Poisson distributed with average frequency $\lambda = f_L$. The probability of drawing $n$ events in any given year is then given by

$$p_n = \frac{\lambda^n}{n!} e^{-\lambda} \tag{A8}$$

and the cumulative severity distribution of the largest loss is simply given by

$$
\begin{aligned}
f_{poisson}(X) &= \sum_{n=0}^{\infty} p_n \left[1-(1-f(X))^n\right] \\
&= \sum_{n=0}^{\infty} \frac{\lambda^n}{n!} e^{-\lambda} \left[1-(1-f(X))^n\right] \\
&= 1-\exp(-\lambda f(X))
\end{aligned}
\tag{A9}
$$

With the power law approximation for $f(X)$, risk capital is given by

$$
RC_{poisson} \approx \left( \frac{\lambda}{-\ln(99.9\%)} \right)^{1/\alpha} = \left( \frac{f_L}{-\ln(99.9\%)} \right)^{p} \tag{A10}
$$

and this is nearly identical to Equation A7 above since $-\ln(CL)$ converges to $1-CL$ when $CL$ is close to 100%. The reason why similar results hold whether or not the annual number $N$ of large events is stochastic is that the variance (and higher-order moments) of $N$ contribute only second- (and higher-) order terms to the aggregate severity distribution. For quantiles in excess of 99.9%, these higher-order terms contribute 1% or less risk capital. Similarly, since frequency correlations impact only the variance (and higher-order moments) of the total frequency, but not the expected frequency itself, they have very little impact on aggregate losses and aggregate risk capital.

One final generalisation is obtained when loss events of different types or in different businesses follow different severity distributions. For example, when $f_{L,1}$ annual events come from a loss distribution with tail parameter $p_1$, and $f_{L,2}$ events come from a distribution with tail parameter $p_2$, the aggregate loss distribution is very nearly equal to

$$
f_{aggregate}(X) \approx f_{L,1} \left( \frac{X}{X_L} \right)^{-\alpha_1} + f_{L,2} \left( \frac{X}{X_L} \right)^{-\alpha_2} \tag{A11}
$$

and risk capital $RC$ at a confidence level $CL$ is the root that solves

$$
1-CL \approx f_{L,1} \left( \frac{RC}{X_L} \right)^{-\alpha_1} + f_{L,2} \left( \frac{RC}{X_L} \right)^{-\alpha_2} \tag{A12}
$$

It takes only slightly more effort to solve this equation numerically – for example, through iteration in a spreadsheet – than to calculate risk capital using the closed formula Equation A7 above.

1 For a broad overview of state-of-the-art operational risk modelling, see the recent conference "Implementing an AMA for Operational Risk", organised and hosted by the Federal Reserve Bank of Boston, May 18–20, 2005. Conference presentations, articles and associated materials are available online at www.bos.frb.org/bankinfo/conevent/oprisk2005/index.htm

2 "Results of the 2004 Loss Data Collection Exercise for Operational Risk", Federal Reserve System, Office of the Comptroller of the Currency, Office of Thrift Supervision, Federal Insurance Deposit Corporation; May 12, 2005, Preprint available at www. bos.frb.org/bankinfo/qau/pd051205.pdf

## REFERENCE

**de Fontnouvelle, P., J. Jordan, and E. Rosengren,** 2006, "Implications of Alternative Operational Risk Modelling Techniques", in M. Carey and R. Stulz (eds), *The Risks of Financial Institutions* (Chicago: NBER/University of Chicago Press), preprint available at URL: http://www.bos.frb.org/bankinfo/qau/pderjj604.pdf

4

# Operational Risk Economic Capital Measurement: Mathematical Models for Analysing Loss Data

**Gene Álvarez**

Fannie Mae

> "When you can measure what you are speaking about, and express it in numbers, you know something about it; but when you cannot measure it, when you cannot express it in numbers, your knowledge is of a meagre and unsatisfactory kind."
>
> – William Thompson, Lord Kelvin

The daily operations of running and supporting a business are not without risk. Every organisation is exposed to human errors, external failures and technology breakdowns, to name just a few potential problems. These events are classified as *operational risk* (OpRisk). Formally, one may define OpRisk as, "The risk of loss resulting from inadequate or failed internal processes, people and systems or from external events. This definition includes legal risk, but excludes strategic and reputational risk" (see BIS, 2004). With this definition, managers can monitor the firm's performance by periodically assessing its personnel and departments to identify strengths and vulnerabilities; keeping a record of loss events that have occurred; analysing these losses to determine what lessons may be learned and to develop strategies for minimising or preventing future problems; and quantifying OpRisk to determine the exposure of a department, business line or firm. Although most risk managers would admit that quantification of OpRisk is fundamentally challenging, I will present a few robust and mathematically rigorous models that simplify this task.

The primary objectives of quantifying OpRisk are, first, to calculate the exposure of a department, business line and firm and, second, to facilitate the processes of minimising, controlling or mitigating adverse risk.[1] Before any calculation can be performed, though, we have to address a major obstacle: understanding the fundamental nature of the collected loss data. In other words, how can we mathematically describe the shape of a given set of loss data? Using robust mathematical functions to describe a dataset allows for great accuracy in all calculations that derive from the data. In the following sections, I will present a probability density function that accurately describes the monetary loss data distribution – or, a "severity distribution" – and then apply the function in three models to calculate potential risk exposures. I will also discuss the process of choosing a frequency probability function to describe the occurrence of losses, and the impact of this choice on operational risk quantification.

## SEVERITY DISTRIBUTION FOR HISTORICAL LOSS DATA

Loss event data play an important role in modelling a firm's OpRisk economic exposure. The collected events represent the monetary amounts the firm has historically lost due to internal failures or inadequacies. In a sense, a loss event reflects the firm's control environment at the time the event occurred. Therefore, the severity distribution is a mathematical indicator of the firm's control environment. In this section, I will discuss one severity distribution and use it throughout the chapter.

### Definition of the tail-adjusted normal and lognormal distributions

For practical purposes, some analysts have assumed that the severity distribution of OpRisk losses is best described by a lognormal function. And, in those situations where the lognormal density does not accurately describe the tail of the monetary loss distribution – even though the body is reasonably depicted – other statistical functions, such as Pareto and extreme-value distributions, are used to describe the tail. Therefore, two functions may be used to express the empirical data. Although it is common practice for

**Figure 1a and 1b** Distinction between the body and tail regions of monetary loss data when represented by either a lognormal or normal distribution

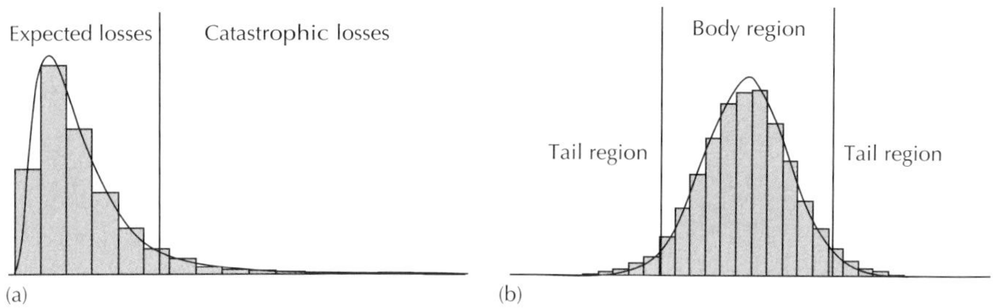


some analysts to use two functions in order to represent the distribution of OpRisk loss data, this practice creates some technical problems. For example, where exactly do the two functions meet? To eliminate the problems that are inherent when disparate functions are used together, we will define a *new* density distribution that will portray the entire dataset.

Although monetary loss data are typically represented by a lognormal distribution (Figure 1a), we will use the normal distribution (Figure 1b) instead because it is simpler to work with. We can use either of these density functions because the lognormal distribution can be changed into a normal distribution via a logarithmic transformation: $y = Log_e|x|$.

Now, we will define the new function. The density distribution we will use for our calculations is a mixture of two well-known functions: the normal and gamma distributions. In mathematical literature, such mixtures are called *compound normal distributions* (see Johnson, Kotz, and Balakrishnan, 1994). The motivation to use the normal–gamma mixture is simple: the two parameters in the normal distribution (mean, $\mu$, and standard deviation, $\sigma$) reasonably describe the body of the loss distribution, and a third parameter – kurtosis, also called the *fourth moment* – satisfactorily depicts the tail. We introduce this third parameter using the gamma distribution. Thus, an OpRisk loss severity distribution is represented by a function with three parameters: mean, standard deviation and kurtosis.[2] From this point forward, I will refer to the mixed distribution as a *tail-adjusted normal* (TAN) *density function*. The TAN probability density function (pdf) is

$$\mathrm{TAN}(\mu,\sigma,\alpha;x)=\int_0^\infty \frac{1}{\sqrt{\varepsilon}\sigma} Z\left(\frac{x-\mu}{\sqrt{\varepsilon}\sigma}\right)\Gamma(\alpha,\alpha^{-1})d\varepsilon \tag{1}$$

where $Z(x)=(\sqrt{2\pi})^{-1}e^{-x^2/2}$ and $\Gamma(\alpha,\alpha^{-1})=\varepsilon^{(\alpha-1)}e^{-\alpha\varepsilon}/\alpha^{-\alpha}\Gamma(\alpha)$. The parameter $\alpha$ will be defined in the next section.

Although I will employ the TAN distribution throughout our discussion, I will also present the tail-adjusted lognormal (TALN) pdf, for reference purposes. The TALN is a lognormal–gamma mixture

$$\mathrm{TALN}(\mu,\sigma,\alpha;x)=\int_0^\infty \frac{x^{-1}}{\sqrt{\varepsilon}\sigma} Z\left(\frac{Log_e|x|-\mu}{\sqrt{\varepsilon}\sigma}\right)\Gamma(\alpha,\alpha^{-1})d\varepsilon \tag{2}$$

where $\mu$ and $\sigma$ are the respective mean and standard deviation of the normally distributed $y=Log_e|x|$. Figure 2 contrasts the standard normal and lognormal probability density functions with their corresponding tail-adjusted counterparts.

### Moments for the tail-adjusted distributions

From Equation 1, we can derive the following expressions:

$$\begin{aligned}
&\text{Mean}=E[x]=\mu\\
&\text{Variance}=E[x^2]-(E[x])^2=\sigma^2\\
&\text{Kurtosis}=E[(x-\mu)^4]/(\sigma^2)^2=3(1+\alpha^{-1})
\end{aligned} \tag{3}$$

**Figure 2a and 2b** Contrast between tail-adjusted normal distribution and the standard normal. a: TAN & normal distributions, b: TAN & normal distributions-tail comparison

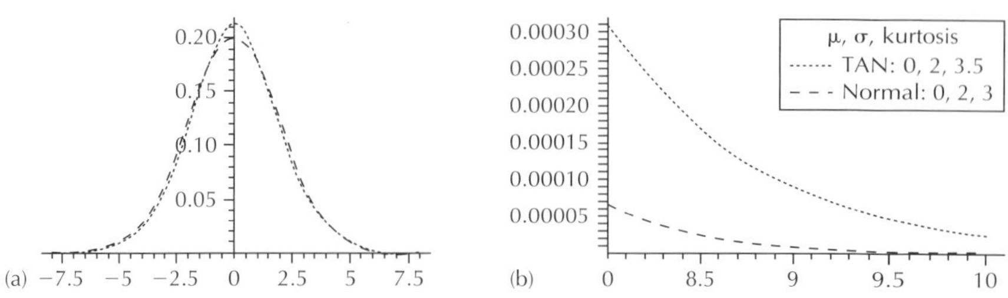

**Figure 2c and 2d** Contrast between tail-adjusted lognormal distribution and the standard lognormal, a: TALN & lognormal distributions, b: TALN & lognormal distributions-tail comparison.
In Figures 2c and 2d, kurtosis is the parameter defined in Equation 31 via α; it is not the fourth moment of the TALN distribution

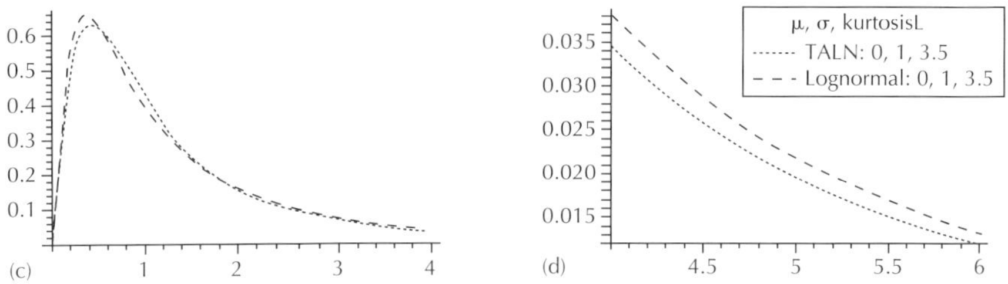


These equations show that the normal–gamma mixture preserves the mean and standard deviation ($=\sqrt{\text{variance}}$) of the normal distribution, while allowing kurtosis to be greater than three because of the following relationship: $\alpha = 3/(\text{kurtosis} - 3) > 0$.

To relate the moments between the TAN and TALN distributions, we will need to know the moments of the lognormal–gamma mixture. Using Equation 2 the $n$th moment is

$$E[x^n] = \left(1 - \frac{n^2\sigma^2}{2\alpha}\right)^{-\alpha} e^{n\mu} \tag{4}$$

One can easily determine the mean ($n = 1$) and variance ($n = 2$) for the TALN distribution from Equation 4.

### Tail-adjusted, normal-distribution, truncated moment equations

Determining the three parameters that depict the TAN distribution for a given set of monetary loss data is critical. We must keep in mind that OpRisk loss data are almost always collected above a truncation threshold because it is impractical to gather losses from zero.[3] Reporting every lost pencil or paperclip, for example, is an impossible task. Therefore, for any given dataset, the measurable quantities – μ, σ, and kurtosis – represent a truncated (conditional) distribution and not a full (unconditional) distribution (see Figure 3).

**Figure 3** Representation of a truncated TAN distribution from the full aTAN distribution (dashed line)

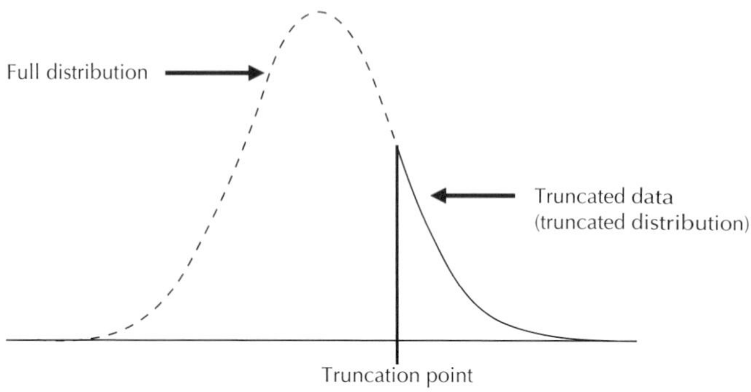


Despite this apparent limitation, we can quantify OpRisk if we use the truncated data's measurable parameters to calculate the full parameters. The procedure is as follows:

(1) calculate the mean, standard deviation and kurtosis of the truncated dataset;
(2) equate each truncated moment expression to its respective truncated measured quantity (eg, the truncated mean is equated to the truncated first moment equation); and
(3) solve the three simultaneous equations.

The solution set to the three truncated simultaneous equations will yield the unconditional parameters. Determining the truncated moment equations is the pivotal step in this process. Without them, it is extremely difficult to determine the unconditional parameters. In the following paragraph, we will derive the truncated TAN moment equations.

First, we must define the pdf of a doubly truncated TAN, which is analogous to a doubly truncated normal distribution. The pdf, with lower and upper truncation points $A$ and $B$, is

$$\int_0^{\infty} \frac{1}{\sqrt{\varepsilon}\sigma} \frac{Z(x')}{\Phi(B') - \Phi(A')} \Gamma(\alpha, \alpha^{-1}) \mathrm{d}\varepsilon, \qquad A \leq x \leq B \tag{5}$$

where

$$\Phi(x) = \frac{1}{\sqrt{2\pi}} \int_{-\infty}^{x} Exp[-t^2/2]\mathrm{d}t,\ x' = \frac{x-\mu}{\sqrt{\varepsilon\sigma}}$$

$$A' = \frac{A-\mu}{\sqrt{\varepsilon\sigma}},\ \text{and}\ B' = \frac{B-\mu}{\sqrt{\varepsilon\sigma}}$$

From Equation 5, we can derive the truncated moment equations for the mean, variance and kurtosis. Using

$$E[x^n \mid \text{truncated}] = \int_A^B \int_0^\infty \frac{1}{\sqrt{\varepsilon\sigma}} \frac{x^n Z(x')}{\Phi(B') - \Phi(A')} \Gamma(\alpha, \alpha^{-1}) \mathrm{d}\varepsilon\, \mathrm{d}x \tag{6}$$

The three expressions are (mean: $n = 1$; variance: $n = 2$; kurtosis: $n = 4$)

$$\mu_{\text{trun}} = \mu + \sigma \int_0^\infty \sqrt{\varepsilon}\, \frac{[Z(A') - Z(B')]}{\Phi(B') - \Phi(A')} \Gamma(\alpha, \alpha^{-1}) \mathrm{d}\varepsilon \tag{7}$$

$$\begin{aligned} \sigma^2_{\text{trun}} = {} & \sigma^2 \left\{ 1 - \left[ \int_0^\infty \sqrt{\varepsilon}\, \frac{[Z(A') - Z(B')]}{\Phi(B') - \Phi(A')} \Gamma(\alpha, \alpha^{-1}) \mathrm{d}\varepsilon \right]^2 \right\} \\ & + \sigma \int_0^\infty \sqrt{\varepsilon}\, \frac{[(A-\mu)Z(A') - (B-\mu)Z(B')]}{\Phi(B') - \Phi(A')} \Gamma(\alpha, \alpha^{-1}) \mathrm{d}\varepsilon \end{aligned} \tag{8}$$

$$\begin{aligned} \text{kurt}_{\text{trun}} = {} & \frac{3\sigma^4}{\alpha} + \sigma \left\{ \int_0^\infty \sqrt{\varepsilon}\, \frac{[(A-\mu)^3 Z(A') - (B-\mu)^3 Z(B')]}{\Phi(B') - \Phi(A')} \Gamma(\alpha, \alpha^{-1}) \mathrm{d}\varepsilon \right. \\ & - 4\sigma \left[ \int_0^\infty \sqrt{\varepsilon}\, \frac{[(A-\mu)Z(A') - (B-\mu)Z(B')]}{\Phi(B') - \Phi(A')} \Gamma(\alpha, \alpha^{-1}) \mathrm{d}\varepsilon \right]^2 \\ & + 3\sigma^2 \left\{ \int_0^\infty \varepsilon^{3/2}\, \frac{[(A-\mu)Z(A') - (B-\mu)Z(B')]}{\Phi(B') - \Phi(A')} \Gamma(\alpha, \alpha^{-1}) \mathrm{d}\varepsilon \right. \\ & \left. \left. + 2 \left[ \int_0^\infty \sqrt{\varepsilon}\, \frac{[(A-\mu)^{1/3} Z(A') - (B-\mu)^{1/3} Z(B')]}{\Phi(B') - \Phi(A')} \Gamma(\alpha, \alpha^{-1}) \mathrm{d}\varepsilon \right]^3 \right\} \right. \end{aligned}$$

$$+\sigma^3 \left\{ 3-8\left( \int_0^\infty \varepsilon^{3/2} \frac{[Z(A')-Z(B')]}{\Phi(B')-\Phi(A')} \Gamma(\alpha,\alpha^{-1}) d\varepsilon \right) \right.$$

$$\left( \int_0^\infty \sqrt{\varepsilon} \frac{[Z(A')-Z(B')]}{\Phi(B')-\Phi(A')} \Gamma(\alpha,\alpha^{-1}) d\varepsilon \right)$$

$$+6\left[ \int_0^\infty \sqrt{\varepsilon} \frac{[Z(A')-Z(B')]}{\Phi(B')-\Phi(A')} \Gamma(\alpha,\alpha^{-1}) d\varepsilon \right]^2$$

$$\left. -3\left[ \int_0^\infty \sqrt{\varepsilon} \frac{[Z(A')-Z(B')]}{\Phi(B')-\Phi(A')} \Gamma(\alpha,\alpha^{-1}) d\varepsilon \right]^4 \right\}\Bigg\} \tag{9}$$

Equations 7–9 are simplified by the fact that monetary loss data are, in most cases, singly truncated. Thus, if the lower truncation point is $A$ and the upper truncation value is assumed to be $B = \infty$, then the corresponding three moment equations for the singly truncated TAN pdf are

$$\mu_{\text{trun}} = \mu + \sigma\,\Psi \tag{10}$$

$$\sigma^2_{\text{trun}} = [(A-\mu)\Psi + \sigma(1-\Psi^2)] \tag{11}$$

$$\text{kurt}_{\text{trun}} = \frac{3\sigma^4}{\alpha} + \sigma[(A-\mu)^3\Psi - 4\sigma(A-\mu)^2\Psi^2 + 3\sigma^2(A-\mu)(X+2\Psi^3)$$
$$+\ \sigma^3(3-8X\Psi+6\Psi^2-3\Psi^4)] \tag{12}$$

where

$$\Psi = \int_0^\infty \sqrt{\varepsilon} \frac{Z(A')}{1-\Phi(A')} \Gamma(\alpha,\alpha^{-1}) d\varepsilon \qquad X\int_0^\infty \varepsilon^{3/2} \frac{Z(A')}{1-\Phi(A')} \Gamma(\alpha,\alpha^{-1}) d\varepsilon \tag{13}$$

*Example: Tail-adjusted, normal-distribution, truncated moment equations*

As an illustration, consider two TAN distributions with parameters ($\mu$, $\sigma$, kurtosis) = (−3.50, 1.50, 3.15) and (−4.00, 1.80, 3.80). For each distribution, 100,000 points were randomly generated above a truncation threshold of $x = -3.69$ (see Figures 4a and 4b). The truncated $\mu$, $\sigma$, and kurtosis parameters were calculated and the simultaneous

**Figure 4a and 4b** Histogram of randomly generated losses for the (μ, σ, kurtosis)= (−3.50, 1.50, 3.15) TAN density function. a: Generated tail-TAN distribution, b: Generated tail-TAN distribution

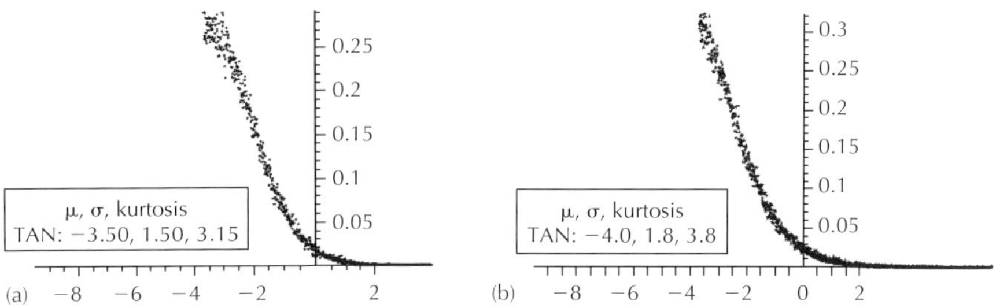


**Table 1** Comparison of known unconditional parameters with parameters obtained from solving simultaneous truncated moment equations

| | TAN distribution parameter values | | | | | |
|---|---|---|---|---|---|---|
| | **Given** | | **Truncated** | | **Solved** | |
| **μ** | −3.50 | −4.00 | −2.43 | −2.39 | −3.49 | −4.03 |
| **σ** | 1.50 | 1.80 | 0.95 | 1.10 | 1.49 | 1.81 |
| **kurtosis** | 3.15 | 3.80 | 4.06 | 5.86 | 3.16 | 3.69 |

truncated moment equations 10–12 were solved after each expression was set equal to its respective measured truncated value (eg, the truncated variance is equated to the truncated second moment equation). As we can see from Table 1, the values obtained from solving the TAN simultaneous equations are in good agreement with the starting parameters. The difference is attributable to numerical rounding in solving the equations.

### Confidence intervals for tail-adjusted normal parameters

Before performing any analysis, we must collect data. At this stage, we must choose an appropriate truncation threshold, keeping in mind the institution's ability to gather data and the potential statistical size of the dataset. An extremely low economic cut-off may overwhelm the data collectors, while a very high threshold may yield a dataset with too few losses to analyse accurately.

Even if a large number of data are collected, an institution will be working with a *sample* dataset because, as we have stressed in other sections, it is impractical to expect that a firm will record every loss it incurs. Also, any sample set collected will be one of many possible datasets for a given institution, and will have parameters different from the parameters of other possible sample sets. Although, theoretically, Equations 10–12 will exactly solve for the unconditional values, slight differences between the possible sample datasets will influence the results of our calculations. This difference is a natural characteristic of calculations dependent on datasets, but we can work around it if we determine how much the parameters of the sample dataset differ from the theoretical values of the full distribution. We test the precision of the estimated values by applying sampling theory to calculate the confidence interval[4] for the three parameters. A confidence interval indicates the precision of an estimated value. The interval represents the range of values, consistent with the data, which is believed to encompass the "true" value with high probability. Wider intervals indicate lower precision, while narrow intervals indicate greater precision.

To derive the respective confidence intervals for $\mu$, $\sigma$, and kurtosis, we will assume that loss events are described by a TAN distribution. This being the case, the joint density function for $N$ observed losses is

$$(\sqrt{2\pi}\sigma)^{-N}\prod_{i=1}^{N}\int_{0}^{\infty}\varepsilon^{-1/2}e^{-x_i^2/2\varepsilon\sigma^2}\,\Gamma(\alpha,\alpha^{-1})d\varepsilon \tag{14}$$

where $\Pi$ indicates a series of products. It is similar to $\Sigma$ – the summation of a series – but uses multiplication rather than addition. For simplicity, we assume the theoretical mean to be zero, the theoretical standard deviation to be $\sigma$, and kurtosis to be $\alpha$. Because a closed-form analytical solution to Equation 14 is difficult to obtain, we must simplify our task. It can be shown that the expression is bounded from above by

$$\begin{aligned}&(\sqrt{2\pi}\sigma)^{-N}\prod_{i=1}^{N}\int_{0}^{\infty}\varepsilon^{-1/2}e^{-x_i^2/2\varepsilon\sigma^2}\,\Gamma(\alpha,\alpha^{-1})d\varepsilon\\&\le(\sqrt{2\pi}\sigma)^{-N}\int_{0}^{\infty}\varepsilon^{-N/2}e^{-\Sigma x_i^2/2\varepsilon\sigma^2}\,\Gamma(\alpha,\alpha^{-1})^{N}\,d\varepsilon\end{aligned} \tag{15}$$

Using $\Sigma_{i=1}^{N} x_i^2 = N(\bar{x}^2 + m_2)$, where $\bar{x}$ is the sample mean and $m_2$ is the second sample moment about the mean, we will expand the gamma function and rewrite the right-hand side of Equation 15 as

$$\left(\frac{\alpha^{\alpha}}{\sqrt{2\pi}\sigma\Gamma(\alpha)}\right)^{N} \int_{0}^{\infty} \varepsilon^{-N(\alpha-3/2)} e^{-N\alpha\varepsilon} e^{-N(\bar{x}^2+m_2)/2\varepsilon\sigma^2} \, d\varepsilon \tag{16}$$

From Equation 16 we can now derive all the probability distributions needed to calculate the confidence intervals for the three parameters. The general steps to derive the probability densities that describe the mean and variance distributions are similar when we assume a normal parent population. For brevity, I will simply state the results in the next two sections and refer the reader to Keeping (1995) for the details.

*Mean confidence interval*

The confidence interval for the mean is calculated using

$$\mu_{CI} = \mu \pm \sigma t_p N^{-1/2} \tag{17}$$

where $t_p$ is obtained from solving

$$1-p = 2\int_{0}^{t_p} N^{-1/2} B\left(\frac{1}{2}, \frac{N}{2}\right)^{-1} \left(1+\frac{t^2}{N}\right)^{-(N+1)/2} dt \tag{18}$$

for a given probability $p$. The integrand of Equation 18 is the Student's $t$ distribution, where $B(m, n) = \Gamma(m)\Gamma(n) / \Gamma(m+n)$ is the beta function. An astute reader will note that Equation 18 yields the same result whether we assume a normally distributed parent dataset or a TAN distribution. This is expected because the shape of the distribution does not affect the position of the TAN density. However, because the standard deviation of the TAN density is influenced by the gamma distribution, we expect a different probability distribution that determines the confidence interval for $\sigma$.

*Standard-deviation confidence interval*

The confidence interval for $\sigma$ can be calculated from

$$\int_{\chi_1^2}^{\infty} f(\chi^2) d\chi^2 = \frac{P}{2} \qquad \int_{0}^{\chi_2^2} f(\chi^2) d\chi^2 = \frac{p}{2} \tag{19}$$

where

$$f(\chi^2) = \frac{1}{2}\frac{[N^{\alpha}\Gamma(\alpha)]^N}{(N\alpha)^{(N-1)}}\left\{\Gamma\left[\frac{1}{2}(N-1)\right]\Gamma[N(\alpha-1)+1]\right\}^{-1}\left(\frac{\chi^2}{2}\right)^{(N-3)/2}$$
$$\times\int_0^{\infty}\varepsilon^{(1-N)/2}\Gamma(\alpha,\alpha^{-1})e^{-\chi^2/2\varepsilon}d\varepsilon \quad \textbf{(20)}$$

Therefore, the lower and upper confidence limits for $\sigma^2$ are given by

$$\sigma_l^2 = \frac{(N-1)}{\chi_1^2}\sigma^2 \qquad \sigma_u^2 = \frac{(N-1)}{\chi_2^2}\sigma^2 \quad \textbf{(21)}$$

As the reader will observe, Equation 20 resembles the chi-squared distribution. In deriving Equation 20, it was necessary to use a known $\alpha$ or, equivalently, a specific kurtosis value, in order to simplify the derivation. In practice, we will use the unconditional kurtosis value obtained from the solution set of the simultaneous truncated moment equations when calculating the confidence interval for $\sigma$.

*Kurtosis confidence interval*

Deriving the probability distribution that describes the kurtosis parameter is an extremely difficult exercise. If we use the formal or the *k*-statistics kurtosis definition, re-expressing $\alpha$ in Equation 16 yields a complicated equation that is difficult to work with. To get around this derivational impasse, let us recall the mathematical form of the TAN density. As defined in Equation 1, we know the gamma function will influence both the $\sigma$ and kurtosis parameters. Since that is the case, we will hypothesise that the gamma has an equal influence on both parameters. Therefore, we will assume that the ratio between the limits of the standard-deviation confidence interval and the solved $\sigma$ value will hold true for the limits of the kurtosis confidence interval and the solved kurtosis value. Mathematically, the lower and upper confidence limits for kurtosis are given by

$$\text{kurt}_l = \frac{\sigma_l}{\sigma}\text{kurt} \qquad \text{kurt}_u = \frac{\sigma_u}{\sigma}\text{kurt} \quad \textbf{(22)}$$

*Example: Confidence intervals for tail-adjusted normal parameters*

To illustrate this point, let us calculate the confidence interval for each parameter: $\mu$, $\sigma$, and kurtosis. Suppose that a TAN distribution is characterised by the parameters $\mu = -3.75$, $\sigma = 1.60$, and kurtosis = 3.55. Let us further assume that the truncation threshold is $x = -3.69$ and the sample size is 300 data points. For the sample dataset, the calculated truncated parameters are ($\mu_{trun}$, $\sigma_{trun}$, $kurt_{trun}$) = (−2.45, 0.92, 4.28). Given the truncated parameters and the cut-off, the solution set to Equations 10–12 is ($\mu$, $\sigma$, kurtosis) = (−3.26, 1.36, 3.40). Solving Equations 17, 19 and 22, the respective 99% confidence intervals for the parameters are: $-3.28 \le \mu \le -3.25$; $1.32 \le \sigma \le 1.64$; and $3.29 \le$ kurtosis $\le 4.09$.

### Tail-adjusted, normal-distribution, maximum-likelihood estimation

Maximum-likelihood method is an analytic maximisation procedure to estimate the parameters that make the known *likelihood* function a maximum. The likelihood function is defined as the joint density

$$L(X;\vartheta) = \prod_{i=1}^{n} PDF(x_i;\vartheta) \tag{23}$$

of the observations $x_i$ considered as a function of $\vartheta$. The method is intuitively appealing because we are trying to find the values of the parameters that would have most likely produced the data we in fact observed.

The maximum-likelihood estimator of $\vartheta$ is solved via

$$\partial_\vartheta L(X;\vartheta) = 0 \Rightarrow \hat{\vartheta} = \arg\max_{\vartheta} L(X;\vartheta) \tag{24}$$

For many analysts, maximum likelihood is the preferred parameter estimation method because it yields minimum-variance unbiased estimators as the sample size increases. However, if we wanted to benefit from this advantage in estimating the TAN parameters, we could not because the partial derivatives do not exist due to the Leibniz rule.[5] Thus, the maximum likelihood method cannot be applied to approximate TAN parameters.

## FREQUENCY DISTRIBUTION: HOW TO QUANTIFY THE OCCURRENCES OF LOSS EVENTS

When analysing loss data, it is essential to identify the severity distribution with the functional form that best describes the monetary impact of the data points. But the analysis will not be complete until we have examined the frequency with which the events occur. This analysis is important because risk managers need to have an idea not only of the amount of money at risk but also of the number of events they can expect to see in a given period of time. In this section, we will examine three related discrete distributions, any of which may be used to analyse the frequency of OpRisk losses.

They are the binomial, negative binomial and the Poisson distributions. All three satisfy the same recursive relationship and are described by one parameter or two (see Johnson, Kotz and Kemp, 1993; Klugman, Panjer and Willmot, 1998). The main distinction among the distributions is the relationship between the mean and the variance. For the binomial distribution, the variance is less than the mean; for the negative binomial distribution, the variance is greater then the mean; and, for the Poisson distribution, the variance and the mean are equal.

### Binomial distribution

Suppose that a trial, or experiment, whose outcome can be classified as either a "success" or a "failure" is performed. The probability function for $n$ number of successes is described by

$$\binom{n}{k} p^k q^{n-k}, \qquad k = 0, 1, 2, \ldots, n \tag{25}$$

where the probability of success at each trial is $p$ $(0 < p < 1)$ and the probability of failure is $q = 1 - p$. Equation 25 is called the *binomial distribution*. The mean and variance of the binomial distribution are

$$\text{Mean} = np \quad \text{Variance} = np(1 - p) \tag{26}$$

### Negative binomial distribution

Suppose that independent trials each having probability $p$ of being a success are performed until $r$ successes are accumulated. The probability function for $n$ trials required for the number of accumulated successes is

$$\binom{n-1}{r-1} p^r q^{n-r}, \qquad r = 0, 1, 2, \ldots \tag{27}$$

Equation 27 is called the *negative binomial distribution*. The mean and variance of the negative binomial distribution are

$$\text{Mean} = \frac{n(1-p)}{p} \qquad \text{Variance} = \frac{n(1-p)}{p^2} \tag{28}$$

**Poisson distribution**

A random variable $x$ ($x = 0, 1, 2, \ldots$) is said to be a Poisson random variable with parameter $\lambda$ if for some $\lambda > 0$ the probability function is given by

$$\frac{\lambda^x e^{-\lambda}}{x!} \tag{29}$$

The mean and variance of the binomial distribution are

$$\text{Mean} = \lambda \qquad \text{Variance} = \lambda \tag{30}$$

## ECONOMIC CAPITAL CALCULATION

Because calculations of capital-risk exposure are sensitive to the tail of the distribution, the tail must be correctly parameterised, or risk exposure values will be under- or overestimated. Therefore, in the analysis of loss data, a closed, analytical function is advantageous because it gives a continuous depiction of the underlying dataset. The analytical function can be evaluated to obtain values of the function or of its inverse (if one exists), for various numerical calculations. In practice, with an accurate functional representation of the dataset in question, the calculations for capital-risk exposure can be carried out with mathematical certainty. To illustrate the point, I will present three capital-exposure models that employ the TAN probability density function.

Before we proceed, we must note that, although empirical data can be grouped in discrete monetary buckets to calculate values such as probabilities, this practice must be used with caution. If we limit our discussion to probability calculations we will under- or overestimate the probabilities and produce inaccurate values, unless the data are smooth throughout the entire data capture range, and are of statistical significance to estimate probabilities with small errors. And, if a probability value beyond the captured monetary range is needed, interpolation of the data definitely may result in erroneous numbers. One of the virtues of a parameterised functional form is that these shortcomings can be avoided.

Having laid the foundation for our discussion on modelling OpRisk economic capital exposure, I can present the general outline for the three models. The common steps for the models are as follows.

(1) *Measure truncated parameters*: Using the collected OpRisk data, calculate the truncated mean, standard deviation and kurtosis.
(2) *Determine full parameters by solving truncated moment equations*: Using the measured truncated parameters and truncation threshold value, solve the truncated moment equations to arrive at the full (unconditional) parameters of the TAN density that best describes the dataset.
(3) *Determine confidence interval for each parameter*: Once the full parameters are known, test the precision of the estimated values by calculating the confidence intervals for the three parameters.
(4) *Estimate the yearly frequency of losses*: From the collected dataset, approximate the number of losses that are likely to occur each year above a monetary threshold.
(5) *Calculate or simulate the capital-at-risk (CaR)*: Using the solved parameters, with their respective confidence intervals, and the estimated yearly occurrence of losses, use an analytical method to calculate or a Monte Carlo engine to simulate the CaR for a given confidence level (eg, 99%).
(6) *Approximate CaR error*: Estimate the uncertainty in the CaR figure.
(7) *Calculate the CaR stress figures*: Using the solved parameters, with their respective confidence intervals, calculate the CaR stress figures.

With the general model characteristics summarised, we can proceed in presenting the three models.

**Figure 5** The employment of the loss probability and frequency to simulate probable operational risk losses in calculating the OpRisk economic capital

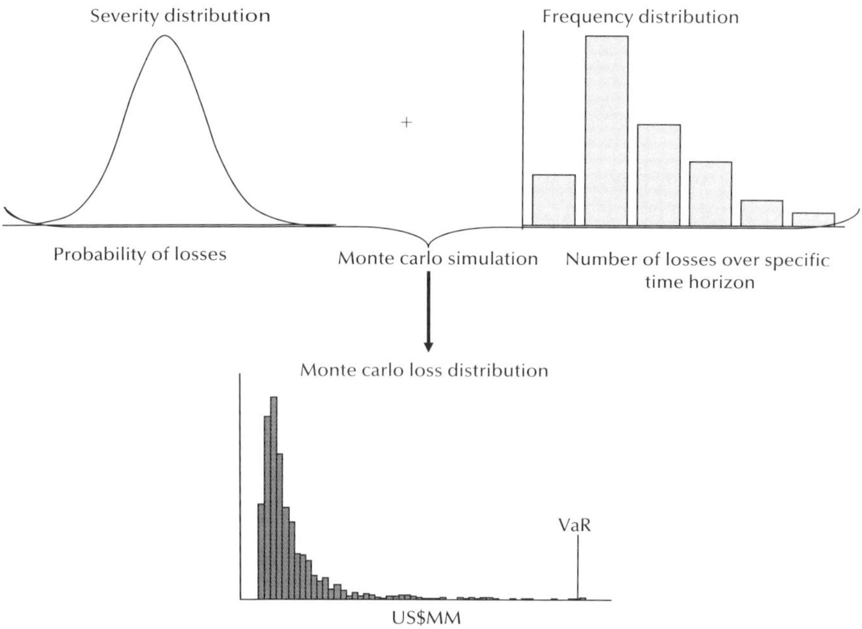


## OpRisk economic capital model I

The first method I will employ to calculate the operational risk exposure is value-at-risk (VaR): the capital amount that may be lost over some time horizon, at a specific confidence level (CL). There are several approaches that can be used to calculate VaR. For the upcoming discussion, we will limit ourselves to Monte Carlo simulation. For illustrative purposes, Figure 5 depicts the use of the severity and frequency of OpRisk loss distributions in calculating the OpRisk economic capital via Monte Carlo simulation.

A Monte Carlo model is a statistical simulation that utilises sequences of random numbers to perform statistical sampling experiments on a computer. The power of the Monte Carlo technique is that it can be applied to problems with no probabilistic content, as well as to those with inherent probabilistic structure (see Dowd, 2002). For our discussion on economic capital exposure, we employ the severity and frequency distributions and parameter

**Figure 6** Illustration of the three determined unconditional TAN parameters used in a stochastic monte carlo engine to generate a family of TAN distributions

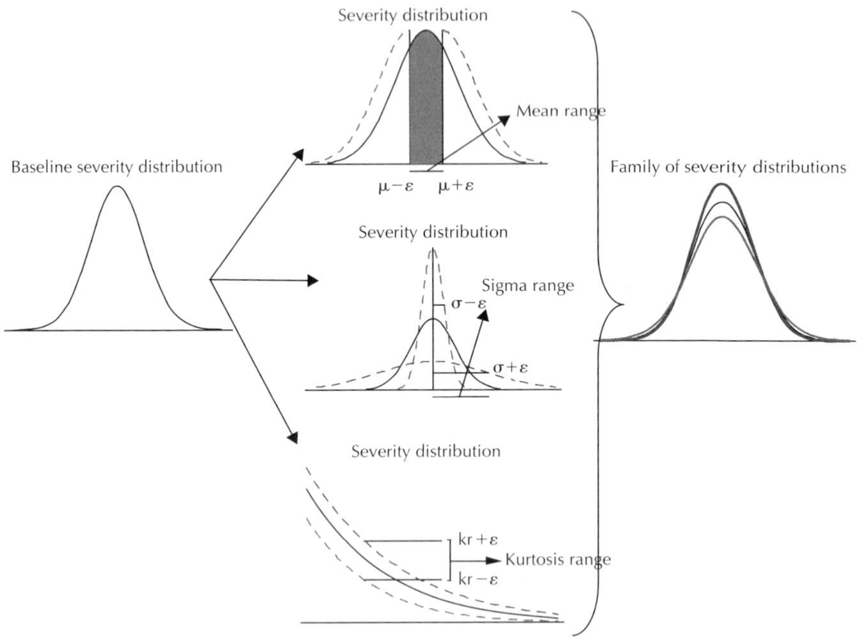


confidence intervals for a loss dataset. The parameter confidence intervals are used because they facilitate the utilisation of a stochastic Monte Carlo simulation engine, as shown in Figure 6. In general, the steps for one Monte Carlo simulation are these:

(a) Generate pseudorandom severity parameters from their respective confidence interval.
(b) Generate a pseudorandom number $m$ for the frequency of losses from the frequency population described by the frequency distribution.
(c) Generate $m$ pseudorandom losses from the severity population described by the pseudorandom severity parameters.
(d) Add the $m$ pseudorandom losses.

To produce multiple simulations, Steps (a)–(d) are iteratively repeated $N$ times. After $N$ simulations are completed, the resultant sums are ranked in ascending order. Finally, the VaR value for a given percentile (confidence limit) is determined from the ordered list.

Although in Step (c) we may apply the inverse or acceptance-rejection method (see Fishman, 1996) to generate a TAN pseudorandom number, the most efficient algorithm to generate a pseudorandom number from the TAN population is $\mu + a\sqrt{b}\sigma$, where $a$ is a pseudorandom number from the unit normal distribution, $N(\mu = 0, \sigma = 1)$, and $b$ is a pseudorandom number from the gamma distribution, $\Gamma(\alpha, \alpha^{-1})(\alpha = 3/(\text{kurtosis} - 3))$.

To illustrate Model I, as well as the other two models to be presented, the TAN distribution will be used to parameterise the severity distribution for a set of monetary loss data.

*Example: Model I*

We will now work an example to clarify the seven steps for Model I. Suppose *a priori* we know that a full monetary loss distribution is characterised by the parameters $\mu = -4.00$, $\sigma = 1.75$, and kurtosis = 3.60. These parameters are given in logarithmic terms.[6] In real dollar terms, the mean represents an average loss of US$121,000. And, as mentioned previously, suppose that real business considerations and limitations do not allow us to collect data on losses below US$25,000; this, then, is our truncation threshold. Let us further assume that, after one year of firm-wide data collection, we have recorded 300 operational risk loss events. Figure 7 illustrates the 300 data points.

Step 1: Measure truncated parameters

The first step in our model is to calculate three basic statistical values of a firm's internally collected truncated data. These statistics, which will allow us to determine the best TAN distribution to portray the dataset, are the mean, standard deviation and kurtosis. Specifically, for a dataset of $n$ elements, the values are computed using

$$\mu = \frac{1}{n}\sum_{i=1}^{n} x_i \tag{31}$$

$$\sigma = \left[\frac{1}{n = 1}\sum_{i=1}^{n}(x_i - \mu)^2\right]^{1/2} \tag{32}$$

$$\text{kurt} = \frac{\dfrac{1}{n-2}\displaystyle\sum_{i=1}^{n}(x_i - \mu)^2}{\sigma^4} \tag{33}$$

**Figure 7** Histogram of the 300 randomly generated losses for the ($\mu$, $\sigma$, kurtosis) = (−4.00, 1.75, 3.60) TAN density function above the truncation threshold of −4.20. Losses were grouped in monetary buckets of US$25,000. The histogram is normalised to unity

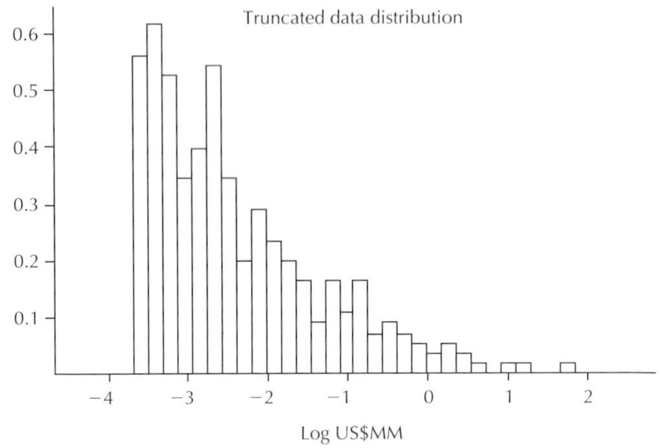


In practice, it is recommended to convert the monetary losses to units of millions (eg, US$15,000 = US$0.015 million) before the losses are re-expressed in logarithmic terms (eg, $\text{Log}_e(0.015) \approx -4.20$). For our dataset, the calculated truncated parameters are ($\mu_{trun}$, $\sigma_{trun}$, $\text{kurt}_{trun}$) = (−2.46, 1.08, 4.31). In real dollar terms, the truncated mean is approximately US$205,000.

Step 2: Solve the TAN truncated moment equations
Given the truncated parameters ($\mu_{trun}$, $\sigma_{trun}$, $\text{kurt}_{trun}$) = (−2.46, 1.08, 4.31) and the monetary cut-off of US$25,000, the solution to the simultaneous truncated moment Equations 10–12 is ($\mu$, $\sigma$, kurtosis) = (−3.84, 1.77, 3.05). Let us emphasise that the solution set represents a TAN distribution that expresses both high-frequency/low-severity and low-frequency/high-severity events.

An astute observer will note that the solved parameters do not equal the parameters of the known distribution. This is to be expected because we are dealing with a small dataset – in this case 300 losses. Ideally, if an infinite number of data points were collected above the monetary threshold of US$25,000, the truncated parameters would have been (−2.43, 1.05, 5.51). However, since an

**Figure 8** Normality assumption for a generic TAN distribution parameter

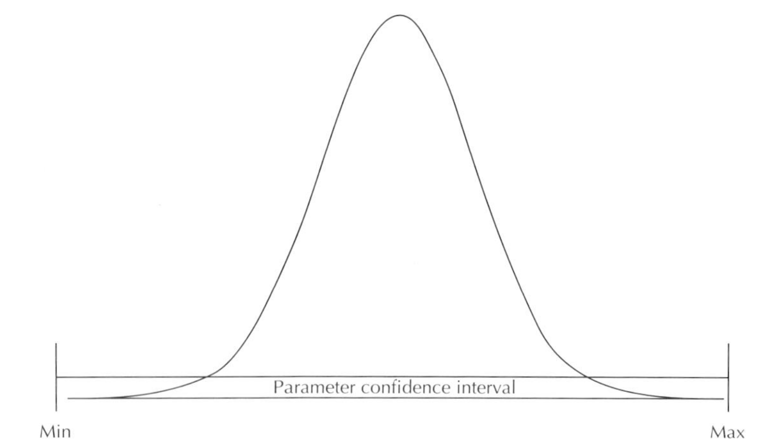


infinite dataset is not attainable, we must settle for a *sample* dataset. The collected, finite dataset in our example is one of many representative data samples for the known distribution. As a result, we must determine how the three calculated parameters differ from the theoretical values of the full distribution. This leads us to step three.

Step 3: Determine parameters' confidence interval and random generation

Solving Equations 17, 19 and 22, the respective 99% confidence intervals for our example are: $-3.86 \leq \mu \leq -3.83$; $1.62 \leq \sigma \leq 2.00$; and $3.00 \leq$ kurtosis $\leq 3.43$. In our simulation engine, we will assume the parameters are normally distributed along their respective confidence interval.[7] This will give the stochastic Monte Carlo engine the mechanism to randomly sample the confidence intervals to generate pseudorandom variates for the severity parameter values. Figure 8 graphically depicts the distribution assumption for an arbitrary parameter.

Step 4: Determine frequency of losses

The fourth step is to estimate the number of losses that will occur each year above a chosen monetary cut-off. Generally, the losses above the monetary threshold are grouped by year when the event occurred, and the mean and variance of the frequency dataset are then calculated. Equations 31 and 32 (variance = $\sigma^2$) are used to perform the computations. After the calculations, the appropriate frequency distribution discussed in the section "Frequency distribution: how to quantify the occurrences of loss events" above is chosen. If there is only one year of data, then the variance computation is not required because we will assume the mean and variance are equal to the number of events above the cut-off and, thus, a Poisson distribution will characterise the frequency in the Monte Carlo simulator. For our example, only one year of data were collected; therefore, let us assume that 68 events above US$100,000 occur each year. Although we assumed that the truncation point for our dataset was US$25,000, we will use a higher cut-off in this step, to reduce the time needed to execute the Monte Carlo simulation.

Step 5: Simulate VaR

Using the information determined by Steps 2 through 4, we can now quantify the potential capital exposure to catastrophic operational risk events. To determine the VaR at the 99% CL – indicating the second largest loss out of 100 losses – we will generate pseudo-random severity distributions from the confidence intervals determined in Step 3 (the family of distributions illustrated in Figure 9) and simulate 68 loss events above US$100,000. Our Monte Carlo engine will assume a Poisson distribution for the frequency of

**Figure 9** Depiction of potential severity distributions when the $\mu$, $\sigma$ and kurtosis confidence intervals are considered. a: TAN comparison, b: Tail comparison

The black graph represents TAN($\mu$, $\sigma$, kurtosis) = (−3.84, 1.77, 3.05); the dark gray represents TAN($\mu$, $\sigma$, kurtosis) = (−3.86, 1.62, 3.00), while the light gray is TAN($\mu$, $\sigma$, kurtosis) = (−3.83, 2.00, 3.43)

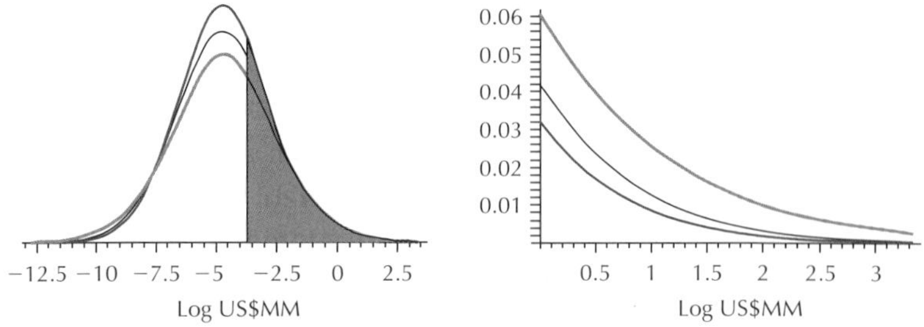

**Table 2** Comparison of the operational risk quantification model results between a randomly generated data set and a known distribution. VaR results represent a Monte Carlo simulation of 10,000 years using a Poisson mean frequency of 68 loss events per year above US$100,000

| | **Truncated parameters ($\mu$, $\sigma$, kurtosis) Values are in logarithmic term** | **Full parameters ($\mu$, $\sigma$, kurtosis)** | **Confidence intervals** | **VaR values are in millions of dollars** |
|---|---|---|---|---|
| Known distribution | (−2.43, 1.05, 5.51) | (−4.00, 1.75, 3.60) | N/A | 170 |
| 300-point dataset | (−2.46, 1.08, 4.31) | (−3.84, 1.77, 3.05) | $-3.86 \leq \mu \leq -3.83$<br>$1.62 \leq \sigma \leq 2.00$<br>$3.00 \leq$ kurtosis $\leq 3.43$ | 130 |

**Figure 10** Comparison between TAN probability distribution function whose parameters were obtained from solving simultaneous truncated moment equations for the 300 data sample, and the original TAN probability distribution function (solid curve)

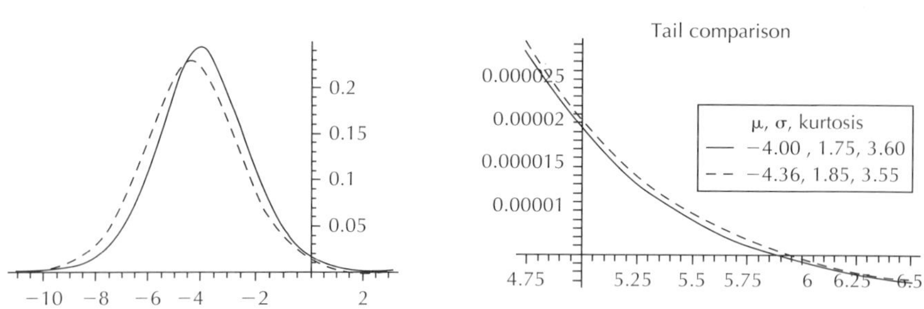


losses. The result after simulating 10,000 years at the 99% confidence level is US$130 million.

As a comparison, we can calculate VaR at the 99% CL for the *a priori* loss distribution ($\mu$, $\sigma$, kurtosis) = (−4.00, 1.75, 3.60). Using the same frequency and momentary truncation values as above, the simulated VaR for the known density is US$170 million. Therefore, the data sample of 300 losses resulted in a VaR number that is in good agreement with the known distribution. Table 2 summarises our example and Figure 10 illustrates how the derived densities approach the known distribution as the number of data points increases.

Step 6: Approximate VaR error

All measurements and computational results have inherent errors. However, determining all the errors and estimating their size can be a strenuous exercise. Hence, only the major errors need to be considered. The proprietary model presented here estimates the error of the calculated VaR figure. The approximate error has three components:

(a) severity distribution ($e_1$);
(b) frequency of losses ($e_2$); and
(c) number of Monte Carlo iterations ($e_3$).

The error for (a) is determined by calculating the ratio of the areas between the two severity distributions defined by the end points of the parameter confidence intervals (the ratio between the red and blue graphs in Figure 9). In our example, the error is approximately 10%.

The error for (b) is estimated from the inaccuracy in observing 68 losses per year. Because we assumed a Poisson distribution, we will estimate the Poisson error. In our example, this value is roughly 24%.

Finally, the third error takes into account the number of Monte Carlo simulations. It is impractical to simulate tens of thousands of iterations and as a result the simulation error is given by $1/\sqrt{M}$. In our example, the error is approximately 3.2%.

Given the three errors, we obtain the overall error ($E_{Total}$) by adding the values in quadrature (as expressed by Equation 34). The total error is estimated to be 26%. This implies that the calculated VaR of US$130 million actually ranges from US$96 to US$164 million.

$$E_{Total} = [e_1^2 + e_2^2 + e_3^2]^{1/2} \tag{34}$$

Step 7: Calculate VaR stress figures

Stress testing is important because it gauges the potential vulnerability to exceptional but plausible events. With respect to operational risk, one is stressing a firm's control environment. Accordingly, Model I calculates the stress figures by multiplying the number of losses and the 99 percentile monetary loss value above the truncation point for each pseudorandom severity pdf (ie, generated in Step 5).

**Figure 11** The stress value $y$ represents the 99th percentile of the PDF's area above the truncation point

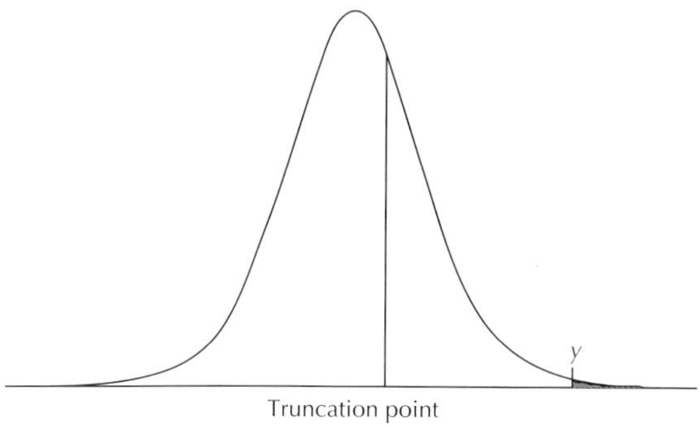


**Table 3** Stress test results

| Stress test results (values in millions of dollars) | | | | |
|---|---|---|---|---|
| Percentiles | | | | |
| **10th** | **25th** | **50th** | **75th** | **99th** |
| 648 | 804 | 1,156 | 1,605 | 2,222 |

Figure 11 graphically depicts the stress figure labelled by $y$, while Equation (35) represents the mathematical expression to solve for the stress value $y$. Each iteration in our example, the stress figure is 68*$y$.

$$\int_{tp}^{y} \text{TAN}(\mu, \sigma, kr; x)\text{d}x = 0.99 * (\text{Area Above Truncation Threshold})$$

$$= 0.99 * \int_{tp}^{\infty} \text{TAN}(\mu, \sigma, kr; x)\text{d}x \quad \textbf{(35)}$$

Ranking the 10,000 stress results, we can determine various stress results. In our example, the stress figures range from US$648 to US$2,222 million (as shown in Table 3).

Summarising our computational results, given a dataset of 300 loss events above US$25,000, the calculated VaR is US$130 million with an approximate 26% error in its determination (VaR range: US$96–164 million) and the VaR stress range is US$648–2,222 million.

## OpRisk Economic Capital Model II

In the prior section, we thoroughly discussed calculating VaR using Monte Carlo simulation. Albeit Monte Carlo simulation has a long and rich history in risk-management calculations, its application in our prior model is numerically intensive because of all the pseudorandom number generations required to perform the $N$ simulations. To lessen the calculation time in generating VaR, we will introduce an alternative calculation methodology that has fewer computational steps.

In contrast to Model I, the second OpRisk economic model is less time-consuming in determining VaR. Model II does follow the general steps (1) to (4) but the time saving comes from taking advantage of how we implemented step (7) in Model I. Without loss of generality, Equation 34 may be rewritten as

$$\int_{tp}^{y} \text{PDF}\,\mathrm{d}x = \text{Confidence Level} * \int_{tp}^{\infty} \text{PDF}\,\mathrm{d}x \qquad \textbf{(36)}$$

Expression 36 allows us to calculate the monetary loss value $y$ above the truncation point $tp$ for a desired confidence level. Performing this calculation for a family of percentiles yields a set of loss amounts.

Another difference between Models I and II is how we utilise the estimated yearly number of losses. In Model I, we generated pseudorandom numbers corresponding to the discrete distribution we chose to describe the frequency of losses. Instead, in Model II we calculate the *quantile* for each CL that was used in the severity calculation. This alternative approach removes the randomness in determining the potential number of losses (eg, values smaller or larger than or equal to the yearly figure) by a known number based on a percentile.

After we evaluate the monetary loss and frequency values, a table can be constructed where the rows are the monetary losses and the columns are the frequency amounts (or visa versa), and each table cell is the product of the $m$th row and $n$th column. Performing the cell-by-cell multiplication yields a $m$-by-$n$ table of VaR figures.

To determine the range of VaR figures, we can perform the described methodology to the end points for the three parameter confidence intervals. As for the errors associated with Model II,

**Table 4** Model II VaR results using TAN($\mu$, $\sigma$, kurtosis) = (−3.84, 1.77, 3.05) and a Poisson mean frequency of 68 loss events per year above US$100,000

| | Severity percentile (values in millions of dollars) | | | | |
|---|---|---|---|---|---|
| **Frequency percentile** | **50th** | **75th** | **90th** | **95th** | **99th** |
| **50th** | 15 | 28 | 58 | 94 | 258 |
| **75th** | 16 | 30 | 62 | 101 | 277 |
| **90th** | 17 | 32 | 67 | 110 | 300 |
| **95th** | 18 | 34 | 70 | 114 | 312 |
| **99th** | 19 | 36 | 75 | 122 | 334 |

they are similar to Model I except that we do not account for the number of Monte Carlo iterations since there are none. Hence, Equation 34 contains only the first two terms: $e_1$ and $e_2$.

Leveraging our previous effort, we will make use of the unconditional TAN and the frequency value used in the subsection "Example: Model I" for our Model I numerical example. Furthermore, we will use 50%, 75%, 90%, 95% and 99% as the CLs of interest. Performing the various calculations, we display the Model II VaR results are displayed in Table 4.

In addition to the computational speed, another advantage of the second OpRisk economic capital model is obtaining a range of VaR values as a function of CL. This allows us to ascertain the sensitivity of the VaR figures as the percentiles vary for the severity and frequency distributions.

*Example: VaR results from binomial and negative binomial distributions*

In the two prior numerical examples, I have used the Poisson distribution to describe the frequency of monetary losses. The fictitious dataset was constructed to represent one year of losses. In this subsection, we will consider the hypothetical case of five years' worth of loss data. Having data span over multiple years provides the opportunity to study how the choice of frequency distribution impacts the measurement of operational risk economic capital.

Maintaining continuity with the other two VaR examples, we will use the unconditional TAN parameters $\mu = -3.84$, $\sigma = 1.77$,

**Table 5** Model II VaR results using TAN ($\mu$, $\sigma$, kurtosis) = (−3.84, 1.77, 3.05) and a binomial mean frequency of 68 ($n$ = 170 and $p$ = 0.4) loss events per year above US$100,000

| | Severity percentile (values in millions of dollars) | | | | |
|---|---|---|---|---|---|
| **Frequency percentile** | **50th** | **75th** | **90th** | **95th** | **99th** |
| **50th** | 15 | 28 | 58 | 94 | 258 |
| **75th** | 16 | 29 | 61 | 100 | 273 |
| **90th** | 16 | 31 | 65 | 106 | 289 |
| **95th** | 17 | 32 | 67 | 110 | 300 |
| **99th** | 18 | 34 | 71 | 115 | 315 |

and kurtosis = 3.05 and the yearly mean of losses to be 68. This continuity will allow us to fairly compare the VaR results for the three discrete distributions.

Using the binomial and negative binomial functions, instead of the Poisson distribution, to represent the frequency of monetary losses, we repeated the steps of Model II to arrive at the VaR figures listed in Table 5 and Table 6. Comparing the results in Tables 4, 5 and 6, we can conclude that VaR is sensitive to the choice of discrete distribution in depicting the frequency of loss data. This result is not unexpected due to the distinct mean–variance relationship for the three discrete functions (as discussed earlier).

### OpRisk Economic Capital Model III

We discussed calculating the operational risk economic capital exposure using the concept of VaR earlier. Even though VaR is common throughout the risk-management community, there is a limitation to its use.[8] VaR only informs us about the amount of capital that can be lost at a certain CL (ie, 99%) and not about what can be lost on the remaining occasion (1%). This shortcoming may result in a firm's undercapitalising its exposure to catastrophic OpRisk events. To address this limitation, we will use another concept to determine the economic capital risk exposure for operational risk: *expected tail loss* (ETL) (see Dowd, 2002).

ETL is the expected loss value, $L$, if the loss is in excess of VaR: $ETL = E[L|L>VaR]$. Thus, ETL informs us what amount can be lost if a tail event does occur. This alternative economic capital concept

**Table 6** Model II VaR results using TAN($\mu$, $\sigma$, kurtosis) = (−3.84, 1.77, 3.05) and a negative binomial mean frequency of 68 ($n$ = 102 and $p$ = 0.6) loss events per year above US$100,000

| | Severity percentile (values in millions of dollars) | | | | |
|---|---|---|---|---|---|
| **Frequency percentile** | **50th** | **75th** | **90th** | **95th** | **99th** |
| **50th** | 15 | 28 | 58 | 94 | 258 |
| **75th** | 16 | 31 | 64 | 104 | 285 |
| **90th** | 18 | 34 | 70 | 114 | 312 |
| **95th** | 19 | 35 | 73 | 119 | 327 |
| **99th** | 20 | 39 | 80 | 130 | 357 |

allows us to ascertain the excess with respect to a monetary figure associated with a given percentile.

Before we can proceed in presenting the third OpRisk economic capital model, a more formal definition for ETL will help us arrive at a general technique in evaluating ETL. Keeping in mind with what was stated in the previous paragraph, ETL can be defined as the probability-weighted average of tail losses that is larger than some monetary figure (such as VaR). Because ETL depends on the *probability-weighted average*, the definition suggests using the pdf of the parameterised severity distribution. This realisation is critical because the pdf characterises the probability weight of a distribution. Therefore, for continuous functions, the following expression

$$\mathrm{ETL} = \frac{\int_{y}^{\infty} x\mathrm{PDF}\,\mathrm{d}x}{\int_{y}^{\infty} \mathrm{PDF}\,\mathrm{d}x} \tag{37}$$

is mathematically equivalent to our ETL definition. Two points should be highlighted: (1) $y$ in the above formula is determined from Equation 36 – TAN distribution or any other pdf; and (2) an expression analogous to Equation 37 can be defined for discrete distributions.

With a formula to calculate ETL, the procedure for Model III is straightforward. In actuality, the procedure is similar to Model II. The only difference between Models III and II is one more computation.

**Figure 12** Graphical depiction of the relationship between VaR and ETL

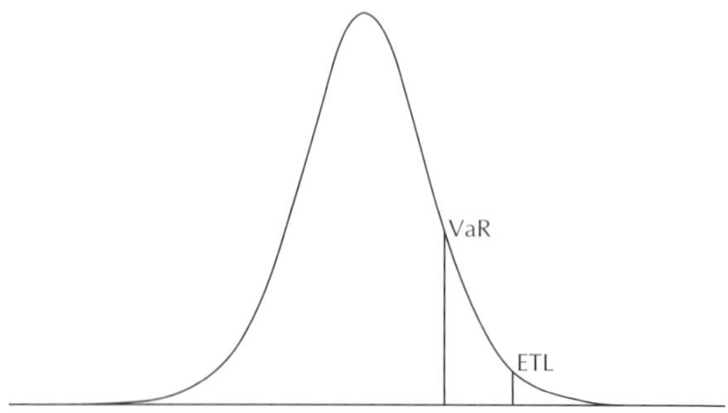


**Table 7** ETL results for OpRisk Economic Capital Model III

| | Severity percentile (values in millions of dollars) | | | | |
|---|---|---|---|---|---|
| **Frequency percentile** | **50th** | **75th** | **90th** | **95th** | **99th** |
| **50th** | 34 | 59 | 112 | 175 | 445 |
| **75th** | 37 | 63 | 121 | 188 | 477 |
| **90th** | 40 | 68 | 131 | 204 | 516 |
| **95th** | 41 | 71 | 136 | 211 | 536 |
| **99th** | 44 | 76 | 145 | 227 | 575 |

Model III requires solving the monetary loss value in Equation 36 and then substituting $y$ into Expression 37 to calculate the ETL. As with Model II, the ETL and the frequency amount for every percentile under consideration are calculated and a table similar to Table 4 is constructed. For illustrative purposes, Model III results are listed in Table 7 for the unconditional TAN and the frequency value used in the subsection "Example: Model I".

Comparing Tables 4 and 7, we see that the economic capital results from Model II and Model III are quite different, as anticipated. ETL is a quantitative approach that provides a firm more insight on the potential exposure to operational risk.

### Qualitative adjustments

Once the economic capital has been calculated, qualitative adjustments may be applied to the value to reflect the present risk-management environment. Since the analysis was performed on historical data, conditions that led to some of the losses – such as weaknesses in the control environment – may have changed. To account for better risk-management practices and improvement of the control framework, as measured by audit, control self-assessment, key indicator or issue resolution results or an OpRisk quality rating, the calculated capital charge may be adjusted. This adjustment may be performed, for example, by selectively sampling the severity distribution parameters' confidence interval based on a *qualitative adjustment value* that is measured on a numeric scale between 1 and 5, where 1 is the best score and 5 the worst.

In the sample case in the subsection "Example: Model I", let us assume that the control environment has been improved through the implementation of new policies and procedures that effectively eliminate or minimise the occurrence of losses. If we assign this change a qualitative adjustment score of 1, the stochastic Monte Carlo engine will generate severity parameters closer to the lower end of the confidence intervals. These "smaller" parameter values will lower the simulated VaR figure to reflect this improvement. If, on the other hand, management has made no effort to reduce the possibility of losses, we will use a qualitative adjustment score of 5, and the resulting parameter values will be closer to the upper end of the confidence intervals. This qualitative adjustment will increase the simulated VaR figure to account for the managers' lack of responsiveness. Figure 13 illustrates this point.

Another way to articulate the discussion of qualitative adjustment is as follows. With the improvement of a business lines' or organisation's control environment, the stochastic Monte Carlo engine simulates smaller volatility values and thinner tails, whereas failure to improve the control framework leads to the simulation of larger volatility values and heavier tails. The former case will yield smaller VaR figures, while the latter will produce larger VaR numbers.

The qualitative adjustment factor may be incorporated into the stochastic Monte Carlo simulation via the use of the two-parameter Weibull distribution (see Johnson, Kotz and Balakrishnan, 1994). One parameter determines the *shape*, while the other describes the *scale*. If we set the shape parameter to five,[9] the quality rating may be used as the scale parameter to determine the location along the severity distribution parameters' confidence interval. Then, the stochastic Monte Carlo engine randomly selects the confidence

**Figure 13** Qualitative adjustment illustration: the severity distribution reflects the strength or weakness of a department's, business unit's, or firm's control environment

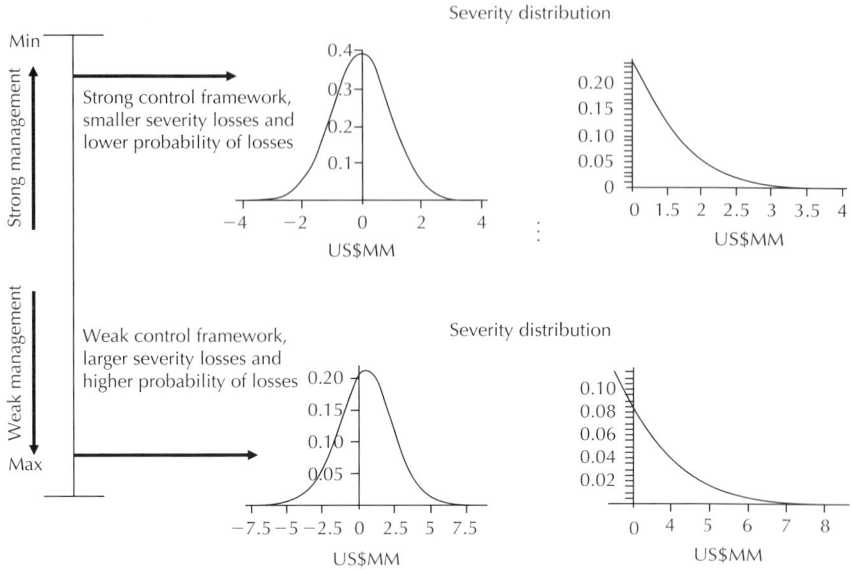


interval range covered by the Weibull distribution. Figure 14 is a depiction of how different quality ratings may be used to select the appropriate range of the parameter confidence interval.

For the other two economic capital models, we can similarly sample the confidence intervals as described above to arrive at the severity parameters for the calculations.

## Application to multiple business lines

The OpRisk economic capital models presented in the sections "OR Economic Capital Model I" through "OR Economic Capital Model III" may be applied to a firm's collective set of internal monetary losses, and can also be put to use for the distinct business lines in the firm, provided that there are sufficient data for such delineation. For example, suppose an institution has $i$ business lines. Then, a listing of the calculated results, like Table 8, may be obtained.

## Economic capital integrity checks

As an institution collects data over time, economic capital computational integrity checks may be performed to confirm the robustness

**Figure 14** Illustration of how the quality rating focuses on a segment of the parameter confidence interval

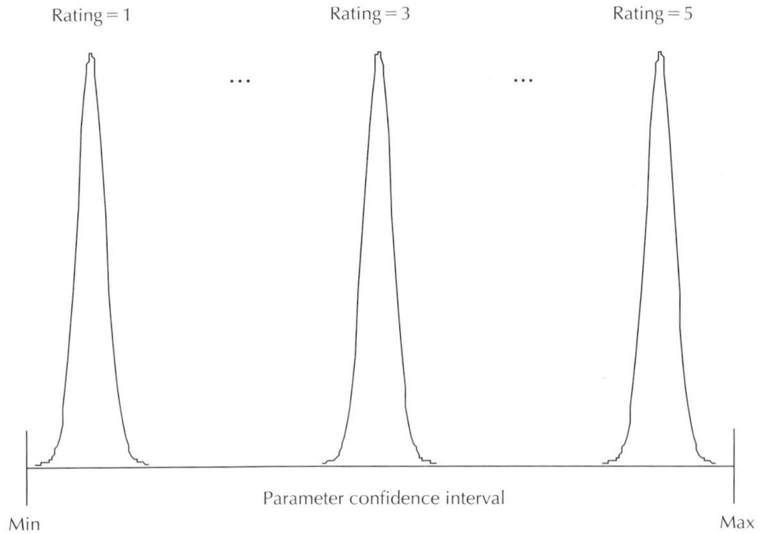


**Table 8** A listing of parameters and CaR results for *i* business lines

| Parameters | Monetary threshold | Mean ($\mu$) | Sigma ($\sigma$) | Kurtosis (kurt) | Frequency (f) | Economic capital |
|---|---|---|---|---|---|---|
| 1st Business Line | $MT_1$ | $\mu_1$ | $\sigma_1$ | $kurt_1$ | $f_1$ | $CaR_1$ |
| 2nd Business Line | $MT_2$ | $\mu_2$ | $\sigma_2$ | $kurt_2$ | $f_2$ | $CaR_2$ |
| : | : | : | : | : | : | : |
| $i^{th}$ Business Line | $MT_i$ | $\mu_i$ | $\sigma_i$ | $kurt_i$ | $f_i$ | $CaR_i$ |

of the calculation. One method to verify the integrity of the calculation is to bucket the monetary loss events by year and to calculate the capital-at-risk[10] (CaR) per year. Comparing the yearly CaR figures to the result for the entire dataset will allow a risk manager to study how CaR is changing over time. This comparison will reflect on the effectiveness of the institution's OpRisk management programme.

The following approach provides another option for checking the integrity of the CaR calculation. If a firm has $N$ years of loss event data, it can use data from the $N - 1$ previous years to predict the capital figure for the $N$th year. Assuming there was no major catastrophic event (such as the terrorist attack of September 11, 2001) in the *N*th year dataset, the severity distribution and confidence intervals determined by the $N-1$ previous years' data may account for the *N*th year. If the "prediction" is not reasonable, this may suggest a potential problem with the *N*th year's monetary loss data.

## OPERATIONAL RISK ECONOMIC CAPITAL DIVERSIFICATION

As discussed in the subsection "Application to multiple business lines" above, the economic capital models presented here may be applied to the discrete business lines within an organisation. Calculating the CaR for each business line allows the firm to allocate economic capital more equitably, instead of dividing a firm-wide figure among the business lines. However, one point needs to be taken into account that will impact the calculated value per business line. The calculations should address the dependencies across and between business lines for operational risk losses. These dependencies are called *correlations*. In this section, I will present and discuss an approach for estimating correlations across and between business lines.

### Correlation and covariance

Correlation measures the degree of relationship, or linear dependence, between two variables. The correlation value varies from 0 (random relationship) to 1 (perfect linear relationship) or –1 (perfect negative linear relationship).

A positive correlation indicates that, when the value of one variable increases, the value of the other variable will also increase. A negative correlation indicates that, when the value of one variable increases, the value of the other variable will decrease. A correlation value close to 0 indicates no association between the variables. The expression to calculate the correlation between two variables of $n$ observations is

$$cor(x,y)=\frac{1}{n-1}\sum_{i=1}^{n}\frac{(x_i-\mu_x)}{\sigma_x}\frac{(y_i-\mu_y)}{\sigma_y} \tag{38}$$

It is worthy of note that, since correlation is symmetrical ($cor(x,y)=cor(y,x)$), we do not have evidence to decipher which variable causes the relationship.

Equation 38 *standardises* the $x$ and $y$ variables, so changes in scale or units of measurement will not affect the correlation value. Standardisation is the process of making variables comparable in magnitude and dispersion: one subtracts the mean from each variable and divides by its standard deviation, giving all variables a mean of 0 and a standard deviation of 1.

The variance between two variables is a measure of the deviation between the two variables. This measure is defined to be the *covariance*.

$$cov(x, y) = \sum_{i=1}^{n} (x_i - \mu_x)(y_i - \mu_y) \tag{39}$$

Generalising covariance to multiple variables, as we would need to do when analysing several business lines, we define a covariance matrix Z (Equation 40). Similar to our observation about correlation, Z is a symmetric matrix: $cov(x, y) = cov(y, x)$.

$$Z = \begin{vmatrix} \zeta_{11} & \zeta_{12} & \cdots & \zeta_{1k} \\ \zeta_{21} & \zeta_{22} & \cdots & \zeta_{2k} \\ \vdots & \vdots & \vdots & \vdots \\ \zeta_{k1} & \zeta_{k2} & \cdots & \zeta_{kk} \end{vmatrix} \tag{40}$$

**Business-line diversification**

Applying the information from the previous section in determining the covariance relation between business lines, we define the parameter $\eta$ for each business line.

$$\eta = \frac{\mu}{\sigma[1 + \text{Max}(0, \text{kurtosis} - 3)} \tag{41}$$

$\eta$ is a dimensionless value that incorporates the three parameters of the business unit's severity distribution. To come up with the covariance matrix Z from a collection of $\eta$'s for $i$ business units over $m$ years, we construct the $\eta$-matrix H (Equation 42) by performing the pair-wise calculation defined by Equation 39.

$$H = \begin{vmatrix} \eta_{11} & \eta_{12} & \cdots & \eta_{1m} \\ \eta_{21} & \eta_{22} & \cdots & \eta_{2m} \\ \vdots & \vdots & \vdots & \vdots \\ \eta_{i1} & \eta_{i2} & \cdots & \eta_{im} \end{vmatrix} \tag{42}$$

*Method 1*

Complex firms typically have multiple business lines. Thus, the challenge of obtaining a diverse organisational economic capital value must be addressed. In this section, we will discuss four OpRisk economic capital diversification methodologies that may be used to calculate a firm-wide economic capital figure.

The most straightforward and conservative approach for determining a firm's enterprise-wide operational risk economic capital figure is to sum the CaR amounts that were calculated (Equation 43) for the individual business lines.

$$CaR_{Firm} = \sum_{i=1}^{n} CaR_i \tag{43}$$

This methodology assumes that the correlation between business units is 1.

*Method 2*

The second approach incorporates the measured covariance between the business lines as discussed earlier. After computing each business line's CaR figure, the diversification calculation is

$$CaR_{Firm} = \sqrt{\sum_{k=1}^{i} \sum_{l=1}^{i} \zeta_{kl} CaR_k CaR_l} \tag{44}$$

where $\zeta$'s are the respective Z matrix elements.

*Method 3*

The following approach is a variation of Method 1 and it is applicable only to Model I. Assuming the correlation between the business units is 1, the steps to obtain the firm-wide VaR are as follows.

(a) Sum the corresponding $N$ scenarios across the $i$ business lines (Equation 45).
(b) Rank aggregate losses in ascending order.
(c) Determine the corresponding value of the desired confidence limit (eg, 99%).

$$\begin{bmatrix} x_{11} \\ x_{12} \\ \vdots \\ x_{1N} \end{bmatrix} + \begin{bmatrix} x_{21} \\ x_{22} \\ \vdots \\ x_{2N} \end{bmatrix} + \cdots + \begin{bmatrix} x_{i1} \\ x_{i2} \\ \vdots \\ x_{iN} \end{bmatrix} = \begin{bmatrix} \sum_{j=1}^{i} x_{j1} \\ \sum_{j=1}^{i} x_{j2} \\ \vdots \\ \sum_{j=1}^{i} x_{jN} \end{bmatrix} \tag{45}$$

*Method 4*

The fourth option is analogous to Method 3 and, once again, the approach is applicable only to Model I. The calculation in Equation 45 is modified to incorporate the $Z$ matrix elements, as defined by Expression 46.

$$\begin{bmatrix} x_{11} \\ x_{12} \\ \vdots \\ x_{1N} \end{bmatrix} + \begin{bmatrix} x_{21} \\ x_{22} \\ \vdots \\ x_{2N} \end{bmatrix} + \cdots + \begin{bmatrix} x_{i1} \\ x_{i2} \\ \vdots \\ x_{iN} \end{bmatrix} = \begin{bmatrix} \sum_{j=1}^{i} \sum_{l=1}^{i} \zeta_{kl} x_{k1} x_{l1} \\ \sum_{k=1}^{i} \sum_{l=1}^{i} \zeta_{kl} x_{k2} x_{l2} \\ \vdots \\ \sum_{k=1}^{i} \sum_{l=1}^{i} \zeta_{kl} x_{kN} x_{lN} \end{bmatrix} \tag{46}$$

To complete the calculation and determine VaR, steps a and b, as outlined above, are performed.

## SCENARIO ANALYSIS

Because every institution has a unique risk profile and control environment, every institution will experience operational risk incidents differently. Nevertheless, some scenarios, such as discrimination and employment-practices litigation, cyber attacks such as viruses and worms, or external incidents such as natural disasters, may be similar in many institutions. The qualitative analysis of risk scenarios that have occurred at companies with similar business profiles can help an organisation to derive lessons learned from the incidents, and apply those lessons to its own operational risk management framework.

**Figure 15a and 15b** The left-hand graph is a fictitious dataset depicting no "tail events"; the right-hand graph is a distribution of external loss events. a: Internal loss data, b: External loss data

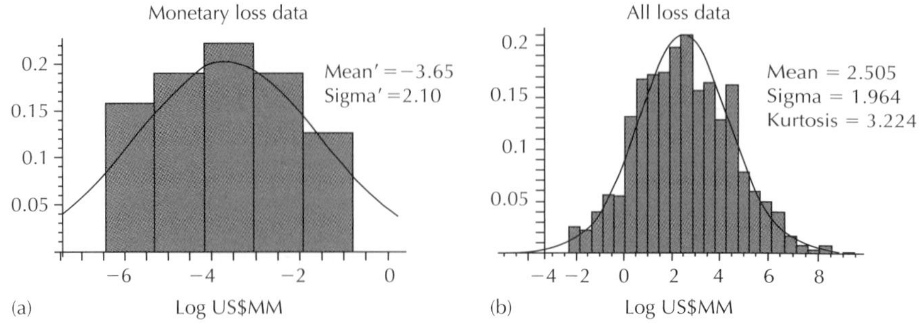


Quantitatively, data on external scenarios may be beneficial in modifying the severity or frequency distributions that are used in the Monte Carlo stochastic engine. For example, an institution may use the measured parameters from external loss data to gauge whether their internal loss data parameter confidence intervals incorporate catastrophic events observed in the financial industry. If the assessment concludes that the confidence intervals determined from internal loss data do not account for catastrophic events, then one can modify the confidence intervals to conform with external loss data parameters.

To illustrate the point, consider Figures 15a and b. The left-hand graph depicts a fictitious internal dataset lacking "tail events". An institution may execute any of the three models based on the calculated parameters and their corresponding confidence intervals. However, because of the small size of the data sample, the firm will not simulate catastrophic tail events. As Figure 15b shows, this exclusion will yield a low CaR estimate. To accommodate the deficiency in the internal data, the kurtosis parameter and the confidence interval measured from external loss data may be used in the simulation or calculation. This method is preferable to "cherry picking" external loss data events for inclusion with internal loss data points because it does not distort the internal loss severity distribution. Instead, this technique allows for the variability of the kurtosis parameter, or either of the other two parameters ($\mu$ and $\sigma$) if they should be varied.

## EVENT CLASSIFICATION

### When data are poorly organised

We have now seen the importance of properly characterising the severity distribution of monetary loss data and determining the probability that losses will occur. With a precise mathematical depiction of the data one is analysing, calculations become meaningful and precise. However, regardless of the tools at one's fingertips and the mathematical rigour of those tools, if the data under analysis are suspect, then the results are meaningless. If losses are categorised haphazardly, any values derived from the dataset will reflect its irregularity. That is why good classification of data is vital. It must be done consistently, and it must follow a logical pattern.

When we talk about categorising data, we mean that we are grouping loss events based on their causes. Some classifications schemes advocate grouping events by their effects, but this system does not give us useful information about where losses come from. Such categorisation methods lead to logical inconsistencies and yield misleading calculated values.

Before we proceed, we must understand the distinction between *cause* and *effect* categories. The cause of an event is the action or set of circumstances that led to the event. The effect is the monetary or non-monetary loss that is incurred as a consequence of the event. In this discussion, we will not examine non-monetary losses, because they are inherently difficult to quantify.

Let us consider the following example of the importance of accurately classifying loss events. We will assume that we have only two cause categories, fraud and sales misrepresentation, and two effect categories, regulatory fines and lawsuit settlements. If we followed an *effect* classification scheme, we would analyse events based on whether they led to fines or settlements, and would risk losing sight of the fact that fraud and sales misrepresentation are distinct from a management perspective and must be addressed differently.

To quantify this point, let us analyse four examples. We will employ the following two TAN distributions: ($\mu$, $\sigma$, kurtosis) = (−3.50, 1.50, 3.15) and (−4.00, 1.80, 3.80). Assume the first distribution represents fraud-related losses, while the second represents losses caused by sales misrepresentation. We randomly generate 100,000 points for each distribution, and then use those data points to analyse four distinct scenarios. The first two scenarios examine misclassification of losses above a US$50,000 threshold. The second pair examines losses with amounts greater than US$100,000. For each pair of scenarios, the first example will show the results when sales misrepresentation losses are mixed into the set of fraud events. In the second example, fraud losses will be mixed into the sales misrepresentation losses. Because the four examples are analogous, we will outline the applied procedure for one, then state the results for all in Table 9.

Let us begin with the first scenario, in which sales misrepresentation events are categorised with fraud cases. In our example, sales misrepresentation loss events above US$50,000 in the ($\mu$, $\sigma$, kurtosis) = (−4.00, 1.80, 3.80) TAN distribution are one-third of the time collected with events from the fraud ($\mu$, $\sigma$, kurtosis) = (−3.50, 1.50, 3.15) TAN distribution, and the total number of losses (in this example, 200,000) remains the same. As a result, the two distributions are now altered – their parameters differ from what they should actually be. The original sales misrepresentation distribution, which lost events above US$0.05 million, has been transformed into a severity density with parameters (−5.01, 2.03, 3.91). The fraud density, which gained events above US$0.05 million, has been transformed into a TAN density with (−2.93, 1.33, 3.96) for its parameters.

The impact of the misclassification of loss events is profound. As Table 9 illustrates, the VaRs calculated at the 99.9% CL[11] for the two "new" TAN density functions are starkly different from the known TAN distributions. The VaR results increased approximately three times from the original results. Many analysts recommend resolving this problem by combining the altered VaR numbers via a correlation analysis to arrive back at the original VaR figures. This "solution" is flawed because it assumes *a priori* knowledge of the original VaR results, which we all know is not possible: if monetary losses and their occurrence could be predicted with certainty, there would be no need for a risk management department.

A similar metamorphosis of the severity distribution will occur if we do not properly identify a loss event and its corresponding monetary impact. Let us consider, for example, a case in which a few loss events above US$100,000 are not identified as one event, but as several different events, even though they are all classified in the same category.

**Table 9** Four scenarios that demonstrate the effect on VaR figures when losses are randomly mixed between two known TAN severity distributions

| | | Results of mixing losses from two known TAN distributions TAN distribution parameters (μ, σ, kurtosis) | | | | | |
|---|---|---|---|---|---|---|---|
| | | Given | | Truncated: before mixture | Truncated: after mixture | Solved | |
| **Scenario 1: A random selection of losses greater than US$0.05 million from (−4.00, 1.80, 3.80) are mixed into (−3.50, 1.50, 3.15). VaR figures are in millions of dollars** | | | | | | | |
| | A | (−4.00, 1.80, 3.80) | | (−2.39, 1.10, 5.86) | (−2.53, 1.08, 6.38) | (−5.01, 2.03, 3.91) | |
| | B | (−3.50, 1.50, 3.15) | | (−2.43, 0.95, 4.06) | (−2.32, 0.98, 4.78) | (−2.93, 1.33, 3.96) | |
| | | A | B | | | A | B |
| VaRs: | Mean | 12.27 | 5.25 | | | 23.39 | 7.11 |
| | 95.5% CL | 30.44 | 10.26 | | | 45.67 | 15.09 |
| | 99.9% CL | 461.38 | 30.74 | | | 1266.71 | 100.82 |
| **Scenario 2: A random selection of losses greater than US$0.05 million from (−3.50, 1.50, 3.15) are mixed into (−4.00, 1.80, 3.80). VaR figures are in millions of dollars** | | | | | | | |
| | C | (−3.50, 1.50, 3.15) | | (−2.43, 0.95, 4.06) | (−2.56, 0.94, 4.35) | (−4.22, 1.69, 3.02) | |
| | D | (−4.00, 1.80, 3.80) | | (−2.39, 1.10, 5.86) | (−2.31, 1.07, 5.56) | (−3.11, 1.50, 4.27) | |
| | | C | D | | | C | D |
| VaRs: | Mean | 5.25 | 12.27 | | | 4.47 | 11.58 |
| | 95.5% CL | 10.26 | 30.44 | | | 8.93 | 26.10 |
| | 99.9% CL | 30.74 | 461.38 | | | 26.17 | 378.12 |

**Table 9** (continued)

| | | Results of mixing losses from two known TAN distributions TAN distribution parameters (μ, σ, kurtosis) | | | | | |
|---|---|---|---|---|---|---|---|
| | | **Given** | | **Truncated: before mixture** | **Truncated: after mixture** | **Solved** | |
| **Scenario 3: A random selection of losses greater than US$0.1 million from (−4.00, 1.80, 3.80) are mixed into (−3.50, 1.50, 3.15). VaR figures are in millions of dollars** | | | | | | | |
| | E | (−4.00, 1.80, 3.80) | | (−2.39, 1.10, 5.86) | (−2.55, 1.02, 7.19) | (−4.65, 1.85, 4.31) | |
| | F | (−3.50, 1.50, 3.15) | | (−2.43, 0.95, 4.06) | (−2.30, 1.02, 4.39) | (−3.08, 1.45, 3.56) | |
| | | E | F | | | E | F |
| VaRs: | Mean | 12.27 | 5.25 | | | 24.04 | 7.55 |
| | 95.5% CL | 30.44 | 10.26 | | | 44.02 | 15.94 |
| | 99.9% CL | 461.38 | 30.74 | | | 1121.34 | 84.48 |
| **Scenario 4: A random selection of losses greater than US$0.1million from (3.50, 1.50, 3.15) are mixed into (−4.00, 1.80, 3.80). VaR figures are in millions of dollars** | | | | | | | |
| | G | (−3.50, 1.50, 3.15) | | (−2.43, 0.95, 4.06) | (−2.57, 0.89, 4.88) | (−4.03, 1.54, 3.10) | |
| | H | (−4.00, 1.80, 3.80) | | (−2.39, 1.10, 5.86) | (−2.28, 1.11, 5.12) | (−3.38, 1.66, 3.76) | |
| | | G | H | | | G | H |
| VaRs: | Mean | 5.25 | 12.27 | | | 4.04 | 12.27 |
| | 95.5% CL | 10.26 | 30.44 | | | 7.80 | 27.61 |
| | 99.9% CL | 30.74 | 461.38 | | | 27.95 | 273.43 |

The VaR figures are a result of a simulation of 100,000 years, with Poisson mean frequencies of 13 and 17 monetary loss events per year above US$100,000.

**Table 10** A scenario that demonstrates the effect on VaR figures when one randomly splits losses from a known TAN severity distribution

| | Results of splitting losses from a known TAN distribution | | | |
|---|---|---|---|---|
| | TAN distribution parameters ($\mu$, $\sigma$, kurtosis) | | | |
| | **Given** | **Truncated: before split of losses** | **Truncated: after split of losses** | **Solved** |
| | (−4.00, 1.80, 3.80) | (−2.39, 1.10, 5.86) | (−2.01, 1.28, 2.42) | (−3.83, 2.17, 3.00) |
| VaRs: | Mean | 12.27 | | 10.55 |
| | 95.5% CL | 30.44 | | 28.30 |
| | 99.9% CL | 461.38 | | 166.02 |
| Number of events | | 100,000 | | 118,562 |

The VaR figures were generated from a simulation of 100,000 years, with a Poisson mean frequency of 15 loss events per year above US$100,000 for the TAN density, and a Poisson mean frequency of 12 loss events per year above US$100,000 for the normal density.

Using the ($\mu$, $\sigma$, kurtosis) = (−4.00, 1.80, 3.80) TAN distribution, we randomly chose events with monetary amounts greater than US$100,000 and divided these amounts into two or three components. The new truncated parameters are (−2.01, 1.28, 2.42). For the new truncated parameters, there was no solution to the truncated TAN moment equations. Consequently, we had to solve the truncated normal moment equations. When we solve the simultaneous equations, the parameters for the new dataset are ($\mu$, $\sigma$) = (−3.83, 2.17). This time, the TAN distribution is transformed into a normal distribution, and the VaR at the 99.9% CL was greatly underestimated, as shown in Table 10. The Monte Carlo simulation did take into account the new frequency of loss events above US$100,000 that resulted from splitting the losses.

The two arguments just presented illustrate that, when operational risk managers collect data, they must use a logical and consistent classification scheme, with mutually exclusive categories, and coherent definitions for losses and their corresponding monetary impacts. Quantitative analysis is only as good as the data upon which it is based, and, if operational risk calculations are done using an unsound classification scheme, any results will be suspect.

**Figure 16** Histograms depict the change to a TAN distribution (solid curve) when losses are spilt (dash curve)

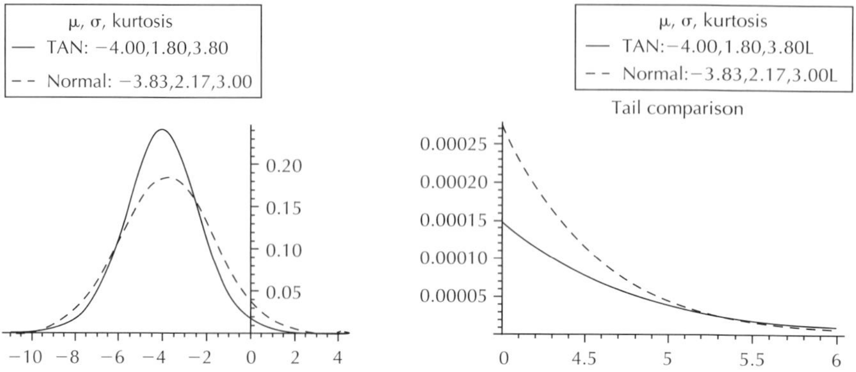


## Loss data classification scheme

It is essential to clearly define an "operational risk loss event" and its corresponding "monetary impact", and to categorise events in statistically non-overlapping groups. As with any analysis, the concept of GIGO – garbage in, garbage out – applies. To keep from producing "garbage", I propose that OpRisk loss events be grouped into the following five major categories, according to the cause of the loss event.

(1) *External*: The risk of loss due to damage to physical property or assets from natural or non-natural causes. This encompasses the risk presented by actions of external parties, such as the perpetration of fraud, or in the case of regulators, the execution of change that would alter the firm's ability to continue operating in certain markets. External risks tend to be factors that an organisation cannot control. Operational risk management focuses on reducing the impact of such events, rather than trying to prevent them.

(2) *People*: The risk of a loss intentionally or unintentionally caused by an employee or involving employees, such as in the area of employment disputes. This risk class covers internal organisational problems and losses. People risks arise from the action or inaction of an individual or a small group of people within the firm.

(3) *Process*: The risks related to the execution and maintenance of transactions, and the various aspects of running a business, including products and activities. Process risks are problems that are systemic in an institution or group, or inherent in a business process.
(4) *Relationship*: The risk arising from the relationship or contact that a firm has with its clients, shareholders, third parties or regulators. Although relationship risks include a human element, they are distinct from people-risk incidents because they are based on the interaction between the firm and outside entities or, in some cases, the connection among groups within the firm.
(5) *Technology*: The risk of loss caused by piracy, theft, failure, breakdown or other disruption in technology, data or information; also includes technology that fails to meet business needs. Technology risks can occur in any department, not just those that manage the firm's technology infrastructure.

The five proposed risk categories apply to a wide spectrum of business activities, and naturally lend themselves to subcategories that are mutually exclusive. For example, a few subgroup members of the people risk class are *human-resource issues*, *employee mistakes* and *wrongful acts*. Within each subcategory, more granular keywords can be defined: the wrongdoing subgroup, for example, could include such branches as fraud, disclosure issues, and trading misdeeds.

Regardless of the categorisation scheme we use, adhering to a logical categorisation format, and assigning only one cause to each event, will prevent us from splitting monetary losses into multiple groups.

## MIXING INTERNAL DATA WITH EXTERNAL DATA

Many of the OpRisk quantification models that are presently in use in the OpRisk management community borrow the idea of mixing external monetary losses collected from the public domain with internal data. This concept was proposed by the operational risk team at Bankers Trust (see Hoffman and Johnson, 1997), which in the 1990s laid the foundation for this branch of risk management. Mixing is done to increase the internal data sample size and, more importantly, to augment the low-frequency, high-impact losses in the tail of the distribution. Conceptually, mixing the two datasets seems reasonable because the combined dataset will be more "universally" representative of the institution's OpRisk losses. It is assumed that the "statistically more meaningful" dataset will give risk analysts and managers a better predictive model to measure the financial impact of potential catastrophic losses. Such an understanding is vital to the risk-management decision process, as it allows managers to determine an appropriate strategy for mitigating or minimising potential OpRisk losses. But, appealing though the mixing concept may be, contemporary OpRisk literature has not addressed the validity of combining external and internal losses. To determine the validity of this practice, we must examine the quality and integrity of the collected external losses. Because most institutions will not have a large dataset that encompasses the broad range of financial losses, it is vital to understand some of the general characteristics of the external data and how the data might impact any quantitative analysis. To initiate this discussion, I will present a preliminary work that tests this practice.

As we have previously seen, many operational risk quantification models rely on mixing internal data with large monetary losses from the public domain, in an effort to depict the tail of the loss distribution. It is well understood that economic capital calculations are sensitive to the heaviness of the tail, so external data points are added to internally collected data to fill in the tail. The belief is that the resulting mixture will provide risk managers with a more robust picture of the firm's OpRisk exposure. From a qualitative perspective, this idea may be valid. Quantitatively, though, using external data has three serious flaws: (1) disclosure bias, (2) reporting bias and (3) search bias.

"Disclosure bias" refers to an institution's unwillingness or inability to publicly reveal losses. If a firm is not required to report an incident, it will have little incentive to do so. As a result, the losses that are disclosed are usually the high-profile ones that must be revealed. Even when incidents are disclosed, they may not be reported in publications that are widely available: this filtering is "reporting bias". The third factor that affects the external loss distribution is "search bias": an individual's ability to research and record all losses available in the public domain. Each of these biases takes some unknown number of losses out of the pool of public data, and reduces the accuracy of the resulting severity

**Figure 17** The figure on the left illustrates the a *priori* lognormal distribution, while the figure on the right illustrates the a *priori* normal distribution

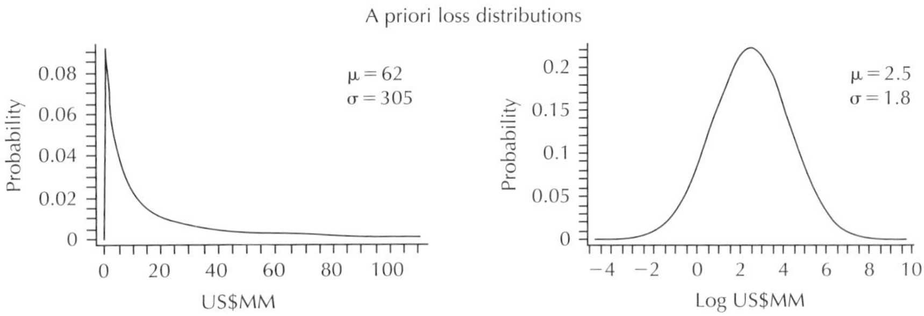


distribution. Consequently, calculations based on the public loss distribution become less and less accurate as the data pool thins.

To illustrate this important consideration, we will randomly generate a dataset with 10,000 losses above US$1 million, and randomly remove some of the data points to show the effect of the biases. To start with, we will assume that the monetary losses are characterised by a normal distribution. For our example, we will speculate that each bias eliminates half of the available data. After three such reductions, we are left with 12.5% of the original data, or 1,250 losses. Let us suppose the *a priori* normal distribution we will use to generate the random losses will have for its parameters $(\mu, \sigma) = (2.5, 1.8)$. These parameters are given in logarithmic terms. In real dollar terms, $\mu$ represents an average loss of US$62 million and $\sigma$ represents a volatility of US$305 million. Figure 17 depicts the *a priori* normal distribution.

Figure 18 illustrates the overlay of the *a priori* normal distribution and the 10,000 generated data points over US$1 million, while Figure 19 shows the overlay of the original 10,000 losses and the 1,250 filtered losses – the remaining, randomly selected 12.5% from the parent sample.

The mean and standard deviations of the 1,250 data points are 2.87 and 1.51. Using these truncated values to solve the normal truncated equations for the parameters of the full normal distribution we get $\mu = 2.66$ and $\sigma = 1.71$. The derived mean is 6% greater than the initial value of 2.5, and the difference between the standard

**Figure 18** Overlay of the randomly generated 10,000 points with the *a priori* normal distribution

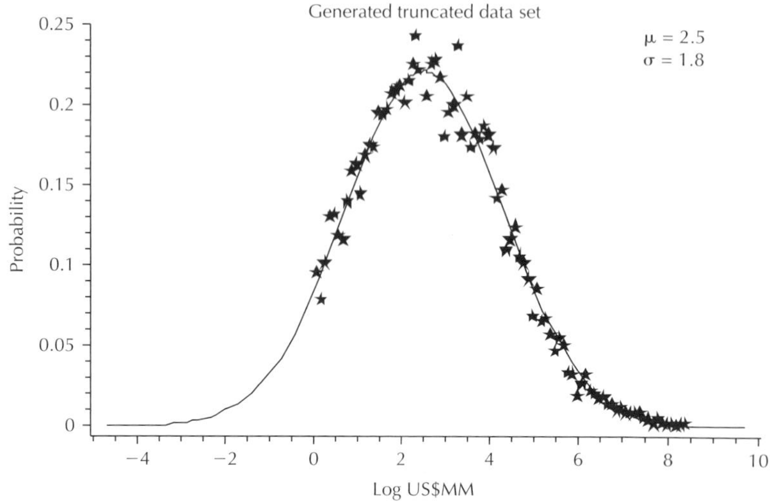


deviations is a decrease of 5%. As Figure 20 shows, the difference between the standard deviations is noticeable when we examine the tails of the distributions. Intuitively, this tells us the volatility of the observed data sample underrepresents the "true" distribution and will not accurately portray the potential occurrence of low-frequency, high-impact losses.

In the previous example, we assumed the losses were characterised by a normal (and equivalently a lognormal) distribution. However, in spite of its numerical and analytical advantages, this assumption does not accurately depict the tail of monetary loss events. To give a more realistic portrayal of the heaviness of the tail, we will use the TAN distribution and carry out another example. As before, let us define the parameters for the *a priori* distribution: ($\mu$, $\sigma$, kurtosis) = (2.5, 1.6, 3.5). In real dollar terms, the mean is US$51 million and standard deviation is US$3,861 million. Figure 21 depicts the *a priori* TAN distribution.

Similar to Figures 18 and 19, the following two graphics (Figures 22 and 23) illustrate the overlays of the randomly generated 10,000 data points over US$1 million with the *a priori* distribution and the randomly selected 1,250 data points with the original 10,000 points.

**Figure 19** Overlay of the randomly selected 1,250 points with the original 10,000 points

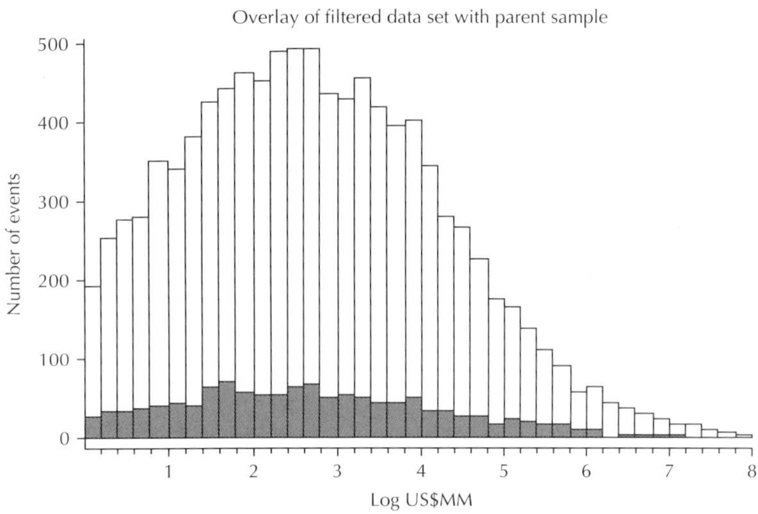


The measured parameter values for the 1,250-point dataset are ($\mu$, $\sigma$, kurtosis) = (2.73, 1.42, 3.44). Using these values to solve for the TAN truncated moment equations, the full TAN has a mean of 2.52, standard deviation of 1.61 and kurtosis of 3.71. Figure 24 compares the original parameters with the ones obtained. As the figure illustrates, the three parameters from the 1,250-point dataset result in a TAN distribution that overestimates the tail when compared to the original distribution. For example, let us compare the relative increase in the probability for two arbitrary loss amounts between the parameter sets. A loss greater than 6 is 10% more likely to occur using the measured parameters instead of the original ones, while the disparity is more dramatic for losses greater than 10.5 where the probability increases more than twice as much.

Our two examples lead us to state preliminarily that external data, which are gathered above a truncation threshold, will not represent the "true" distribution because the three biases – disclosure bias, reporting bias and search bias – dramatically alter the characteristics of the parent set of external loss data. Because of the inaccuracy inherent in biased data, we should be wary of mixing external data with internally collected losses.

**Figure 20** The solid curve is the original normal distribution whose parameters are $(\mu, \sigma) = (2.5, 1.5)$, while the dotted curve is the resulting normal distribution (2.66, 1.71) as determined from the truncated parameters

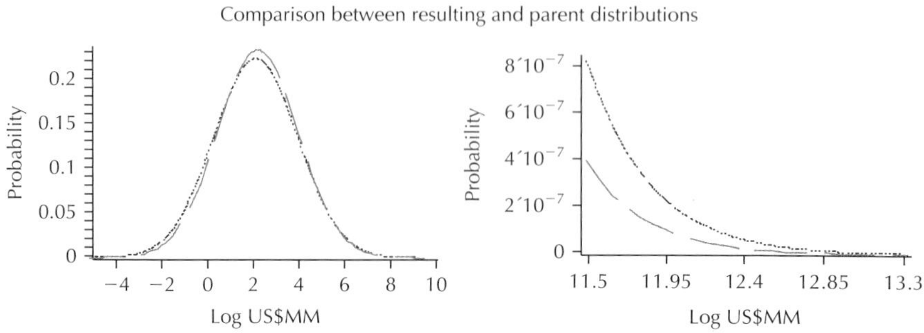


**Figure 21** The figure on the left illustrates the *a priori* tail-adjusted lognormal distribution, while the figure on the right illustrates the *a priori* tail-adjusted normal distribution

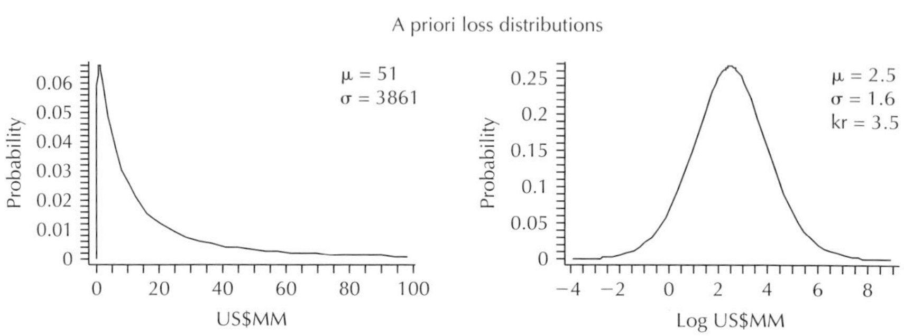


Furthermore, there are other issues that arise when internal and external datasets are combined. One is scaling losses from different-sized outside organisations to correspond to the size of the institution performing the analysis. Although some preliminary work has been done to understand the relationship between loss amount and an institution's asset or revenue size, there remain questions about the accuracy of scaled data. First, what measure of financial size should be used to define the relative sizes of institutions? This consideration is fundamental: one could present valid arguments

**Figure 22** Overlay of the randomly generated 10,000 points with the *a priori* normal distribution

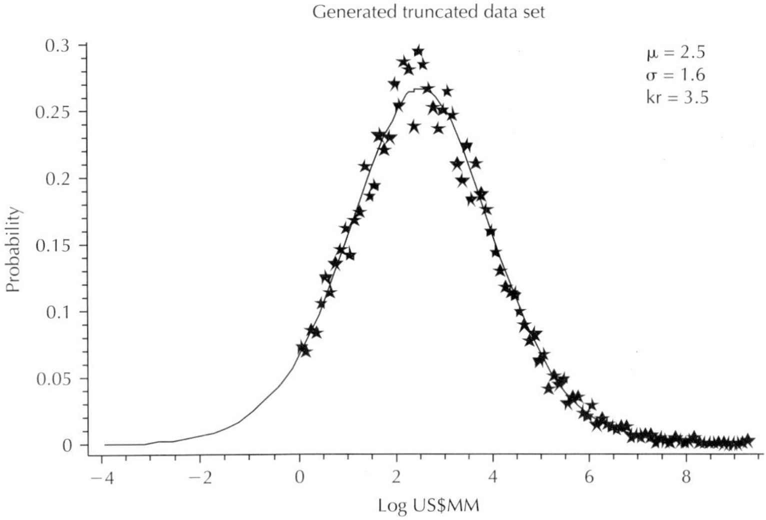


**Figure 23** Overlay of the randomly selected 1,250 points with the original 10,000 points

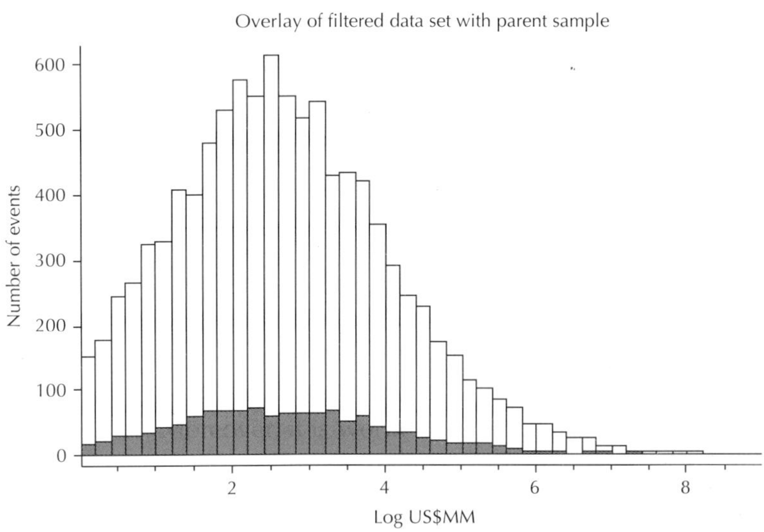

**Figure 24** The solid curve is the original tail-adjusted normal distribution whose parameters are ($\mu$, $\sigma$, kurtosis) = (2.5, 1.6, 3.5), while the dotted curve is the resulting tail-adjusted normal distribution (2.52, 1.61, 3.71) as determined from the truncated parameters

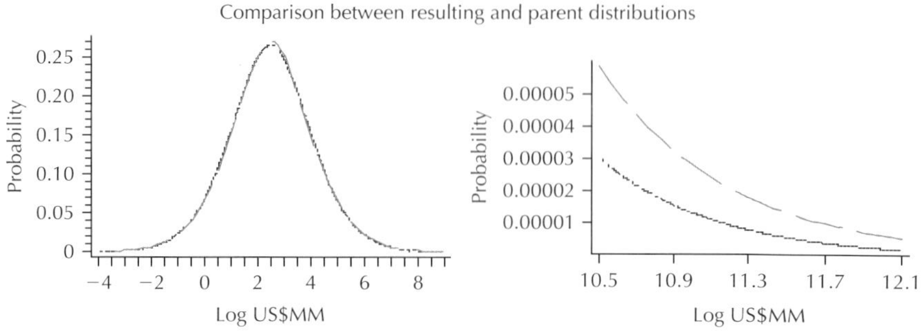


for using any of a number of accounting principles and, with each definition, the scaling relationship will differ.

A second scaling-related problem that is not addressed in the existing body of research is whether different types of OpRisk losses require different degrees of scaling. For example, is there some intangible factor that makes technology-related losses more severe than cases of employee fraud? Current conventions dictate that all types of OpRisk loss be scaled by the same amount, but this one-ratio-fits-all approach may have hidden inaccuracies.

Finally, a third concern about mixing internal and external data is the amount of external data to be mixed with the internal sample. The best one can do to determine the ratio between external and internal data is make an educated guess; anything more would require an understanding of the dataset's severity distribution. Such an understanding contradicts the premise of using external data in the first place – if we knew the severity distribution, we would not need to augment the dataset with external losses.

Although I do not advocate mixing external and internal data because of the quantitative imperfections, external loss information is valuable to risk managers as a qualitative educational tool. If details of significant incidents are available – specifically, what factors triggered or contributed to the losses, how the events were handled, what lessons were learned – managers can apply that knowledge to their own operations. A sound historical understanding of the nature of operational risk provides them with tools that are vital in the decision-making process, and equips them to keep sight of their risks when planning business objectives.

Even though mixing external and internal monetary losses may appear to be a reasonable idea, the examples presented in this section show that the biases inherent in externally gathered losses prevent these data from accurately representing the universal dataset. Additionally, we discussed three questions about external–internal mixtures that have not been adequately answered – these points must be further developed from a quantitative point of view. Given the results presented in this section, an institution that uses external data to augment its internal monetary losses should reconsider this practice and look for alternative quantitative models that will help risk analysts and managers to measure the firm's potential capital exposure to operational risk.

## CONCLUSION

As economic globalisation becomes a reality and our reliance on technically skilled people, computer technologies and telecommunications grows, the execution of business becomes more intricate and competitive. With these changes comes an increased exposure to operational risk. Firms have always been vulnerable to problems in the realm of OpRisk, but only recently have they begun to classify them as such. Managers face pressure from many sources, both inside and outside their organisation, and are expected to raise profits, minimise financial losses and promote institutional efficiency, in spite of these pressures. To achieve these goals, risk managers cannot rely solely on intuitive understanding of risk. They must have at their disposal tools or methodologies that help them to comprehend their OpRisk exposure. One such tool is mathematical analysis.

To fully understand their own risks, firms must perform rigorous quantitative analysis. For this purpose, the most relevant results are obtained using only internal data. The generic seven-step OpRisk quantification model outlined in this chapter can be applied to a small dataset, so an institution can begin to make economic capital exposure and stress-test calculations soon after it begins to record its losses. Furthermore, I presented a classification scheme that categorises OpRisk events by their cause – the action or set of circumstances that led to the event – helping us avoid some of the pitfalls of overlapping datasets, and preventing the inconsistency that arises when events are grouped by the type of loss incurred. As the dataset grows, the calculations will become more precise. But, in the early stages of internal OpRisk measurement, even a sample as small as 100 data points can provide a basic picture of the firm's risk-management environment, along with a starting point for effective OpRisk management. As more data points are included in the calculations over time, the model will yield increasingly accurate results. As their understanding of risk grows, managers will be able to refine their strategies for controlling or minimising operational risk, and achieve the goals of higher profits, lower financial losses and greater institutional efficiency.

1 Risk is defined to be the combination of the severity and frequency of a potential result over a given time horizon.

2 In statistical literature, the three parameters – mean, sigma, and kurtosis – are generally referred to as location, scale and shape.

3 The choice of monetary threshold may be the same, or it may vary across business lines.

4 A probability distribution that is used to determine whether a measured value is within an interval of acceptance with respect to a theoretical value.

5 $\partial_\alpha \varphi(\alpha) = \int_{u_1}^{u_2} \partial_\alpha f(x,\alpha)\mathrm{d}x + f(u_2)\frac{\mathrm{d}u_2}{\mathrm{d}\alpha} - f(u_1)\frac{\mathrm{d}u_1}{\mathrm{d}\alpha}$, where $\varphi(\alpha) = \int_{u_1}^{u_2} f(x,\alpha)\mathrm{d}x$.

6 $\mathrm{Log}_e|\text{loss amount}/1{,}000{,}000|$.

7 One may also assume a uniform distribution, or any other distribution, to compare results.

8 Other VaR limitations are discussed in Dowd (2002).

9 The value was chosen to preserve a "bell-shaped" distribution.

10 For our discussion, a generic phrase for either VaR or ETL.

11 A higher confidence level is used to highlight the effect of the misclassification.

## REFERENCES

**BIS,** 2004, "Basel Committee on Banking Supervision International Convergence of Capital Measurement and Capital Standards", June.

**Dowd, K.,** 2002, *Measuring Market Risk* (New York: John Wiley & Sons).

**Fishman, G.,** 1996, *Monte Carlo: Concepts, Algorithms, and Applications* (New York: Springer-Verlag).

**Hoffman, D. G. and M. Johnson,** 1997, "The Development of Operational RAROC at Bankers Trust", submission for Treasury and Risk Management's Alexander Hamilton Award, September.

**Johnson, N. L., S. Kotz, and N. Balakrishnan,** 1994, *Continuous Univariate Distributions,* Volume 1 (2nd edn) (New York: John Wiley & Sons).

**Johnson, N. L., S. Kotz, and A. W. Kemp,** 1993, *Univariate Discrete Distributions* (2nd edn) (New York: John Wiley & Sons).

**Keeping, E. S.,** 1995, *Introduction to Statistical Inference* (New York: Dover Publications).

**Klugman, S. A., H. H. Panjer, and G. E. Willmot,** 1998, *Loss Models: From Data to Decisions* (New York: John Wiley & Sons).

# Section Three

# Modelling Challenges

This section gets down to discussing some of the thorniest problems of OR modelling in some depth.

In the first chapter, executives from Wachovia describe how they have constructed their loss data capture systems. While this may seem like an unusually practical chapter for a book that has more than its share of the Greek alphabet dotting its pages, I decided to include it because loss data capture is an essential element for any operational risk manager to get his or her head around before even thinking about actual modelling. The chapter describes one approach – certainly there are others. But hopefully it will provide a basis for discussion and debate about how best to capture the data that will provide the foundation for any modelling approach.

The second chapter, by the University of Trento's Marco Bee looks at the fraught area of maximum-likelihood estimation of log-normal severity distributions with censored and truncated data – a significant problem in most op risk datasets. The third chapter explores another incomplete-data issue: the effect of data gaps on parameter estimates, and calculations of expected and unexpected loss. The fourth chapter looks at how extreme-value theory can be used to help mitigate some of the data problems associated with operational risk modelling.

While none of this could be considered "light reading", the chapters are written clearly and with a fair amount of explanation, so that readers who have a basic background in modelling should be able to find them understandable and useful. The goal is to provide some guidance for executives struggling with these issues. While not all questions will be answered – in a field as new and rapidly evolving as operational risk this is nearly impossible – the chapters do provide useful guidance for getting to grips with these specific challenges and should provide readers with a basic understanding of the issues.

5

# *Breaking Ground on the Loss Data Challenge: Wachovia's Approach to Loss Data Capture and Validation*

**Dee Harris, Tom Longstroth**

Wachovia Corporation

How does a company successfully integrate loss data into its operational risk management (ORM) framework? How do you build a comprehensive and consistent approach to collect data from multiple lines of business and subsystems? How do you ensure data integrity? How do you avoid expensive investments in additional resources? Wachovia considered these and other questions as we began development of a new operational-loss data approach in 2002.

Wachovia is the fourth-largest bank in the United States with US$521 billion in assets, 94,000 employees and banking operations from Connecticut to Florida and west to Texas. Wachovia's retail brokerage firm, Wachovia Securities, LLC, serves clients through offices in 49 states and five Latin American countries, and its Corporate and Investment Bank serves clients in selected industries nationwide. Global services are offered through 40 offices around the world. Creating a comprehensive loss data framework was an important, yet complicated, component of Wachovia's ORM objective: to create and sustain a competitive advantage through lower earnings volatility, greater customer satisfaction and enhanced reputation.

## ESTABLISHING ORM OBJECTIVES

Wachovia's Corporate ORM Group focused on three key objectives in formulating its loss data collection approach: (1) leveraging existing processes, (2) ensuring data integrity and (3) improving analysis, reporting and decision making. The intent was to create a simple yet comprehensive loss data approach without significantly affecting business team resources. We did not want a process that would burden business units with capturing and reporting operational-loss events. At the same time, it was necessary for loss data to integrate with other ORM tools in Wachovia's enterprise ORM framework, such as risk assessments, issue/action plans and risk profiles.

**Leveraging processes**

Much of Wachovia's operational loss data existed in organisational silos. For example, Human Resources captured losses on worker's compensation claims. Legal captured litigation losses, and Loss Management captured losses regarding fraud. The Corporate Insurance Group used a tracking system for all claims and losses involving property damage, car accidents and general liability. Each organisation had processes and case-management systems to capture and house loss event data elements, which enabled detailed analysis and reporting. Rather than disrupt these existing processes by attempting to merge multiple discrete data flows and systems into one data-collection process, Wachovia decided to use the existing systems to feed operational loss data to the Operational Risk Management Suite (ORMS), Wachovia's integrated operational risk system. ORMS was developed by Centerprise and houses modules for operational loss data and other ORM components.

Each case-management system presented distinct interfacing challenges. For example, some system interfaces required engagement from external vendors responsible for managing those systems. To overcome these challenges, Corporate ORM developed data standards and file specifications for each data silo and built automated interfaces that pulled data into a central database created in ORMS. By leveraging existing processes, ORM was able to quickly gain access to the necessary data without imposing significant requirements or resource demands on business units.

Case-management systems did not capture all operational-loss events occurring across the enterprise. The majority of losses not captured in a case-management system were the result of business processes, and were recorded directly to the general ledger (GL). In order to capture these losses, an automated interface was built

**Figure 1** General ledger mapping assistant

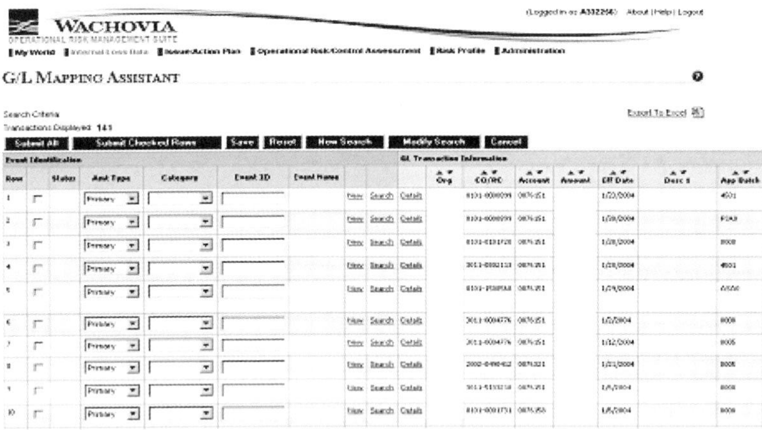


between ORMS and the GL designed to extract transaction details from designated loss accounts. This information is now imported automatically into ORMS on a monthly basis.

Using a feature of ORMS called the GL Mapping Assistant (see Figure 1), designated line of business risk managers can review GL transactions for the month, group them by Basel category and input non-financial event information such as description, event date, discovery date, reputation impact and customer impact. In addition, ORMS has the capability to manually add loss events if a financial loss was not captured in a case-management system or on the GL.

## Ensuring data integrity

Data integrity is an essential component of Wachovia's operational-loss data framework (see Figure 2). Business leaders, regulators and auditors need confidence that the loss data in ORMS are complete and accurate. In creating our approach, we needed to ensure: (1) the data were consistent and complete, (2) data were transferred accurately, and (3) no duplicate loss events existed in the database. To ensure ORM could consistently identify operational losses across the company, existing accounting policies and procedures had to be updated to reflect the new terminology and definition of operational risk (OR) as mandated by Basel II and

**Figure 2** Loss data flow

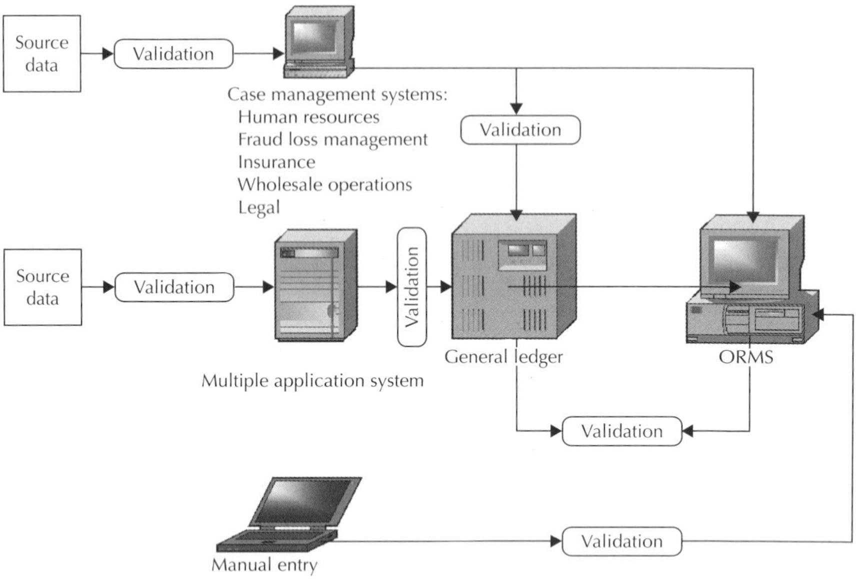


adopted by Wachovia. ORM partnered with Corporate Finance to overhaul the operational loss GL accounts along with the policies for their use. These revised policies addressed what was considered an operational loss and defined which GL account to use. We then prepared leadership announcements, reference materials, question-and-answer sheets, decision trees and case-study examples, along with classroom and on-line training to inform and educate select audiences in the new policies and procedures.

To ensure integrity between the multiple sources of loss data, the ORM Group built a validation process to strengthen the accuracy of data in ORMS. This involves validating the data loaded into ORMS with control totals supplied by the source of the data. This is referred to as a *source file validation* and requires the cooperation of the case-management system owners and, in some cases, outside vendors. ORMS also employs filters to screen out duplicate data, since some loss events received from case-management system source files may also be included in feeds from the GL. For data imported directly from the GL to ORMS, Corporate ORM created a monthly reconciliation of ORMS financial data to selected accounts on the GL. In addition, an automated workflow in ORMS requires that all loss events over a certain dollar threshold be reviewed and approved by a line of business operational risk managers. This review confirms that all significant losses are captured in ORMS, supports proper event categorisation (such as Basel category, risk type), and ensures that significant loss events are given appropriate attention from management.

While 100% reconcilement of ORMS data to the GL is not yet possible, efforts are under way to move in that direction. Until full reconciliation is achieved, targeted reconciliations, data validation and systemic controls over manual entries provide assurance that the data are complete and accurate.

### Improving data analysis and reporting

The transfer, validation and aggregation of data enables more accurate comparisons, analysis and reporting. With ORMS, a comprehensive and comparable loss profile can be built for each line of business and sub-unit. Before ORMS, a manager had to go to separate departments to obtain data for each loss type. Each of these departments had different definitions, thresholds and assumptions, making comprehensive analysis and reporting difficult. ORMS has fostered a common language and understanding across the company, resulting in greater effectiveness and consistency in business unit and Executive reporting.

### Creating a foundation to drive value

As we contemplated a new loss data approach, Wachovia's ORM Group knew that comprehensive loss data collection and analysis would be challenging. Multiple complex processes and systems compounded the difficulties. ORMS has enabled a flexible and sustainable framework for managing OR loss data by leveraging existing processes and resources. Our data validation and review processes provide confidence in the data. We continue to work across the company to enhance our processes, strengthen data integrity and improve analysis and reporting. This work is performed with our primary objective in mind – to use loss data and other ORM tools to strengthen business processes and better manage risk, delivering greater value to customers and shareholders.

6

# *Estimating the Parameters in the Loss Distribution Approach: How Can We Deal with Truncated Data?*

**Marco Bee**[1]

University of Trento

Operational risk presents peculiar features with respect to other areas of financial risk management and, as a consequence, its measurement and management require different tools. In particular, the distribution of losses is usually modelled directly because, unlike losses caused by market or credit events, operational losses are not related to underlying financial factors. This characteristic has been the key to the development of a purely statistical approach that assumes a fully parametric model for the losses and estimates its parameters using historical observations.

The Basel II accord contemplates three approaches to the measurement of operational risk, in increasing order of mathematical complexity. The third level, called the *Advanced Measurement Approach* (AMA) is in turn subdivided in two levels: the *Internal Measurement Approach* and the *Loss Distribution Approach* (LDA); in this chapter, we focus on the LDA, which is the most sophisticated and prescribes to estimate the whole loss distribution for each business line by modelling the frequency and the severity of losses separately.

The typical probabilistic models proposed to describe the loss severity are the Lognormal, Gamma, Weibull and Pareto distributions. Tail thickness is probably the most important feature to be considered when choosing a model for the severity; we know from extreme value theory that the Pareto distribution is long-tailed, the Lognormal and Gamma distributions are moderately tailed (in the sense that they are both in the domain of attraction of the Gumbel distribution, also called the type-II Generalised Extreme Value Distribution), whereas the Weibull corresponds to the type-III Generalised Extreme Value Distribution, which is short-tailed. In general, operational risk data is moderately to long-tailed, so that the Weibull distribution should be ruled out; moreover, the Gamma and the lognormal distributions have similar tail heaviness, but the latter is analytically more tractable, so that in recent years it has become the most popular model. Finally, the Pareto distribution is mainly used when data is definitely long-tailed.

As for the frequency, we follow the common approach of modelling it as a Poisson distribution. This hypothesis is justified when the data provides empirical evidence for the equality of mean and variance; when the variance is significantly larger than the mean, the negative binomial distribution may be more appropriate. However, the Poisson–lognormal model is now considered the standard. From a methodological point of view, the LDA is based on the techniques developed in the non-life insurance field, where losses are represented by claims; see Klugman *et al* (1998) or Mikosch (2004) for a thorough analysis of these methods, which represent the starting point for the LDA.

The most important risk measure used in the operational risk framework is the Unexpected Loss, which is computed as the $(1-\alpha)$th quantile minus the expected value of the loss distribution over a specified time horizon. The Basel II accord defines it as the capital-at-risk (CaR).

There are at least two reasons why statistical analysis is challenging. First, for measuring risk one has to determine the aggregate loss, as given by the combination of frequency and severity: the distribution of this quantity is the convolution of $k$ independent continuous random variables, where $k$ is the realisation of a discrete random variable. The resulting distribution is usually difficult to work with, so that, in order to compute loss and risk measures, simulation techniques are called for.

Second, statistical inference about the parameters of the severity distribution cannot be performed along the familiar lines, because losses below a certain threshold are usually not recorded: according to whether these "small" losses are not measured (but their number is known) or completely discarded (so that even their number is unknown), data is respectively left-censored or left-truncated.

In this chapter we study the problem of maximum likelihood estimation of the aggregate loss distribution with censored and truncated observations. In order to simplify the terminology, from now on the truncated and censored setups will be called the *incomplete-data setup*, whereas we will call the framework where all data is fully recorded the *complete-data setup*.

Estimation with incomplete data is more difficult than estimation with complete data: no closed-form estimators are available and even numerical maximisation of the likelihood function is not straightforward. We show that the EM algorithm provides a solution that is both theoretically well founded and easily implementable; in addition, it has two features that make it preferable with respect to commonly used algorithms: (i) it produces an estimate of the number of truncated observations, which is essential for the estimation of the parameters of the frequency distribution; (ii) in the censored case, if the proportion of missing data is large, the likelihood function has a disturbing feature that causes underflows when using algorithms that attempt a direct maximisation of the function. In this situation the EM algorithm is not affected by the problem. More details about both of these issues will be given in the following.

This chapter is organised as follows. In the first section we describe the data-generating process of operational losses, review the estimation techniques in the complete-data setup and quantify, in terms of bias and mean squared error of the estimators, the consequences of ignoring the truncation process. Next we derive the EM algorithm to find the maximum likelihood estimators (MLEs) of the parameters in the case of both censored and truncated lognormal losses. Then we use the algorithm to measure risk and investigate the impact of truncation on CaR estimation. In the last section we discuss the results and provide conclusions.

## MODELLING AND ESTIMATING OPERATIONAL LOSSES: COMPLETE DATA

To describe the mathematical approach to CaR measurement in the LDA formally, we start by introducing the loss distribution, the simulation procedure and the estimation methodology with complete data. The total loss over a predetermined time horizon is given by the random sum

$$S = \sum_{i=1}^{K} W_i \tag{1}$$

where $K$ is a random variable with a counting distribution and $W_1, \ldots, W_K$ are independent and identically distributed continuous positive random variables, also independent from $K$. The corresponding cumulative distribution function is

$$\begin{aligned} F_S(w) &= P(S \leq w) \\ &= \sum_{k=0}^{\infty} p_k P(S \leq w | K = k) \\ &= \sum_{k=0}^{\infty} p_k F_W^{*k}(w) \end{aligned}$$

where $p_k = P(K = k)$ and $F_W^{*k}(w)$ is the $k$-fold convolution of the cumulative distribution function of $W$; the distribution of $S$ is commonly known as a *compound distribution*.

The LDA can be formulated, more generally, in continuous time. In this setup, the total loss is a stochastic process $S(t)$, $0 \leq t \leq T$, represented as

$$S(t) = \sum_{i=1}^{K(t)} W_i, \qquad 0 \leq t \leq T \tag{2}$$

where $K(t)$ is a counting process and $W_1, \ldots, W_K$ are independent and identically distributed continuous random variables. $S(t)$ is a *compound counting process* and the pair $\{t_k, W_k\}_{k \in \mathbb{Z}}$, where $t_k$ are the points of jump and $\mathbb{Z}$ is the set of integers, is a *marked point process*. In particular, if we assume that $K(t)$ is a Poisson process with parameter $\nu$, Equation (2) is called a *Poisson compound process*; from the basic properties of the Poisson process (see, eg, Durrett (1996, p 145)), if we fix $t^* \in [0, T]$, the compound counting process (2) reduces to the compound distribution (1), where the parameter of the Poisson distribution is $\lambda = \nu \cdot t^*$.

The joint distribution $f_{K,W}(k, w)$ of the two sources of randomness $K$ and $W$ in (1) is quite intricate, so that almost invariably simulation techniques are the only possibility to deal with it; to this aim, we have to use the following factorisation of the joint distribution of $K$ and $S$: $f_{K,S}(k, s) = f_{S|K}(s|k) \cdot f_K(k)$. In this way, the simulation has been split into two simpler problems: simulating $K$ and $S|K$. The latter can be written as

$$(S \mid K = k) = \sum_{i=1}^{k} W_i$$

which may or may not be analytically tractable depending on the distribution of $W$, but can easily be simulated as long as we can simulate $W$. If $W \sim Logn(\mu, \sigma^2)$, and conditionally on $K$, this distribution is the convolution of $k$ lognormal random variables; if we further assume that $K \sim Pois(\lambda)$, random number generation from $f_{K,S}(k, s)$ can be accomplished by performing the following steps:

(i) simulate a random number $k$ from the $Pois(\lambda)$ distribution;
(ii) simulate $k$ random numbers $w_1, \ldots, w_k$ from the $Logn(\mu, \sigma^2)$ distribution and compute $s = \sum_{i=1}^{k} w_i$.

Repeating these two steps $B$ times, we get a random sample of size $B$ from the density $f_{K,S}(k, s)$. This is the approach commonly adopted to compute CaR, which is given by the appropriate quantile of the empirical distribution minus its mean.

From the point of view of statistical inference, the parameters of the frequency and of the severity distribution can be estimated separately either by maximum likelihood or by percentile matching. Whereas this is straightforward in principle, a major difficulty is given by the fact that loss data is usually left-censored or, more frequently, left-truncated: according to whether data is censored or truncated, specific inferential procedures are required. Before moving on, we recall the appropriate definitions (Klugman *et al* 1998, p 132).

**Definition 1.** *Data is said to be* censored *when the number of observations that fall into a given set is known, but the specific values of the observations are unknown; data is said to be censored from below when the set is all numbers less than a specific value.*

**Definition 2.** *Data is said to be* truncated *when observations that fall into a given set are excluded; data is said to be truncated from below when the set is all numbers less than a specific value.*

The importance of considering the truncation mechanism in estimation becomes clear when considering what happens if truncated data is ignored. To this aim, suppose that $W \sim Logn(\mu, \sigma^2)$ and that losses whose severity is less than $c$ are discarded; suppose further that the logarithmic transformation $V = log(W)$ is used, so that $V \sim N(\mu, \sigma^2)$. With complete data, the MLEs of the parameters are given by

$$\hat{\mu} = \frac{1}{N}\sum_{i=1}^{N} V_i, \quad \hat{\sigma}^2 = \frac{1}{N}\sum_{i=1}^{N}(V_i - \hat{\mu})^2 \tag{3}$$

In the truncated case, we only observe $N_1 < N$ logarithmic losses; the remaining $N_2 = N - N_1$ observations are discarded, so that both $N$ and $N_2$ are unknown. If we just ignore the truncation and use the $N_1$ recorded observations to compute the MLEs (3), we get

$$\tilde{\mu} = \frac{1}{N_1}\sum_{i=1}^{N_1} V_i^*, \quad \tilde{\sigma}^2 = \frac{1}{N_1}\sum_{i=1}^{N_1}(V_i^* - \tilde{\mu})^2$$

where $V_i^* = \{V_i : V_i > c\}$. The expected value of $\tilde{\mu}$ is given by

$$E\left(\frac{1}{N_1}\sum_{i=1}^{N_1} V_i^*\right) = E(V_i^*) = \int_c^{\infty} xf^*(x)\,dx$$

where $f^*$ is the density of a normal random variable left-truncated at $c$; a standard result from elementary probability theory gives

$$E(\tilde{\mu}) = \mu + \sigma\frac{\phi(c)}{1-\Phi(c)}$$

where $\phi$ and $\Phi$ are, respectively, the probability distribution function and the cumulative distribution function of the standard normal distribution. Similarly, the expected value of $\tilde{\sigma}^2$ is the variance of a normal random variable left-truncated at $c$, which is given by

$$E(\tilde{\sigma}^2) = \sigma^2\left\{1 + \frac{c\phi(c)}{1-\Phi(c)} - \left[\frac{\phi(c)}{1-\Phi(c)}\right]^2\right\}$$

For the standard normal case, the bias of the two estimators is thus equal to

$$E(\tilde{\mu}) = \frac{\phi(c)}{1-\Phi(c)}$$

$$E(\tilde{\sigma}^2 - 1) = \left\{1 + \frac{c\phi(c)}{1-\Phi(c)} - \left[\frac{\phi(c)}{1-\Phi(c)}\right]^2\right\} - 1 \tag{4}$$

and is shown in Figure 1.

The biases computed in (4) obviously have an impact on CaR computation; we measure this later.

## MODELLING AND ESTIMATING OPERATIONAL LOSSES: INCOMPLETE DATA

To give a motivation for the later developments of the chapter, we first sketch the difficulties associated with maximum likelihood estimation in the incomplete-data setup.

The likelihood function corresponding to the density of the severity distribution when the observations are left-censored is given by (Maddala 1983, p 5):

$$L(\mu, \sigma^2; c, \mathbf{y}) = \text{constant} \cdot [\Phi(c^*)]^{N_C} \cdot \prod_{i=1}^{N_U} L(\mu, \sigma^2; y_i) \tag{5}$$

where $y_i$ ($i = 1, \ldots, N_U$) is the logarithm of the uncensored observations, $L(\mu, \sigma^2; y_i)$ is the normal likelihood function, $N_U$ and $N_C$ are the number of uncensored and censored observations, respectively, $c$ is the censoring threshold, $c^* = (c - \mu)/\sigma$ and the constant does not depend on unknown parameters. Maximising this function is rather complicated: analytical differentiation is impossible because of the presence of the normal cumulative distribution function, and numerical differentiation is computationally heavy. For this reason, standard gradient-based optimisation methods are likely to give unstable results, and it is preferable to introduce algorithms that are better suited for the solution of this problem.

### The EM algorithm

The EM algorithm (Dempster *et al* 1977; McLachlan and Krishnan 1996) is an iterative method for computing MLEs with incomplete data. Typically, the algorithm is particularly convenient in cases

**Figure 1** Bias of the MLE of (a) $\mu$ and (b) $\sigma^2$ as a function of the truncation threshold $c$

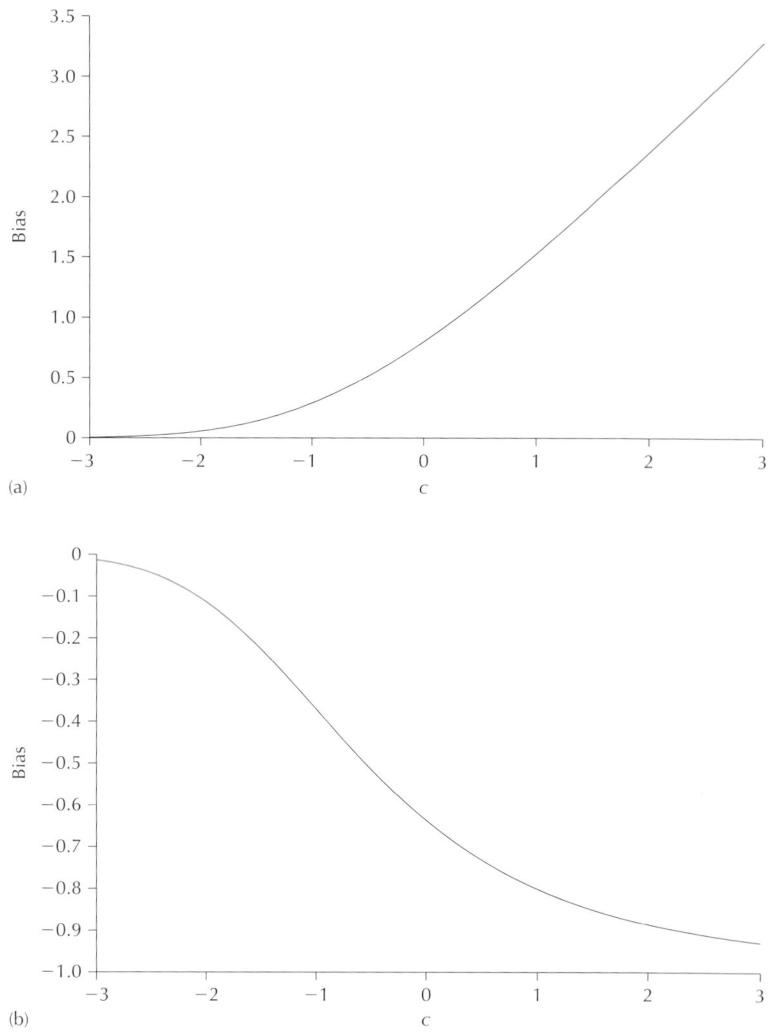


when, if the missing data was known, estimation would be straightforward.

Roughly speaking, the algorithm consists of maximising a hypothetical likelihood based not only on the observed data but also on a "proper replacement" of the missing data. The maximisation of the latter function, called the complete likelihood function, is often much easier than the maximisation of the observed likelihood.

More formally, let $\mathbf{Y}$ be the random vector of the observed data; let $g(\mathbf{y}; \boldsymbol{\theta})$ and $l(\boldsymbol{\theta})$ be its density and log-likelihood function, respectively, where $\boldsymbol{\theta}$ is the vector of all parameters. Then let $\mathbf{X}$ be the vector containing the missing data, whose elements are unobservable; finally, let $\mathbf{Z} = (\mathbf{X}', \mathbf{Z}')'$ be the complete-data vector, with density and log-likelihood denoted by $g_c(\mathbf{z}; \boldsymbol{\theta})$ and $l_c(\boldsymbol{\theta})$, respectively.

The first step of the algorithm (called the *E*-step, where *E* stands for expectation) consists of computing the conditional expectation of the complete log-likelihood function $l_c(\boldsymbol{\theta})$, given the current value of $\boldsymbol{\theta}$ and the observed sample $\mathbf{y}$. The second step (called the *M*-step, where *M* stands for maximisation) maximises, with respect to $\boldsymbol{\theta}$, the conditional expectation of the complete log-likelihood computed in the *E*-step.

The structure of the algorithm can be described as follows: let $\boldsymbol{\theta}^{(0)}$ be the initial value of the parameter vector; the *E*-step consists of computing

$$Q(\boldsymbol{\theta}; \boldsymbol{\theta}^{(0)}) = E_{\theta^{(0)}}\{l_c(\boldsymbol{\theta}) \mid \mathbf{y}\} \tag{6}$$

Then $Q(\boldsymbol{\theta}; \boldsymbol{\theta}^{(0)})$ is maximised with respect to $\boldsymbol{\theta}$, namely $\boldsymbol{\theta}^{(1)}$ is chosen such that

$$Q(\boldsymbol{\theta}^{(1)}; \boldsymbol{\theta}^{(0)}) = \max_{\theta} Q(\boldsymbol{\theta}; \boldsymbol{\theta}^{(0)}) \tag{7}$$

The procedure is then repeated, that is, (6) and (7) are recomputed using $\boldsymbol{\theta}^{(1)}$ in place of $\boldsymbol{\theta}^{(0)}$. The two steps are iterated until some convergence criterion is met.

From the numerical point of view, the EM algorithm has interesting properties (see McLachlan and Krishnan (1996, Chapter 3)). The actual form of (6) and (7) depends on the specific problem at hand and on the assumptions on the distribution of the data: in the following we develop the algorithm for left-censored and left-truncated lognormal data. The next two sections are rather technical; readers mainly interested in the practical implementation of the algorithm may skip directly to Equations (10)–(13) for the censored case and Equations (16)–(19) for the truncated case.

### Censored data

Let $W_1, \ldots, W_N$ be a sample of independent losses from a lognormal population with parameters $\mu$ and $\sigma^2$; as usual with lognormally distributed observations, one can use the transformation $Y_i = log(W_i) \sim N(\mu, \sigma^2)$ and restrict attention to the normal case. Let $N_U$ and $N_C = N - N_U$ be respectively the number of uncensored and censored observations, and let $\mathbf{y} = (y_1, \ldots, y_{N_U})'$ be the vector of uncensored observations. Similarly, let $\mathbf{x}$ be the missing data, that is, $\mathbf{x} = (x_1, \ldots, x_{N_C})'$; the numerical values of the data are unobservable, but the number of the data $N_C$ is known. Finally, let $\mathbf{z} = (\mathbf{y}', \mathbf{x}')'$ be the complete data. Note that we can also write $\mathbf{y} = \{z_i : z_i \geq c\}$ and $\mathbf{x} = \{z_i : z_i < c\}$, $i = 1, \ldots, N$, where $c$ is the logarithm of the truncation threshold.

The complete likelihood function is given by the hypothetical likelihood we would observe if no data was missing:

$$L_c(\mu, \sigma^2; \mathbf{z}) = \prod_{i=1}^{N} L(\mu, \sigma^2; z_i), \quad \mu \in \mathbb{R},\ \sigma^2 \in \mathbb{R}^+$$

where $L(\mu, \sigma^2; z_i)$ is the normal likelihood function evaluated at $z_i$. The observed likelihood can be written as

$$\begin{aligned} L_{obs}(\mu, \sigma^2; c, \mathbf{y}) &= \text{constant} \cdot \prod_{i=1}^{N_U} L(\mu, \sigma^2; y_i) \cdot [P(Y \leq c)]^{N_C} \\ &= \text{constant} \cdot \prod_{i=1}^{N_U} L(\mu, \sigma^2; y_i) \cdot [\Phi(c^*)]^{N_C}, \ \mu \in \mathbb{R},\ \sigma^2 \in \mathbb{R}^+ \end{aligned} \quad \textbf{(8)}$$

where $c^* = (c - \mu)/\sigma$ and $L(\mu, \sigma^2; y_i)$ is the normal likelihood, so that

$$\begin{aligned} & L_{obs}(\mu, \sigma^2; c, \mathbf{y}) \\ & = \text{constant} \cdot \prod_{i=1}^{N_U} \left\{ \frac{1}{\sqrt{2\pi}\sigma} \exp\left( -\frac{1}{2} \left( \frac{y_i - \mu}{\sigma} \right)^2 \right) \right\} \cdot [\Phi(c^*)]^{N_C} \end{aligned} \quad \textbf{(9)}$$

The $E$-step is given by the conditional expectation of the complete log-likelihood function given the observed data and the current numerical values of the parameters. Putting $\tau = \sigma^2$ to simplify notation, at the $t$th iteration we have

$$E[L_c(\mu,\tau;\mathbf{z})\,|\,\mathbf{y},\mu^{(t)},\tau^{(t)}] = \prod_{i=1}^{N_U} L(\mu,\tau;y_i)\cdot\prod_{i=1}^{N_C} E[L_{miss}(\mu,\tau;c,x_i\,|\,y_i,\mu^{(t)},\tau^{(t)})]$$

Now the distribution of the missing data $X_i$, $i = 1,\ldots,N_C$, is right-truncated normal, because the $X_i$ are normal and smaller than $c$, so that they have density

$$f_X(x) = \frac{1}{\Phi(c^*)}\cdot\frac{1}{\sqrt{2\pi}\sigma}\exp\left(-\frac{1}{2}\left(\frac{x-\mu}{\sigma}\right)^2\right),\qquad x \le c$$

and $L_{miss}$ is the likelihood of the right-truncated normal distribution. The computation of the conditional expectation $E[L_{miss}(\mu,\tau;c,x_i\,|\,y_i,\mu^{(t)},\tau^{(t)})]$ is simplified by the fact that the complete log-likelihood function is linear in $X$ and $X^2$; thus, it amounts to computing $E(X\,|\,\mu^{(t)},\tau^{(t)},y_1,\ldots,y_{N_U})$ and $E(X^2\,|\,\mu^{(t)},\tau^{(t)},y_1,\ldots,y_{N_U})$. These two quantities are given by the well-known formulae for the expected value and the variance of the right-truncated normal distribution. We get

$$E(X\,|\,\boldsymbol{\theta}^{(t)},\mathbf{y}) = \mu^{(t)} - \sigma^{(t)}\cdot\alpha(c^{*(t)}) \tag{10}$$

$$E(X^2\,|\,\boldsymbol{\theta}^{(t)},\mathbf{y}) = \tau^{(t)}\cdot[1 - c^{*(t)}\cdot\alpha(c^{*(t)}) - (\alpha(c^{*(t)}))^2] + [E(X\,|\,\boldsymbol{\theta}^{(t)},\mathbf{y})]^2 \tag{11}$$

where $\alpha(c^*) = \phi(c^*)/\Phi(c^*)$. As for the $M$-step, we just have to use the formulae of the MLEs of the normal distribution, with missing data replaced by (10) and (11):

$$\mu^{(t+1)} = \frac{1}{N}\left(\sum_{i=1}^{N_U} y_i + N_C\cdot E(X\,|\,\boldsymbol{\theta}^{(t)},\mathbf{y})\right) \tag{12}$$

$$\tau^{(t+1)} = \frac{1}{N}\left(\sum_{i=1}^{N_U} y_i^2 + N_C\cdot E(X^2\,|\,\boldsymbol{\theta}^{(t)},\mathbf{y})\right) - (\mu^{(t+1)})^2 \tag{13}$$

Finally, MLEs of the parameters are given by iterating (10)–(13) until convergence.

### Truncated data

In practical applications, truncated data is more frequent than censored data; deriving the relevant equations of the algorithm in this case is slightly more tricky, but the practical implementation remains as easy as with censored observations. The following calculations are based on the way of reasoning followed by McLachlan and Krishnan (1996, Section 2.8) in a model with grouped and truncated data.

The setup needs to be modified as follows. Let $W_1, \ldots, W_{N_U}$ be a sample of independent losses from a truncated lognormal population with parameters $\mu$ and $\sigma^2$; again, we use the transformation $Y_i = log(W_i) \sim N(\mu, \sigma^2)$ and restrict attention to the normal case. $N_U$ is now the number of untruncated observations and $\mathbf{y} = (y_1, \ldots, y_{N_U})'$ is the vector containing this data. We also know that $N_T$ observations are smaller than $c$ and have been discarded, but $N_T$ is unknown. It follows that the missing data is now given by $\{N_T, \mathbf{x}\}$, where $N_T$ is the number of truncated observations and $\mathbf{x} = (x_1, \ldots, x_{N_T})'$. As before, let $\mathbf{z} = (\mathbf{y}', N_T, \mathbf{x}')'$ represent the complete data, where $\mathbf{y} = \{z_i : z_i \geq c\}$, $N_T = \#\{z_i : z_i < c\}$ and $\mathbf{x} = \{z_i : z_i < c\}$, $i = 1, \ldots, N$.

The complete likelihood function is as in the previous section:

$$L_c(\mu, \sigma^2; \mathbf{z}) = \prod_{i=1}^{N} L(\mu, \sigma^2; z_i), \quad \mu \in \mathbb{R}, \sigma^2 \in \mathbb{R}^+ \tag{14}$$

where $L(\mu, \sigma^2; z_i)$ is the normal likelihood function evaluated at $z_i$. The observed likelihood is given by

$$\begin{aligned} L_{obs}(\mu, \sigma^2; c, \mathbf{Y}) &= \prod_{i=1}^{N_U} L_{trunc}(\mu, \sigma^2; c, y_i) \\ &= \prod_{i=1}^{N_U} \left\{ \frac{1}{1-\Phi(c^*)} \cdot \frac{1}{\sqrt{2\pi}\sigma} \exp\left( -\frac{1}{2}\left( \frac{y_i - \mu}{\sigma} \right)^2 \right) \right\}, \\ &\mu \in \mathbb{R}, \sigma^2 \in \mathbb{R}^+ \end{aligned} \tag{15}$$

For the implementation of the algorithm, it is convenient to rewrite (14) using the factorisation

$$f(y, n_T, x) = f(y) \cdot f(n_T \mid y) \cdot f(x \mid n_T, y)$$

To compute the conditional expectation of the complete log-likelihood function, we need to determine the distribution of $N_T|Y$ and of $(X|Y, N_T)$.

Denoting with $Z$ the random variable having the complete-data distribution, that is, $Z \sim N(\mu, \sigma^2)$, it can be shown (McLachlan and Krishnan 1996, pp 76–77) that $N_T|Y$ has the negative binomial distribution with parameters $N_U$ and $\pi$, where $\pi = P(Z > c) = 1 - \Phi(c^*)$. The conditional expectation is thus given by $E(N_T|Y) = N_U \cdot (1 - \pi)/\pi$.

Concerning $(X|Y, N_T)$, the quantities $E(X|Y, N_T)$ and $E(X^2|Y, N_T)$ can be computed as in the preceding section; in summary, the $E$-step is given by

$$\begin{aligned} E(N_T \mid Y) &\stackrel{\text{def}}{=} \hat{N}_T = N_U \cdot (1-\pi)/\pi \\ E(X \mid \boldsymbol{\theta}^{(t)}, Y) &= \mu^{(t)} - \sigma^{(t)} \cdot \alpha(c^{*(t)}) \end{aligned} \tag{16}$$

$$E(X^2 \mid \boldsymbol{\theta}^{(t)}, Y) = \tau^{(t)} \cdot [1 - c^{*(t)} \cdot \alpha(c^{*(t)}) - (\alpha(c^{*(t)}))^2] + [E(X \mid \boldsymbol{\theta}^{(t)}, Y)]^2 \tag{17}$$

As for the $M$-step, the equations are analogous to the censored case, with $N_C$ replaced by $N_T^{(t)}$:

$$\mu^{(t+1)} = \frac{1}{N_U + N_T^{(t)}} \left( \sum_{i=1}^{N_U} y_i + N_T^{(t)} \cdot E(X \mid \boldsymbol{\theta}^{(t)}, \mathbf{y}) \right) \tag{18}$$

$$\tau^{(t+1)} = \frac{1}{N_U + N_T^{(t)}} \left( \sum_{i=1}^{N_U} y_i^2 + N_T^{(t)} \cdot E(X^2 \mid \boldsymbol{\theta}^{(t)}, \mathbf{y}) \right) - (\mu^{(t+1)})^2 \tag{19}$$

These equations are then iterated until convergence to get the MLEs.

As usual, the maximisation of the likelihood function can also be performed by means of standard optimisation tools. However, gradient-based algorithms (eg, Newton–Raphson, Scoring, Broyden–Fletcher–Goldfarb–Shanno (BFGS)), are not particularly efficient in this case: the log-likelihood functions (9) and (15) are not differentiable analytically. On the other hand, numerical differentiation is computationally heavy: this fact, in addition to slowing the algorithm, is likely to cause unstable results, in particular as concerns the Hessian matrix.

In the class of deterministic optimisation methods, a direct search method such as, for example, the Nelder–Mead (NM) simplex algorithm may be more appropriate. The algorithms in this family do not require any gradient information, so that they are usually less efficient in terms of speed of convergence, but they may be very useful when the function to be maximised is "ill-behaved". The three algorithms will be compared in the next section.

What happens under different distributional assumptions for the severity distribution? As mentioned in the introduction, alternative distributions sometimes considered in the literature are the Gamma, the Weibull and the Generalised Pareto; in all of these cases, complete-data maximum likelihood estimation is not particularly convenient because no closed form solution exists for the likelihood equations. On the basis of the description of the EM algorithm given above, it should be clear that in such a case it loses much of its appeal: consider, indeed, that at each iteration of the algorithm, the $M$-step would require another numerical optimisation and this considerably slows down the algorithm. Although the likelihood function under hypotheses different from lognormality is more involved than (5), and its maximisation becomes more complicated, it can still be performed, for example, with the NM algorithm (see Klugman *et al* (1998, pp 134–135) for the details of the Weibull case).

In conclusion, in our opinion the Poisson–lognormal model should be preferred in the censored and truncated data setups, at least with moderately tailed data, for the same reasons of analytical tractability that made it the standard model in the complete-data case.

## EMPIRICAL APPLICATIONS

### Operational risk data

In this section we apply the methodology developed so far to some modified real operational losses. The data is shown in Figure 2; Table 1 reports estimates of the parameters obtained with the EM algorithm and standard errors.

As the computation of standard errors in the EM framework is somewhat involved (McLachlan and Krishnan 1996, Chapter 4), we prefer to assess them using the non-parametric bootstrap; see Bee (2005) for details on the implementation of the bootstrap in this setup.

For comparison purposes, we also applied the algorithm for the censored case; we used the same data, treating the estimated

**Figure 2** Histogram of losses ($N_U = 782$)

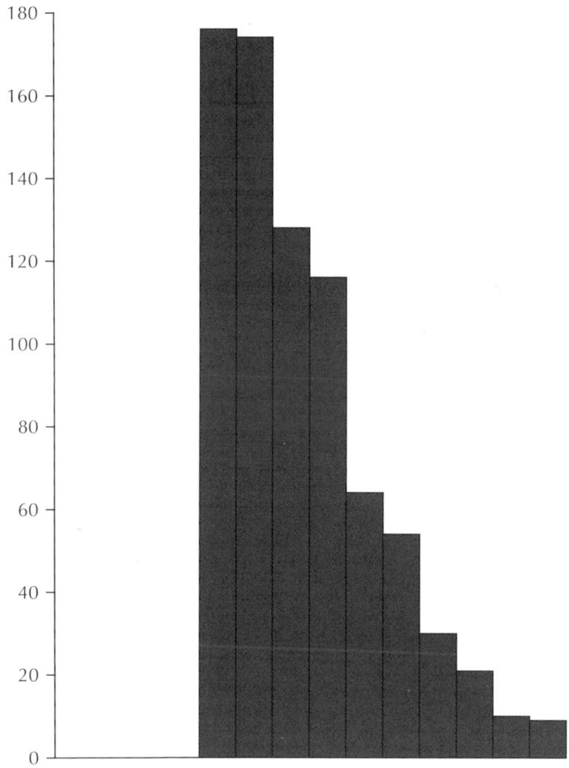


**Table 1** Estimates and standard errors

| | $\lambda$ | $\mu$ | $\sigma^2$ | $N_T$ |
|---|---|---|---|---|
| Truncated case | 6.931 | 1.404 | 2.823 | 950.63 |
| | (1.189) | (0.313) | (0.409) | (295.252) |
| Censored case | 6.932 | 1.403 | 2.823 | – |
| | (0.14) | (0.053) | (0.159) | – |
| Complete-data MLE | 3.128 | 2.878 | 0.953 | – |
| | (0.11) | (0.034) | (0.054) | – |

number $\hat{N}_T$ of truncated observations (rounded to the nearest integer) as the true number of censored observations. Finally, we employ complete-data maximum likelihood estimation, ignoring the truncation.

As expected on the basis of (4), the complete-data MLE of $\mu$ is biased upwards whereas the MLE of $\sigma^2$ is biased downwards. The large estimated number of truncated data, which is not surprising on the basis of Figure 2, has two consequences: (i) the bias is large; (ii) standard errors in the truncated case are rather large.

The fact that data are truncated has an impact on the estimation of the parameter $\lambda$ as well: the MLE of $\lambda$ is indeed the number of losses observed in one year, but with truncated data we do not know the number of losses smaller than $c$. However, the EM algorithm gives an estimate of this number, $\hat{N}_T$, so that the MLE of $\lambda$ is $\hat{\lambda} = \hat{N}_T + N_U$. It is worth noting that when using the BFGS and NM algorithms, no estimate of $N_T$ is available and thus maximum likelihood estimation of $\lambda$ is impossible.

We also used the BFGS and the NM simplex method to maximise the log-likelihood function. The BFGS algorithm is probably the most popular method in the class of quasi-Newton algorithms: its main strength is fast convergence, but the initial guess must be sufficiently good or it does not converge at all. Moreover, numerical differentiation is usually needed, and this may be a source of instability. The NM algorithm, on the other hand, is entirely based on function evaluations, so that it does not require derivatives; for this reason its use is mainly recommended for the maximisation of highly discontinuous functions. For details about both algorithms we refer the interested reader to Press *et al* (1992, Chapter 10) and to the references therein; for the NM algorithm, see also Klugman *et al* (1998, Appendix C).

Whereas in the truncated case BFGS and NM give the same point estimates as EM, in the censored case they do not converge. The problem has to do with the number of censored data being too large: the term $[\Phi(c^*)]^{N_C}$ is very small in the log-likelihood function (8) when $N_C$ is large, so that the numerical value of the function is a large negative number and the algorithms break down because of an underflow. In such a situation, the EM algorithm has the advantage of finding the MLEs without performing a direct maximisation of the likelihood function, so that it is not affected by the problem; Bee (2005) provides simulation results about this issue.

The histogram of the data with the estimated density superimposed is shown in Figure 3. The histogram is built using $\hat{N}_T$ as the frequency of the first bin $[0, c]$. Figure 4 shows the contour plot of

**Figure 3** Loss distribution and fitted lognormal distribution

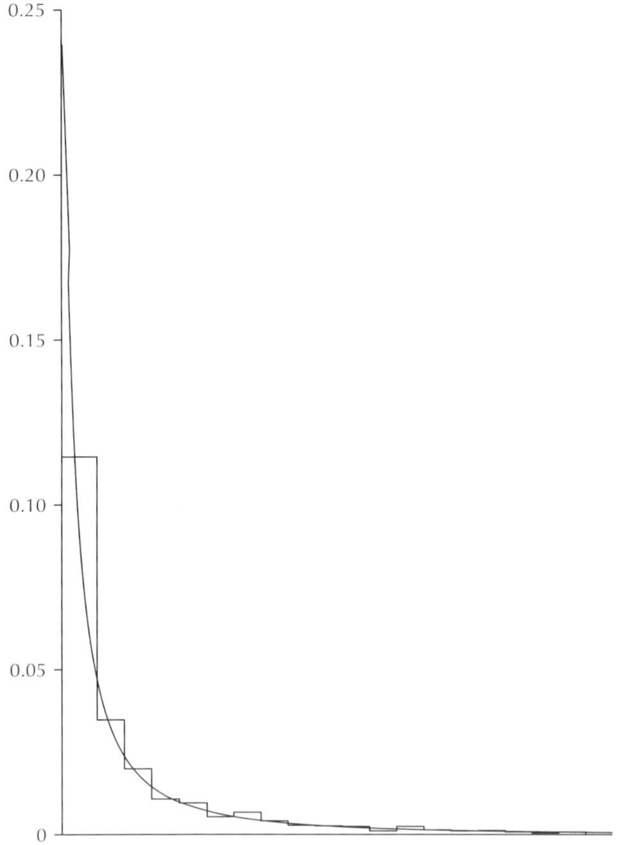


the likelihood function; the dot marks the maximum found by the algorithms.

Finally, CaR is computed using both the estimates obtained with the EM algorithm and the complete-data MLEs. The goal consists in assessing "how wrong" things can go when parameter estimates are biased; the results are displayed in Table 2.

Notice that, *a priori,* it is rather difficult to predict the impact on CaR deriving from the use of complete-data MLEs; even the direction of this impact is uncertain, because the bias in mean is positive whereas the bias in variance is negative, and the combined effect is

**Figure 4** Contours of the likelihood function

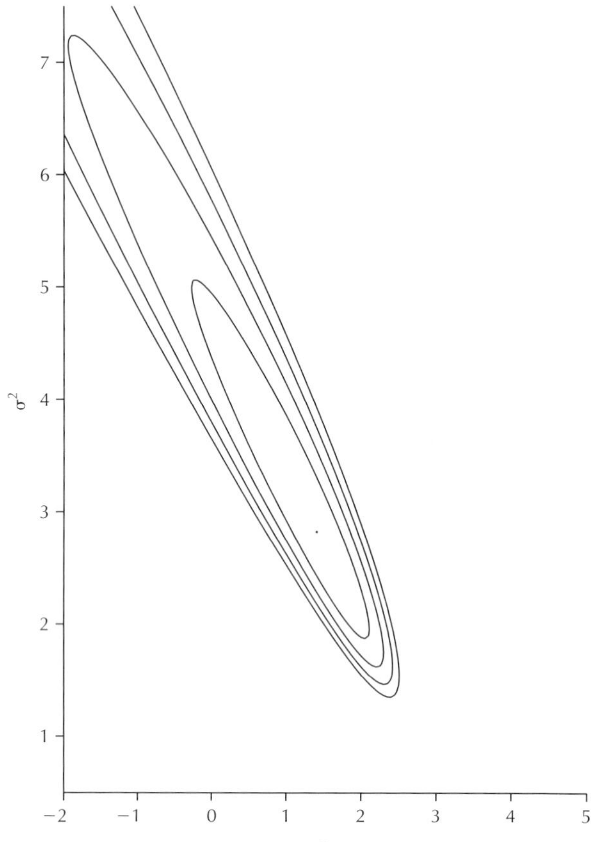


not easy to assess. From Table 2 we see that the CaR estimated on the basis of plain MLEs is largely overestimated; in the next section we will perform a thorough simulation study to gain more insight into the relationship between the percentage of truncated data and the CaR measure.

## A Monte Carlo study

It has been seen that using complete-data MLEs to compute CaR gives biased parameter estimates, and that it is difficult to assess *a priori* the combined effect of the bias on CaR computation. In this section we investigate this issue by means of a simulation study.

**Table 2** Daily CaR at the 95% level, with 10,000 Monte Carlo replications

| | Daily CaR(€) |
|---|---|
| Truncated data | 98,720 |
| Censored data | 100,630 |
| Plain MLE | 155,780 |

**Table 3** Daily expected loss and CaR (at the 95% level)

| $c$ | Expected $\text{loss}_{\text{EM}}$ | Expected $\text{loss}_{\text{plain}}$ | $\text{CaR}_{\text{EM}}$ | $\text{CaR}_{\text{plain}}$ |
|---|---|---|---|---|
| 0.5 | 71,020 | 78,520 | 106,130 | 102,960 |
| 1.0 | 67,470 | 83,850 | 96,540 | 112,490 |
| 1.5 | 68,840 | 88,460 | 96,570 | 125,440 |
| 2.0 | 66,730 | 91,410 | 95,260 | 128,940 |
| 2.5 | 66,630 | 93,670 | 93,910 | 135,740 |
| 3.0 | 69,130 | 95,740 | 100,620 | 145,840 |
| 3.5 | 70,920 | 97,170 | 102,630 | 148,540 |
| 4.0 | 71,580 | 98,240 | 109,650 | 153,580 |
| 4.5 | 66,900 | 98,870 | 94,860 | 159,040 |
| 5.0 | 66,630 | 99,430 | 96,680 | 166,710 |
| 5.5 | 71,380 | 100,050 | 102,490 | 170,190 |

To this aim, we simulate data from a lognormal distribution whose parameters are given by the MLEs obtained in the previous section for the data at hand. Then we truncate the distribution using different thresholds $c$: more precisely, the thresholds go from 0.5 to 5.5 in steps of 0.5. This implies that the fraction of truncated observations ranges approximately from 11% when $c = 0.5$ to 56% when $c = 5.5$. The results are shown in Table 3 and Figure 5.

Not surprisingly, the consequences of ignoring the truncation are more relevant as the threshold increases; in particular, for the largest thresholds considered in the experiment, the CaR measure obtained with standard MLEs is almost twice as large as the CaR based on the EM estimates. Moreover, it is worth stressing that expected loss and CaR based on the EM estimates are essentially stable for all values of $c$. This result can be taken as a confirmation that the EM algorithm works well even with a large number of truncated data.

**Figure 5** Daily CaR at the 95% level based on EM estimates and on complete-data MLEs

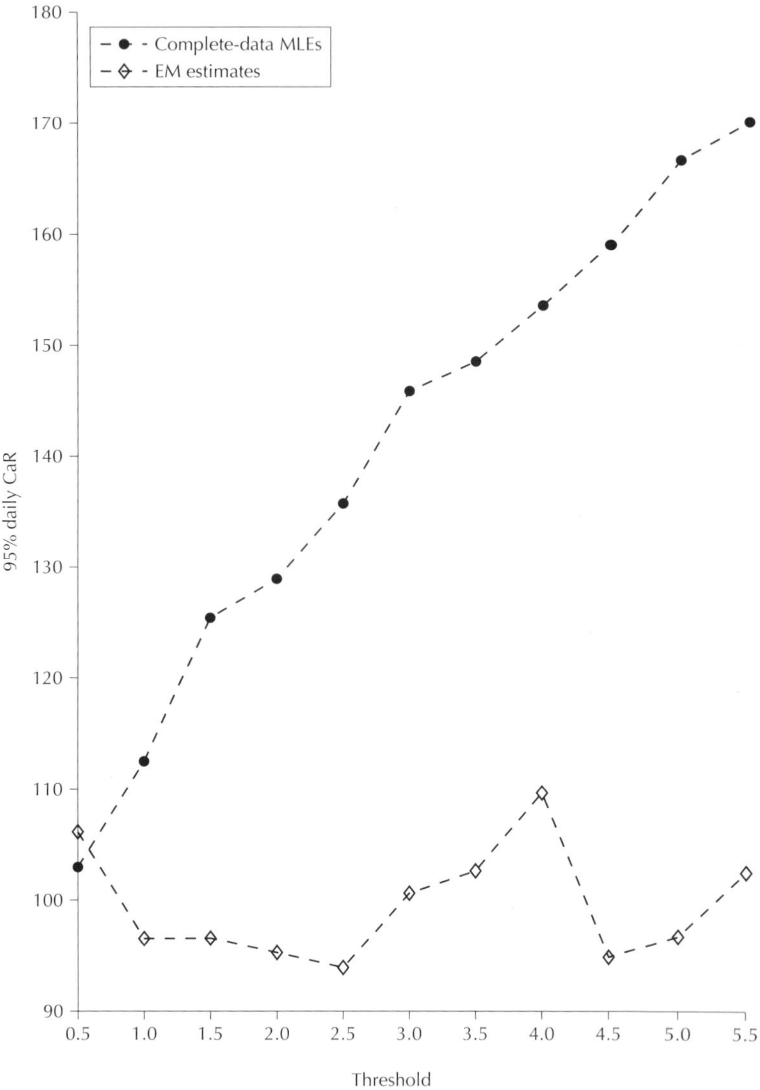


## CONCLUSION

In this chapter we have analysed the problem of maximum likelihood estimation of lognormal severity distributions with censored and truncated data. Using real operational losses, we computed estimates of the parameters, standard errors and Capital at Risk. The EM algorithm was compared to the BFGS algorithm and the NM simplex algorithm, and it turned out that it has at least two advantages: (i) unlike BFGS and NM, in the truncated case it gives an estimate of the number of truncated observations, which is essential for the estimation of the frequency distribution and for the computation of risk measures; (ii) in the censored case, when the sample size is large and the fraction of censored data is not sufficiently small, BFGS and NM break down; in such a setup, the EM algorithm converges normally.

Several problems are still open to future research; in our opinion, it is worth mentioning at least two issues. First, estimation of parameters in the LDA is now a relatively well-studied topic in the univariate case, but the appropriateness of the lognormal model should not be taken for granted, and a more detailed analysis of maximum likelihood estimation in the LDA with Generalised Pareto severity would probably require further research.

Second, the real challenge is probably the extension of the techniques to the multivariate case. Given the analytical intractability of the univariate distributions, a multidimensional model should likely be based on copulas (Lindskog and McNeil 2003). Construction of models and analysis of estimation techniques in this setup are probably going to constitute the main object of investigation in the future.

1 E-mail: marco.bee@economia.unitn.it

**REFERENCES**

**Bee, M.**, 2005, "On Maximum Likelihood Estimation of Operational Losses", Discussion Paper 2005.3, Department of Economics, University of Trento.

**Dempster, A. P., N. M. Laird, and D. B. Rubin,** 1977, "Maximum Likelihood from Incomplete Data via the *EM* Algorithm (with discussion)", *Journal of the Royal Statistical Society B*, **39**, pp 1–38.

**Durrett, R.,** 1996, *Probability: Theory and Examples* (Pacific Grove, CA: Duxbury Press).

**Klugman, S. A., H. H. Panjer, and G. E. Willmot,** 1998, *Loss Models – From Data to Decisions* (New York: Wiley).

**Lindskog, F. and A. McNeil,** 2003 "Common Poisson Shock Models: Applications to Insurance and Credit Risk Modelling", *Astin Bulletin*, **33**, pp 209–238.

**Maddala, G. S.,** 1983, *Limited-Dependent and Qualitative Variables in Econometrics* (Cambridge: Cambridge University Press).

**McLachlan, G. J. and T. Krishnan,** 1996, *The EM Algorithm and Extensions* (New York: Wiley).

**Mikosch, T.,** 2004, *Non-Life Insurance Mathematics. An Introduction with Stochastic Processes* (New York: Springer).

**Press, W. H., S. A. Teukolsky, W. T. Vetterling, and B. P. Flannery,** 1992, *Numerical Recipes in C,* 2nd edn (Cambridge: Cambridge University Press).

# 7

# *Treatment of Incomplete Data in the Field of Operational Risk: The Effects on Parameter Estimates, EL and UL Figures*

**Anna Chernobai; Christian Menn*; Svetlozar T. Rachev; Stefan Trück**; Marco Moscadelli**

University of California; Cornell University and Universität Karlsruhe; Universität Karlsruhe and University of California; Queensland University of Technology and Universität Karlsruhe; Bank of Italy

In the operational risk field, the computation of the capital charge is based, in most cases, on the loss distribution approach, which estimates the aggregated loss distribution and derives from it appropriate figures for the expected losses (EL) and unexpected losses (UL).

The process of computing the aggregated distribution of losses is, from the statistical point of view, very challenging. This occurs for a number of reasons, most relevant of which are these:

(1) In the "conventional" actuarial approach, the severity and frequency components are treated as separate estimation problems; the aggregate distribution is derived as a proper combination of its estimated components. However, as the expression for the aggregated loss is only in rare cases analytically derivable from

*Research support by the German Academic Exchange Service (DAAD) is gratefully acknowledged.

**Rachev gratefully acknowledges research support by grants from Division of Mathematical, Life and Physical Sciences, College of Letters and Science, University of California, Santa Barbara, the Deutschen Forschungsgemeinschaft and the Deutscher Akademischer Austausch Dienst.

the frequency and severity distributions, approximations or simulations are usually called for (for instance, the Monte Carlo procedure). These methods require a large number of scenarios to be generated to get reliable figures of the highest percentiles of the loss distribution.

(2) "Less conventional" approaches, inherited from the engineering field, as the point process, allow us to address in a mutually exclusive manner the problem of estimating the parameters of the frequency and severity of the operational losses. They are different from the conventional approach in that they take into consideration in the estimation procedure the (unknown) relationship between the frequency and the severity of large losses up to the end of the distribution, hence reducing the computational cost and the error related to a non-analytical representation of the aggregated losses. These techniques, however, require specific conditions to be fulfilled in order to be workable.

(3) Operational losses are often recorded in banks' databases starting from a threshold of a specific amount (usually US$10,000 or €5,000). This phenomenon makes the inferential procedures more complicated, and, if not properly addressed, may create unwanted biases of the aggregated loss based statistics.

While the challenges in carrying out "conventional" and "less conventional" approaches for determining the aggregated loss distributions have more recently been a subject of intense study,[1] the inferential problem of dealing with incomplete data has been less investigated.

This chapter moves from an initial study by Chernobai *et al* (2005a), to cover, under a theoretical and practical point of view, all the issues related to the estimation of aggregated loss distribution in the presence of incomplete data available at hand. The main objective of the chapter is to analytically measure the extent of the bias on the EL and UL figures when incorrect statistical approaches are used to treat incomplete data. The chapter is organised as follows. The next section deals with the relevant definitional aspects related to incomplete data, while the next two illustrate, respectively, the theoretical approaches and a specific

MLE algorithm that may be carried out to estimate loss distributions in the presence of missing data. The following two sections focus on a typical operational risk model, the Poisson-lognormal model; for this model the effect of adopting correct and incorrect approaches on the estimate of the figures relevant to the capital charge (frequency and severity parameters, EL, VAR and expected shortfall) is analytically computed and measured. The next section gives some final remarks for a general aggregated loss model and concludes.

## INCOMPLETE DATA: DEFINITIONAL ASPECTS

In general, data's being incomplete means that specific observations are either lost or are not recorded exactly. Based on the definitions adopted from the insurance context (see Klugman, Panjer and Willmot, 2004), there are two main ways in which the data can be incomplete:

(1) *Censored data*: Data are said to be censored when the number of observations that fall in a given set is known, but the specific values of the observations are unknown; data are said to be censored from below (or left-censored) when the set is all numbers less than a specific value.
(2) *Truncated data*: Data are said to be truncated when observations that fall in a given set are excluded; data are said to be truncated from below (or left-truncated) when the set is all numbers less than a specific value.

While the "left-censored" definition would point out that only the number of observations under the threshold has been recorded (the frequency), the "left-truncated" definition would point out that neither the number (the frequency) nor the amounts (the severity) of such observations have been recorded.

In fact, in the operational risk field, the second scenario is the more common. The truncated data refer to the recorded observations all of which fall above a positive threshold of a specific amount, while the missing data identify the unrecorded observations falling below the known threshold. The latter are usually called "non-randomly missing data", to distinguish them from the "randomly missing data" that may instead affect the observations that fall over the entire range of the data and can be caused, for example, by an inadequate loss-data-collection process.

## APPROACHES WITH INCOMPLETE DATA

All statistical approaches become somewhat ad hoc in the presence of incomplete data. That is because the estimation process must account for the specific nature of the modifications. From the definition above, it is clear that the presence of censored data does affect the process of estimation of the severity distribution, but not that of the frequency; the presence of truncated data instead affects the process of estimation of both the frequency and severity distributions.

In light of the operational risk peculiarities, in the subsequent study, we address the worst situation, the truncated-data problem, meaning that the number and the amounts of the observations below the set threshold are unknown.

In general, we identify four possible approaches that banks may undertake to estimate the parameters of the frequency and severity distributions in the presence of missing data. As we will see, only the last approach (Approach 4) is correct, or, to be more precise, is the best we can do under the given conditions on the data.

### Approach 1 ("naïve")

*Fit "unconditional" severity and frequency distributions to the data over the threshold*

The term "unconditional" means that the missing observations are ignored and the observed data are treated as a complete dataset during the process of fitting the frequency and severity distributions. We refer to it as the "naïve" approach, because no account is given to the missing data in the estimations of both distributions.

### Approach 2

*Fit "unconditional" severity and frequency distributions to the data over the threshold, and adjust the frequency parameter(s)*

The first step of such an approach is identical to the previous one: unconditional distributions are fitted to the severity and frequency of the observed data.

In the second step the incompleteness of the number of data is recognised and the frequency parameter(s) is adjusted according to the estimated fraction of the data over the threshold, which is

**Figure 1** Fraction of missing data ($A$) and observed data ($B$)

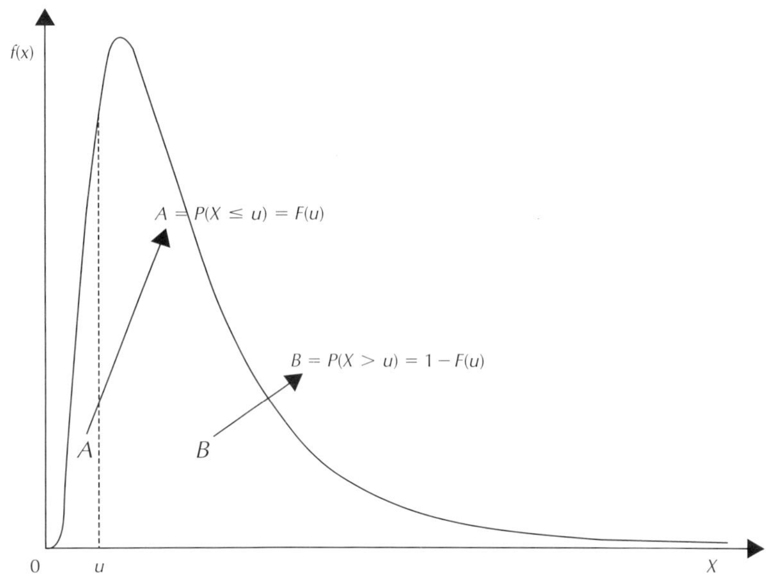


obtained using the parameters of the information provided by the severity distribution.

In general, if all data were duly recorded (that is to say, if the dataset was complete), fitting unconditional severity distributions to such data would provide a correct estimate of the parameters of the severity distribution. Each range of data (we are dealing with continuous distributions) generated from such distribution would have a probability of:

- ❑ falling under a fixed threshold $u$ (area denoted by $A$ in Figure 1) equal to the distribution function computed at $u$, $F(u)$; and
- ❑ falling over the threshold $u$ (area denoted by $B$ in Figure 1) equal to the complement of the distribution function computed at $u$, $1-F(u)$.

The areas $A$ and $B$, as pointed out by the unconditional severity distribution, correspond to the fraction of missing and observed data, under the Approach 2.

In light of that, the frequency parameter estimate(s), based on the observed data, must be adjusted for the probability of these data to occur, that is $1-F(u)$. The frequency parameter(s) adjustment formula under Approach 2 may be then expressed by the following:

$$\hat{\theta}_{adj} = \frac{\hat{\theta}_{obs}}{1-\hat{F}_{uncond}(u)} \tag{1}$$

where $\hat{\theta}_{adj}$ represents the adjusted frequency parameter(s) estimate and indicates the estimate of the intensity rate of the complete data, $\hat{\theta}_{obs}$ represents the unconditional (observed) frequency parameter(s) estimate, and $\hat{F}_{uncond}(u)$ represents the estimated unconditional severity distribution computed at the threshold $u$.

### Approach 3

*Fit "conditional" severity and "unconditional" frequency distributions to the data over the threshold*

Differently from Approaches 1 and 2, in this approach, the incompleteness of data is explicitly taken into account in the estimation of the severity distribution. The latter is indeed estimated "conditionally" on the fact that the observed data are now recognised as actually truncated dataset and no longer a complete dataset. Under the reasoning, the truncated-loss severity distribution is fitted to the observed data, with the density expressed as follows:

$$f_{cond}(x) = \begin{cases} f(x)/(1-F(u)) & \text{for } x > u \\ 0 & \text{for } x \leq u \end{cases} \tag{2}$$

According to this approach, the unconditional frequency distribution is fitted, analogously to Approach 1, to the observed data in order to estimate the unconditional frequency parameter(s). No further adjustments are made. In Figure 2 the density functions for the unconditional and conditional severities are illustrated.

In this approach, it is assumed that no losses under the threshold $u$ have occurred, and the aggregated loss distribution is derived solely from the losses that are observed (above $u$).

**Figure 2** Unconditional and conditional severity densities

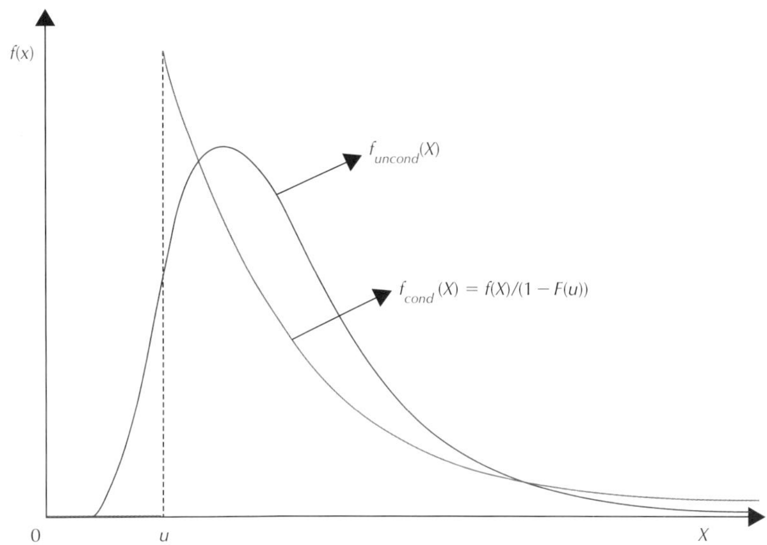


## Approach 4

*Fit "conditional" severity and unconditional frequency distributions to the data over the threshold, and adjust the frequency parameter(s)*

The incompleteness of data is explicitly taken into account in the estimates of both the severity and frequency distributions under this approach. These distributions are indeed estimated "conditionally" on the fact that the observed dataset is now recognised as actually truncated datasets and no longer a complete dataset. As in Approach 3, the estimated severity distribution is the "conditional" one, and as in Approach 2 the frequency parameter(s) adjustment formula may be expressed by the following:

$$\hat{\theta}_{adj} = \frac{\hat{\theta}_{obs}}{1 - \hat{F}_{cond}(u)} \tag{3}$$

where $\hat{\theta}_{adj}$ represents the adjusted (complete-data) frequency parameter estimate(s), $\hat{\theta}_{obs}$ the unconditional (observed) frequency parameter estimate(s), and $\hat{F}_{cond}(u)$ represents the estimated conditional severity distribution computed at the threshold $u$. In the framework of operational risk modelling, this is the only relevant and correct approach, out of the four proposed. Since *all* loss data, both observed and missing, are essential for the aggregated loss derivation and subsequent estimation of EL and UL, both severity and frequency distributions are estimated in such a way that the complete loss data come into play.

## PARAMETERS ESTIMATION PROCEDURE

In general, different statistical methods may be carried out to estimate the parameters of the frequency and severity distributions. The method that has the majority of attractive properties, and for this reason the one most widely used in practice, is the *maximum-likelihood estimation* (MLE), which is based on two steps: finding the functional form of the likelihood function of the data and finding the parameter value that maximises it.

Unfortunately the MLE is more complex if the available dataset is incomplete, either censored or truncated. The incompleteness of data is reflected in a restricted ability to both identify the expression for the likelihood function and maximise it. In particular, as analytical differentiation is often impossible in estimating the parameters, the computationally heavy numerical differentiation and the usual gradient-based algorithms, such as Newton–Raphson, can be used for these purposes.

Additionally, a specific algorithm has been designed for MLE with incomplete data. The *expectation-maximisation algorithm* (EM), developed by Dempster in 1977, is particularly convenient in cases when the range of the missing data is known, and when the MLE estimates have a closed-form solution. The algorithm has been used in a variety of applications such as probability density mixture models, hidden Markov models, cluster analysis, factor analysis and survival analysis.

A detailed explanation of the theoretical and practical elements of the EM is outside the purpose of this chapter. Nevertheless, two fundamental aspects of the EM can be mentioned:

- The intuition behind EM consists in maximising a hypothetical likelihood function, called *complete likelihood*, instead of the likelihood based on the observed data (either if censored or truncated), and is based on the combination of the expectations of the observed-data likelihood and the missing-data likelihood functions. The EM is a two-step iterative procedure that, starting from initial assigned values to the parameters to be estimated, computes and maximises at each step the conditional expectation of the complete (log)likelihood function.

- Regardless of whether applied to truncated or censored data, the EM has some desirable properties: (a) it is simple to apply even when the form of the likelihood function is complicated, (b) it increases the likelihood at each step and, most importantly, (c) it is much less sensitive to the choice of the starting values than the direct numerical integration methods applied to Equation (2) (this means that the EM converges even for very bad initial choice values of the parameters).

## IMPACT OF USING INCORRECT APPROACHES ON PARAMETER ESTIMATES

The correct estimation of the parameters of the frequency and severity distributions is the key to determining accurate capital-charge figures. Any density misspecification and/or incorrect estimation procedure would lead to biased estimates of the distribution parameters, which, in turn, would result in misleading figures of both EL and UL.

As observed earlier, four possible approaches may be used by banks to deal with incomplete data. Only Approach 4 appears to be correct.

The first approach – ignoring the missing data and treating the observed data as a complete dataset – determines the highest biases in the estimates of the parameters of both the severity and frequency distributions; *unfortunately, this is the approach most followed by practitioners.*

The second approach – fitting unconditional severity and frequency distributions and adjusting the frequency parameter(s) – even though it improves the previous situation, produces biases in the parameter estimates of the severity distribution, unconditionally estimated. Consequently, these biases are reflected in the adjusted frequency parameter estimate, as it becomes incorrectly adjusted.

The third approach – fitting conditional severity and unconditional frequency distributions – produces a smaller bias, which comes from the unadjusted estimate of the parameters of the frequency distribution.

The fourth approach results in the minimum bias of the capital charge, and may be due only to the fact that the number of missing data is estimated rather than explicitly available. Still, the bias is expected to be at zero under the approach.

In order to fully appreciate the effect of incorrect approaches on the estimate of the parameters, we here consider a typical situation and derive an analytic expression of the biases in the parameters. We focus on two approaches: Approach 1 ("naïve") and Approach 4.

The typical situation is represented by a Poisson(λ)–lognormal(μ, σ) model for the frequency and severity distributions, respectively. We are aware that such a model may not be the best one in depicting the actual behaviour of the operational risk data, as coming from the analysis of the QIS3 loss data (the cited Bank of Italy working paper puts in evidence that the operational risk losses usually follow a binomial negative-lognormal model for the EL, and a heavy-tailed point process model for the UL). However, as it will be clearer later, the outcomes from such a model may be easily generalised also to different (heavier-tail) operational risk models.

Given the Poisson-lognormal model, it is then possible to express analytically the bias for the frequency and severity parameters when Approach 1 (as mentioned, the one most commonly followed by practitioners) is adopted. Using the relation between the fractions of observed and missing data to derive the true λ parameter, and using the closed-form expressions for the MLE estimates of μ and σ, it is possible to get the following expressions for the biases of the three parameters (in the ideal case, the estimates of μ and σ would correspond to the true parameters):

$$bias(\hat{\lambda}_{obs}) = -\lambda\Phi\left(\frac{\log u - \mu}{\sigma}\right) < 0 \qquad \textbf{(4)}$$

$$bias(\hat{\mu}_{obs}) = \sigma\frac{\varphi\left(\frac{\log u - \mu}{\sigma}\right)}{1-\Phi\left(\frac{\log u - \mu}{\sigma}\right)} > 0 \qquad \textbf{(5)}$$

$$bias(\hat{\sigma}^2_{obs}) = \sigma^2 \left( \frac{\log u - \mu}{\sigma} \frac{\varphi\left(\frac{\log u - \mu}{\sigma}\right)}{1 - \Phi\left(\frac{\log u - \mu}{\sigma}\right)} - \left( \frac{\varphi\left(\frac{\log u - \mu}{\sigma}\right)}{1 - \Phi\left(\frac{\log u - \mu}{\sigma}\right)} \right)^2 \right) < 0 \text{ (since usually } \log u < \mu) \quad \textbf{(6)}$$

where $\varphi$ and $\Phi$ denote the density and distribution function of the standard normal law and $u$ is the threshold.

What is important to note is that the "naïve" Approach 1 would lead to an underestimation of the Poisson frequency parameter $\lambda$, an overestimation and an underestimation of, respectively, the location ($\mu$) and the scale ($\sigma$) parameters of the lognormal law. While the magnitude of this effect depends on the threshold level and on the values of the true (unknown) parameters, it is interesting to examine how using the fourth approach would reduce such biases.

We illustrate such idea for the severity parameters, using true hypothetical values for $\mu$ and $\sigma$ ($\mu_0$ and $\sigma_0$) in the range 4–6.5 and 1.5–2.7, respectively, and use the threshold $u$ to truncate the initially complete dataset (the threshold is assumed to be equal to 50). The true fractions of missing data under such specifications are stated in Table 1.

Figures 3 and 4 demonstrate the ratios of the estimated parameters of the truncated data under Approach 1 (left) and Approach 4 (right), for different $\mu_0$ and $\sigma_0$ combinations. The ratio being closer to one indicates more accurate parameter estimate corresponding to the complete data, and a smaller bias.

**Table 1** True fractions of missing data for various combinations of $\mu_0$ and $\sigma_0$

| $\sigma_0$ \ $\mu_0$ | 4 | 5 | 6.5 |
|---|---|---|---|
| 1.5 | 0.48 | 0.23 | 0.04 |
| 2.0 | 0.48 | 0.29 | 0.10 |
| 2.7 | 0.49 | 0.34 | 0.17 |

**Figure 3** Effects of using Approach 1 ("naïve") and Approach 4 on the $\mu$ estimate

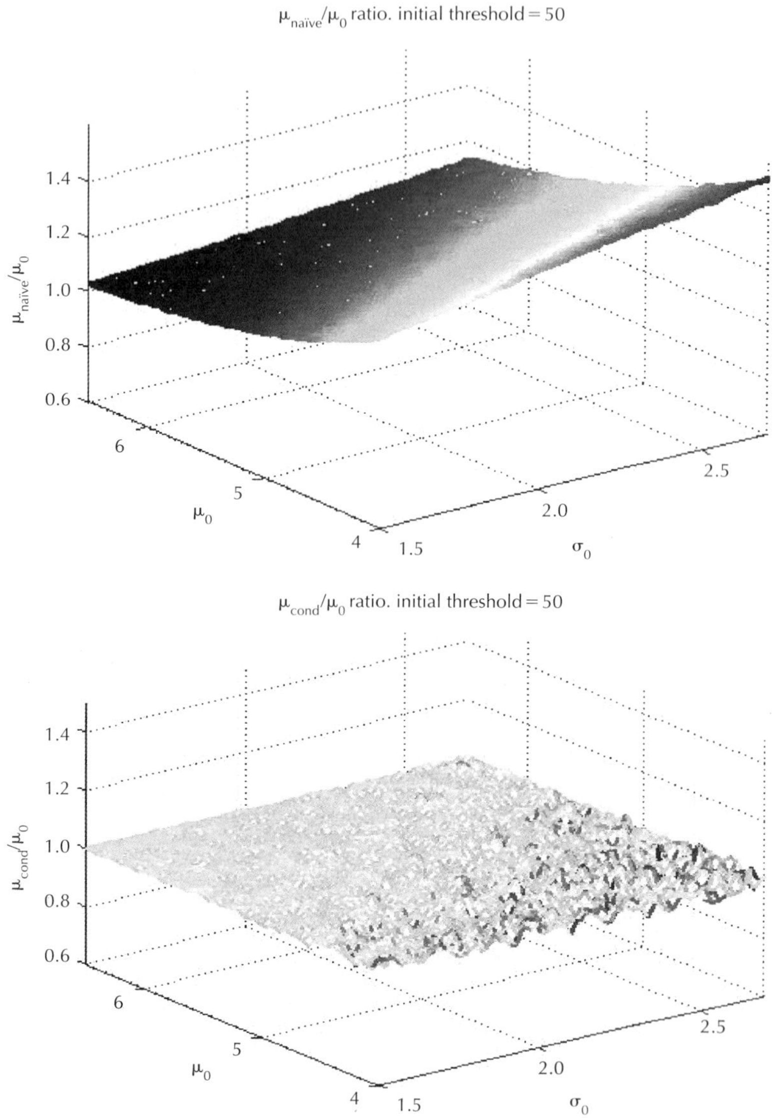

**Figure 4** Effects of using Approach 1 ("naïve") and Approach 4 on the $\sigma$ estimate

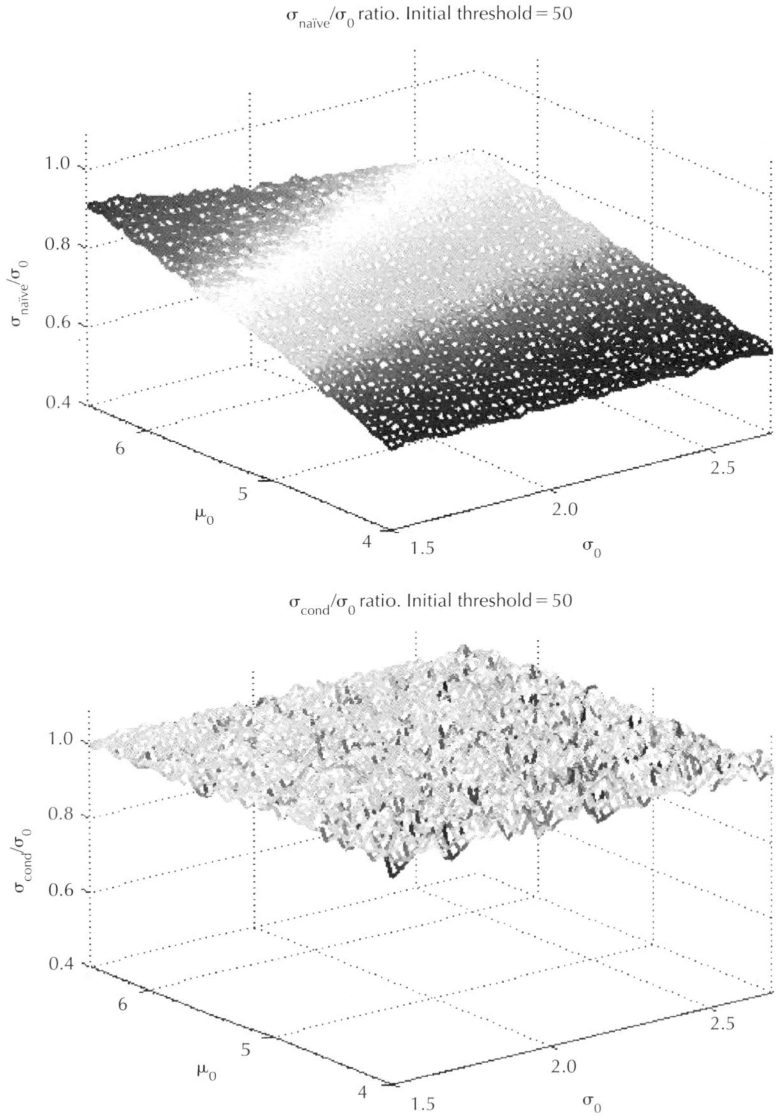

What is remarkable is that, while, in general, the extent of the bias increases for lower values of the $\mu_0$ parameter and higher values of the $\sigma_0$ parameter, Approach 1 produces significant biases in most of the possible combinations of the (true) parameters of the lognormal law; in the worst case, it overestimates $\mu$ and underestimates $\sigma$ by nearly 40–50%. If, instead, Approach 4 is adopted, highly accurate figures for $\mu$ and $\sigma$ are obtained for the majority of the combinations of the true lognormal parameters (that is, the ratio is 1); when the bias occurs, overestimation of $\mu$ and underestimation of $\sigma$ is roughly by at most 5%.

The results illustrated in the above figures would by all means hold in different models other than the Poisson–lognormal. In fact, the pattern was observed when other loss distributions were considered (the results are omitted from this chapter): overestimated location parameter and underestimated scale parameter, with the effect being more severe for heavier-tailed distributions (see Chernobai *et al*, 2005b and 2005c). Applying Approach 4, in turn, would result in highly accurate estimates and would closely reflect the true nature of the complete data.

## IMPACT OF THE BIASED PARAMETER ESTIMATES ON THE EL, VAR AND EXPECTED SHORTFALL FIGURES

The question that arises now is the impact – namely, magnitude and sign – the described biases would have on the EL and UL figures, which represent at the end of the day the ultimate target of the estimation process. In particular, we will explore the effects on EL, VAR and expected shortfall figure.

### Impact on EL

The expression for EL of an aggregated loss process is easily obtainable in the case when the conditions of homogeneity of the actuarial risk model are fulfilled, that is, with the loss severity variable independent and identically distributed and independent from the loss frequency variable. In such cases, EL is obtainable as the simple product of the expected frequency (EF) and the expected severity (ES). The problem is thus to assess the impact of the biases on the EF and ES figures. If we use the arithmetic mean as an estimator of EF and ES,[2] the expressions for EF and ES in the

Poisson-lognormal model for a unit time interval (usually, one year) with $\lambda$, $\mu$ and $\sigma$ being the true model parameters, are the following:

$$EF_{Poi} = \lambda \tag{7}$$

$$ES_{LogN} = \exp\left\{\mu + \frac{\sigma^2}{2}\right\} \tag{8}$$

Hence the EL becomes:

$$EL_{Poi-LogN} = \lambda \exp\left\{\mu + \frac{\sigma^2}{2}\right\} \tag{9}$$

If Approach 1 is adopted for the estimation of the parameters, each parameter enters the EL formula together with its bias, as discussed earlier. Therefore, the expression for the estimated EL will read:

$$\hat{E}L_{Poi-LogN} = (\lambda + bias(\hat{\lambda}_{obs}))\exp\left\{\mu + bias(\hat{\mu}_{obs}) + \frac{\sigma^2 + bias(\hat{\sigma}^2_{obs})}{2}\right\} \tag{10}$$

where the biases may be expressed in terms of the true parameters $\lambda$, $\mu$ and $\sigma$ and the threshold $u$, as in Equations (4), (5) and (6).

Given the estimate (10), it is important to evaluate the sign and the extent of the bias, that is whether $\hat{E}L$ overestimates or underestimates the true $EL$, and the magnitude of such eventual bias. For this purpose, we compare the $\hat{E}L$ estimates under Approaches 1 and 4 with the true $EL$ values for a variety of simulated scenarios that involve different combinations of the parameters $\mu$ and $\sigma$. In particular, $\mu$ and $\sigma$ are assumed to vary almost continuously in plausible ranges (50 × 50 combinations of $\mu_0$ and $\sigma_0$, considered within the range of 4–6.5 and 1.5–2.7, respectively). The threshold is fixed at 50, as earlier. Figure 5 compares the ratios of the unconditional (Approach 1, "naïve") and conditional (Approach 4) $\hat{E}L$ estimates to the true $EL$ value, for the wide range of true $\mu$ and $\sigma$ of the initial complete data (and any value of $\lambda$, as it cancels out inside the ratio). The exercise shows that Approach 1 always *underestimates* the true value of $EL$: the bias is on average 35% and assumes its maximum (approximately 60%) in the presence of the lowest considered values of $\mu$ and the highest considered values of $\sigma$. Given its role of

**Figure 5** Effects of using Approach 1 ("naïve") and Approach 4 on the μ estimate

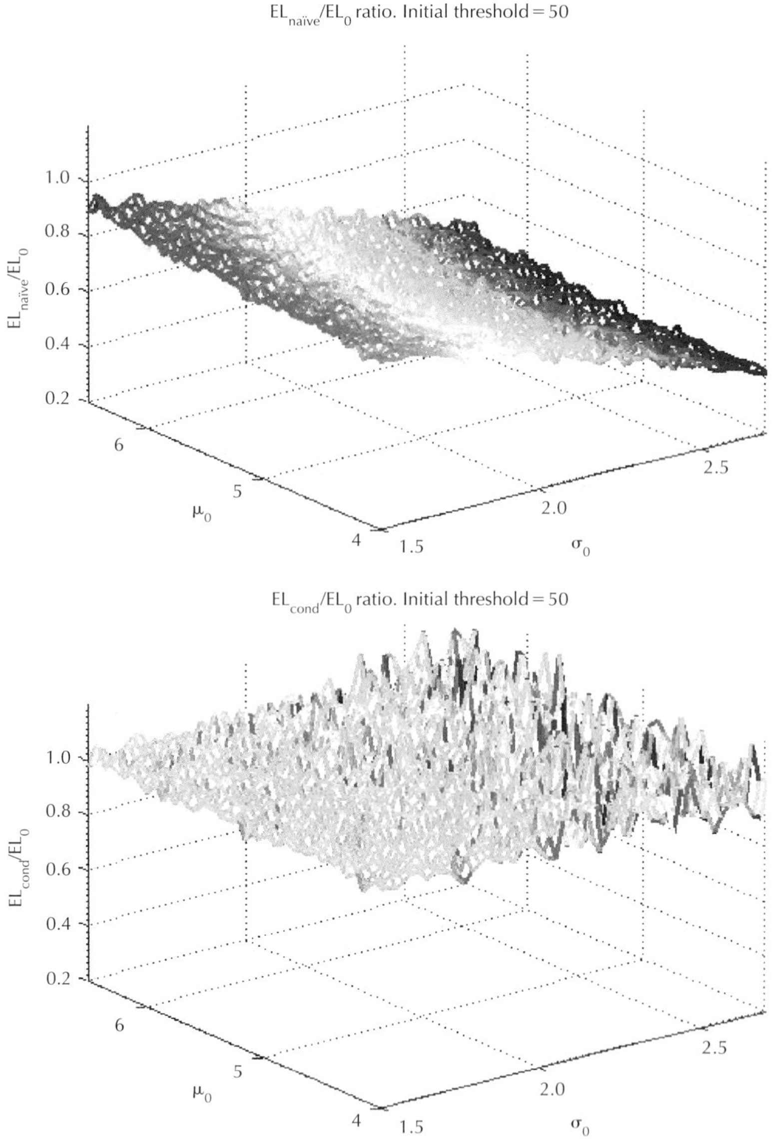

scale in Equation (10), the frequency does not affect the bias in relative terms, but only affects in absolute terms.

**Impact on the VAR**

In regard to VAR, its expression is analytically derivable from the fact that the lognormal distribution belongs to the class of subexponential distributions. Following the tail approximation of the compound Poisson process given in Embrechts Klüppelberg and Mikosch (1997), the following formula holds (for a unit of time):

$$VaR_{Poi-LogN,1-\alpha} \approx \exp\left\{\mu + \sigma\Phi^{-1}\left(1 - \frac{\alpha}{\lambda}\right)\right\} \tag{11}$$

where $\Phi^{-1}$ denotes the standard normal quantile and $(1 - \alpha) \times 100$ the confidence level.

If Approach 1 is adopted for the estimation of the parameters, each parameter enters the VAR formula together with its bias, as computed in the expressions (3), (4) and (5) above. Therefore, the expression for the estimated VAR will turn to:

$$V\hat{a}R_{Poi-LogN,1-\alpha} \approx \exp\left\{\mu + bias(\hat{\mu}_{obs}) + \lesssim \sigma + bias(\hat{\sigma}_{obs}))\ \Phi^{-1}\left(1 - \frac{\alpha}{\lambda + bias(\hat{\lambda}_{obs})}\right)\right\} \tag{12}$$

where the bias may be expressed in terms of the true parameters $\lambda$, $\mu$ and $\sigma$ and the threshold $u$.

Analogously to the EL case, an exercise is carried out to find the sign and the extent of the bias for $V\hat{a}R$, that is whether $V\hat{a}R$ overestimates or underestimates $VaR$, and the magnitude of such, eventual, bias. The $V\hat{a}R$ estimates are thus compared with the true $VaR$ values for different combinations of the complete-data parameters $\lambda$, $\mu$ and $\sigma$. Using the same scenario, combinations and ranges adopted in the EL case are here reproduced ($50 \times 50$ combinations of $\mu$ and $\sigma$ in the range of values, respectively, 4–6.5 and 1.5–2.7), for four cases of $\lambda$ ($\lambda = 50, 100, 150, 200$). The threshold is fixed at 50. Figure 6 illustrates the effects of using the "naïve" (Approach 1) and conditional (Approach 4) models on the ratios of estimated $V\hat{a}R$ to the true VAR, for $\alpha = 0.05$.

**Figure 6** Effects of using Approach 1 ("naïve") and Approach 4 on the VAR estimates

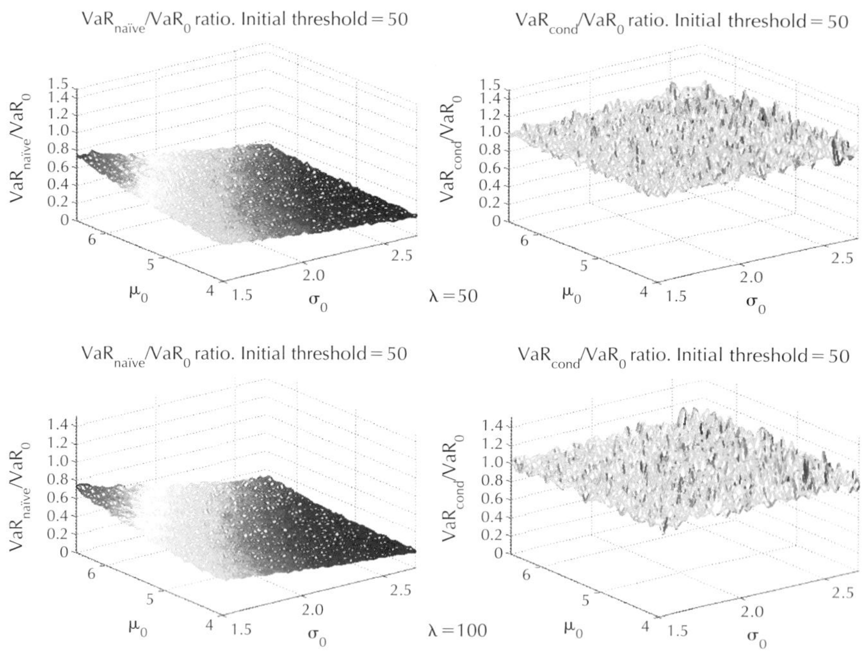


The exercise shows that Approach 1 (unconditional) always underestimates the true value of the VAR-based capital charge: the bias is on average 50% and attains its maximum (approximately 80%) in the presence of the lowest considered value for $\mu$ and the highest for $\sigma$. The frequency has a limited impact on the bias: the highest frequency scenario ($\lambda = 200$) determines an increase of the bias of around 4% in comparison to the lowest frequency scenario ($\lambda = 50$).

### Impact on the expected shortfall (or CVAR)

Much attention in recent literature has been given to the use of the expected shortfall (or the conditional VAR, CVAR) as a measure of risk superior to VAR. As argued by Artzner *et al* 1997 and 1999, CVAR is a coherent measure of risk because it satisfies the sub-additivity property, while VAR can violate it. Even more importantly,

**Figure 6** (continued)

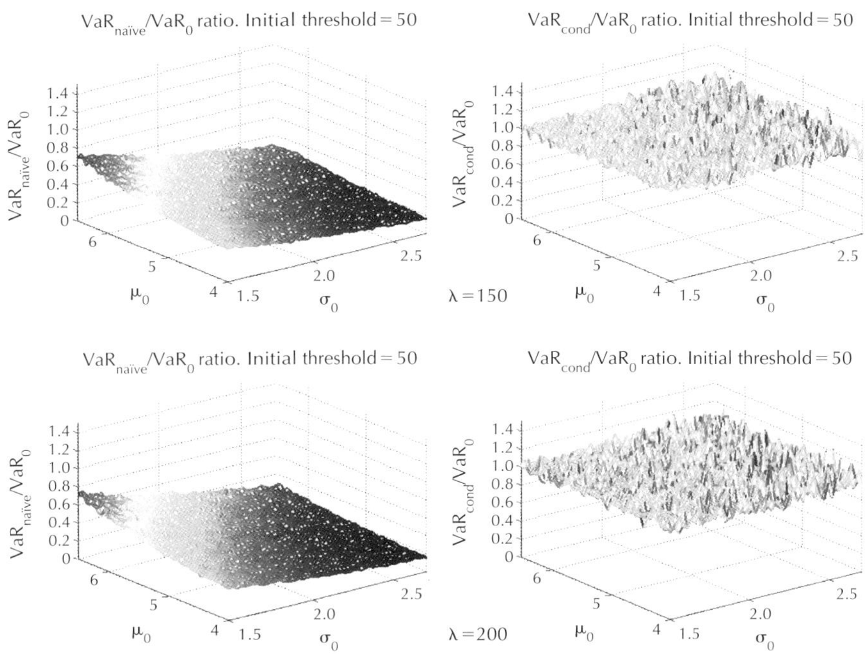


CVAR is able to capture the tail behaviour of losses much better than VAR. The use of CVAR has been emphasised in financial models. Recent references include Rachev, Menn and Fabozzi (2005). CVAR is defined as the expected value of loss, given that the loss exceeds VAR. It is expressed as:

$$\begin{aligned} CVaR_{Poi-LogN,1-\alpha} &= \mathrm{E}[L \mid L \geq VaR_{Poi-LogN,1-\alpha}] \\ &= \frac{\mathrm{E}[L; L \geq VaR_{Poi-LogN,1-\alpha}]}{\alpha} \end{aligned} \qquad \textbf{(13)}$$

Analytical expression in a simple form exists only for the normally distributed losses. For other cases, Monte Carlo simulations or other techniques must be used.

The $C\hat{V}aR$ estimates are further compared with the true $CVaR$ values for the same large number of combinations of the complete-data parameters $\lambda$, $\mu$ and $\sigma$. Figure 7 illustrates the effects of using

**Figure 7** Effects of using Approach 1 ("naïve") and Approach 4 on the CVAR estimates

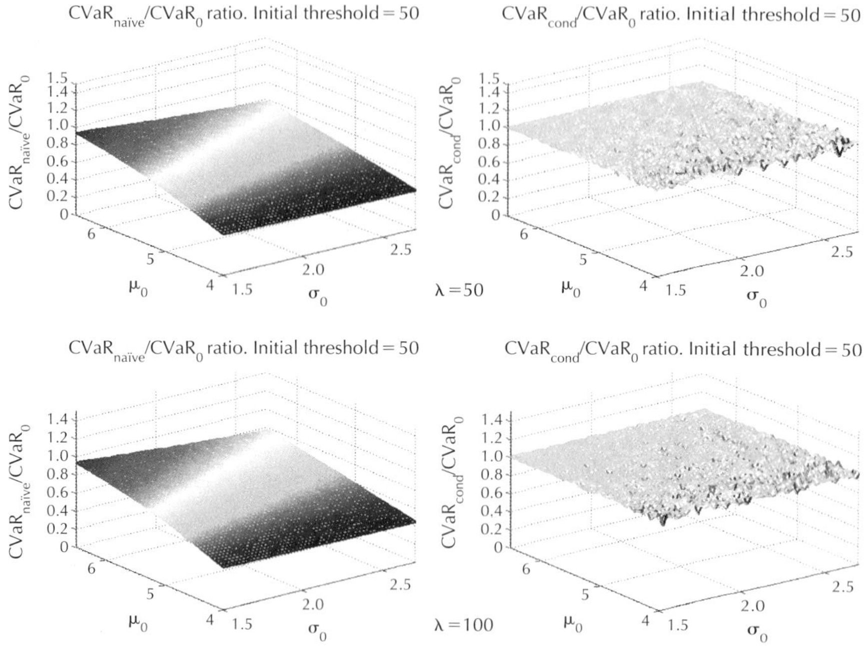


the "naïve" (Approach 1) and conditional (Approach 4) models on the ratios of estimated CVAR to the true CVAR, for $\alpha = 0.05$.

The exercise results in similar conclusions about the effect on CVAR to those said about the effect on VAR. The "naïve" approach often highly underestimates the true CVAR while the conditional model captures the true CVAR remarkably well.

## CONCLUSIONS

This chapter deals with the problem of estimation of the aggregate operational loss distribution in the presence of incomplete data. The existence of data unrecorded under a seemingly low threshold (of, for instance, US$10,000 or €5,000) has serious implications on the operational capital-charge-relevant figures, if not duly accounted for.

In the first part of the chapter, some definitional aspects were addressed: a clear distinction between "non-randomly missing data" (eg, data that fall under a threshold of a specific amount) and

**Figure 7** (continued)

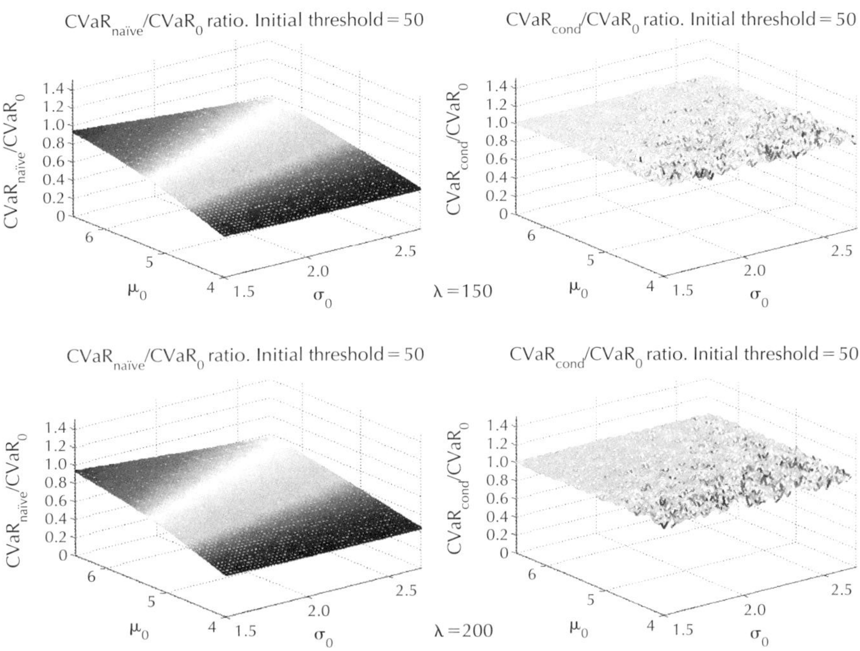


"randomly missing data" (observations that are missing randomly over the entire range of the data, and are caused, for example, by an inadequate loss data collection process) was made. Within the first category, a clear line was also put between the categories of censored and truncated data, sometimes incorrectly treated as synonymous terms: while with the censored data the information loss refers only to the severity, in the truncated data the information loss occurs in both the frequency and severity.

For the truncated data (the worst case), the chapter illustrated possible approaches that may be carried out to estimate the parameters of the frequency and severity distributions: four approaches were depicted, from the fully "unconditional", which ignores the missing observations and treats the observed data as a complete dataset (the "naïve" approach), to the fully "conditional", where the incompleteness of data is explicitly taken into account in the estimation of both severity and frequency distributions.

A specific algorithm, the expectation-maximisation (EM) algorithm, was then introduced as a robust iterative procedure designed for maximum-likelihood estimation with incomplete data; in particular it was highlighted that the EM algorithm is easy to apply even when the form of the likelihood function is complicated, and results in an increased likelihood value at each iteration and, most importantly, convergence to the true parameter values is achieved even for very bad starting values.

In the second part of the chapter, the effects of the use of the stated approaches on the correctness of the estimate of the capital-charge-relevant figures was described, analytically derived and measured.

In particular it was stressed that the "naïve" approach – the one most followed by practitioners – determines the highest biases in the estimates of the parameters of both severity and frequency distributions. This is confirmed by the Poisson ($\lambda$)-lognormal ($\mu$, $\sigma$) model, for which the sign and the extent of the bias were computed and then measured for a large number of the true $\lambda$–$\mu$–$\sigma$ combinations. The model demonstrates that the extent of the bias increases for lower values of the location parameter ($\mu$) and higher values of the scale parameter ($\sigma$); in the worst case it overestimates $\mu$ by 50% and underestimates $\sigma$ by 40%. On the other side, when the fully "conditional" approach is adopted, the estimates of $\mu$ and $\sigma$ coincide with the true values for the majority of scenarios, and, when the bias occurs, it stays under 5%.

Finally, the bias on the estimate of the EL and VAR (and expected shortfall) figures generated under the "naïve" approach in the case of the Poisson–lognormal model was first analytically expressed and then measured. The exercise shows that this "naïve" approach always underestimates the true values of EL and VAR (and expected shortfall): the bias is on average 35% and 50%, respectively, and attains its maximum at roughly 60% and 80%. The frequency has a negligible impact on the bias in relative terms, but has an impact in the absolute ones. Equivalently to the conclusion made regarding the parameter estimation, correct (or minimally biased) figures for EL and VAR (and expected shortfall) would be obtained if the conditional distribution were fitted to the incomplete data, by adopting the expectation-maximisation algorithm or, alternatively, direct numerical integration.

The exercise also shows that the underestimation of EL and VAR (and expected shortfall) figures rises when $\mu$ decreases and $\sigma$ increases; this means that the bias is driven, other than by the fraction of missing data, by the asymmetry and the heavy-tailness of the model. Therefore, if instead of the Poisson–lognormal case, models with a higher level of asymmetry and tail-heaviness were used (for instance negative binomial-generalised Pareto), the bias would significantly amplify, possibly up to figures bigger than 100%.

The recommendation for practitioners stemming from the depicted exercise is to fix the thresholds as low as possible and use a correct approach to estimate the parameters of the frequency and severity distributions in order to determine the EL and VAR (or expected shortfall) figures. By doing so, in addition to avoiding the information loss carried by the missing data, one would be able to produce accurate estimates of the operational capital charge.

1 For a theoretical and practical comparison of the two approaches, see Moscadelli (2004).

2 In the context of the Basel Accord, there is no definition of EL, hence of its components EF and ES. Even if in this study we use the arithmetic mean as a measure of EL, this does not necessarily mean that it represents the best candidate for EL. Depending on the shape and characteristics of the data, alternative, more robust, measures (as the median or the trimmed/winsorised means) could be called for to represent the typical loss experience of the bank.

## REFERENCES

**Artzner, P., *et al*,** 1997, "Thinking Coherently", *Risk Magazine*, **10**, pp 68–71.

**Artzner, *et al*,** 1999, "Coherent Measures of Risk", *Mathematical Finance*, **9(3)**, pp 203–28.

**Chernobai, A., C. Menn, S. Rachev, and S. Trück,** 2005a, "A note on the Estimation of the Frequency and Severity Distributions of Operational Losses", *Mathematical Scientist*, **30(2)**.

**Chernobai, A., K. Burnecki, S. Rachev, and S. Trück, R. Weron,** 2005b, "Modelling Catastrophe Claims with Left-Truncated Severity Distributions", forthcoming in the *Journal of Computational Statistics*.

**Chernobai, A., C. Menn, S. Rachev, and S. Trück,** 2005c, "Estimation of Operational Value-at-Risk in the Presence of Minimum Collection Thresholds", Working Paper.

**Dempster, A. P., N. Laird, and D. Rubin,** 1977, "Maximum Likelihood from Incomplete Data via the EM Algorithm", *Journal of the Royal Statistical Society*, **39(B)**, pp 1–38.

**Embrechts, P., C. Klüppelberg, and T. Mikosch,** 1997, *Modelling Extremal Events for Insurance and Finance* (Heidelberg: Springer).

**Klugman, S. A., H. H. Panjer, and G. E. Willmot,** 2004, *Loss Models: From Data to Decisions* (New York: John Wiley & Sons).

**Moscadelli, M.,** 2004, "The Modelling of Operational Risk: Experience with the Analysis of the Data Collected by the Basel Committee", Bank of Italy, working paper.

**Rachev, S. T., C. Menn, and F. J. Fabozzi,** 2005, *Fat-tailed and Skewed Asset Return Distributions: Implications for Risk Management, Portfolio Selection, and Option Pricing* (New York: John Wiley & Sons).

# 8

# *Tests of Extreme-Value Theory Applied to Operational Risk Data*

**Giulio Mignola, Roberto Ugoccioni**

Operational Risk Management, Sanpaolo IMI*

In this chapter, we test the applicability of the asymptotic extreme-value theory (EVT) to operational risk data. We performed the analysis in a so-called *controlled* environment (an environment in which everything is *a priori* known) consisting of a lognormal severity distribution and a Poisson frequency distribution, chosen to reproduce the features observed in operational risk loss data. We show how the use of the EVT in this case could lead to a substantial overestimate of the risk figures. In addition, we test the application of the same EVT scheme in the case of a generalised Pareto distribution (GPD) with a Poisson frequency distribution. In this latter case, where we know that the theory is exact and hence holds for the whole distribution, the results, although as expected not biased, show a very high uncertainty.

In operational risk data analysis, the following approach has become widespread (see de Fontnouvelle, Jordan and Rosengren, 2005; Moscadelli, 2004): frequency and severity distributions are analysed separately; the latter is divided into two areas: the body, up to a threshold, and the tail. The body is often used to build an empirical distribution function, or sometimes parameterised with a lognormal distribution, while the tail is modelled using extreme-value theory's (EVT) peaks-over-thresholds (POT) approach.

*The views expressed in this chapter are those of the authors and do not involve the responsibility of the bank.

The aim of this chapter is to test the predictive power of this common practice scheme (in particular, focusing our interest in the EVT tail modelling) with respect to the yearly addition of more data. The scheme is here applied to a few known, and therefore in principle completely under-control, cases: the loss-data collection and analysis process is simulated within this controlled environment, and results on expected loss (EL) and capital-at-risk (CAR, here defined as the 99.9% quantile) are compared to exact values.

In the next section, the method used is described in detail; in the following section, results from several test cases are presented and discussed; conclusions are drawn at the end.

We intend to simulate a medium-size bank collecting and analysing loss data along the years. Synthetic data drawn from a completely known distribution, and for which therefore exact values for EL and CAR are known, are used to populate a historic loss-data base. Subsequently, the inference scheme is applied and yearly results are compared with the *a priori* known exact values.

In more detail, the procedure used is the following.[1]

(1) A specific business line is chosen, loss data of all event types pooled, an average gross income for that business line taken from known sources.
(2) An average frequency is computed based on the number of data points. This value is taken as the parameter $\lambda$ of a Poisson distribution.
(3) A severity probability density $f(x)$ is chosen and a set of parameters identified, such that the aggregate loss resulting from the chosen distribution compounded with the Poisson frequency distribution gives an average aggregate loss of the same order of magnitude as is obtained from the data alone and a 99.9% quantile of the same order of magnitude as 12% of the gross income.
(4) From the severity $f(x)$ and the Poisson frequency, exact (ie, not limited by statistics) values of the aggregate expected loss and CAR are computed.
(5) A set of size $N$ (equal to the integer part of $\lambda$) of synthetic data is generated according to the chosen severity.
(6) An empirical distribution function, $Q_N(x)$, is built from the synthetic data, and a set of thresholds is chosen in order to

investigate 100, 150, 200, . . . , 1,000 excesses: 100 excesses is the minimum number recommended in McNeil and Saladin (1997) for EVT analysis; 1,000 excesses is a case rarely achieved in practice. For each threshold $u$, a ground-up GPD,

$$G(x;u)=1-\left(1+\xi\frac{x-u}{\sigma}\right)^{-1/\xi} \quad (1)$$

is fitted to the exceedances: the shape ($\xi$) and scale ($\sigma$) parameters are estimated by maximum likelihood methods.

(7) For each threshold, the aggregate annual loss distribution (see Klugman, Panjer and Willmot, 2004) is computed, using characteristic functions and fast-Fourier-transform techniques, from the aforementioned Poisson and a piecewise severity distribution $P(x;u)$, built as follows:

$$P(x;u)=\begin{cases} Q_N(x), & x\le u; \\ Q_N(u)+[1-Q_N(u)]\,G(x;u), & x>u \end{cases} \quad (2)$$

Finally, EL and CAR are calculated as the usual expected value and 99.9 percentile of the aggregate annual loss distribution.

(8) Another set of $\lfloor\lambda\rfloor$ data is generated as in Step 5 and added to the previous data, thus simulating another year of accumulated losses ($N \rightarrow N + \lfloor\lambda\rfloor$). The process is then repeated from Step 6 for ten times, thus simulating ten years of data taking *from the same, known distribution*.

Notice that we work with data above a minimum threshold (€20,000) consistently, both in the known severity and in the synthetic data. In this way, left-truncation does not play a role in comparing those results. It is, however, foreseen to explore the effect of left-truncation on EVT in a forthcoming chapter.

In this chapter, we carry out the analysis and present results starting from the third year, the minimum provisional requirement according to Basel II (see Basel Committee on Banking Supervision, 2004). All computations have been performed using the "R" system (see R Development Core Team, 2005).

A word of caution is in order here. For the low-frequency scenarios analysed in what follows, the thresholds corresponding to a large number of excesses (of order of a few hundred to a thousand) cover much more than just the tail of the severity distribution (as can be seen by the relevant graphs). For these particular cases[2] we should not expect the asymptotic approximation to hold and hence the EVT to be applicable; nevertheless, we show the results to keep consistency with the high-frequency cases.

### Lognormal

As a first step, severity is modelled with a shifted lognormal distribution, which is a quite common and good description of the bulk of loss data. It is known that convergence to a GPD is slow (see Embrecht, Kluppelberg and Mikosch, 1999), but it is interesting to explore the effects of this feature on the risk measures.

The density function is:

$$f_{\ln}(x) = \frac{\exp(-z^2/2)}{(x-s_0)\sigma\sqrt{2\pi}}, \quad \text{with} \quad z \equiv \frac{\ln(x-s_0)-\mu}{\sigma}, \quad x \geq s_0 \tag{3}$$

The parameters used are detailed in Table 1: cases (A) and (B) present a high-frequency and a low-frequency situation, respectively, applied to the same-severity distribution (other cases in the Table will be discussed later). The resulting (exact) EL and CAR are also listed.

Results are presented as a function of the threshold above which the EVT approach is applied. We start by discussing case (A): in Figure 1, the shape plot for the test case after ten simulated years is shown. Within EVT (see Coles, 2001), the constancy of the shape $\xi$ when changing the threshold is considered a necessary condition for applicability (indicating that the tail is already in the asymptotic regime). From the plot, two areas can be identified where $\xi$ is constant. It is interesting to point out that the lognormal distribution (independently of the value of the parameters) belongs to the class whose limiting tail behaviour is described by an exponential (see McNeil and Saladin, 1997; Johnson, Kotz and Balakrishnan, 1995), that is, a generalised Pareto with $\xi = 0$, while the Maximum Likelyhood Estimate (MLE) values of the shape parameter range between 0.7 and 0.9.

In Figure 2, the expected loss and the 99.9% quantile are plotted for each year. Estimates with a number of excesses slightly above the minimum are seen to come closer to the exact values; this corresponds to the plateau on the right-hand side of Figure 1, while the plateau for lower thresholds gives larger fluctuations. Fluctuations decrease as more and more years are analysed, meaning that adding more data

**Table 1** Distributions and parameters used in the simulation. A star (*) in the last two columns indicates units of $10^6$

| Distribution | Parameters | | | $\lambda$ | EL | CAR |
|---|---|---|---|---|---|---|
| A lognormal | $s_0 = 20{,}000$ | $\mu = 7.1$ | $\sigma = 3$ | 2,700 | 287* | 3,706* |
| B lognormal | $s_0 = 20{,}000$ | $\mu = 7.1$ | $\sigma = 3$ | 120 | 15.2* | 508* |
| C lognormal | $s_0 = 20{,}000$ | $\mu = 6.1$ | $\sigma = 2.2$ | 2,700 | 66.7* | 91.2* |
| D lognormal | $s_0 = 0$ | $\mu = 0$ | $\sigma = 1$ | 2,700 | 4,452 | 4,907 |
| E GPD | $s_0 = 20{,}000$ | $\xi = 0.85$ | $\tilde{\sigma} = 20{,}200$ | 2,700 | 315* | 7,256* |
| F GPD | $s_0 = 20{,}000$ | $\xi = 0.85$ | $\tilde{\sigma} = 20{,}200$ | 120 | 16.5* | 509* |
| G GPD | $s_0 = 20{,}000$ | $\xi = 0.6$ | $\tilde{\sigma} = 20{,}200$ | 2,700 | 122* | 245* |
| H GPD | $s_0 = 0$ | $\xi = 0.85$ | $\tilde{\sigma} = 1$ | 2,700 | 11,600 | 355,100 |

**Figure 1** Shape plot for case (A).
The lines illustrate 95% confidence bands on the parameters (obtained by MLE errors, supposed normal)

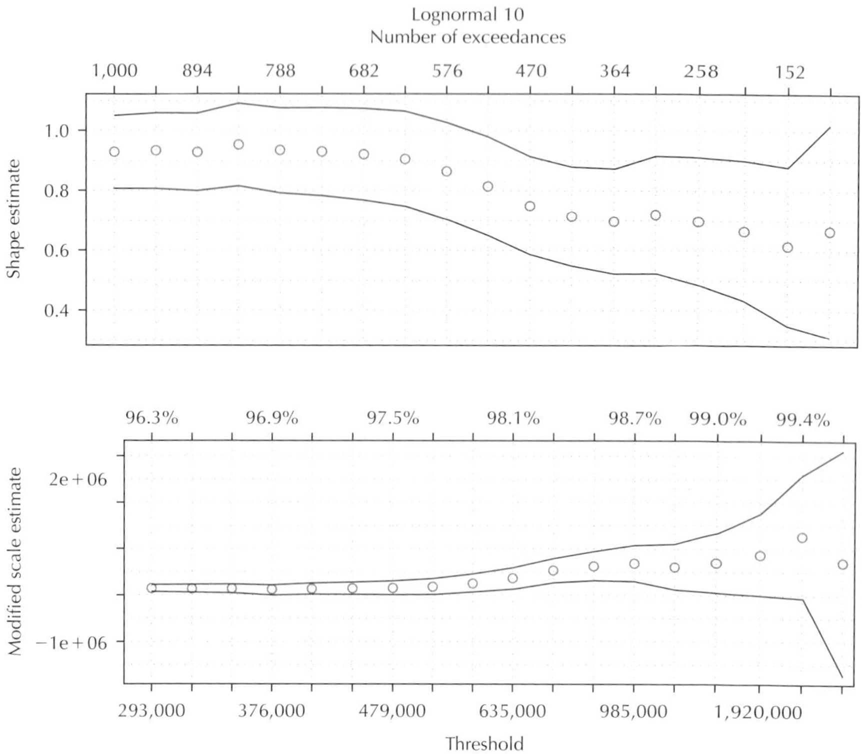


improves the situation. However, even after ten years the numbers are 13–15% too low (for EL) and 40–50% too low (for CAR); after five years, on the other hand, one obtains values that overshoot the exact value of the expected loss by 20% and of the quantile by more than 200%. We have investigated this issue further, checking whether prolonging data taking helps converging to the exact value: we added ten more simulated years to the process, and found that the results keep oscillating around the ten-year values, and not the exact values.

The situation appears worse in the low-frequency case (B), Figure 3: the shape plot is never flat and therefore EVT is not applicable. Nevertheless, we carried out the analysis of EL and CAR to have a feeling for the type of results one can obtain. As

**Figure 2** Expected loss and 99.9% quantile of aggregate loss for case (A). Each symbol represents a different number of years of data (see legend); solid lines are drawn to guide the eye. The dashed horizontal lines mark the exact values of EL and CAR

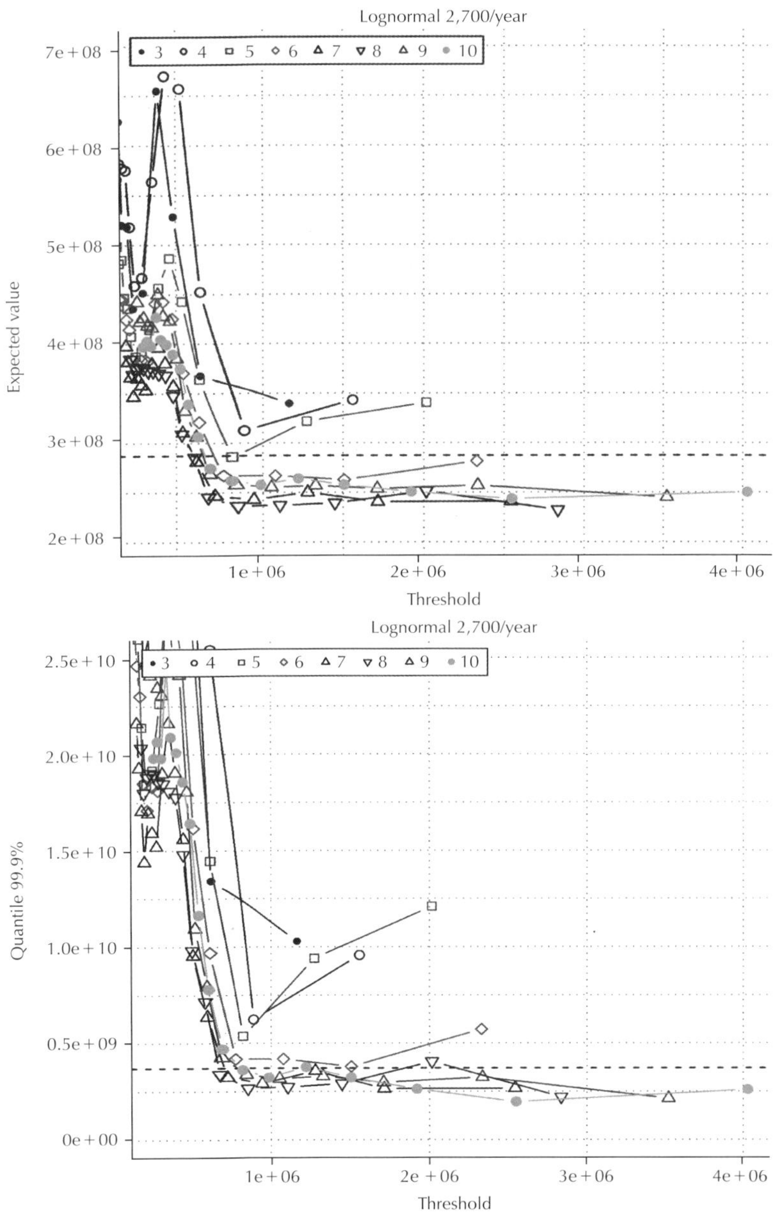

**Figure 3** Shape plot (a) and 99.9% quantile of aggregate loss (b) *vs* thresholds for case (B).
Each symbol represents a different number of years of data (see legend); solid lines are drawn to guide the eye. The dashed horizontal lines mark the exact values of the CAR

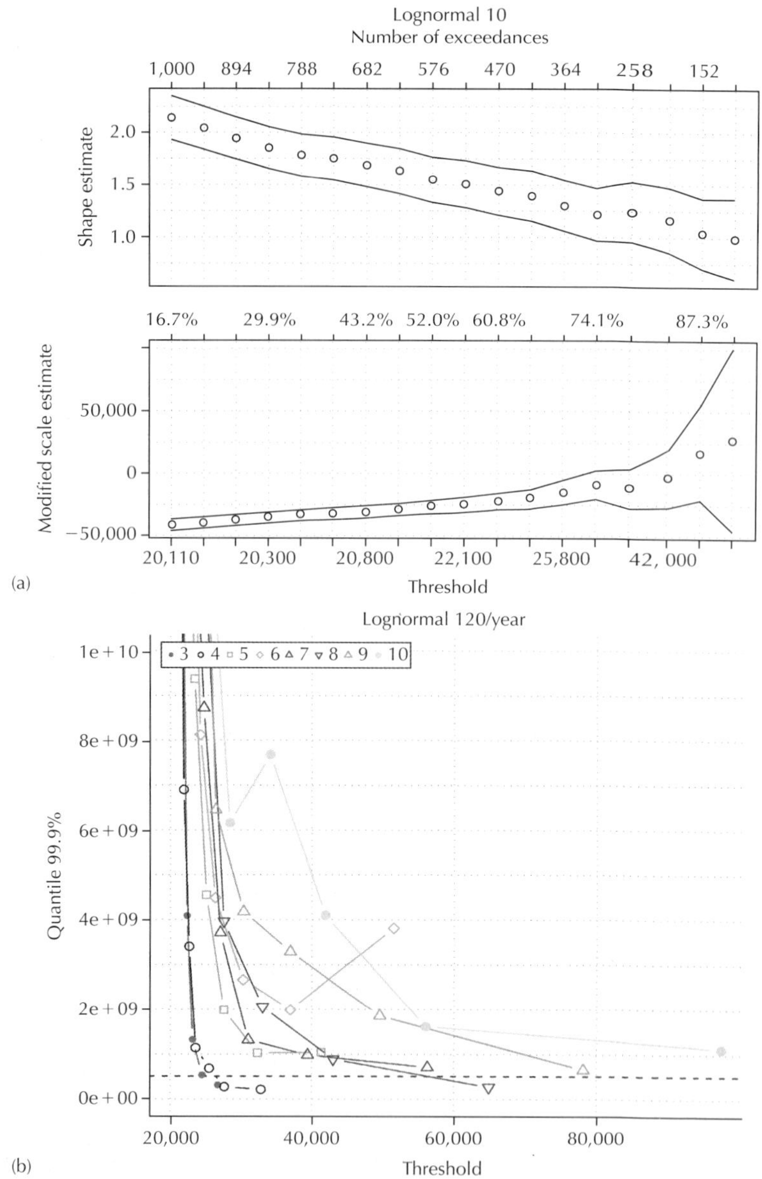

expected, the right-hand panel of Figure 3 shows hardly any convergence, although by pure chance the ten years point at the highest threshold is right on the spot.

In view of the disappointing results of the analysis described up to now, further investigations have been carried out. It should be noticed that, in the treated case, the exact single loss quantile of the chosen distribution is a very significant part of the exact aggregate quantile (see Embrecht, Kluppelberg and Mikosch, 1999): that is, solving

$$\int_{S_0}^{x} f_{\ln}(x)\,\mathrm{d}x = 1-\frac{10^{-3}}{\lambda}$$

with the parameters of case (A) one has already $x$ close to 92% of the CAR. Thus we modified the parameters so that the exact single loss quantile amounts to about 50% of the CAR. In the outcome of this exercise, whose parameters are in line (C) of the table, the shape parameter is still far from the theoretically expected value, and is flat with a large number of excesses rather than with a small number. EL is 1% below the exact value and CAR varies from +20% to −10%.

A standard lognormal distribution – case (D) in the table – has also been investigated, to check whether convergence depends on the scale parameters of the distribution. In this textbook case everything works well: the shape plot is flat (although never near 0, the asymptotic value); EL and CAR do not vary more than 1% from the exact value.

It thus appears that the method is largely sensitive to the underlying distribution. This matter is now further probed by replacing the lognormal distribution with the Pareto distribution.

**Pareto**

It is well known that for data from the GPD, the EVT approach is always applicable, because excesses do follow a GPD with the same shape $\xi$ (but not necessarily the same $\tilde{\sigma}$) as the full data (see Coles, 2001);

$$f_{\mathrm{GPD}}(x) = \frac{1}{\tilde{\sigma}}\left(1+\xi\frac{x-S_0}{\tilde{\sigma}}\right)^{-1/\xi-1}$$

Again, parameters are chosen as in Step 3 (see row (E) in Table 1). A low-frequency case is then investigated (F), as well as a case in which the single loss quantile is roughly 50% of the exact CAR (G) and a case in which the scale is set to 1 (H).

We see in general (eg, Figure 4 shows case (E); other cases are not shown due to lack of space), that the shape plot is flatter than in the lognormal case, and the values are close to the $\xi$ of the original distribution. However, large oscillations are seen in the graphs both of EL and CAR (see Figure 5), even when the scale is $\tilde{\sigma} = 1$. It should be noticed that setting also $\xi = 0$ as well as $\tilde{\sigma} = 1$ does give nearly perfect results (not shown): EL and CAR are estimated to 0.1% or better already from the third year.

### Other distributions

The two examined distributions, lognormal and GDP, are two extremes: the former is known to converge very slowly to its asymptotic

**Figure 4** Shape plot for case (E).
The lines illustrate 95% confidence bands on the parameters (obtained by MLE errors, supposed normal)

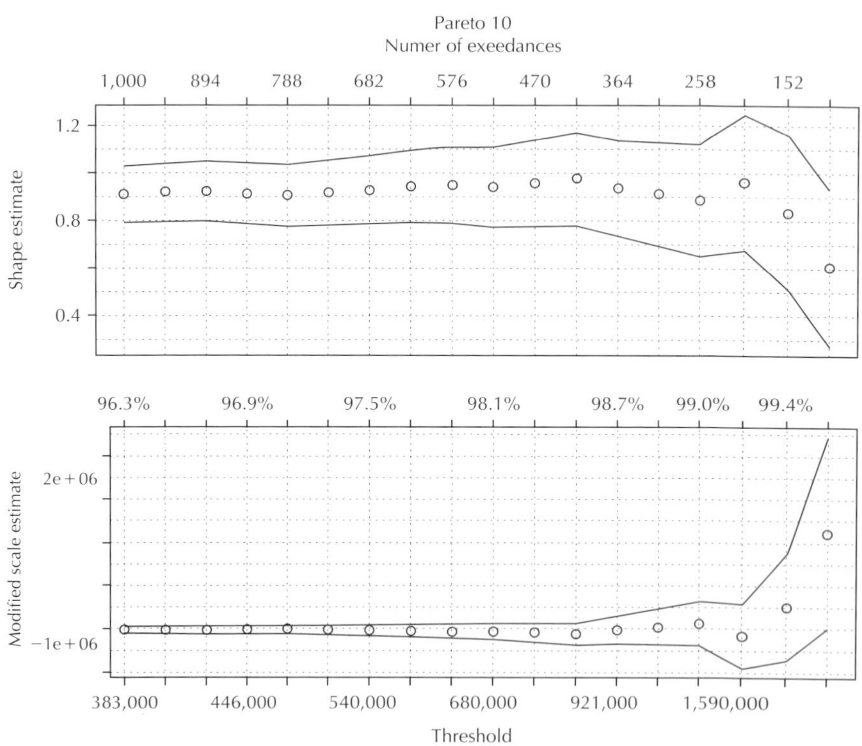

**Figure 5** Expected loss and 99.9% quantile of aggregate loss for case (E).
Each symbol represents a different number of years of data (see legend); solid lines are drawn to guide the eye. The dashed horizontal lines mark the exact values of EL and CAR

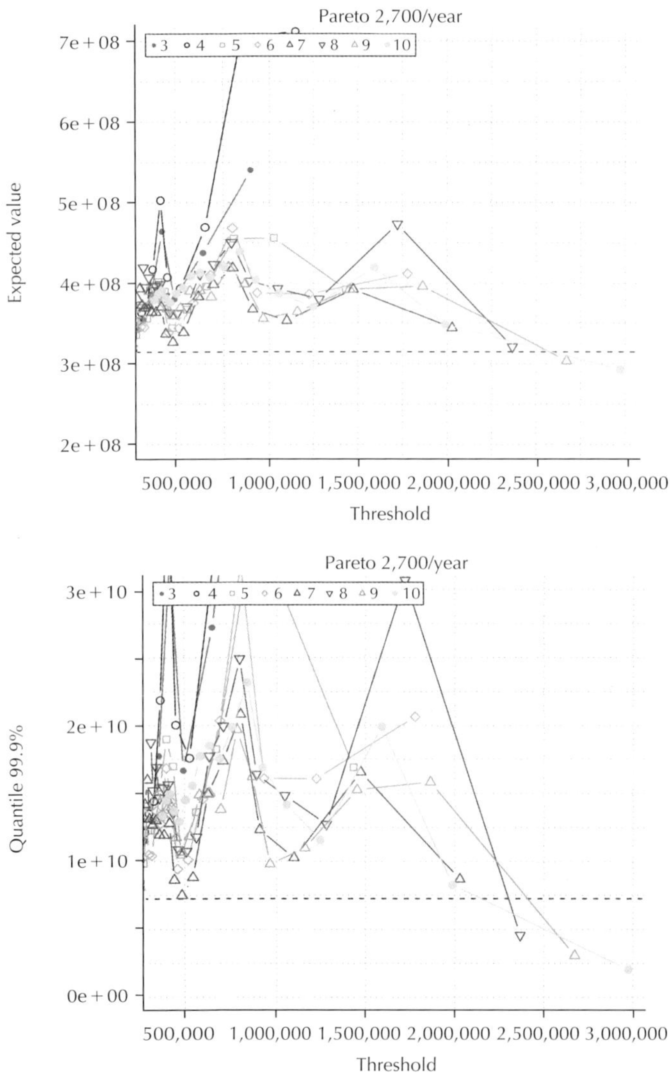

regime, while the latter has the assumed behaviour everywhere. To complete the analysis we tested the log-gamma distribution with rate parameter 2, which implies convergence (faster than the lognormal) to the maximum domain of attraction of the Fréchet distribution with tail parameter 1/2 (see Embrecht, Kluppelberg and Mikosch, 1999). Our results show, following the trend of the lognormal analysis, that the estimated shape parameter of the GDP ($\xi \approx 0.9$) is still far from its asymptotic value (0.5).

## Was it bad luck?

We have examined only a few instances, in particular one instance for each case. We might appear to be particularly unlucky,

**Figure 6** Box plots and strip plots of the CAR after five and ten simulated years. These results come from 100 different runs of case (A). Notice that, contrary to previous figures, we are plotting the number of excesses on the x axis instead of the thresholds, which are unevenly distributed

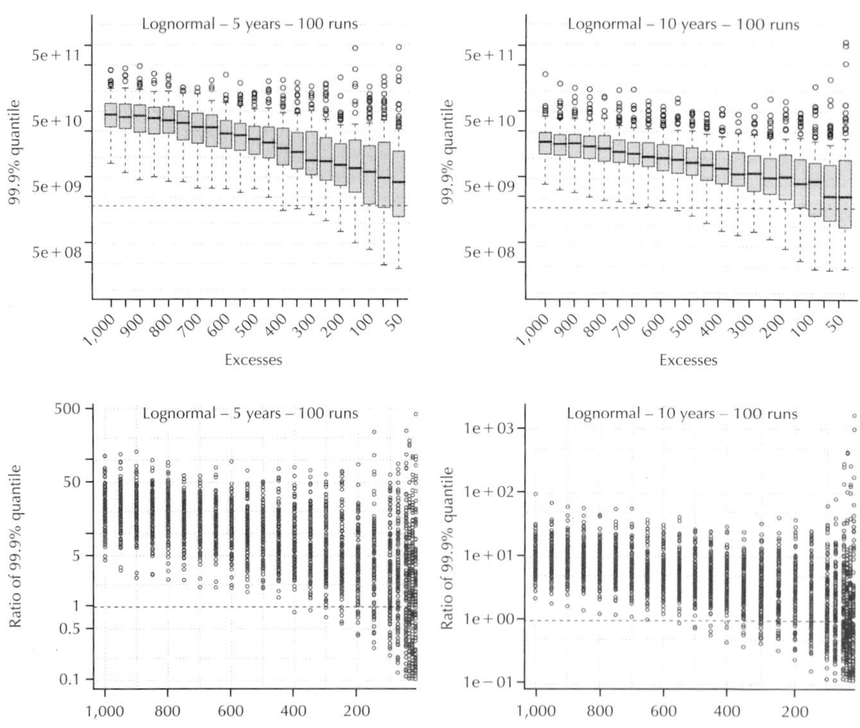

so scenario (A) was run 100 times, and statistics collected in Figure 6, even going to a smaller number of excesses (higher thresholds). It can be seen that estimates vary wildly, as one could have concluded from the discussion in the previous sections. As a general comment, we observe that where the uncertainty is smaller the model overestimates the quantile, and in the far tail nothing can be said since the uncertainty is too large. The same holds for the log-gamma distribution (not shown here).

In Figure 7 the same exercise was performed for case (E), using a GPD: here large uncertainties are the dominant feature giving rise to configurations that are even thousands of times the exact value.

**Figure 7** Box plots and strip plots of the CAR after five and ten simulated years. These results come from 100 different runs of case (E). Notice that, contrary to other figures, we are plotting the number of excesses on the x axis instead of the thresholds, which are unevenly distributed

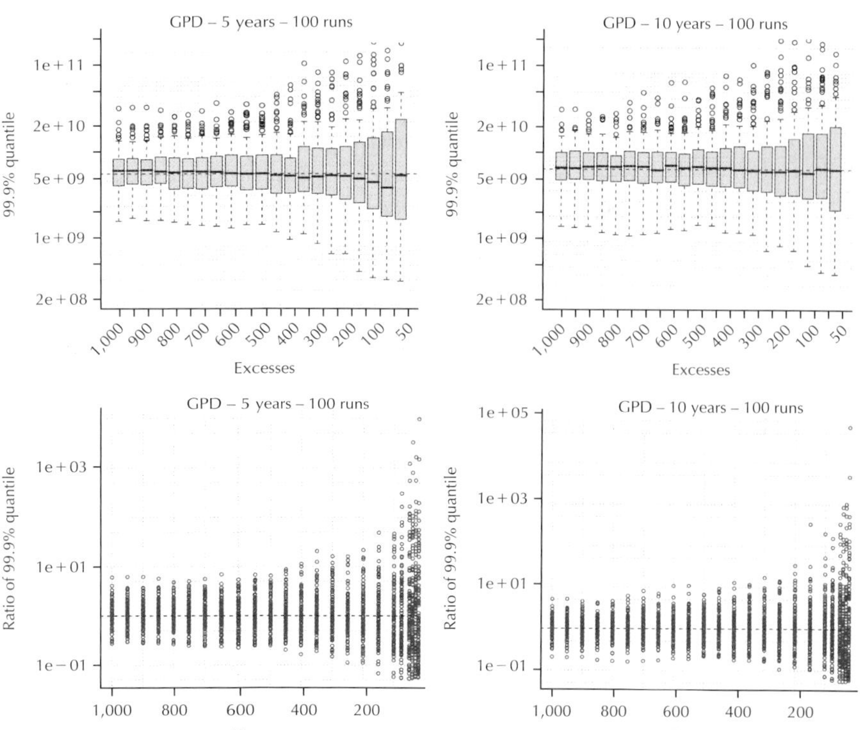

## CONCLUSIONS

In this chapter, we have tested the peaks-over-thresholds (POT) approach for estimating high quantiles of distributions typical of operational risk. The result is somewhat disappointing, as both high quantiles and mean values are not computed correctly even with a large dataset. This situation should be compared to textbook distributions, with standard parameters, where excellent results are obtained. Furthermore, when estimates are performed in the far tail – that is, using only the last hundreds of data – a large dispersion of results is observed, as a direct outcome of the sizable uncertainty on the parameters of the GPD. Our conclusion is that applicability of the method depends strongly on the shape of the underlying distribution, as well as on its scale and location features. This suggests that caution should be used in applying EVT to unknown distributions, where the aforementioned parameters are not under control and a method for ascertaining the reaching of the asymptotic regime is not available. As we have shown in the case of the lognormal distribution, the POT approach, apart from the uncertainty due to the small number of data points used in the estimation process, systematically overestimates the percentile of the aggregate annual distribution.

At this point, extrapolating from a distribution that interpolates well the majority of available data – in the sense of classical goodness-of-fit tests, especially if one considers those that give more importance to the tail (see Klugman, Panjer and Willmot, 2004; Rioux and Klugman, 2004) – and hence reduces the uncertainty of the parameters, does not appear to stand on weaker grounds: it is hard to argue that the generalised Pareto is a preferred method for fitting the tail of distributions encountered in operational risk data analysis in all cases.

1 Steps 1 to 3 are there in order to remain as close as possible to a "realistic" case.

2 This, unfortunately, is the situation that is closely matched by reality for some combination of event type, business line as defined in the Basel II accord, where the typical observed frequencies could be of the order of few tens per year.

## REFERENCES

**Basel Committee on Banking Supervision,** 2004, "International Convergence of Capital Measurement and Capital Standards. A Revised Framework", June.

**Coles, S.,** 2001, *An Introduction to Statistical Modeling of Extreme Values* (London: Springer Verlag).

**de Fontnouvelle, P., J. Jordan, and E. Rosengren,** 2005, "Implication of Alternative Operational Risk Modeling Techniques", NBER working paper 111036, unpublished, URL: http://www.nber.org/papers/w11103

**Embrecht, P., C. Kluppelberg, and T. Mikosch,** 1999, *Modelling Extremal Events for Insurance and Finance* (Berlin: Springer Verlag).

**Johnson, M. L., S. Kotz, and N. Balakrishnan,** 1995, *Continuous Univariate Distributions*, Volume 2, 2nd edn (New York: John Wiley and Sons).

**Klugman, S. A., H. H. Panjer, and G. E. Willmot,** 2004, *Loss Models: From Data to Decisions*, 2nd edn (New York: John Wiley & Sons).

**McNeil, A. J. and T. Saladin,** 1997, "The Peaks Over Thresholds Method for Estimating High Quantiles of Loss Distributions", Proceedings of the XXVIIth International ASTIN Colloquium, Cairns, Australia, pp 23–43.

**Moscadelli, M.,** 2004, "The Modelling of Operational Risk: The Experience with the Analysis of the Data Collected by the Basel Committee", Banca d'Italia, Temi di discussione del Servizio Studi (517), July.

**R Development Core Team,** 2005, "R: A Language and Environment for Statistical Computing", R Foundation for Statistical Computing, Vienna, URL: http://www.R-project.org

**Rioux, J. and S. Klugman,** 2004, "Toward a Unified Approach to Fitting Loss Models", Unpublished, URL: http://www.iowaactuariesclub.org/library/lossmodels.pdf

# Section Four

# Alternative Modelling Approaches

While the use of internal and external data in OR modelling is essential, most experts now believe that this is not where an AMA programme's quantification element should end. It is being recognised by experts that the very nature of OR makes it essential that qualitative elements be incorporated with quantitative elements to produce a more accurate understanding of the risks.

To this end, I have included three chapters that take on more qualitative subjects: scenario analysis, key risk indicators and the challenges of quantifying an issue such as technology risk. There are dozens of other subjects I could have included here but, hopefully, these three will provide a general framework for thinking about qualitative elements and their role in modelling, as well as providing specific guidance in the three subjects covered.

The chapter on scenario analysis kicks off with a literary discussion of a tale of a mythical novel "in which all possible developments and endings are told and which is, as such, at the same time, infinite and incomplete". A horror story? Possibly, but this is also a very accurate description of the challenges that OR managers conducting scenario analysis face – for example, how many different kinds of event could kick a firm's business continuity programme into place, and how different would the impact of each of those events be? Author Sergio Scandizzo walks readers through the benefits and difficulties posed by scenario analysis.

The second chapter, on key risk indicators, is authored by the gurus of the subject from Risk*Business*, who have started a key-risk-indicator library in partnership with the Risk Management Association in the United States. This useful chapter takes the reader through the definition of a KRI, how KRIs should be used and incorporated into an OR framework.

The last chapter, by Advanta's Eric Holmquist, looks at the difficulties inherent in quantifying a rather woolly subject such as technology risk. By and large, the industry hasn't even really agreed on a definition of "technology risk", although most experts recognise that it is one of the most significant risks that a firm faces. This chapter suggests a strategy for exploring the implications of technology risk and the impact that it could have on a firm's economic capital calculations.

# 9

# *Scenario Analysis in Operational Risk Management*

**Sergio Scandizzo**

European Investment Bank*

*Dejo a los varios porvenires (no a todos) mi jardín de senderos que se bifurcan.*
(I leave to the various futures (not to all) my garden of forking paths)

J. L. Borges, "*El jardín de senderos que se bifurcan*"[1]

In his beautiful and intriguing tale of multiple futures, Jorge Luis Borges writes about a mythical novel in which all possible developments and endings are told and which is, as such, at the same time, infinite and incomplete. To the risk manager, this fascinating and unsettling idea is a metaphor for the innumerable multiplicity of events that lie ahead as well as for the impossibility for any analysis to be exhaustive.

Nevertheless, trying to say something nontrivial about the various ways things can turn out is at the core of what risk managers do, and it is not so much about predicting what is going to happen, as it is about identifying the most troublesome combinations of circumstances and being prepared for them.

The analysis of scenarios has existed for as long as mankind has tried to act strategically, albeit that it is only recently that its practice has been endowed with the panoply of mathematical and computing tools that financial risk managers are now used to. In all human endeavours, from agriculture to sea voyages, from politics to warfare, people have tried to imagine multiple possible outcomes

*The views expressed in this chapter are those of the author and do not necessarily reflect those of the European Investment Bank.

and prepare themselves against the adverse ones. Modern scenario analysis, like many other management techniques, can be traced back to World War Two, first in the military and later in the civil domain. The RAND Corporation and subsequently the Hudson Institute developed this approach through the seminal work of Herman Kahn (1967). It was then adopted as a key planning tool by most large corporations (see, for example, van der Heijden, 1996, for a history of its introduction at Shell) as well as for smaller ones (see Linneman and Kennel, 1997 for an application to small enterprises).

Within modern financial risk management, scenario analysis has not been so far widely employed except in the form of stress testing, notably for market risk (the interested reader can consult *Modern Risk Management: A History*, various authors, Risk Books, 2003), although the two terms are used sometimes in combination. According to the Financial Services Authority, "Stress test typically refers to shifting the values of individual parameters that affect the financial position of a firm and determining the effect on the firm's business. Scenario analysis typically refers to a wider range of parameters being varied at the same time." (See FSA, 2005.)

However, unlike in market risk, where we can shift market parameters individually or simultaneously to gauge the effect on the resulting exposure, in most operational risk models all we can vary is likelihood and impact of the event itself. Furthermore, in operational risk the distinction made above between stress testing and scenario analysis blurs considerably as one takes into account the peculiarities of operational risk assessment. As operational risk measurement is concerned mainly with assessing the likelihood and impact of individual events, it is in essence a form of systematic and, hopefully, comprehensive scenario analysis. This is true regardless of which quantification methodology is chosen. Whether we measure operational risk by applying statistical techniques to historical data, through scoring risk and controls[1] or by relying on managers' self-assessment, we are always analysing scenarios in each of which a specific event takes place. In fact, what some authors call *scenario-based risk measurement techniques* (see for example Anders and van der Brink, 2004) should be really classified under self-assessment. The following passage from the Federal Reserve Bank of New York (2003) clearly expresses the substantial identity between the two terms in the context of operational risk management: "Scenario analysis is a systematic process of obtaining expert opinions from business managers and risk-management experts to derive reasoned assessments of the likelihood and impact of plausible operational losses consistent with the regulatory soundness standard."

The New Basel Accord 2004 (see BCBS, 2004, Section 675) has most appropriately introduced not so much a different definition, but an emphasis on focusing scenario analysis on that component of operational risk where statistical data are minimal and consequences potentially catastrophic.

> A bank must use scenario analysis of expert opinion in conjunction with external data to evaluate its exposure to high-severity events. This approach draws on the knowledge of experienced business managers and risk management experts to derive reasoned assessments of plausible severe losses. For instance, these expert assessments could be expressed as parameters of an assumed statistical loss distribution. In addition, scenario analysis should be used to assess the impact of deviations from the correlation assumptions embedded in the bank's operational risk measurement framework, in particular, to evaluate potential losses arising from multiple simultaneous operational risk loss events. Over time, such assessments need to be validated and re-assessed through comparison to actual loss experience to ensure their reasonableness.

It is interesting to note that the Basel Committee for Banking Supervision (BCBS) keeps the self-assessment of likelihood and severity in its recommendation while focusing on high-severity events and linking those to "multiple, simultaneous loss events". In this context, scenario analysis is a strategic tool because it focuses on long-term, large-scale consequences. It is not about calculating value-at-risk (VAR) to the *n*th decimal digit, nor does it purport to predict what is actually going to happen. Scenario analysis can support decision making by focusing managers' minds on the consequences of certain combinations of events that would otherwise go ignored on the grounds either that they are extremely unlikely or that they have never happened. Unfortunately, very little guidance is available on how to practically choose the risk drivers that will cause tail events, how to imagine breakdowns leading to unexpected consequences and how to construct scenarios that have never happened.

In this chapter I discuss the application of scenario analysis to operational risk assessment and propose a methodology to perform it systematically throughout a banking organisation. First, I introduce scenario analysis as the main element in an operational risk assessment methodology. In the following section, I discuss scenario analysis in relation to high severity events. Then I develop a methodology for applying scenario analysis to extreme events and finally I discuss some case studies.

## SCENARIO-BASED RISKS ASSESSMENT

As scenario-based risk assessment is essentially a form of management self-assessment of risks (and related controls), it is not surprising that the key to its effective implementation lies mainly in how the events to be assessed are identified. The identification of the events requires a mapping of the risks within the business process and/or unit and this in turn corresponds to a systematic extraction of task-specific information on the various ways a given process can fail.

Experts' contribution should therefore focus on the following dimensions:

- scenario configuration (which event or combination of events);
- impact assessment (how much can it cost); and
- likelihood estimation (admittedly the least reliable piece of information).

In a recent paper (Scandizzo, 2005) I have proposed a methodology for the identification of events and losses in a given business process which is based on the following concepts.

- The drivers of operational risk are also the key resources present in each banking activity: people, process, technology and external factors.
- An operational failure will occur every time one or more of these resources is/are inadequate to the task being performed. This may happen because the resource is insufficient either in quality or in quantity (capacity and capability), unavailable at a critical stage (availability and criticality), or because they break down altogether.

By following this line of reasoning it is then possible to identify an event category for each failure and one or more corresponding loss(es). By systematically reclassifying the identified risks, a map can be created to produce a Basel-compliant loss event model, which in turn can form the basis for self-assessment. The resulting structure will resemble the one in Table 1 (example developed for a trading business).

The information contained in the last two columns (event and loss category) can then be provided to management for self-assessment.

*Probability assessment*: The probability that an operational failure may occur has to be assessed for each identified risk exposure. This assessment can be expressed as the expected frequency of occurrence of the related operational event.

*Impact assessment*: Impact is the potential loss that could be realised should the operational failure occur. This can be expressed in terms of expected loss and worst-case loss given an operational failure.

Results will reflect a structure similar to that reported in Table 2.

This is done by estimating, on the basis of management experience and historical information, the parameters of the probability distributions of operational events and those of the conditional probability distribution of operational loss severity given an operational event. The two distributions are then aggregated using standard statistical techniques and the resulting statistics of the aggregate distribution of losses calculated.

In order to fully assess the operational risk exposure, the information on likelihood and severity of each operational risk event needs to be combined into an overall measure of operational risk. To do so we would need to estimate the correlation between the various risk exposures. This also requires more data on operational losses than most banks currently have. Therefore the BCBS recommends a conservative approach by assuming that all correlations are equal to 1 and that all individual risk exposures are added up to generate the overall risk exposure of the Bank.

The assessment process can be summarised as in Figure 1.

Although the Basel Accord does not specify which methodology banks should use in order to implement an acceptable advanced measurement approach (AMA), it does provide some guidance both in terms of the capabilities the regulators are expecting and the key components any solution should have in order to qualify. In particular, whatever specific approach a bank chooses to implement,

**Table 1** Risk-mapping matrix – deal negotiation and conclusion

| Risk driver | Risk factor | Risk | Loss | Basel loss event category (Level 3) |
|---|---|---|---|---|
| People | Quantity (sufficient staff) | Failure to conclude deals and missing of targets | Opportunity loss/lost clients | Transaction capture, execution and maintenance |
| | Quality (competent staff) | Loss due to mistakes (ie, incorrect hedging) | Market loss (eg, due to higher than intended VAR) | Transaction capture, execution and maintenance |
| | Criticality (key staff) | Foregone clients/business due to loss of key individuals | Opportunity loss/lost clients | – |
| | Failure (unauthorised behaviour) | Rogue trading, fraud, etc | Direct financial loss or unanticipated market loss | Unauthorised activity |
| Process | Quantity (existing process can handle all instances) | Foregone business (ie, inability to obtain approval) | Opportunity loss/lost clients/ unauthorised deals/ unsuitable products | Suitability, disclosure and fiduciary |
| | Quality (appropriate processes) | Foregone business (ie, delays in process) | Opportunity loss/lost clients | Transaction capture, execution and maintenance |
| | Criticality (appropriate process unavailable) | Failure to conclude deals (ie, key process unavailable and no backup) | Opportunity loss/lost clients | Transaction capture, execution and maintenance |
| | Failure | Rogue trading, fraud, etc | Direct financial loss or unanticipated market loss | Unauthorised activity |
| Technology | Quantity (system capacity) | Failure to conclude deals (ie, trading platform too slow) | Opportunity loss/lost clients | Transaction capture, execution and maintenance |

| | | | | |
|---|---|---|---|---|
| | Quality (incorrect market info) | Error (ie, wrong pricing) due to incorrect info | Market loss (eg, due to higher-than-intended VAR) | Transaction capture, execution and maintenance |
| | Criticality (critical application) | Failure to conclude deals (ie, trading platform unavailable) | Opportunity loss/lost clients | Transaction capture, execution and maintenance |
| | Failure (infrastructure breakdown) | Inability to conduct business | Opportunity loss/lost clients | Systems |
| External dependencies | Clients | Foregone business due to loss of key clients | Opportunity loss/lost clients | – |
| | Regulators | Compliance failure | Fines or other sanctions | Improper business or market practices |
| | Suppliers | Unavailability of key inputs | Opportunity loss or market loss | Vendors and suppliers |
| | Competitors | Foregone business | Opportunity loss | – |

**Table 2** Results of management's assessment – deal negotiation and conclusion

| Basel loss event category (Level 3) | Probability | Expected severity (US$) | Worst-case loss (US$) |
|---|---|---|---|
| Transaction capture, execution and maintenance | 10 times a year | 10,000 | 1,000,000 |
| Unauthorised activity | One every 5 years | 50,000,000 | 1,000,000,000 |
| Systems | 30 times a year | 50,000 | 750,000 |

**Figure 1** Scenario-based assessment

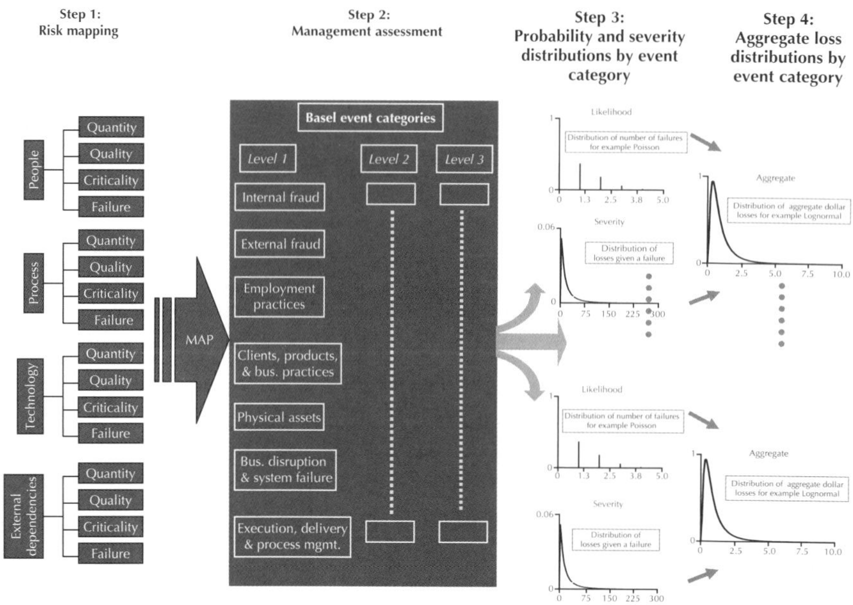


this must provide quantitative estimates at a 99.9% confidence level, classified and mapped according to Basel loss and business categories. Such an approach should derive the quantitative measure of operational risk on the basis of a reasoned combination of:

- internal data;
- external data;
- scenario analysis; and

- ❑ factors reflecting the business environment and internal control systems.

The key challenge in building a measurement process on the basis of the elements and according to these criteria lies in the need for integrating information of a very diverse nature. The overall measurement process comprises the following key steps:

1. *Risk mapping*. Risks and controls are identified and mapped with reference to business activities and related risk factors.
2. *Management assessment*. Risks and controls are assessed by management in terms of probability and impact during an interactive exercise with the business units concerned.
3. *Value-at-risk*. Probability and impact data are then fed into a statistical model[2] to derive an overall measure (by loss event category and by business unit) of operational risk. This measure is based on a one-year holding period and corresponds to the 99.9th percentile of the estimated distribution of operational risk losses (for a complete methodological review see Cruz, 2002).
4. *Statistical information*. In the form of historical frequency and severity of losses, can be used by managers both as a basis for assessment and to periodically adjust estimates as new information becomes available over time. Bayesian inference (see Bayes, 1763) provides a theoretical basis for integrating management's estimates with loss data by systematically updating loss distributions with empirical data.[3]
5. *External data*. The updated results are then integrated by the operational risk function on the basis of the information contained in a database of external operational losses for those loss categories that either have not been identified in the management's assessment or for which internal data are insufficient.
6. *Business environment and internal control factors*. The resulting measure is further updated on the basis of the results of the operational risk scorecard and on the basis of the results of the statistical analysis of historical operational losses.

The quality of the business and control environment can be factored in through a set of key risk indicators covering operational risk across the main dimensions of business activities and controls. An operational risk scorecard is a structured set of indicators of the exposure to operational risk supported by a consistent aggregation

**Table 3** Operational risk scorecard

| | Corporate finance | | | Trading & sales | | | Retail banking | | | Commercial banking | | | Payment and settlement | | | Agency services & custody | | | Asset management | | | Retail brokerage | | |
|---|---|---|---|---|---|---|---|---|---|---|---|---|---|---|---|---|---|---|---|---|---|---|---|---|
| | Ind | Unit | Weight | Ind | Unit | Weight | Ind | Unit | Weight | Ind | Unit | Weight | Ind | Unit | Weight | Ind | Unit | Weight | Ind | Unit | Weight | Ind | Unit | Weight |
| Risk driver | | | | | | | | | | | | | | | | | | | | | | | | |
| Activity | | | | | | | | | | | | | | | | | | | | | | | | |
| Complexity | | | | | | | | | | | | | | | | | | | | | | | | |
| People | | | | | | | | | | | | | | | | | | | | | | | | |
| Process | | | | | | | | | | | | | | | | | | | | | | | | |
| Systems | | | | | | | | | | | | | | | | | | | | | | | | |
| Aggr indicator | | | | | | | | | | | | | | | | | | | | | | | | |
| | N | | Weight | N | | Weight | N | | Weight | N | | Weight | N | | Weight | N | | Weight | N | | Weight | N | | Weight |
| Corrective actions | | | | | | | | | | | | | | | | | | | | | | | | |
| New procedures | | | | | | | | | | | | | | | | | | | | | | | | |
| Information systems | | | | | | | | | | | | | | | | | | | | | | | | |
| HR and training | | | | | | | | | | | | | | | | | | | | | | | | |

**Figure 2** Scenario-based AMA

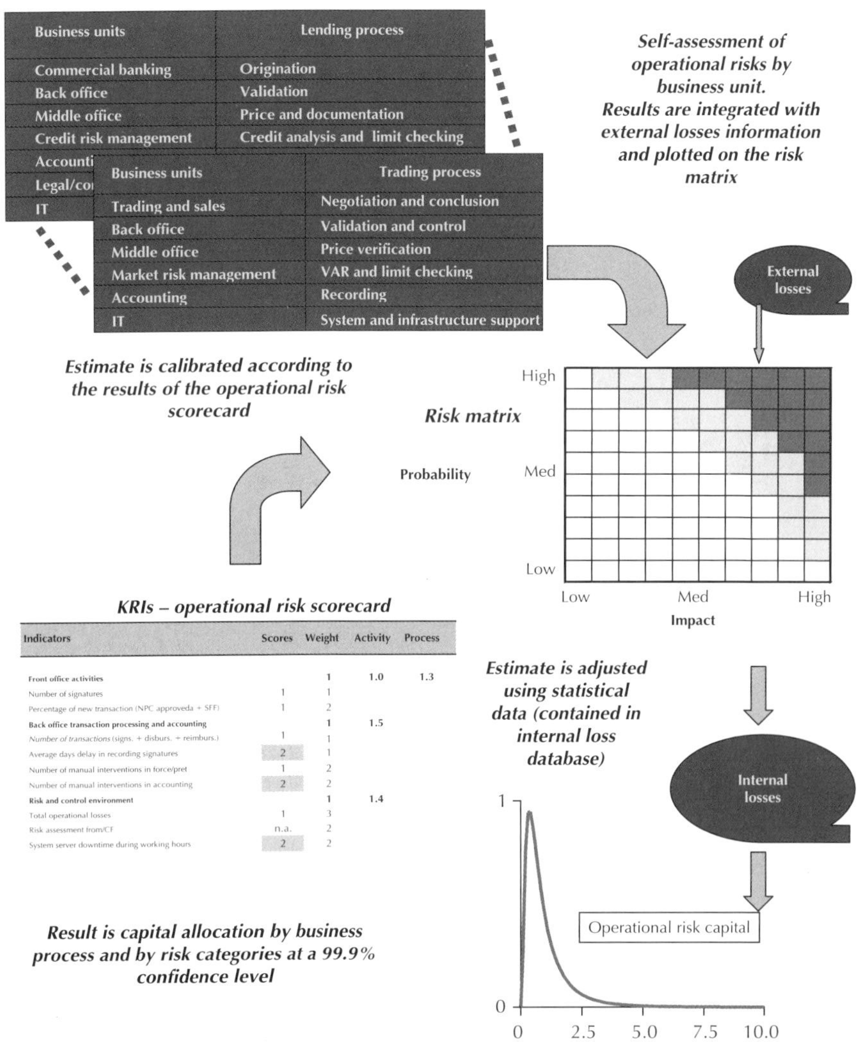


mechanism that can produce one or more summary scores of risk. In a previous paper (Scandizzo and Setola, 2003) I have explored the application of a scorecard approach to the measurement of operational risk, assessing both its reliability as a risk-management tool and the practicalities of its implementation. Table 3 provides a sample structure for an operational risk scorecard.

Scores by business unit can be used to calibrate estimates of risk capital and account for changes in the business and control environment in a forward-looking way. Figure 2 outlines the key steps in a scenario-based AMA process of operational risk assessment.

## SCENARIO ANALYSIS AND HIGH-SEVERITY EVENTS

It should be clear from the discussion in the previous section that scenario analysis is a very expensive and in general not very efficient process. It involves collecting very heterogeneous data, historical and statistical as well as operational, and combining them with intelligence, qualitative and quantitative, about the future. Therefore, it requires complex and cumbersome data processing, but also the contribution of experts, people who can provide suggestions, estimations and educated guesses about what might happen in certain contexts. Such experts will be required to take time off their day jobs to provide insights on scenarios, but it will be risk managers' responsibility to ask the right questions and to make the best use of their (limited) time.

It follows that scenario analysis is a tool that should not be abused and that should be applied where it can add the most value. There is no point in constructing scenarios around well-known situations or about events that have already happened several times. Very little could be added by interrogating experts whose judgement will be inevitably biased by the existing historical information. On the other hand, experts' assessment may be invaluable when it comes to high-impact events whose likelihood can only be guessed.

High-frequency, low-severity (HFLS) losses are normally linked to repetitive transactions and somewhat caused by the failure of getting some part of the process to work flawlessly. For example, to the extent that some manual activity cannot be automated, performing such activity in a transaction-intensive business will give rise to a certain error rate. That is how the majority of losses in the settlement/payment area are generated.[4]

Low-frequency, high-severity (LFHS) losses, on the other hand, are due to substantial failures that should not have happened in the first place, to breakdowns, not only unexpected, but that are not part of the normal course of operations and for which by definition no reliable statistics are available. They happen because something has gone very wrong not only where the actual loss has taken place, but also at a higher and more fundamental level. In other words, it is never just a mistake, a software bug, a process design flaw – although all of the above do normally happen – but also, and more critically, a strategic mistake, a hole in the internal control system, a flaw in corporate governance.

Another important point about extreme losses is the relevant role that they play in shaping the overall risk profile and, as a consequence, in determining any economic capital requirement. As shown by Jenkins and others in an instructive series of simulations (see Jenkins, Slade and Street, 2005), not only is economic capital mainly driven by extreme losses, but also, for the same increase in the confidence level, the capital requirement for extreme losses increases much faster then that for HFLS ones. In a simulation with a portfolio of two extreme and ten HFLS exposures they show how the two extreme risks account for 80% of the overall capital requirement at 99.9% confidence level, whereas an increase in the confidence level from 99% to 99.9% implies a threefold increase in the capital required for the two extreme losses.

This point can be more intuitively shown by looking at a classical model, nowadays of widespread use in operational risk measurement: the compound distribution model for aggregate losses. Imagine losses are generated by a certain category of operational events whose probability distribution has mean $M_e$ and variance $V_e$. Imagine also that severity of loss resulting from each event follows a probability distribution with mean $M_l$ and variance $V_l$. The compound distribution is the distribution of the aggregate losses for that event category and will have parameters:[5]

$$M = M_e \times M_l$$

$$V = M_e \times V_l + M_l^2 \times V_e$$

The variance, and hence the spread around the mean, of the resulting distribution will therefore vary with the square of the average severity of losses and only linearly with the other three parameters.

This has consequences on measurement as well as on management. Our results are especially sensitive to our estimate of the severity of losses and more so for the more severe ones. But the more severe ones are also the least frequent and therefore precisely those whose estimates are less reliable, because they are based on fewer observations. It also means that as we get closer to the tail of the distribution, for example in going from 99% to 99.9% confidence, a much larger portion of our estimate depends on fewer and less reliable information.

The other problem with extreme events is that statistics would be of little use even if plenty of historical data were available. Out of all decisions taken with the intent of strengthening the risk-and-control environment, the most forceful, and presumably incisive, are taken following high-severity events. Such decisions may affect the risk profile in a number of different ways (through changes in control procedures, systems, personnel, to name but a few), none of which any measurement model can capture in a simple and direct way. Statistical approaches will be at a loss in taking into account such changes, since historical data will reflect a risk-and-control environment that by and large no longer exists.[6] The requirement of the new Basel Accord – to base risk assessment on five years of historical data – if taken too literally will have banks generating risk capital charges on the basis of information largely unrelated to the current and, even less, the future risk-and-control environment.[7]

The true value-added of scenario analysis lies in helping us conceive the unconceivable, in giving us a glimpse of certain possible futures that would otherwise not even be taken into consideration. Anything short of this is equivalent to replacing statistical data with management's assessment on a predefined set of either historical events or abstract categories.

## A METHODOLOGY FOR THE ANALYSIS OF EXTREME SCENARIOS

We have seen earlier how the key resources that allow a bank to manage a business are also its main risk factors. People, process, technology and eternal events are at the same time at the source of operational risk and the very (and only) assets available to manage it. This happens because, unlike market and credit risk, operational risk is not product-specific. The market risk of a derivative contract depends strictly on the contract's features and on the relevant market risk factors. Once the deal is concluded, the underlying process, as well as the people and the technology involved, by and large does not matter to the related market risk exposure. It is impossible, on the other hand, to analyse the operational risk in the trading activities of a bank without a thorough understanding of the whole trading process from initial negotiation to final accounting. So we should expect the drivers of extreme risks to be the very same elements a bank should manage to build a strategy to manage those risks.

The question of how to identify (one might say conceive) extreme events, or unknown unknowns, as they have also been called, is tightly linked to the question on how to manage them. But what are the risk factors behind financial disaster? Is it possible to build a model of extreme risk drivers that is at the same time a model of the resources governing the long-term future of a bank? All the major financial disasters of the last 25 years have been the subject of extensive coverage in both popular and scholarly publications. The works briefly discussed below represent of course only a limited selection of the vast literature available.

Tschoegl (2004) discusses three famous financial debacles (Barings Brothers, Daiwa Bank and Sumitomo Corporation) and finds that in all three cases fundamental failures in governance allowed unauthorised behaviour to happen and go unnoticed for a long time.

Kimball (2000) analyses evidence from a similar set of cases (Baring Brothers, Metalgessellschaft, Sumitomo Corporation, Chase Manhattan/Drysdale and Orange County) to point out how each case exemplifies one or more fundamental failures in the risk-management process.

Jensen (1993) finds a strong relation between firms' failures and ineffective internal controls systems and has identified internal controls as one force capable of mitigating the agency problem between managers and shareholders.

Stultz (1996) discusses two cases (Metalgessellschaft and Daimler Benz) where risk-management programmes turned out to be taking large market positions eventually leading to very large losses. He also suggests that the primary goal of risk management is to eliminate the probability of costly, lower-tail outcomes, in other words, extreme scenarios.

Finally, the complex subject of how deeply flawed financial strategies can be devised from apparently reasonable assumptions, and at the hands of the best minds in the industry, has been analysed in a number of interesting works, one of the most fascinating of which is that of Taleb (2004).

What all these works consistently show is that financial disasters systematically stem out of a small number of key risk factors and that these factors correspond to the institutional and organisational tools companies put in place to mitigate risks. A number of common elements appear in all the analyses as the key determinants of the (extreme) financial losses. These can be described as business strategy, internal controls, risk management and overall corporate governance of the institution and can be seen as the high-level institutional equivalent of the classical set of operational risk factors (people, processes, systems and external events).

Table 4 summarises the key extreme risk drivers in relation to some of the most high-profile financial scandals of the last twenty years.

Once we have identified the key risk drivers and failures that are systematically behind extreme events, we shall consider that those failures can occur again and be more severe than in the past and, most importantly, happen simultaneously. The combination of such events can be seen in time as well as in space. Events that have occurred only elsewhere can happen in our institution together with events that have happened to us already, and sequentially as well as simultaneously. This process of combining events across time and space dimensions can be pictured as in Figure 3.

It follows that an essential set of building blocks for extreme scenario analysis will consist of the following items:

- ❑ database of internal events and losses (by risk category and by business unit);
- ❑ database of external events and losses (by risk category and business unit, industry-wide);
- ❑ risk and internal control map; and
- ❑ connectivity map.

In order to consistently build a set of extreme scenarios, we should, for each business unit and for each loss event category, do the following.

(1) Select the worst loss event from the internal and/or external database or, alternatively, select a potential worst-case loss event based on management opinions. This second alternative may be used in the case of new products, systems or business practices.

**Table 4** Major banking disasters – risk drivers

| | Corporate governance | Internal control framework | Risk management | Business strategy |
|---|---|---|---|---|
| Metalgesellschaft | Lack of communication and poor understanding of risks at senior executive level | – | No effective limits system | Delivery contracts (non-marked to market) hedged with futures swaps (marked to market) |
| Barings | No board supervision | Same person in charge of front and back office | No independent verification of positions | Naked exposure to Nikkei's volatility |
| Sumitomo | Lack of supervision/ involvement by senior manager | Trade confirmation sent directly to the head trader, Mr Hamanaka (bypassing back office) | No limit monitoring or independent reporting of positions | Hedging forward sales by selling out-of-the-money puts, resulting in huge gamma risk on copper prices |
| Daiwa | Failure to supervise and, subsequently, to disclose | Same person in charge of trading and back office | No independent check of custody accounts | – |
| NatWest | – | Lack of back office checks and escalation of exceptions | No independent verification of implied volatilities[8] | Hard push towards investment banking[9] |
| Credit Lyonnais | Political interferences, state guarantees and government-run bailouts | Poor internal controls leaving the bank exposed to internal and external fraud | Gross underestimation of the bank's true risk position | Expansive strategy resulting in a massive portfolio of low-quality assets |
| Allied Irish Banks | Unclear responsibilities and reporting lines between AIB and Allfirst (the mother company) | Rusnak convinced back office staff to forego normal procedures and not systematically request trade confirmations | Lack of independent VAR calculation | – |

**Figure 3** Events combination across time and space

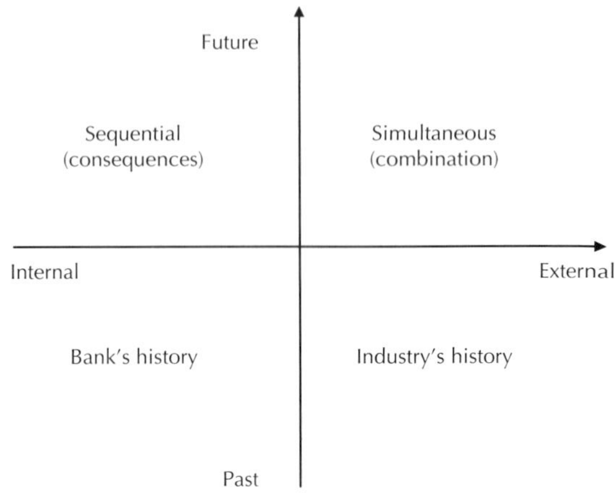


(2) Identify the key elements in strategy, governance, internal controls and/or risk management that ideally should prevent a disastrous outcome – and assume they fail altogether.

(3) Spell out the consequences of each failure, also taking into account connectivity and indirect consequences. A bank is not just a collection of businesses, as its various components work together and are interdependent. The overall impact of a single failure can go well beyond the loss taken in the unit that originally failed.

(4) Analyse the combined impact. The whole can be larger than the sum of its parts and it is usually this nonlinearity of consequences that provides the most devastating surprises.[10] The ability to explore such consequences lies at the heart of scenario analysis and it is far from being a codified technique. However, a good way of proceeding, at least of making sure the tail of the loss distribution has been thoroughly explored, is to consider a catastrophic loss (the minimum loss necessary to wipe out the company's capital and cause bankruptcy) and ask whether such a loss could be caused by the scenario in question. If the answer is yes, the assessment is made; if it is no, then one can work backwards by reducing the amount until a more reasonable amount is estimated.

In the context of operational risk capital calculation, the results of this analysis can be used, as suggested in the Basel Accord, in two ways. One possibility is to supplement the estimate of the aggregate distribution of losses derived for each loss event category through the methodology described earlier. This can be done by interpreting the resulting impact as, for instance, the loss corresponding to the 99.9th (or other) percentile thereby "adding a tail" to the distribution.

The other possibility is to repeat steps 1 to 3 a number of times in order to construct a scenario that is made up of simultaneous extreme events. The result is a scenario that does not correspond to a single loss event category and that can rather be used as a sort of stress test of the basic assumptions of the operational risk model employed by the bank.

The following section discusses some case studies where failures of a diverse nature and from different parts of the business combine to produce catastrophic scenarios.

## SCENARIO IDENTIFICATION – CASE STUDIES

I have selected the following case studies to exemplify the methodology discussed in the previous section. None of them corresponds in full to a specific historical event, but in each of them the reader will easily find elements of some famous cases. This is a key feature all scenarios share, as it is extremely difficult to construct scenarios out of events that have never happened. On the other hand, known events and circumstances can happen in conjunction with entirely new ones and can combine, giving raise to totally new, and unexpected, consequences. For each case I identify the key failures, the individual consequences, the related losses as well as the overall final impact of the resulting scenario.

### Scenario 1: Lending and investment banking

Imagine a bank that is active in both investment banking and lending. Its investment banking arm advises a major client in the chemical industry on a strategy to hedge the risks of movements in the price of key raw materials based on the usage of complex derivative products. At the same time its commercial banking arm finances the same company in the construction of a large industrial facility.

Unfortunately, raw-material prices move in such a way as to reveal a large gap between the way the hedging solution works in practice and the company's management understanding of it. As a consequence, the hedge is unwound at great cost. At the same time a completely unforeseen environmental damage caused by the new industrial facility causes a wave of litigation that, given its high profile (and its deep pockets), the bank cannot manage to avoid. It also emerges that an early leak of information about such impending litigations had come out from commercial banking to the investment banking side, leading to a substantial sale of shares of the company the bank was holding. Entities and events are depicted in Figure 4.

In terms of individual failures the situation can be summarised as follows:

- flawed business decision – unsuitable derivative products – market loss – client sues for damages;
- poor risk assessment – project causes environmental damage – third party sues for damages; and
- internal control failure – ineffective Chinese wall – regulators impose penalties.

Table 5 summarises the analysis of this scenario.

In itself, each individual failure, although potentially expensive, is not fatal. Regulatory fines are incurred all the time for noncompliance and lending departments routinely overlook the potential for damage to third parties or to the environment, as this is not, strictly speaking, the bank's responsibility. Also, the sale of unsuitable hedging products, although potentially damaging to the bank's reputation, would normally result in a settlement or in punitive damages to be paid.

However, in this case the combined impact of regulatory intervention, client and third-party litigation generates a catastrophic loss of reputation, forcing senior management to bow out. The subsequent loss of confidence in the market allows a rival to perform a successful takeover. Similar dynamics have been at work in the cases of Arthur Andersen and Refco, where the actual financial losses were in no way threatening company's existence, but where the market reacted (overreacted, perhaps?) by questioning the very soundness of the business.

**Figure 4** A lending/investment banking scenario

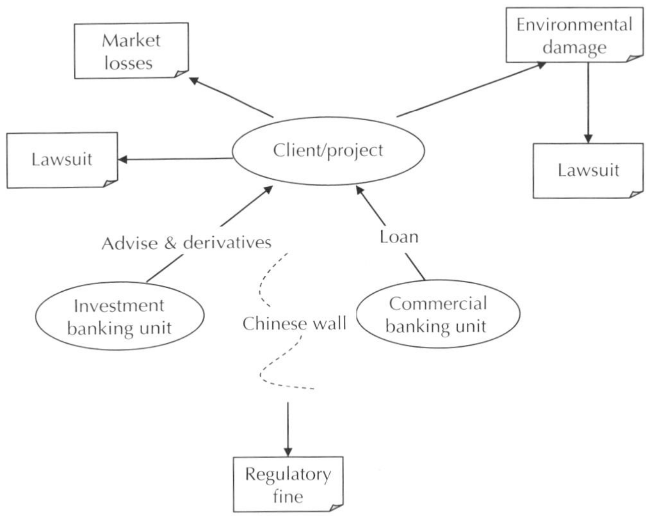


**Table 5** Lending/investment banking – scenario analysis

| | Failure | Immediate consequences | Loss events | Scenario impact |
|---|---|---|---|---|
| Corporate governance | – | – | – | – |
| Internal control framework | Ineffective Chinese wall | Bank trades on insider (client) information | Regulator imposes penalties | Major reputation fallout forces management's resignation with subsequent drop in share price and competitors' takeover |
| Risk management | Poor risk assessment | Project causes environmental damage | Third party sues for damages | |
| Business strategy | Unsuitable derivative products sold to client | Client suffers market loss | Client sues for damages | |

### Scenario 2: Trading

The following scenario will sound familiar to most readers in the operational risk trade. Imagine a senior trader who is in charge of both front and back office. The bank has no independent assessment of market positions, because risk management relies on data provided by the front office itself. Top management does not

**Figure 5** A trading scenario

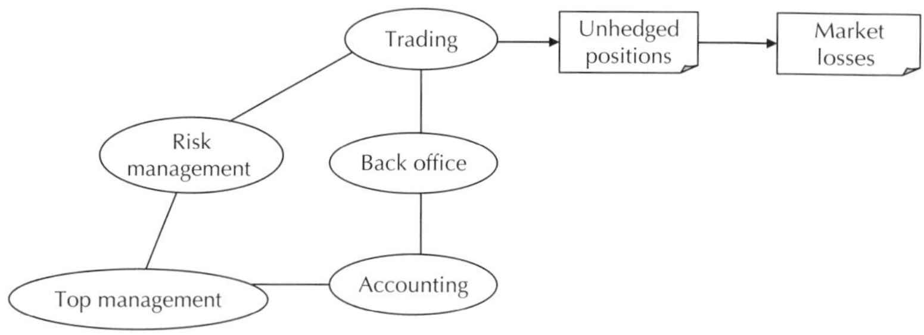


bother to supervise the trading desk as far as it continues to post high profits. Following some embarrassing but totally inconsequential market losses, the senior trader decides to conceal the losses and to engage in riskier and riskier trades in an attempt at recovery. Needless to say, losses pile up without being reported while huge, unhedged market positions continue to grow. Entities and events are depicted in Figure 5.

When finally the size of the losses is such that they can no longer be concealed it appears that the bank's own funds are not enough to ensure it remains a going concern and bankruptcy is inevitable.

Table 6 gives the usual summary of the scenario.

### Scenario 3: Trading, Continued

Imagine a trade executed by the funding desk on behalf of the equity desk to fund an equity deal with an external counterpart. A ticket is generated in the front office; it is confirmed and settled in the back office; profit-and-loss data are generated in the middle office. A technology group, which in turn buys part of its products and services form an external vendor, supports all of these units.

Not only can a failure in any point of this network cause a financial loss, but also the impact can go well beyond the unit where the original failure took place. The inability of one of the external vendors to provide a timely service can lead to a failure in the technology group. A failure in technology can cause a failure in the back office and as a consequence a loss for the funding desk. But this can at the same time impact the equity desk transaction, causing an additional loss, and make external counterparts dissatisfied,

**Table 6** Trading – scenario analyses

<table>
<tr><th></th><th>Failure</th><th>Immediate consequences</th><th>Loss events</th><th>Scenario impact</th></tr>
<tr><td>Corporate governance</td><td>No board supervision of trading activities</td><td>Audit reports and "abnormal" profits go unchecked</td><td rowspan="4">Catastrophic market loss</td><td rowspan="4">Insufficient capital to absorb losses. Controlled administration and eventually takeover from another bank</td></tr>
<tr><td>Internal control framework</td><td>No segregation between front and back office</td><td>No detection of unauthorised trades</td></tr>
<tr><td>Risk management</td><td>No independent pricing and position risk measurement</td><td>No reporting of VAR limit breaches</td></tr>
<tr><td>Business strategy</td><td>Sale of "naked" options in order to show profits</td><td>Huge unhedged position</td></tr>
</table>

causing the bank to forgo future business opportunities. We can represent this web of interrelationships graphically in the following way.

Now imagine that the IT vendor systematically fails to deliver on its service level agreement and that, as a consequence, a multiplication of the settlement failures takes place. The problem is detected only after a long delay because there is no independent check on the correct and successful execution of payments. This is not promptly reported to senior management outside back office because the operational risk function reports only capital-at-risk numbers without any information on the underlying operational failures. Furthermore, as neither IT nor back office takes responsibility for managing the relationship with the vendor, the situation is allowed to continue uncorrected. Entities and events are depicted in Figure 6.

Eventually, counterparty claims and front-office complaints make the situation impossible to ignore, but when finally corrective actions are taken – replacing the vendor, reviewing the outsourcing strategy, redrafting back-office and risk-management procedures – a substantial damage has already been done in the form of direct losses, lost business and loss of key employees in the front office. In the long run the loss of reputation with counterparts and potential employees thwarts the bank's plans to build a successful proprietary trading

**Table 7** Trading continued – scenario analysis

| | Failure | Immediate consequences | Loss events | Scenario impact |
|---|---|---|---|---|
| Corporate governance | Unclear roles and responsibilities | No action to ensure vendor's compliance with SLAs | Penalties and interest | Failure to build a successful proprietary trading desk and loss of share price |
| Internal control framework | Lack of back office controls | Late detection of failures | Foregone business | |
| Risk management | Inadequate operational risk management | No timely information to senior management | Loss of key employees | |
| Business strategy | Flawed outsourcing strategy | Repeated settlement failures | | |

**Figure 6** Another trading scenario

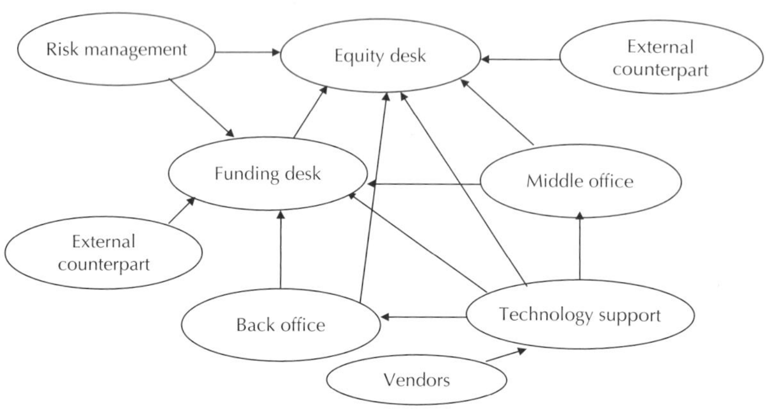


desk with a substantial loss of value to shareholders. Table 7 gives a summary of the scenario.

## CONCLUSIONS

In this chapter we have examined scenario analysis in the assessment of operational risk within the framework provided by the advanced measurement approach envisaged in the second Basel Accord.

From the practitioner's perspective, the advantages of scenario analysis can be summarised in the following way.

- It provides for a lesser need for historical information. Scenario analysis is mainly based on management assessment and in this context even a very scarce set of statistical information could be used to supplement management's judgement and to provide useful backtesting information.
- It is forward-looking. Managers will be the best-placed individuals to be aware and anticipate changes in the business environment and will know whether or not a past event can repeat itself in light of current procedures and controls.
- Can incorporate key risk indicators (KRIs) and business and control environment information. KRIs and scorecards can be used to effectively refine management assessment by providing detailed and focused information directly into the scenario analysis process.
- Can be used to build the tail of a distribution. Scenario assessment can be used to correct the estimate of the loss distribution, and hence of the capital requirements, by providing theoretical "extreme values".

Several disadvantages of course exist and can be described as follows.

- *Subjective and potentially unreliable.* No matter how well prepared and executed, it is inevitable that the same exercise performed with different people will give different results. Choosing the right stakeholders, ensuring a proper validation process and constantly updating the results are all key steps in ensuring the reliability of scenario-based estimates.
- *No way to know it is comprehensive.* Especially when it comes to extreme events, constructed scenarios may never happen as they are foreseen or never happen at all. Also, the possibility will always exist that something entirely unforeseen and unimagined will happen.
- *Time- and resource-consuming.* Scenario analysis is people-based and it adds more value the more competent and prepared such people are. Staff with these characteristics are expensive and scarce. Also, the processes to ensure data and result quality are

more cumbersome than with other techniques and hence more expensive as well.

Although, as already widely adopted in the industry, scenario analysis can be successfully applied in conjunction with management assessment of elementary scenarios corresponding to the individual event loss categories defined in the Basel Accord, a key contribution of this technique is in identifying and analysing complex and catastrophic combination of events. Such extreme scenarios are normally overlooked in risk-management reports on the grounds that they are difficult to conceive, let alone assess, given the lack of available specific data, such as historical losses.

Nevertheless the discipline of constructing complex and entirely new scenarios from simpler historical occurrences and variations thereof is not only technically feasible, but also very worthwhile, as it can afford management a window on the elusive "fat tails" that lie behind so many financial disasters. Furthermore, it provides a means to systematically address what a substantial body of financial literature identifies as the key value-added of risk management: the prevention or avoidance of financial distress.

1 This is called either the *scorecard approach* or the *risk drivers and controls approach*.

2 The distribution of the *aggregate losses*, a term taken from the insurance industry, like most of the mathematics involved, may then be derived in a number of ways, both analytically and numerically. Alternatives, especially useful with more complex combinations of distributions, are the use of convolution integrals or Monte Carlo simulations. By analogy with market and credit risk, the percentile of the resulting distribution corresponding to the desired level of confidence is then called *operational value at risk*.

3 Bayesian inference is a statistical inference in which probabilities are interpreted not as frequencies or proportions or the like, but rather as degrees of belief. It uses an estimate of the degree of belief in a hypothesis before the advent of some evidence to give a numerical value to the degree of belief in the hypothesis after the advent of the evidence. Bayes's theorem also provides a method for adjusting degrees of belief in the light of new information.

4 Conversely, there are activities that are normally performed automatically, but at the expense of certain controls, such as cheque clearing below a threshold amount, which makes the clearing of a certain number of forged cheques inevitable, albeit without too severe consequences most of the time.

5 The interested reader can consult Klugman, Panjer and Willmot (1998) for a thorough mathematical treatment of this subject.

6 This may be seen as a risk-management equivalent of the famous Lucas Critique (Lucas, 1976), whereby Nobel prizewinner R. E. Lucas argued that using a model with fixed coefficients estimated from historical data to evaluate the consequences of new policies would mislead because (i) the change in policy will affect expectations and (ii) the estimated coefficients are sensitive to changes in expectations.

7 Think, for example, of how much the recent overhaul in corporate governance, enshrined in US legislation by the Sarbanes–Oxley Act, will impact the risk and control environment of most large banks and of how irrelevant extreme loss data predating such changes already are.

8 The key input in the pricing of NatWest option portfolio.

9 Although this was not proved by any subsequent investigation, public perception was widespread that the severe mistakes in option pricing were in part due to NatWest's attempt to break into a business for which it was not fully prepared.

10 When Hurricane Katrina struck the Gulf Coast of the United States in August 2005, the expected consequences of a Category 5 hurricane were well known, as were those of a breach in the levees protecting New Orleans from the waters of Lake Pontchartrain. However, nobody (at least nobody in a position of responsibility) had seriously considered what would happen in the case that both events happened at the same time.

## REFERENCES

**Anders, U. and G. J. van der Brink,** 2004, "Implementing a Basel II Scenario-Based AMA for Operational Risk", in M. K. Ong (ed), *The Basel Handbook* (London: Risk Books).

**Bayes, T.,** 1763, "An Essay Towards Solving a Problem in the Doctrine of Chances", *Philosophical Transactions of the Royal Society of London* **53**.

**BCBS,** 2004, "International Convergence of Capital Measurements and Capital Standards", Basel, June.

**Borges, J. L.,** 1941, "El jardín de senderos que se bifurcan", Buenos Aires, Sur.

**Cruz, M.,** 2002, *Modelling, Measuring and Hedging Operational Risk* (New York: J. Wiley & Sons).

**Federal Reserve Bank of New York,** 2003, "Supervisory Guidance on Operational Risk, Advanced Measurement Approaches for Regulatory Capital", New York, July.

**FSA,** 2005, "Stress Testing", Discussion Paper, May.

**Jenkins, T., J. Slade, and A. Street,** 2005, "A Practitioner's Guide to the Advanced Measurement Approach to Operational Risk Under Basel II", Institute of Actuaries of Australia 2005 Biennial Convention, 8–11, May.

**Jensen, M. C.,** 1993, "The Modern Industrial Revolution, Exit and the Failure of Internal Control Systems", *Journal of Finance* **48(3)**, pp 831–80.

**Kimball R. C.,** 2000, "Failures in Risk Management", New England Economic Review, pp 3–12, January.

**Lucas, R. E.,** 1976, "Econometric Policy Evaluation: A Critique", in K. Brunner and A. H. Meltzer (eds), *"The Phillips Curve and Labor Markets"*, Carnegie–Rochester Conference Series on Public Policy, Vol. 1, pp 19–46, Reprinted in R. E. Lucas, Jr, 1976, *Studies in Modern Business Cycle Theory* (Cambridge, MA: MIT Press), pp 104–30.

**Kahn, H.,** 1967, *The Year 2000: A Framework for Speculation on the Next Thirty-Three Years* (New York: Macmillan).

**Klugman, S. A., H. H. Panjer, and G. E. Willmot,** 1998, *Loss Models, From Data to Decisions* (New York: J. Wiley & Sons)

**Linneman, R. E. and J. D. Kennell,** 1997, "Shirt-Sleeve Approach to Long-Range Plans", *Harvard Business Review* **55(2)**, p 141, March/April.

**Scandizzo, S.,** 2003, "Connectivity and the Measurement of Operational Risk: An Input–output Approach", *Soft Computing* **7(8)**, pp 516–25, August.

**Scandizzo, S.,** 2005, "Risk Mapping and Key Risk Indicators in Operational Risk Management", *Economic Notes* **34(2)**, pp 231–56, July.

**Scandizzo, S. and R. Setola,** 2003, "Mark up the Scorecard", *Operational Risk* **4(12)**, December.

**Stultz, R.,** 1996, "Rethinking Risk Management", *Journal of Applied Corporate Finance*, pp 8–24, Fall, reprinted in C. L. Culp and M. H. Miller (eds), 1999, *Corporate Hedging in Theory and Practice: Lessons from Metallgesellschaft* (London: Risk Publications), and in G. W. Brown and D. H. Chew (eds), 1999, *Corporate Risk: Strategies and Management* (London: Risk Publications).

**Taleb, N. N.,** 2004, *Fooled by Randomness* (New York: Thomson, Texere).

**Tschoegl, A. E.,** 2004, "The Key to Risk Management: Management", in M. Frenkel, U. Hommel and M. Rudolf (eds), *Risk management: Challenge and Opportunity* (Berlin**[AA1]**, Springer Verlag).

**van der Heijden, K.,** 1996, *Scenarios: The Art of Strategic Conversation* (New York: John Wiley & Sons).

**Various Authors,** 2003, "Modern Risk Management: A History" (London: Risk Books, London).

# 10

# *Key Risk Indicators – Their Role in Operational Risk Management and Measurement*

**Jonathan Davies, Mike Finlay, Tara McLenaghen, Duncan Wilson**

Risk*Business* International Ltd

In comparison with other operational risk management and measurement tools such as loss data (internal, public and consortium), risk-and-control assessments, capital allocation and performance measurement, key risk indicators (KRIs) remain one of the outstanding action items on most firms' to-do lists, along with scenario analysis. KRIs are not new, but, up until recently, attempts to implement such programmes have often been characterised as less than effective. We believe that there are emerging best practices for KRI programmes that overcome some of the traditional challenges in KRI implementations. Further, we believe that investment in KRI programmes will reap many benefits, including the ability to clearly convey risk appetite, optimise risk and return, and improve the likelihood of achieving primary business goals through more effective operational risk management.

In this chapter, we will seek to demystify KRIs, understand the basic fundamentals in identifying, specifying, selecting and implementing quality indicators, and consider how to monitor and report on them, in conjunction with other useful operational risk management information, to create powerful management reporting. We will also examine the potential for more advanced applications of KRIs, touching on the measurement of risk for correlation purposes, and the potential for composite indicators as well as KRI benchmarking. Finally, we will overview an industry KRI initiative which can help many firms get their own KRI programmes started.

## THE FUNDAMENTALS OF A KRI PROGRAMME

As with so many aspects of operational risk management, one of the biggest challenges in creating a KRI programme is communication – both in understanding how market practice is evolving and in explaining objectives and policy internally. In this section, we will describe what KRIs are, how they can be used, as well as the importance and value of establishing a common language and structure to support KRI programme implementation. We will then outline the main steps and considerations in selecting KRIs, as the foundation for any KRI programme.

### What is an indicator?

KRIs are measurable metrics or indicators that track exposure or loss, or, as one person put it, "trouble". Anything that can perform this function may be considered a risk indicator. The indicator becomes key when it tracks an especially important exposure, or it does so especially well, or ideally both. In operational risk, we are interested in KRIs that monitor operational risk. Operational risk can be defined as the risk of loss resulting from inadequate or failed processes, systems, human performance or external events.

The number of customer complaints is an example of a *risk* indicator. As customer complaints increase, the probability that there are some underlying and potentially systemic mistakes and errors of judgement being made is likely to rise. In other words, there is a rationale for thinking that, at least in some ranges, changes in the value of this indicator are likely to be associated with changes in operational risk exposure or operational loss experience.

The number of customer complaints is also an example of a *common* indicator – an indicator that would seem to be relevant at most points of risk in an organisation. Similarly, staff turnover and the number of audit points may also be considered common indicators. Most indicators are not common, but, rather, specific to individual businesses or processes. For example, the frequency of unmatched trades would be a predictor of losses arising from the settlement process within a retail brokerage but is irrelevant to other businesses.

**Figure 1** Uses for KRIs

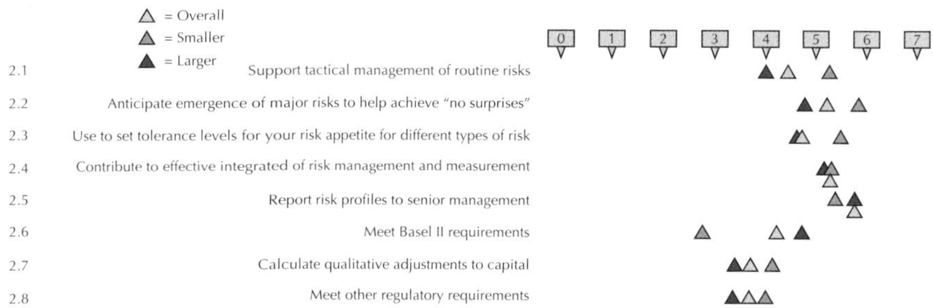


0 = *"unimportant"*; 7 = *"very important"*

The frequency of unmatched trades is also an example of a *performance* indicator – in this case, of performance in the trade-matching activity. In fact, one person's KRI is another's performance indicator (KPI) and a third person's control-effectiveness indicator, Key Control Effectiveness Indicator (KCI). The preferred terminology depends on the user's perspective and the activity in which they are engaged, but, not unexpectedly, there is often some overlap.

## Uses for KRIs

Financial institutions are interested in KRI programmes for many reasons. The Risk Management Association (RMA) conducted a survey of 38 financial institutions in May 2005 on the subject of KRI programmes.[1] As shown in Figure 1 they found that, while most are still in planning stages, they intended to pursue virtually all of the specified objectives for such programmes (see Risk Management Association, 2005).

The highest priority programme objective among respondents to this survey was to use KRIs to report risk profiles to senior management. The next-highest objectives were to create a no-surprise environment and to integrate risk management and measurement effectively. If KRIs are focused on the areas of most significant risk, then they should provide managers with reasonably clear direction as to what levers to pull to reduce exposure, as well as quick feedback on their effectiveness.

Communicating risk appetite (through the setting of KRI thresholds and triggers for action) and the day-to-day management of

**Figure 2** How KRIs help

= Overall

| | | Not started at all | Planned | Underway | Mostly finished or rolled out |
|---|---|---|---|---|---|
| 9.1 | At the tactical level in day-to-day management for | | | | |
| 9.1.1 | Identifying disquieting activity patterns | 12 | 12 | 6 | 6 |
| 9.1.2 | Escalating risk-taking decisionmaking | 13 | 15 | 7 | 1 |
| 9.1.3 | Escalating situation management decisionmaking | 14 | 15 | 6 | 2 |
| 9.1.4 | Reporting control performance | 10 | 13 | 11 | 2 |
| 9.1.5 | Monitoring process improvement impact | 14 | 15 | 4 | 3 |
| 9.1.6 | With specific thresholds that trigger intervention or escalation | 11 | 18 | 6 | 2 |
| 9.2 | At the corporate level for | | | | |
| 9.2.1 | Aggregating, analysing and reporting risks profile changes | 9 | 18 | 5 | 4 |
| 9.2.2 | Aggregating, analysing and reporting control performance | 11 | 20 | 4 | 1 |
| 9.2.3 | Estimating capital | 20 | 10 | 3 | 2 |
| 9.2.4 | With specific triggers for senior management intervention | 14 | 18 | 1 | 4 |

*Note*: The numbers of respondents are shown in each cell

routine risks in various financial services processes were also viewed to be important objectives.

The RMA survey also asked respondents to indicate how they expected KRIs to help them achieve specific business-related objectives. Again, most financial institutions were still in the planning stages, but expressed their intent for virtually all of the specified objectives. In addition to those *planning* for these objectives (one-third to one-half of respondents), a further one-sixth to two-fifths were already rolling out plans to achieve these same objectives, or they had completed their implementation. The most popular objectives are to aggregate, analyse and report risk profile changes at the corporate level and to report control performance at the business-unit level. Also, most organisations intend or already use KRIs with specific thresholds that trigger intervention or escalation. The only objective that received notably lower focus was that of estimating capital, where the majority of respondents indicated that they have not started to think about this potential application of KRIs.

### Value of a common language and structure for KRIs

KRIs are not new, but they are very topical at the moment, being widely viewed as having the potential to make operational risk management a more effective discipline. Financial services regulators in particular have expressed interest in KRIs as a potentially important tool to manage operational risk. However, up to this point, the promise has not been realised for a number of reasons:

- it has been difficult to show that KRIs really track losses well;
- there is no consistency in the way organisations use KRIs – various units track the same thing but call it something different, and calculate it differently;
- KRI specifications are often incomplete or inaccurate; and, as a consequence,
- it has been difficult to aggregate, compare or interpret KRIs in a systematic way.

Clearly, the challenge is to implement KRIs in such a way as to improve consistency, relevance, transparency and completeness. To achieve this, we believe some standardisation is required across the firm and, ideally, across the financial services industry, in terms of both language and approach to KRI implementation. Increased standardisation is increasingly being demanded by regulators and supervisors (who need confidence in metrics used for capital adjustments and other purposes), rating agencies (who need defensible comparative metrics for their models) and stakeholders and auditors (as a way to develop a true understanding of exposure, on the road towards improving corporate governance).

The first step in standardisation should be use of a common language around risks, business activities and products or business lines. A logical place to begin in the development of this language is with the risk types and business lines specified in the "International Convergence of Capital Measurement and Capital Standards – a Revised Framework", commonly referred to as Basel II, although this is only a starting point. Most organisations find they need greater granularity in risk categories and business lines and they would also benefit from standardisation in the definition of specific business activities, as well as in the definitions and specification of KRIs. Benefits to the firm in developing this kind of common understanding include:

- permitting indicators to be related to specific risks in a clear and consistent way;
- permitting alignment of internal and external loss data, risk-and-control assessment results, capital and scenario analysis with KRI data for much more powerful management information and operational risk management reporting capabilities;

- reducing confusion when it comes to ensuring robust, complete coverage of all risks, be it for self-assessment, KRIs or collection and classification of loss data; and
- with the use of common KRI definitions, both internal and external benchmarking becomes much easier.

Similarly, a common structure for KRI implementation in terms of the approach used to assess risk, develop indicators, set thresholds and protocols and aggregate and report results across the whole organisation has many benefits. It:

- conveys strong sponsorship at senior levels of the organisation and a commitment to risk management;
- can be used to establish and communicate risk appetite in a deliberate and meaningful way;
- facilitates meaningful aggregation and reporting;
- allows meaningful (internal and external) comparisons;
- ensures efforts to develop KRIs and monitor risk are relevant and focused on areas of highest risk;
- provides greater consistency and assurance in the way risk issues are managed across the organisation;
- ensures robust coverage while reducing duplicative efforts in tracking and monitoring risk; and
- permits systematic adjustments to capital estimates with enhanced credibility.

So, if we can agree that there is great potential business value for a KRI programme, particularly if it is implemented in a systematic way across the organisation, with a common language and structure, then let us proceed to some of the fundamentals in getting such a programme started.

**Properties of a good indicator**

Key to the effectiveness of any KRI programme is the quality of the KRIs themselves. An assessment of KRI effectiveness largely depends on expert opinion, which is based, in turn, on knowledge of how specific business functions and processes work, where they are vulnerable, and what can affect that vulnerability. Given the inherent subjectivity implicit in most KRI programmes, there is a strong case for establishing a framework for assessing effectiveness.

**Table 1** Criteria for good KRIs

| Effectiveness | Comparability | Ease of use |
|---|---|---|
| Indicators should:<br>❑ apply to at least one specific risk and one business function or activity;<br>❑ be measurable at specific points in time;<br>❑ reflect objective measurement rather than subjective judgement;<br>❑ track at least one aspect of the loss profile or event history, such as frequency, average severity, cumulative loss or near-miss rates; and<br>❑ provide useful management information | Indicators should:<br>❑ be quantified as an amount, a percentage, or a ratio;<br>❑ be a reasonably precise and definite quantity;<br>❑ have values that are comparable over time;<br>❑ be comparable internally across businesses;<br>❑ be reported with primary values and be meaningful without interpretation to some more subjective measure;<br>❑ be auditable; and<br>❑ be identified as comparable across organisations (if in fact they are) | Indicators should:<br>❑ be available reliably on a timely basis;<br>❑ be cost-effective to collect; and<br>❑ be readily understood and communicated |

We believe that the ideal features of KRIs are that they are effective in tracking the risk, they are comparable within and outside the organisation and they are practical and easy to use. Table 1 provides some criteria for assessing indicators against these three objectives.

Along with a framework for assessing KRIs, it is helpful to develop some standards for fully specifying an indicator. It is our experience that a relatively high degree of detail is beneficial in minimising misunderstandings and in ensuring a high degree of quality and efficiency in the implementation of KRIs. This detail should include:

- ❑ full definition and description of what is collected;
- ❑ how to measure and calculate (in detail); and
- ❑ guidance for implementation (sources, collection, uses and so forth).

For example, staff turnover as an indicator could be described as the turnover percentage across all categories of permanent staff during the preceding month. It is a measure of risk due to inadequate or failed human performance. It would rate relatively high on the KRI assessment criteria listed above. It can be measured against multiple dimensions, including location, country, business unit, product or service group and job function. It should probably be measured for full-time and part-time employees separately. We should also have some rules for the period of time to be assessed and the frequency of measurement, and some specifics of who should be included and excluded in the count (eg, it may be that contractors should be excluded). There should also be rules for scaling the indicator to allow comparisons with differently sized units (not applicable for this indicator) and aggregation of results within a line of business or the organisation as a whole.

### Leading, lagging and current indicators and trending indicators

Indictors can be leading, lagging or current in nature. Most managers want leading or preventative indicators – to predict problems far enough in advance to prevent or eliminate them or at least mitigate the damage. Unfortunately, prevention of incidents is a desired but rarely achieved forward-looking aspect of operational risk management.

Accordingly, current and lagging indicators also have their place. Current indicators provide a snapshot or current view of operational risk exposures. They may identify a situation that may require attention to reduce exposure or minimise loss. Lagging indicators can be considered as more "detective" in nature, and can provide useful information regarding the historical causes of loss or exposure. They may also be useful where losses are initially hidden from view, or where changes in historical trends can reflect changes in circumstances, which may in turn have predictive value. An example of a current indicator could be the number of threatened legal actions or the number of customer complaints. An example of a lagging indicator could be the number of critical system outages.

In our experience, leading indicators are generally environmental indicators, or they are based on causal analysis or expert opinion. Environmental factors are the most common leading measures of operational risk. These are measures of the state of people, process, technology and the market that affect the level of risk in a particular organisation. A leading or preventative KRI can be something as simple as the number of limit breaches on market or credit risk exposures, or cash movements, or the average length of delays in executing a transaction. In themselves, such limit breaches may not be incidents, but, if the number of breaches and their value starts to increase, this may point to the potential for a higher frequency or severity of incidents: unauthorised breaches, or impending failures in other processes.

One misconception about leading indicators is the assumption that establishing or projecting future values from historical trends results in a leading indicator of risk. While this may be the case where sophisticated techniques such as charts and dynamic anomaly pattern response are used, in general, trending does not produce leading indicators, which need to provide useful information about future events in and of themselves, generally through the use of thresholds and triggers, which are discussed later in this section.

However, it *is* beneficial to measure KRIs over time, in order to detect trends and provide contextual information. For example, consider the KRI for late-trade processing for Firm X, shown in Figure 3. In May, the percentage of late trades is 9% for London and Singapore and 10% for New York, which in the face of those facts alone might lead us to conclude that New York has a slightly riskier operation. However, further analysis of the trends suggests that, in fact, Singapore may have an emerging problem.

But, again, if we check the absolute trade volumes of these various locations (see Figure 4), we learn that New York's late trades have risen only slightly against a significant increase in volumes, and Singapore's increase in late trades is based on a very low volume of trades. Context is everything! It is usually beneficial to know the underlying trend of an indicator, as well as to look at it in the context of other KRIs and other management information, in order to really understand the story the numbers are suggesting.

## KRI selection

Having a good understanding of the desirable characteristics of a KRI, we now come to the stage where they must be selected and bundled into a programme for a business area or unit or the organisation overall. Most practitioners believe that KRIs are of highest use when applied at a fairly granular level within the organisation,

**Figure 3** Late-trade processing

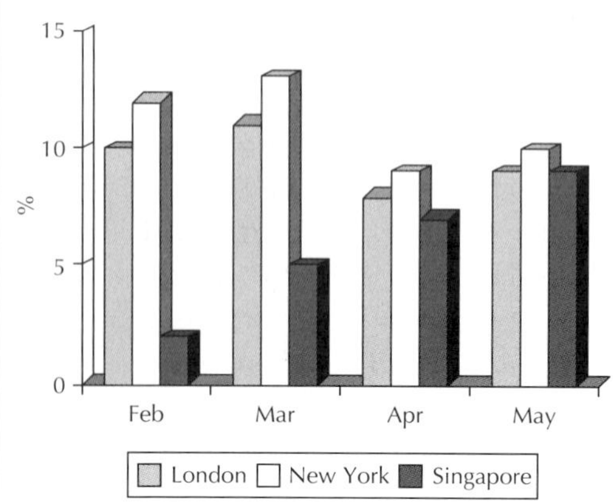


**Figure 4** Absolute trade volumes

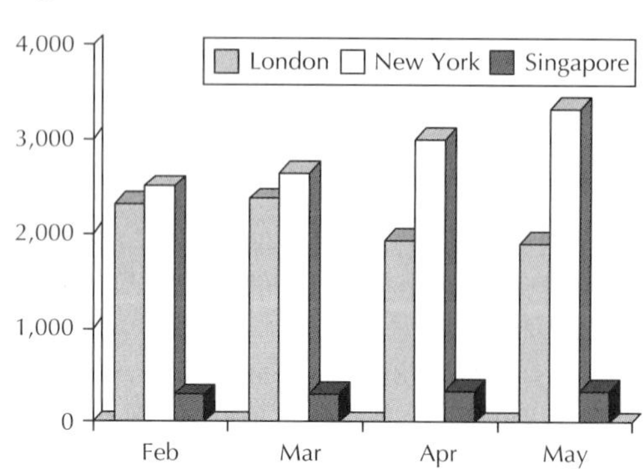


used by middle managers to monitor and manage day-to-day risks. They can then be filtered and aggregated for reporting to more senior management. Accordingly, the construction of a KRI programme ideally starts with an individual business unit.

Because KRIs are supposed to track key risks, the first step in KRI selection is to identify areas of highest risk for the business unit in question. It is important to have a consistent and comprehensive approach to this analysis. It can be done by risk mapping or profiling each business unit, or leveraging risk-and-control assessment programmes already in place. The analysis should focus on component processes or business functions within each business, considering how they work, and where a material loss has been or could be experienced.

Participants in the assessment should assess *residual* risk, after the impact of current controls is taken into account. It is helpful to ask them to focus on the expected loss in the worst year over an understandable time horizon, for example, 10 years – this captures the effect of a typical economic cycle on risks, is reasonably easy for most participants to conceptualise and embraces the time horizon of most strategic initiatives and the majority of banking obligations. Generally, we suggest that assessments should include the impact of reputation damage as well, as these are real impacts to the organisation, if a little harder to quantify.

Once high-risk areas are identified, the business needs to consider what existing indicators or metrics could be leveraged or new ones created to help anticipate a loss, monitor an exposure, measure the risk, manage the exposure or loss, or report on the risk and its implications. An inventory of existing KRIs, as well as the identification of the high risks for which there are not currently KRIs in place, is often a good first step in this process. Once gaps are identified, it is important to consider a variety of KRIs against each risk type, as each KRI is reflective of a specific causal element which may come into play if a loss occurs. Figure 5 illustrates this concept.

Ultimately, however, in order to keep the number of KRIs being monitored to a manageable number, it will be necessary to select the few that best reflect the business unit's collective understanding of the key causes of each potential problem. This selection should also be guided by consideration of the quality of the potential indicators against the effectiveness, comparability and ease-of-use criteria discussed above, as well as their contribution to the goal of obtaining a reasonable mix of leading, current and lagging indicators. This is an art rather than a science at the moment, but, in the hands of experienced practitioners in the business, should represent a reasonable start. Of course, fine-tuning the KRIs will naturally occur over time as the business learns and gains experience with these relationships.

Once selected, each indicator needs to be defined and specified as discussed above to ensure clarity of interpretation and implementation. The next step is to establish bands of acceptance that essentially codify risk appetite, and triggers for escalation and/or

**Figure 5** Causal drivers for different types of operational risks

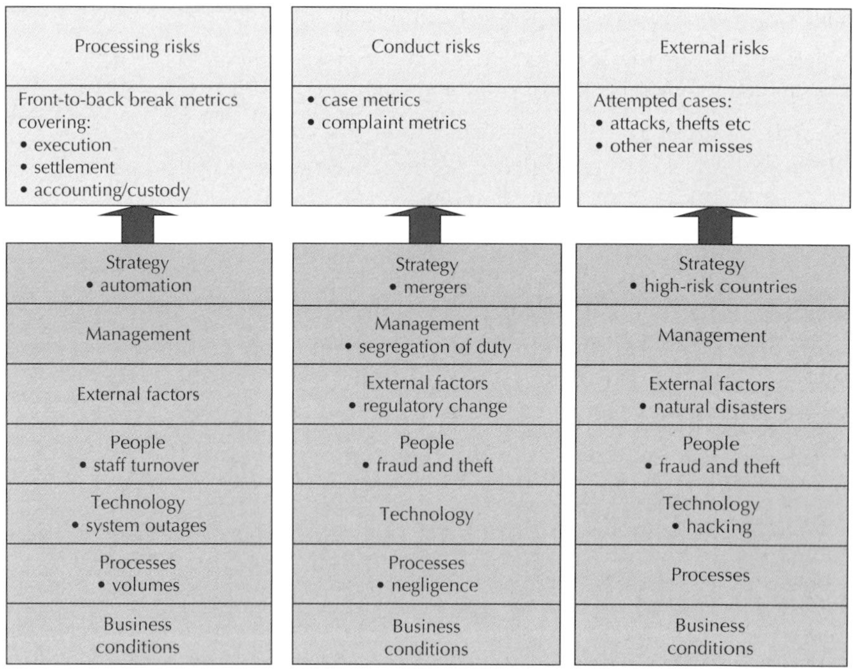


some other form of action. Indicators are then assessed on an ongoing basis against this frame of reference.

In the case of high-frequency, low-impact exposures, it is often useful for managers to think about different *ranges* of indicator value as calling for different kinds of action:

- ❑ low-risk range: no action required;
- ❑ medium-risk range: some action required; and
- ❑ high-risk range: issue to be escalated to management; other actions required urgently to mitigate damage.

Thresholds can be set to define each range and trigger each kind of response. After a threshold is breached, actions taken by managers to accept or mitigate the risk should be recorded.

Thresholds and escalation triggers are an important risk management tool. KRI thresholds will vary from institution to institution, depending on management's risk appetite, as well as strategy and ability. For some risks the thresholds may be quite low and others higher. They can also change over time, if there is a strategic decision to manage risk down (or sometimes up). Managers will become more experienced at setting the appropriate level of threshold over time. This is where art meets science as there can be no one-size-fits-all approach or algorithm for thresholds. It is subjective and based upon the managers' risk appetite and experience, and that of their peers within the firm.

What is a reasonable number of KRIs? Many financial institutions have a very large number. This may be justified by the heterogeneity of operational risks and complexity of financial services and products. We believe that a large diverse institution would reasonably use between several hundred and a few thousand indicators in middle management. Of course, these cannot all be reported to senior levels of management. Accordingly, it is very important to have an appropriate strategy for reporting and aggregating KRIs to senior management and the board.

## AGGREGATION AND REPORTING OF INDICATORS

In the previous section, we explained the basics of KRIs, starting with what is a good indicator, through the need for a common language and, finally, techniques for KRI selection. It is these building blocks that provide the foundation for the aggregation and reporting of KRIs.

Key elements of a robust structure for KRI aggregation and reporting are:

- ❑ clear objectives for the reporting and aggregation mechanism;
- ❑ common data dimensions and classification;
- ❑ content appropriate to the required level of analysis and decision making; and
- ❑ timeliness and accuracy to the required level of materiality.

Let us explore these factors further.

### Clear objectives for the reporting and aggregation mechanism

The objectives of any management information system need to be defined before data are gathered to populate it, otherwise a meaningless paper chase will be delivered with no added value to operational risk management. The objectives can be defined at the business-line level, although some homogeneity of concepts will be essential across the firm to facilitate benchmarking and multidimensional risk analysis.

There is a clear difference between data and management information. Data can be fairly "raw" and of little or no use to any manager. Information is the result of transforming the data into meaningful and incisive management tools for the better management of operational risk exposures in a timely manner. When so-called indicators are being collected without a clear view about what they are reported for, or to whom or where they are reported, the firm has a problem. The data-collection effort will be in vain and any management information will be lost with no value added to the business or firm-wide operational risk management process.

Few KRI reporting frameworks will succeed if they are implemented merely with the objective of regulatory compliance.

Data collection without risk management decision making will provide the businesses and functions with negative added value: they will implement a reporting framework for a cost without benefit. A better and more reasonable objective would be "to better manage operational risk". This will provide the managers in the businesses and functions with information for operational risk management decisions regarding risk acceptance and/or mitigation.

## Common data dimensions and classification

To facilitate aggregation of KRI data in a meaningful way, the firm must have a classification system with appropriate hierarchies reflecting the organisational structure. Ideally, this system of classification and the concepts embedded in it should be common across the operational risk framework, and in many cases with pre-existing management reporting. As we alluded to earlier, most managers have risk *and* performance objectives, so it makes sense to have some commonality of concepts across risk and performance measurement, although the granularity may differ with risk exposure being at a more aggregated level than process efficiency.

Accordingly, we would expect that most firms will have already defined a number of core data dimensions that are integral to aggregating and reporting KRIs, such as:

- ❑ *incident* (historical and potential), normally consisting of:

  - one or more causes;
  - one or more events (as in a chain of events);
  - financial and non-financial (ie, reputational) impact on profit and loss; and
  - risk categories;
- *process*, with a clearly defined hierarchical level consisting of:
  - end-to-end processes, typically referred to as a complete business function;
  - sub-process components;
  - process types;
  - function domains (HR, finance, compliance, IT, communications and so on);
  - shared processes; and
  - hand-offs between departments or business functions;
- *control*, consisting of:
  - control types (ie, reconciliation, accounting, review, management);
  - control attributes (ie, automated, manual); and
  - preventative and detective controls;
- *product*, consisting of:
  - business lines; and
  - product and service groups;
- reporting entity:
  - branch, territory, function, business line, legal entities, joint ventures, outsourcers and so on.

The regulators have defined the scope of operational risk and have provided, for regulatory reporting purposes, an event-type classification. The other data dimensions should be defined by each firm according to its own risk management framework with the appropriate emphasis placed upon each one in relation to the specific attributes of each firm: complexity of business model, global and local operations and management structure, number of product lines and so on.

### Content appropriate to the required level of analysis and decision making

One of the most important challenges in establishing a KRI programme is to ensure that each level and area of management gets the KRI information that is appropriate for its needs and responsibilities. This is a big part of the art of creating management information out of data, as discussed earlier. Each manager should be receiving KRI information that allows them to proactively identify problems within their area of concern, and take appropriate action, even if that is simply to escalate or delegate to the next level up or down. In essence, KRI reporting needs to be customised within each business unit and at each level of the organisation, similar to other kinds of management reporting. While this may seem like a tall order, it is actually a natural part of the KRI programme roll-out within each area of the firm, and, once completed, will represent a very powerful tool in managing operational risk more effectively.

There are several elements to consider when deciding who should see each KRI. We will consider each of these in turn.

*The level of granularity or risk exposure being measured by the KRI*

KRIs can be set at any level of risk exposure. Consider the following examples:

- At a regional level the firm may track the number of actual breaches of specific local laws and regulations for a single process, which are not declared to regulators.
- At the global level it might monitor the number of internal audit points overdue for each business unit.

The management information that these KRIs provide are at two different levels but both are relevant for the management of operational risk. In the first example, the number of undeclared actual breaches of laws and regulations gives an indication of exposure to potential fines if and when the regulators find out during one of their inspections. This means something to the regional head who is managing the reputation of the branch across all business lines, as well as to the manager responsible for the breach. However, it should not impact the CEO's decision making, as the CEO has delegated this responsibility to the regional head, so should not concern themselves with such minutiae.

In the second example, the lack of action regarding implementation of internal audit points is a global KRI, and one that would be of interest to both the head of internal audit and the CEO. These two indicators measure different levels of exposure: one at the individual process level in a region and the other across all processes and exposures within the firm. Generally, the higher the level, the greater the interest to senior managers, provided it relates to their area of purview.

*The breadth of risks represented by the KRI*

When KRIs point at causes that could lead to multiple events across all event types, the CEO will be very interested. In essence, these multi-event indicators, analysed by cause rather than specific potential events, provide early-warning signals regarding unexpected losses and a flag to senior management to start asking some pointed questions.

A good example of a multi-event indicator is the total number of audit points outstanding. Some audit points can easily be related to specific exposures and mapped to the Basel II event types. It is more difficult to do this with others, for example, when they are related to causes such as a lack of appropriate management skills. If a KRI analysis results in the conclusion that there are insufficient management skills in any specific unit or location, this is an issue appropriate for the attention of senior rather than lower levels of management.

*The current "temperature" (red, yellow or green) of the KRI – bottom-up indicators*

Most indicators collected by businesses stay in the business without any reporting to a higher level within the organisation. Senior management delegates the authority to manage most operational risks to appropriate levels and functions and outsourcing service providers throughout the firm. As we discussed earlier, each business unit or function is then responsible for developing its own KRIs based on a bottom-up assessment of the risk in its area. The process level indicator measuring undeclared local law breaches is a typical bottom-up indicator.

However, if a KRI breaches the thresholds or trigger points previously established, then it is usually escalated to the next level of management, depending on the materiality of the situation. The senior manager must then decide whether to accept the risk and increase the threshold or reduce the risk indicated by the management information. Some managers also set triggers at an earlier point, when the indicator *starts* to trend upwards or accelerate towards the threshold level. This is useful if the manager prefers a window to deal with any emerging situation *before* the threshold is actually breached, and they are obliged to report it to more senior management. In some cases, triggers can be set so as to escalate only when a condition persists, or when a certain level of indicator volatility is exceeded. For example, a single breach of a KRI threshold may result in immediate action that is within the delegated authority of the manager, thus not requiring escalation to the next level of management. However, if the condition persists or becomes repetitive, then the trigger is set off, and the problem is escalated. Thresholds should be dynamic, so that when volume increases the thresholds are "scaled up" to take account of the increased volume, otherwise too many excesses over thresholds will be reported.

Of course, if a KRI is considered to represent a particularly significant risk, or it tracks risk in a business unit of significant size or materiality relative to the entire firm, or it exceeds the threshold by a significant amount, this KRI may need to be escalated beyond the immediate senior manager. Ultimately, there may be some bottom-up KRIs that need to be escalated to business or function heads or the CEO. This gives the most senior levels of management a window on emerging areas of significant risk in the organisation as and when they occur.

*The specific risk focus of the KRI – top-down indicators*

Top-down KRIs are generally set in conjunction with group functions and may relate to general causes or specific potential process failures or events. Total outstanding audit points or the state of the overall management skills of an entity are typical examples of top-down indicators set by the heads of internal audit and human resources respectively, for the CEO's review. Other examples set by the heads of group functions are:

- *legal*: the total number and value of legal claims against the firm, in total and by business line and peer group;
- *finance*: the number of incidences of late financial reporting by legal entities within the group, or number of accounting errors or unexplained differences; and
- *IT*: the number of attempted external attacks to the firewall.

Clearly these KRIs are somewhat specialised and generally of interest only to the CEO and the most senior management, particularly within functional areas.

In some cases, top-down and bottom-up KRIs can be directly linked together to form a chain in the operational risk exposure management process. For example, we can imagine a situation where many audit points have arisen from various control-effectiveness reviews. These can be considered bottom-up KRIs as they arise directly from detailed risk analysis of specific processes. The respective process owners/departments will be allocated responsibility for taking remedial action before the audit points are reported to the CEO at the global business level.

However, the cause of the problem of many outstanding audit points may not be within the powers of the individual managers to solve. The individual managers may not have the mandate to address some of the root causes due to their breadth or implications; they may have insufficient resources to carry out the day-to-day operations *and* fix endemic control or system issues that require some modest investment; or they may not have the scope of management information to recognise a larger systemic problem. This is a particular concern in trading and sales businesses where the profit and loss is very short-term-focused and the medium-term operational risk exposures of chronically lagging back offices are often ignored or underinvested. So, at the end of the day, the mitigation of the risk by investment or the acceptance of the exposure needs to be the responsibility of the business unit head or the CEO. The CEO can put pressure on the business unit head based upon the KRI of outstanding audit points. They can also assist with a reallocation of resources as required, if the exposure to operational risk is above that desired.

Ideally, through the application of the above principles, each manager will end up with a portfolio of KRIs that reflects the risks of most importance to their mandate. The manager will also have a clear understanding of the action required when thresholds or trigger are breached, including which KRIs need to be escalated to the next level of management or higher.

### Timeliness and accuracy to the required level of materiality

The final element of a robust reporting and aggregation programme for KRIs is timeliness and accuracy of information. If it takes longer to collect the indicators than the timescale required by the decision-making process, then the indicator has failed the "timely" test. Indicator reporting and aggregation should balance speed with accuracy. The late reporting of indicators achieves nothing. If the systems or manual nature of the reporting process leads to delays, it is better to sacrifice some of the accuracy for speed. In other words, if the indicators are 80% rather than 100% complete or accurate, in many cases that is sufficient information to enable the manager to take appropriate action.

In summary, a strong KRI aggregation and reporting programme will have as its clear objective the effective management of operational risk, and will be founded on data dimensions and a classification system that are common to the entire operational risk framework, as well as many elements of the firm's general management reporting structure. It will also ensure that each manager views those KRIs that are appropriate to their mandate and scope of decision making, and that the KRI data are timely and accurate within reason.

No discussion of KRI aggregation and reporting would be complete without addressing one more issue, namely the concept of the "top ten" indicators to be reported to the CEO and the board of directors.

### The mythical "top 10" KRIs for senior management

Some firms wish to report at the very highest level, the "top 10" KRIs – and the group operational risk team are required to find them. This quest is like searching for the Holy Grail. They will never find what they are looking for but a whole mystical and quasi-religious framework and following will be created in the process. This search will feed itself, resulting in the KRI framework being criticised for lack of added value, the possible withdrawal of investment and a perception that KRI monitoring is an abject failure.

While we understand that senior management desires predictability and conciseness in reporting, every risk manager will know this dream is not achievable through the selection of 10 operational risk KRIs. Businesses constantly change their risk exposure to operational risks as they, and the market and world within which they operate and manage, change. KRIs that were relevant last year may well not be relevant this year. The portfolio of information that is required to communicate these risks will change over time, and will certainly be very different from one business to another.

Of course, there is a role for top-down indicators. Ideally, there will be some support from group functions to set an appropriate number of these in keeping with the perceived risks. It is best practice to have at least two KRIs for each group function: human resources, information technology, legal, finance, compliance, group risk, and audit. There may also be one or two KRIs selected for each main "multi-event" cause. This totals about 12–20 indicators.

In addition to these top-down indicators, as we discussed before, consistent or material breaches of thresholds should be reported to senior management. Those indicators set by managers that are within the thresholds should stay where they are: in the business line or function to be reported and used locally.

## Some final comments on reporting

Many KRIs currently collected by businesses and functions are for managing expected rather than unexpected losses. Therefore, their contribution to capital measurement may be limited, but the value added to the businesses for managing exposures to the range of losses between expected and unexpected is immense.

Setting relevant and reliable indicators is a challenge. They should be linked to the causes of operational risk incidents so that operational risk managers can monitor the drivers of operational risk exposures on an ongoing monthly or quarterly basis. It will not be known whether the indicators are "key" until they are refined in the light of experience. Such experience will require at least two years' worth of complete indicator data and internal incidents. Most firms will not have accumulated such a time series of homogeneous indicators using group-wide concepts and definitions before they have to pass regulatory validation prior to Basel II deadlines. Therefore, this is a challenge both before and after the Basel II validation process. The first gathering of consistent indicators across the firm has commenced in 2006, but the time series necessary to decide on the "key" ones could take another year until 2007.

Nevertheless, firms who do invest in this area will eventually have a dynamic, predictive library of indicators they can interchange depending on the particular business, process, geography or market environment. This target is some way off for most firms today, but we believe the investment will reap many benefits.

## ADVANCED APPLICATIONS FOR KRIs

While the benefits of a robust, dynamic and comprehensive set of KRIs across the organisation coupled with strong aggregation and reporting are worthy objectives on their own, they also open the door to some more "advanced applications" and opportunities. These include the potential for measuring the success of our risk management activities, building risk indexes and benchmarking KRI performance. We will briefly consider each of these in turn.

### Relationships of KRIs with losses and risk and control assessment (RCA) output

In arguing the benefit of KRIs, many risk managers are seeking a strong cause and effect relationship. After identifying certain KRIs and managing them down, does the organisation see a reduction in risk? The answer depends on a number of factors, but in our experience the statistical correlations will be weak even for the more effective measures. This doesn't mean that the indicator is ineffective. It may still achieve its objective – when identified and managed, the management of the indicator produces a reduction in one or more characteristics of the loss profile: frequency, severity or both. The lack of correlation is due in part to the multifactor relationship between losses and their drivers, and also to the variable timing differences between managing the cause and the impact on the recognition of a loss. But these relationships will be improved if the *measure of risk* used is consistent with the KRIs themselves.

What do we mean by that? Well, there are many measures of risk, in fact, an infinite number. This is illustrated by the loss distribution curve in Figure 6. At different confidence intervals, you are assessing the different likelihoods that a firm will suffer one or more events of a certain aggregate impact.

One common measure of risk illustrated in this distribution is the mean or expected loss (depicted at the point "EL"). However, this is not really risk, as the mean is predictable with reasonable accuracy. Another common measure of risk is the 99.9 percentile on

**Figure 6** Appropriate measures of risk

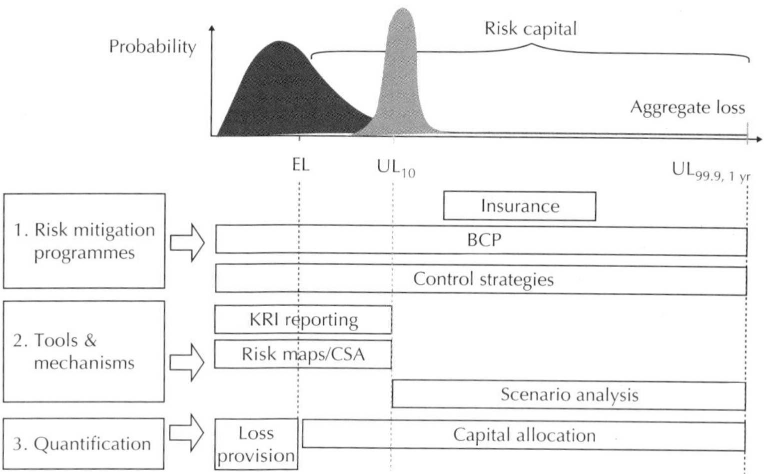


this curve, which is often used to determine capital requirements for the firm. This measure is located on the far right of the curve ($UL_{99.9,\ 1\ yr}$), and shows the aggregate loss at a confidence interval of 99.9% using a one-year holding period. This is equivalent to measuring losses for the single worst year in 1,000 years, for a given loss type. That is almost impossible for management to conceptualise, and in reality very few KRIs are likely to influence such extreme measures of risk.

Which leads us to the question of whether there is a more appropriate measure of risk for *risk management* purposes. Ideally, we would like a measure that addresses that range of exposures between expected and unexpected losses, providing a conceptual or specific target for our risk management activities, and a source of feedback on our success. Well, the answer is a resounding yes!

One possible standard is a measure of the worst year of losses predicted over a 10-year horizon, or $UL_{10}$. This empirical measure is roughly equivalent to a probabilistic risk measure using a confidence interval of between 90% and 95%. This standard would better define the risk that can be reasonably and practically assessed in risk assessment processes and that is the focus of KRIs and much of the risk information currently in use. It may also assist in defining the boundary between management techniques such as risk-and-control assessments and scenario analysis.

Most of the KRIs and management information used to manage the risk-and-control environment identify the more routine "unexpected" risks – those that occur once every 5–10 years – through the typical operational, investment, market, credit or economic cycle. This is appropriate because these are the risks that management can realistically imagine resulting in an event, and that they can actively influence. True, management may also mitigate the less regular operational risks through controls such as business continuity planning, but even these are typically "tested in anger" more frequently than once in 20, 50 or 100 years, making them easier to conceptualise, manage and mitigate than risks that occur even less frequently.

Therefore, we believe that a $UL_{10}$ basis provides a more appropriate measure of risk on which to focus our risk-and-control assessments and KRI frameworks, and one that should correlate more closely to good predictive indicators.

## Collections of indicators and composite or index indicators

We discussed earlier the common desire for a magical "top ten" set of indicators that can inform the firm or business area on the profile of its operational risks. While we believe this is an unrealistic goal, a more realistic possibility may be a set of KRI "indexes" that comprise different measures, which in essence try to represent a score for each specific risk exposure. It is also possible that the classes of these composites or index indicators could be very similar across business lines and possibly across the industry.

Possible indexes might include:

- ❏ process quality index;
- ❏ technology stability index;
- ❏ client satisfaction index;
- ❏ employee satisfaction index;
- ❏ litigation exposure index;
- ❏ ethical quality index; and
- ❏ asset protection index.

For example, to compile an index on process quality, the first step is to identify the underlying KRIs that address the risk drivers impacting process quality, such as the level of automation, the process error rate, the aggregate cost of rework, the number of related client complaints and the costs of restitution. Theses KRIs are then combined into a weighted value that can be tracked over time, and, in aggregate, give a better picture of the risk.

In theory, the "formulas" for these internal indexes could also be agreed externally among peer firms; however, practically speaking, this may be difficult, as establishing such composites is no trivial task. It requires the use of a standardised classification framework across all forms of operational risk information, coupled to factor and multivariate statistical analysis across a relevant data series. Even then, the resultant composite indexes will need to be tested and possibly refined over time in the light of actual experience.

However, one exciting area for operational risk index development currently under exploration is the establishment of indexes for external factors. Examples could include:

- ❑ white-collar crime;
- ❑ blue-collar crime;
- ❑ payment systems stability;
- ❑ weather events; and
- ❑ terrorism ratings.

Many of these exist today as governmental outputs on socioeconomic conditions. They represent information on the external environment in which an institution operates, and the deterioration in such an indicator would surely be a worthy input into a measure of the risk environment of a firm for a location in which it operates. In fact, these indexes themselves could be aggregated into country ratings for any given country to provide information on foreign country risk. They could even be extended to cover political risks as well.

### Internal/external benchmarking

There should be an optimum level of operational risk exposure for a given institution – in theory, being too low could be as costly as being too high. An overcontrolled organisation that continues to make risk investments where the incremental return on increasing controls is actually negative is as risky as the organisation that makes little effort to control such risks.

How do we start to answer the question of whether the level of risk we are implicitly or explicitly accepting is too high or too low? By comparing who is in the newspapers? By comparing loss distributions? By comparing KRIs? Ideally, we could try to mark-to-market operational risk investments, and, perhaps one day, we will be a position to do this. A more practical alternative is to benchmark the risk environment in some fashion either internally against similar business lines, or externally in comparing the performance of business lines across a peer group.

The best operational risk metrics for benchmarking performance are, without doubt, KRIs. KRIs are periodic monitoring mechanisms to identify risk drivers in an objective manner. They make a good basis for comparison because they represent exposure, and business areas relate to them easily. KRIs are likely to be similar in the similar business processes that exist to support similar products. If a common basis is established to measure a KRI across processes within a firm or across institutions, and a process is established to compare performance, then benchmarking is a viable feedback mechanism to compare the riskiness of similar processes across a peer group.

Benchmarking KRIs can provide many benefits to participating firms, including:

- an opportunity to learn from peers and exchange information, ideas and concepts with them;
- an opportunity to assist in developing industry best practice, thereby making it easier to gain internal support and acceptance for risk management principles;
- an increased awareness of risk exposures within the firm, simply through the association with initiatives supported by peers and competitors;
- the ongoing development of standard language and frameworks for the identification, measurement, management, monitoring and mitigation of operational risks; and
- the opportunity to directly compare risk exposures with peers, using exactly the same language and structures, thereby gaining a better understanding of the firm's relative riskiness, and validating or

contradicting any preconceived notions of the conceptual level of risk being run by the firm.

While there is no argument that competition remains a driving force in successful business management, there are equally strong arguments that operational exposures facing one firm also face others, with adjustments for differing cultures and risk appetites. Accordingly, there must be mutual benefit in being able to benchmark your risk profile by comparing specifically focused, standardised risk indicators, especially if these can be compared to the firm's own internal loss history, its current risk-and-control assessment scores, specific scenarios being analysed and the amount of economic and/or regulatory capital being set aside. The benefit becomes even stronger when public loss data published into the public domain and loss consortium data employ the same frameworks and structures, thereby facilitating comparative benchmarking.

Today, the industry has begun to recognise these benefits, and, in fact, there is now a specific industry initiative under way that not only permits KRI benchmarking, but, in essence, represents a library of data and information to support the establishment of KRI programmes for participating firms.

## www.KRIeX.org – THE INDUSTRY KRI REPOSITORY

In 2003, the Risk Management Association, in conjunction with Risk*Business* International Limited, launched an initiative aimed at furthering the use of KRIs across the financial services industry. This followed the publication of several white papers by international rating agencies regarding the inclusion of operational risk effectiveness capabilities into a firm's credit rating, as well as the publication of draft Basel II guidelines that suggested that standardised indicators could be used to adjust a firm's calculated capital reserve requirement under the advanced measurement approach.

This initiative had three specific objectives:

- to establish a common "language" or framework through which areas of greater risk exposure could be identified and measured. This structure is depicted in Figure 7;
- for each such high risk point, to identify, define and establish a standard specification for suitable risk metrics to measure, monitor and manage such exposures; and

**Figure 7** The Risk*Business* Framework

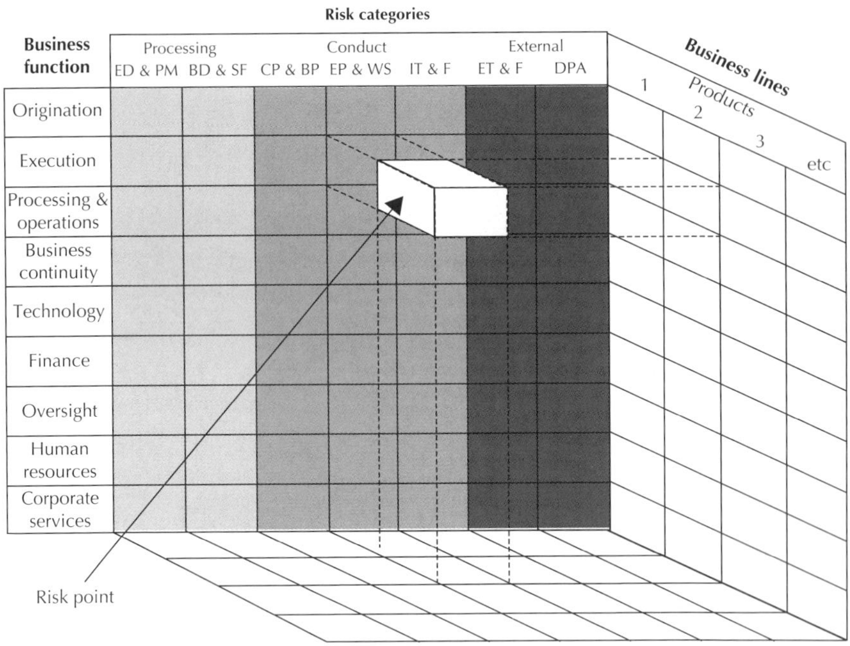


- ❑ to facilitate the formal comparison of such exposures between peer groups, using the standardised specifications in an anonymous manner.

Today, this industry initiative has transformed into best practice around KRIs. With more than 100 global firms participating, common areas of concern around operational risk have been identified, and linked to specific risk categories, product or service areas and business functions (ie, specific areas of business activity where such risks arise for each product or service area considered).

For each of the agreed areas of higher risk, subject matter experts from these leading firms have provided their input in identifying, developing and reviewing detailed specifications for suitable indicators that provide timely, value-added information on the exposure. More than 2,000 of these indicators are now provided through a subscription-based online repository of KRIs maintained by the RMA at http://www.KRIeX.org

**Figure 8** Example of comparative KRI benchmarking

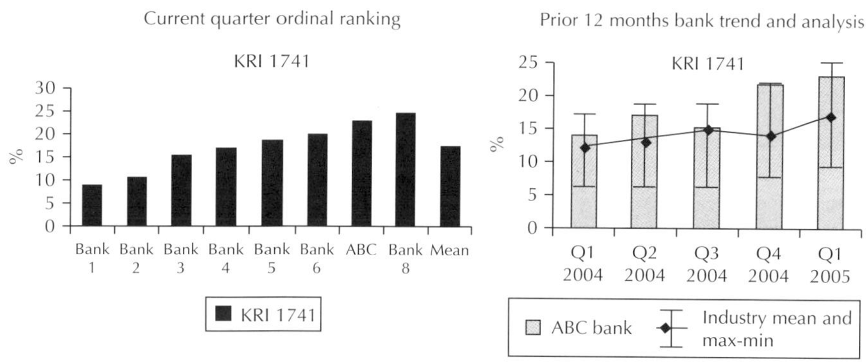


## Benchmarking

As an extension of the original RMA/Risk*Business* initiative, a global set of working groups continue to investigate both changing trends in exposure and changes in the identified risk profiles. These same working groups are involved in extending and maintaining this library of KRIs. At the same time, subscribers who have identified which indicators they wish to compare with their peers are now engaged in collecting indicator information in accordance with agreed specifications, with the purpose of comparing values against their peer group. An example of the kind of reporting to be generated in support of this benchmarking is shown in Figure 8.

In this example, a fictional bank, ABC, is shown as being above the mean for the current analysis period, and historically not only usually above the mean, but tending towards the top end of the exposure distribution. If ABC considered itself relatively risk-adverse, it would expect to be consistently below the mean for any risk measure. So, in this case, ABC management would want to initiate corrective action to reduce relative risk. However, it is possible that, when this indicator was selected internally for management purposes, a threshold range was established that has still not been triggered – it is only through comparison with peers that we can identify that we are out of synch (or have a competitive advantage) relative to the market.

This initiative has proved two things: first, firms *are* prepared to work together to ensure appropriate internal risk management;

second, we all face very similar operational risk issues. We believe that access to the collective experience and knowledge of the entire industry, as represented by more than 2,000 standardised indicators in the KRI Library, as well as through the various regional and business line working groups, is a powerful tool for enhancing any firm's operational risk management.

## CONCLUSION

Today, many firms have, often from necessity, left the establishment of an integrated KRI programme to last in their order of priorities. Many industry participants question the role of indicators, both from a top-down and a bottom-up perspective. Others argue that industry participants would be reluctant to contribute KRI data for benchmarking, due to discoverability issues as well as the potential for gaming.

However, KRIs (or risk indicators in general) have one very specific quality that no other operational risk management or measurement tool offers: quasi real-time exposure information.

- Loss data, whether internal, provided by a public source or obtained from a data consortium, is fundamentally lagging in nature, representing a past state of affairs, which in most cases is repaired long before the data analysis hits the risk manager's desk.
- Risk-and-control assessments are periodic subjective evaluations of the state of affairs, often supported by audit programmes, issue tracking and change management programmes. While important in understanding and anticipating exposures, these periodic evaluations cannot measure ongoing change.
- Scenario analysis allows you to consider what could happen to you, but in isolation tends to be considered as far-fetched, or a measure of the almost impossible – it certainly cannot provide an accurate barometer of real-time conditions.
- Setting aside economic or regulatory capital as a safeguard is the ultimate fail-safe – any firm that gets to the point where it needs to employ these measures is in such deep trouble that it is probably too late to contain much if not most of the collateral damage from what has already happened. Insurance is also an uncertain safeguard, with some potential relief triggered after the event has occurred.

However, similar to the way in which the fuel gauge, oil pressure gauge, engine temperature gauge and speedometer in a motor vehicle all provide you with vital information as to your safety and likelihood of survival, a KRI programme is the only way to provide management with the real-time targeted feedback they need to make mid-course adjustments as required. And that is essential to the achievement of business goals and the safety of the organisation.

1 The Risk Management Association's Web site can be found at http://www.RMAhq.org

**REFERENCE**

**Risk Management Association,** 2005, "Report on a Survey of KRI Programmes" (Web-based survey conducted with 38 respondents comprising banks with a North American, European or global focus), Summer.

11

# *Implementing Operational Risk Measurement at Financial-Services Firms: Quantifying the Operational Risks of Technology*

**Eric Holmquist**

Advanta Bank Corp

If you want to create a spirited discussion over cocktails, and you've somehow run dry on politics or religion, try this one. "Can the operational risks of technology be quantified?" Depending on your audience, the responses will be wildly different in both position and conviction. Add in a few folk with responsibility for the management programme for operational risk (OR) – and several rounds of your favourite libation – and you just might end up with a good old-fashioned bar fight. The arguments both for and against this question have merit, some of which will be discussed here. However, when the dust settles and the wounded are tended to, you are still left with a much, much bigger question, and that is: should it be?

The reality is that the answer, like so many other aspects of risk analysis, is the frustratingly ambiguous "it depends". It depends on how isolated you want the analysis to be. It depends on how you define your assumptions, on what period of time you're considering, on how you define "technology", on how you define OR, and on and on. But, most importantly, it depends on what you're trying to accomplish. I firmly believe that it is in this last question that we stand the best chance of addressing the larger question of "should it be?". Simply put, if your goal is to create a pure, stand-alone, forensic analysis of your technology risks without influence or regard for the human involvement, you're wasting your time.

Technology is simply too deeply integrated into our everyday processes and the consequences of its use are too dependent on the actions of poorly trained, inattentive or unsuspecting individuals who are just trying to do their jobs. In addition, the assumptions are both too many and too quick to change to avoid almost immediate time decay in any analysis, rendering its results questionable.

However, and this is important, if your goal is to understand how technology, in and of itself, influences the risk profile of a set of processes, and whether there may be opportunity to manage or mitigate those risks, than not only can these risks be quantified, but it is the responsibility of every financial institution (FI) to do so. In other words, understanding the unique and (here it is) quantifiable aspects of technology will only serve to make any OR management programme better and stronger.

Unfortunately this topic has received very limited treatment within OR circles. Since most of the risk-management discipline is still relatively new and has, up until recently, been largely focused on credit and market risk, it makes sense that initial OR management efforts would focus on the most intuitive aspect, process. Technology tends to baffle most people, and on top of that IT departments are typically not overtly focused on risk management: they're focused on making sure it works. Therefore, we're somewhat in uncharted waters with this topic, but there is a significant opportunity to improve how we manage our ever-increasing dependency on technology.

Before moving on to the mechanics and application of quantifying technology risk, this question deserves a bit more treatment. There are a number of very practical reasons why these risks can, and should, be analysed.

- ❑ In the field of OR, technology embodies some unique attributes *versus* people, process and external events, attributes which are often misunderstood and misinterpreted. Some of these will be addressed in this chapter. The good news is that, believe it or not, there are actually more constants and fewer unique elements than one might think.
- ❑ Risk assessments that are oriented from a "process" standpoint very often *do* consider the technology that supports that process,

but only within the context of that one process. Some technologies are used to support multiple business processes, often in unrelated business areas. The cumulative amount of risk that is represented by a cross-functional technology is rarely fully captured when you start to consider the potential failure against all of the dependent processes. Only by focusing on a risk-assessment methodology that is centred on the technology itself do you capture the full business risk of a potential failure of that technology.

- Technology-centred "events" tend not to be repeated, unlike people-driven events. Once a weakness is discovered, the root cause is usually identified and fixed. Unfortunately, this has implications on the value of historical loss data when considering potential technology failures.
- As we as a society continue to amass an unprecedented amount of confidential information, information security will for the next decade be at the forefront of all OR discussions. This has become a hot topic with both bank regulators and legislative bodies throughout the world. But, in the field of OR, you cannot fully know your information security risks if you do not know the underlying risks of the technology that you are using to host the data.
- On the positive side, a risk assessment of technology requires a meeting of the minds between IT and business areas. This will be later, but the reality is that the IT staff members are the best at identifying what can go wrong and the business areas are the best at quantifying the effect on the business of those events. Only by bringing these two areas of expertise together can you get a clear picture of your technology risks.
- Finally, risk assessments that involve a technology component often understate the risks for a number of reasons:
  - People by nature have a tendency to assume that a given technology will always work, and despite all evidence to the contrary, are surprised when it fails.
  - IT staff (who are often central to the "assessment" steps because they know the technology), in general, are willing to accept a higher degree of risk than other management. There is more of an attitude of "mitigate the obvious stuff and we'll deal with the rest when it comes up." As a rule, IT staff are typically very bright, and love a challenge.

- ❑ A technology failure may not necessarily be immediately obvious, unlike one that involves a person or an external event. Because businesses often use extensive and complex automation, the time delay before awareness of an event taking place can have profound implications on the impact.
- ❑ The "ripple effect" of a technology failure (one event triggering another and another) is almost always understated. Often it is not the initial "event" that causes the most damage, but the downstream implications, sometimes creating cascading technology failures that can have devastating effects. This is an unavoidable consequence of the reality that we have become irreversibly dependent on technology.
- ❑ People routinely overestimate their ability to recover from a technology failure.
- ❑ Changes to technology, both planned and unplanned, are very often not accurately reflected in existing risk assessments, and can render historical loss data less effective if the new technology involves significant new automation or more leveraged processes, or even if the affected technology contains new design or development flaws not present in prior versions.

Simply put, if the overall OR management programme was a rope, by continually improving the quantification aspects of the operational risk assessments of your technology (including change management), you probably aren't adding new braids to the rope, but you can *significantly* improve its overall strength. The key to success (defined as adding worthwhile incremental value to your overall assessments) is in understanding what *can* be measured and what can't, and in staying focused not on the search for absolute-precision risk numbers but on trying to understand the relative risk that a given technology brings. We can certainly keep our eye on the theoretical goal of "What is the risk of this particular technology?" while being satisfied with an ever-improving response to "What is the risk of this process that involves this technology?" To quote the words of Peter Drucker, "If you can't measure it, you can't manage it."

## DISCLAIMERS

Several disclaimers are worth mentioning. First, in presenting this material it would not be realistic to propose one perfect model for quantifying technology risk. Each organisation is simply too distinctive and, depending on the size of the organisation, OR assessment models can be wildly different and focused on different objectives. Therefore, the structure of this chapter is not based on "use this model" but more like "consider these things when developing your own model". The material presented here is designed to focus on the root elements of assessing technology risk. Take what resonates to you, discard what you don't feel would increment value to your programme, but, in the end, hopefully everyone will take away elements that they can use to strengthen their ability to quantify, and manage, their technology risks.

Second, a large part of the OR world right now is focused on models designed to drive capital allocations, particularly in the larger, multinational institutions. Although the techniques outlined in this chapter could certainly be used to fine-tune models designed for this purpose, the larger practical application is in the other side of OR management, which is identifying risk areas within the organisation, determining whether any of those risks exceed acceptable tolerance levels and determining whether there is opportunity, or need, to further manage or mitigate those risks. The single biggest factor in the success or failure of an OR management programme is awareness at all levels. My number-one law of OR management is that "people can manage only those risks that they understand". Therefore, it is only through the process of clearly understanding the risks that a given technology represents to an organisation that they can properly address those risks.

Finally, the information presented here is primarily focused on technology that is within the control of the organisation. Technology that is used by third parties in the course of providing goods or services to the FI falls within the domain of "external events", because the institution generally does not have authority over the strategic planning, implementation, support or risk mitigation of the technology outside of its walls. To the extent that the institution may have contractual arrangements that allow for its involvement in third-party technology usage, then this assumption should be modified when analysing these risks.

## A METHODOLOGY

The following sections outline a practical set of guidelines for quantifying the operational risks of technology. Again, this does

**Table 1** General operational risk factors

| Component | Risk factors | Quantifiable? |
|---|---|---|
| People | Ability – Is the employee, contractor, vendor skilled at his or her job? Does he or she learn quickly? | Partial |
| | Equipped – Has the person been trained and given a supportive environment? | Partial |
| | Intent – Does the person intend to perform well, or do they intend to defraud the bank? | Minimal |
| Process | Complexity – Is the process understood by only a few staff members? Does it have many dependencies? | Yes |
| | Criticality – Is the process critical to operations? How quickly could the institution recover from a failure? | Yes |
| | Design – Is the process soundly designed? Does it consistently perform as expected, or are errors and unexpected results frequent? | Yes |
| Systems | Complexity – Is the system complex, requiring special staff or training to utilise and support? | Yes |
| | Criticality – Is the system critical to operations? How long could the institution survive without it? | Yes |
| | Quality – Is the system of quality design, construction and durability? Is there support available? It is easy to use? | Yes |

not necessarily represent a standalone assessment model (however, it certainly could for a bank without a comprehensive overall operational risk-assessment model), but instead presents the components that should be considered in evaluating technology risks. This section starts with an overview of how technology risk relates to other operational risk types, a discussion of alternate taxonomies, scenario strategy, assessing impact and mitigation. The remaining sections will deal with applying the risk analysis to the business at a practical level.

When we consider OR, particularly within the context of the Basel segmentations of "people, process, systems and external events", if we are to be at all successful in quantifying our technology risk we have to establish a few founding principles about what drives that risk. Putting aside external events (which are outside of our control) and focusing on the internal components, we can generalise our risk factors, and the extent to which these factors can be quantified, as shown in Table 1.

Although somewhat simplistic, these principles are extremely important, because, as you are developing methods of assessing risk, you need a foundation to fall back on, a reality check if you will, that guides your assessment assumptions. We will refer back to these factors periodically throughout the chapter.

It is interesting to note that the area that is actually the least quantifiable is people, not systems; however, it is not surprising that the largest area of focus within operational risk is in "process", since this is the most intuitive of the three.

## CLASSIFICATION TAXONOMY

The first aspect to consider is the *taxonomy* to be used to group technologies because it is quite obviously impractical to analyse every single piece of individual technology. However, this is the one aspect in this exercise that is wholly dependent on the focus and objective of your analysis. Simply put, the more accurate and detailed the analysis needs to be, the more detailed your taxonomy has to be. If your goal is simply a broad assessment of your general use of technology, than the taxonomy can certainly be broad as well.

However, there is some very good news within this aspect that does not exist when considering people or processes or even external events. That is that similar technologies can be grouped into relatively homogeneous buckets and assessed as a similar unit. In other words, a file server is, for the most part, a file server; a desktop PC is a desktop PC. Individual bits of hardware or software generally don't have dramatically different profiles, unlike individual people or processes that can each be wildly different based on their unique characteristics. Even if all like components (such as servers, PCs, routers) are not identical or close to it, they can typically be grouped into manageable buckets with those of similar properties. Once an institution combines its list of technologies into similar categories, surprisingly, the list of technologies that it uses isn't nearly as long as one would think.

For a detailed risk assessment, particularly where the intent is to match technologies against specific processes, this is the taxonomy level (basically similar component level) that is required. Not only does it allow you to assess risk at a component level, but it is also the most powerful method of incorporating the assessment process into other areas such as change control and strategic planning, which will be discussed later. The consequence is that this can be a significant amount of work and requires a fair bit of planning to establish manageable categorisation. The other benefit to this approach to a taxonomy is that it does not have to include every single piece of technology in order to provide useful data. If all you want to do is assess the risk of a particular system or piece of software, you can use the metrics outlined in this chapter to do so without having to document every other system. This could be valuable if an institution wanted to use a risk model selectively only where they felt that there "may" be risk levels beyond a certain threshold and wanted to prove or disprove that suspicion.

If that level of detail is too granular for the institution's purposes or willingness, there are several other ways to consider in classifying technology. Each loses a level of detail and accuracy, but significantly simplifies the taxonomy. One method would be to group technologies into broad properties as whatever level of detail the institution decided, such as:

- ❑ hardware:
  - ❑ facilities;
  - ❑ servers;
  - ❑ communications systems (voice and data);
  - ❑ computers; and
  - ❑ other.
- ❑ software:
  - ❑ operating systems;
  - ❑ application software; and
  - ❑ data management.

Another approach could be to group technologies into broad functional categories, such as:

- ❑ data management – such as day-to-day operations, MIS, analytics;
- ❑ communications – both voice and data exchange; and
- ❑ security – physical and logical.

Analysing at this level (or even this style broken down even further, but still short of component level) would still give you a sense of your overall technology risks, but would not allow you to analyse the risk of specific technologies. There are pros and cons for each approach, but in the end it is entirely dependent on the goals and objectives of the assessment exercise that will drive the level of detail required in the taxonomy design. However, the more generalised the categorisation, the higher the margin of error in the analysis. So, if the objective is a clear assessment of the risk of given technology, then a higher level of granularity would be recommended.

## EVENT TYPES

The next aspect to consider is event types, which have proved problematic for many institutions for one reason: too much detail. The number of scenarios that can impact a company's technology is so limitless that in a lifetime you could never consider every one. Don't. Another one of the beneficial aspects of technology is that event scenarios can be generalised – again, unlike, say, people who, history has shown, seem to be able to come up with amazingly creative ways of doing something wrong. However, for a piece of technology – say a file server or even a rack of servers – failed means failed. It doesn't really matter if it failed by fire, a system crash or disgruntled employee with baseball bat. Either way, you're done. Once you reduce the exercise to, "What happens if this technology fails?" you are free to focus your energy and resources on assessing the actual impact of that failure. The various ways that the failure can occur is considered in the assessment component later. Scenario analysis can then be a useful means of testing your assessments as opposed to serving as foundation for it.

It is at this point that we reach a fork in the road and you must determine what it is that you want to accomplish with this analysis. If the goal of your assessment is an isolated view of the risk of a given technology, then failure[1] is where the analysis typically begins and ends. The unplanned removal of a given technology from ongoing operations is as close to a pure analysis as you're going to get. However, if the goal of the exercise is to understand the *complete* risk that the technology imposes on the organisation, then you have no choice but to consider not only the technology itself, but how the technology is used, meaning the processes that it touches. It is only in considering this holistic view that we can understand the full *operational risks of technology*. Unfortunately, what we end up with is a good bit of crossover between this analysis (technology-centric) and conventional operational risk assessments, which are process-centric. Hopefully, as software tools evolve in quantifying OR, the dynamics of this will be easier to resolve because the reality is that these are simply two dimensions of the same analysis.

So, assuming that the goal is to capture the full operational risks of some or all of the technology that is in use, then we need a taxonomy for events, just as we needed one for components. Trying to consider every conceivable way a technology is used or abused would be impossible from any practical perspective. Therefore, some suggested categories are the following.

- *System failure*: Unexpected failure or removal of the technology.
- *System attacks*: Any attack upon a technology for destructive purposes (eg, altering or destroying data or introducing a computer virus). This may not require direct access.
- *Unauthorised logical access*: An unauthorised person gaining access to sensitive systems, possibly with the intention of committing fraud or gaining inside information.
- *Theft*: Typically, theft of a system, potentially representing loss of both data and the device.
- *Misuse*: Technology that is used in an unintended way (such as sending threatening or inappropriate messages with e-mail or running an outside business on company computers).

Again, there are pros and cons to this method of categorisation and they may not work for every institution, but they have historically been shown to represent a complete set of risk profiles that capture most, if not all, event scenarios. In other words, it would be difficult to consider a specific scenario that did not share a risk profile with one of the generalisations above. What they do represent, however, is a crossover into other OR areas because each scenario beyond "failure" requires human interaction. It is up to the FI to design their analysis to take this duplication into consideration.

## QUANTIFICATION MEASURES

The next series of components of the analysis are not only much more intuitive by nature, but provide for quantified values fairly easily. These are specifically designed around practical, tangible metrics to capture inherent and net risk values. These risk factors are grouped into four general categories (of which the first three are focused on calculating inherent risk and the last focuses on risk mitigation):

- What is exposed in each general scenario?
- What is the nature of the exposure?
- What is the potential source of the threat?
- How much can the FI mitigate the risk?

The following is a detailed breakdown of the individual risk components in each category. In order to give a practical perspective when reading these categories, assume we are analysing the impact of the theft of, say, a server hosting a data warehouse. Keeping that in mind, the risk elements are as follows:

- *What is exposed*: Each value weighted by the *degree* of the impact:
  - hardware – facilities, equipment;
  - software – operating systems and applications;
  - data – confidential information;
  - personnel – certain technologies can create a high-risk work environment.
- *The nature of exposure*: Each value also weighted by the degree of impact:
  - financial – estimated dollar impact to recover from the event;
  - operational – impact on ongoing operations, including manpower to recover from the event;
  - regulatory – potential impact with regulatory authorities;
  - reputation – estimate of the impact on the FI's reputation.
- *The sources of the threat*: Each weighted by the estimated likelihood of the source:
  - internal person – an employee or contracted third party;
  - external person – an individual outside the company;
  - internal system – one internal system causing damage to another (cascade);
  - external system – an external system causing damage to an internal system;
  - natural disaster – any natural event that could trigger the event.

If each of these parameters is given a risk weight related to the scenario under consideration, the analyst has established an approximate gross risk weight. The parameters above, when combined, are effective at capturing the impact of a disruptive event.

The most important thing to remember here is that there is no benefit in debating minute differences in quantification values (for instance, is potential financial impact a 7.2 or a 7.5?). The reality is that the margin of error is too high and that really isn't the objective. The value of using standardised risk parameters like these is in (1) being able to validate which technologies represent the most risk and which don't, and (2) being able to evaluate incremental risk based on a change in assumptions (such as a proposal to replace a given technology).

It is at this point in the analysis that you should refer back to the summary of risk factors discussed earlier. When considering a general event scenario against a given technology or group of technologies, continue to refer back to the three main considerations, which should drive the assessment values.

- ❑ How complex is the technology?
- ❑ How critical is the technology?
- ❑ What is the quality of the technology?

The answers to these three questions should be generally consistent with the quantification values assigned in the analysis. If they aren't then the analysis should be reconsidered until they are.
The final step in the quantification is to consider the FI's ability to manage and mitigate risk, which is represented in three parameters.

- ❑ *Risk mitigation*: Each weighted by the degree of the FIs ability:
  - ❑ *Prevention*: How much can the scenario be prevented (eg, physically securing equipment, strong security, redundant equipment)?
  - ❑ *Monitoring*: How quickly can the scenario be identified in order to respond?
  - ❑ *Recovery*: How quickly can the FI fully recover from the event?

Figure 1 presents a sample matrix of the above parameters using a series of examples in each of the event scenarios described. This particular model happens to use a five-point scale for each component where 0 = none and 5 = very high. The gross values are summed and then the mitigation values reduce the gross values on a percentage basis to arrive at net values. This particular style of

**Figure 1** Sample risk matrix

Technology risk assesment matrix

| # | Threat | What is exposed | | | | Type of exposure | | | | Source of threat | | | | | Total | Risk mediation | | | Net factor |
|---|---|---|---|---|---|---|---|---|---|---|---|---|---|---|---|---|---|---|---|
| | | Personnel | Facilities & equip. | Op. systems & applications | Information | Financial | Operational | Reputation | Regulatory | Internal human | External human | Natural disaster | Internal systems | External systems | | Prevention | Monitoring | Recovery | |
| 1 | **System failures** | | | | | | | | | | | | | | | | | | |
| | File and print server | 0 | 3 | 3 | 1 | 3 | 1 | 1 | 1 | 4 | 1 | 2 | 2 | 1 | **23** | 4 | 5 | 3 | **6.4** |
| | Exchange mail server | 0 | 3 | 3 | 2 | 2 | 1 | 2 | 1 | 4 | 4 | 2 | 2 | 1 | **27** | 4 | 5 | 3 | **7.6** |
| | Branch router | 0 | 3 | 0 | 0 | 3 | 4 | 3 | 2 | 4 | 2 | 3 | 3 | 2 | **29** | 3 | 5 | 4 | **8.1** |
| | ATM | 0 | 3 | 1 | 1 | 3 | 5 | 5 | 3 | 3 | 4 | 4 | 1 | 1 | **34** | 3 | 4 | 2 | **15.6** |
| | Workstation | 0 | 3 | 1 | 3 | 3 | 1 | 1 | 1 | 4 | 1 | 4 | 2 | 1 | **25** | 4 | 4 | 5 | **5.5** |
| | etc | | | | | | | | | | | | | | – | | | | – |
| 2 | **Unexpected loss** | | | | | | | | | | | | | | | | | | |
| | Theft of laptop or workstation | 4 | 3 | 1 | 4 | 5 | 4 | 5 | 3 | 2 | 5 | 0 | 0 | 0 | **36** | 2 | 4 | 2 | **18.7** |
| | etc | | | | | | | | | | | | | | – | | | | – |
| 3 | **System attacks** | | | | | | | | | | | | | | | | | | |
| | Computer virus | 1 | 4 | 5 | 5 | 5 | 3 | 5 | 4 | 4 | 5 | 0 | 0 | 0 | **41** | 4 | 4 | 2 | **16.4** |
| | etc | | | | | | | | | | | | | | – | | | | – |
| 4 | **Unauthorised logical access** | | | | | | | | | | | | | | | | | | |
| | File and print server | 0 | 1 | 4 | 5 | 5 | 5 | 5 | 4 | 5 | 4 | 0 | 0 | 0 | **38** | 4 | 3 | 2 | **17.5** |
| | etc | | | | | | | | | | | | | | – | | | | – |
| 5 | **Misuse of technology** | | | | | | | | | | | | | | | | | | |
| | E-mail used in illegal fashion | 3 | 0 | 0 | 2 | 5 | 5 | 5 | 3 | 5 | 2 | 0 | 0 | 0 | **30** | 4 | 2 | 2 | **15.6** |
| | etc | | | | | | | | | | | | | | – | | | | – |

analysis allows technology to be viewed on both an inherent and net risk basis.

In addition, this particular model happens to be only two-dimensional based on one set of assumptions. It is certainly possible to expand the model to a range of assumptions and map the results to a set of frequency distributions in order to consider the broad impacts of changing assumptions. This could be particularly useful in a changing environment, such as a potential system integration or strategic acquisition. Once you have normalised the quantification parameters within general event scenarios, the analytic opportunities are effectively limitless. In other words, we start to get pretty close to answering the question, "What is the risk profile of XYZ technology?" with "Fill in the blanks and we'll find out".

In the end, the FI should consider establishing risk tolerances for its technology so that, as environments change and new technology is added, becomes obsolete or is used differently, the FI does not find itself faced with a risk profile that is dramatically different from when the technology was first implemented. It may even choose not to implement a given technology based on the risk profile that it would represent.

## OTHER CONSIDERATIONS

Before moving on to a discussion about applying an OR model for technology to the FI, there are a few additional points worth making with regard to developing a quantification model.

- In order for this exercise to be worthwhile it must have input from IT, operational and business areas, including legal, compliance and customer management. As I stated earlier, all of these areas bring unique insight into the event possibilities as well as the impact of potential events. Each of these perspectives *must* be considered in assigned quantification values.
- An analysis of this nature is never finished. It is as dynamic as the organisation itself. Change is a constant (more on this later) and a risk-assessment model should not only be flexible enough to adapt to change, but should help *understand* the implications of potential change.
- We touched on this earlier, but it bears repeating. A mature organisation with a comprehensive operational risk-assessment process should have already considered technology "events" in their risk assessments. The purpose of the exercise in this instance should never be to replace that analysis, but it should serve to validate or challenge it. If the data that comes from this analysis (focused on technology) differs wildly with the analysis from the OR assessment (focused on process), then something isn't right.
- Never lose sight of the goal of detailed risk assessment, which is to answer the questions, "Are we willing to accept this level of risk?" and, if not, "What can be done to mitigate or transfer part of the risk?"
- Be very cautious about who "owns" a technology risk assessment. Technology, in and of itself, is never strategic: it is only a set of tools designed to facilitate the business objectives, which *are* strategic. An IT risk-management staff member or team certainly can facilitate the assessment process, but, in the end, the business should own the risk.
- Never forget the relationship between a given technology and the controls surrounding that technology. The relative strength or weakness of an operational control should not impact the risk assessment of the technology. A bad control is a bad control,

that's all. In other words, a bad control represents a process risk, not a technology risk.

- ❑ There is way too much focus in the industry on inherent risk and not nearly enough on net risk (after mitigation and transfer). I believe that this is largely attributed to the woeful lack of decent modelling software designed around technology risk, with the consequence of a commensurate lack of awareness of net risk. Even though most FIs have spent significant sums implementing powerful tools, processes and controls to mitigate technology risks, they often remain short-sightedly focused on those same risks, ignoring the reality that other risk areas (especially internal risks) often rate much higher on a net basis.
- ❑ Finally, in order to model the operational risks of technology, the FI must have an understanding of how technology is used specifically to support business processes. It is often the case that the real value in the exercise is as much in the discovery as the end result.

## BUSINESS APPLICATIONS

Now that we have established at least a rudimentary framework for quantifying the operational risks of technology, there are some important implications to the business in its application. Having the ability to measure the risks that are inherent to these tools that have become so critical to our business can have a material benefit to how we manage the business. The following subsections discuss the impact of an OR assessment of technology on areas such as strategic planning, KRIs and change management.

### Strategic planning

When we begin discussing strategy, it is important to distinguish between the corporate strategic plan and the strategic technology plan. Unfortunately, in too many organisations there is a disconnection between these two plans when there should be an inherent symmetry. This can be evidenced by the abundance of IT projects that go unfinished or over budget, that underdeliver or, in any one of a number of ways, fail to bring incremental value to business objectives. If done correctly, the strategic initiatives of the organisation should drive the need for technology spend, where the return on investment (ROI) of any given technology can be derived from the value gained in supporting those objectives. Technology in and of itself is not strategic and it never has been: it is simply a tool to facilitate the business objectives. Once a set of strategic objectives have been established, a process should take place to determine the technology that is best suited to support those objectives.

Too often, however, the analysis begins and ends with, "How much will it cost?" and, "What will it get me?" which is a tragically short-sighted approach to evaluating technology. Go back to several of the observations from the beginning of the chapter about people's perception of technology: (1) it will always work and (2) people will always do the right thing with it. It is amazing how often the question is never asked within the strategic planning process, "What could go wrong?" and, "What would that mean to the organisation?"

Therefore, when developing strategic technology plans, in order to consider properly the potential impact of any proposed technology, you must go beyond the traditional questions of cost[2] and timeline and consider the incremental operational risks. In order to do this the FI must have a quantification model in place to assess the operational impact of the proposed technology. Once a base model has been developed, that same model can be used not only to evaluate the incremental risk of the new technology but also to consider additional scenarios of implementation failures. Depending on the results of this analysis, the FI may need to revisit the assumptions that went into the strategic plan regarding which technologies to consider or even the anticipated ROI of the business initiative itself. The FI may decide that although the project may have very favourable prospects, the new risks inherent in the required technology may exceed risk tolerances for the institution. But, without some form of assessment model in place, the institution is unable to consider the incremental risk profile.

Put another way, the OR assessment of technology should always start with the strategic plan. If the first time that the question, "What is the risk to the FI with this technology?" is being asked is after the technology is in place, then something is very wrong. At that point the FI has already accepted the risk regardless of whether it is within its allowable risk profiles.

Finally, one of the biggest advantages of starting the risk-assessment process of technology right at the strategic-planning phase is that it creates awareness and accountability with the business sponsors. By agreeing to new technology with an awareness of the increment risk that it brings, the FI is never put in a position of something going wrong somewhere along the line and the business areas saying "but you never told me that could happen." It is never too early in a process for awareness and accountability.

### Key risk indicators

Given that this is an area that is still evolving within the financial-services industry, and we are probably a long way from something that looks like best practices, it is still worth mentioning the connection between key risk indicators (KRIs) and assessing technology risks. Many institutions have developed some form of KRI programme, and, despite the fact that there are wildly different thoughts on programme design, the fact remains that FIs have always had risk indicators and always will. At the end of the day you need a set of indicators that tell you if something isn't right. They need be clearly defined and highly correlated to event types.

In addition to serving (by their very nature) as an excellent bridge between the technology and business areas, KRIs actually provide one critical component to effective risk mitigation, and that is that they address change. Risk assessments are all built on a series of assumptions at some point in time. As change is introduced in people, processes, external events and so forth, these changes can have a profound impact on risk profiles, and the FI needs mechanisms in place to capture the impact of those changes. This is particularly true with technology, which often leverages certain processes to the point where failure scenarios can take on epic proportions.

However, one area where KRIs have struggled for traction is in lack of sufficient foundation, or connectivity to a set of assumptions about *why* the indicator maps to a quantifiable risk. Most KRIs are derived by historical experience, such as events and losses, which, for reasons stated above, are not always proper foundation when it comes to technology, as similar events tend not to repeat. This is an area where a solid OR assessment of technology can prove invaluable, because instead of mapping the KRI to empirical (and sometimes anecdotal) data, you can map them to the business assumptions built directly into the assessment model. Once you have completed your assessment of the technology components used by the organisation, a certain percentage of those technologies will present high-risk profiles, either on a gross or net basis. As part of the risk-mitigation process, KRIs may in some cases be established specifically to monitor the higher-risk technologies. One could even argue that, when it comes to your technology, it is effectively impossible to know what is a "key" indicator until you know what are your key risks, as determined by a defensible assessment model. As you can see, there is tremendous value in utilising the symmetry between these two very powerful tools.

Developing KRIs to address technology risks is a bit of both good news and bad news. The good news is that because it involves technology there is much that can typically be automated based on systemic rules (for instance, network uptime, number of invalid login attempts). The bad news is that, with many processes that are leveraged on complex technology, there are cases where, by the time a KRI fires, it may be too late to mitigate the risk. The obvious implications of this are that (1) KRIs will likely have degrees of tolerance values that may require different types of responses and (2) KRIs should never fully replace trained staff who know how to recognise trouble when they see it.

The development of KRIs is fully covered in another chapter, but here are a few tactical points to consider relative to technology risks.

- ❑ Based on the results of technology risks assessments, focus particular attention on any technology that ends up rating as a high risk. Require that your technology staff and business owners work together to develop related KRIs that would signal a potential emerging threat to that technology. As we said before, this is important because the IT staff have the best knowledge of what can go wrong (and what activity would signal that something may be going wrong) and the business areas have the best insight into what the impact of that failure would be to the business. Any exercise that allows IT and business owners to "stand in each other's shoes" so to speak is good for the organisation.
- ❑ Assign specific responsibility for the monitoring of systemic KRIs with clearly defined response requirements based on different tolerances. These tolerance levels should be well documented, communicated and audited.

- Be clear on the audience for all KRIs. Leading indicators will generally be most useful to the IT staff (who are obviously in a position to take corrective action) and lagging indicators will be useful to both IT and business owners, often as a forensic look at how systems could be improved.
- Whatever you decide to measure, monitor. A report that is generated so routinely that nobody really looks at it any more is worse than no report at all. With KRIs consider either exception-only reports or make them visually obvious (graphical heat maps for instance) to indicate when values have changed.
- Any time major changes happen to the technology infrastructure, particularly when new systems are added or obsolete ones removed, revisit the KRI library to determine what changes need to be made to keep the list relevant and accurate.

In the end, the most important thing to ensure when developing KRIs for technology is there is harmony between risk assessments and KRI libraries. Again, risk assessments represent point-in-time data; good KRIs make them dynamic and real-time. Together they represent a powerful tool in OR management.

### Change management

As I have been known to say, "Ironically, change, in and of itself, is a constant." One of the few things of which you can be sure is that change will take place. It is the great destabiliser (which, unfortunately for me, is not even a real word, at least not yet.) When I was consulting for banks over many years I would ask them, "Do you want a ten-second assessment of your operational risks? How much change is going on?" The more change that is taking place within an organisation, the higher the operational risks, and this is particularly true for technology. What risk managers must understand is that, in the light of change, most if not all assumptions become suspect. If you don't have some sort of base model in place to establish your risk profiles, especially for the technology you depend on, you simply cannot have any basis to appreciate the impact that potential change has on those risk profiles. This point is illustrated in Figure 2, which I refer to as the "prism effect of change". If you take an organisation that does the same thing the same way with the same tools every day under the same circumstances, a certain number of things

**Figure 2** The prism effect of change

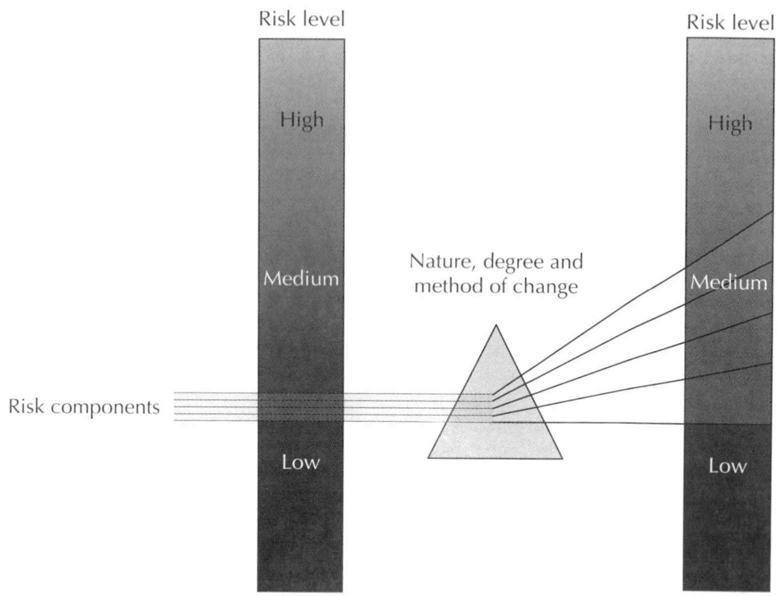


can and will go wrong. This is what we model into our range of "expected losses" that comprise the band on the left side of the figure. But, once we introduce some form of change into the environment, it creates a prism effect on the risk properties, which probably won't make the risk profile go down, but most assuredly will make the risk range go up. If you are going to understand the implications of proposed change on the FI's OR profile, you must have a model to be able to adjust your risk assumptions and evaluate the impact on your technology. This is where an OR assessment model for technology can be absolutely invaluable.

## PRISM EFFECT OF CHANGE

A proper treatment of assessing the operational risk of technology should not end with a point-in-time analysis. No business exists at only a point in time. We live and work in an environment that is constantly changing, and this is no truer than with technology. It is imperative that, in order to fully understand the risks that we accept by using technology that we understand the dynamics that exist when we consider change, whether we invoked or encountered it.

In conclusion, the broad business applications of a sound OR model for technology are significant, more than can be fully covered in this text. However, the areas described above should give the reader a basic understanding of how beneficial this type of model can be, and how it so logically integrates into existing risk tools. It is simply a matter of deciding how the FI wants to approach the process, and how deeply it wants to incorporate it into the overall OR management programme.

## FORWARD TRENDS

Technology, like everything, marches on. Before closing, it is worth mentioning several trends that can be observed, as they both serve to reinforce the need for a quantification model and may influence its design and application.

- *Complexity*: Most technology, in order to be more functional, user-friendly, cost-effective and so forth, continues to grow exponentially more complex. Operating systems and software applications of today contain billions of lines of computer code, requiring ever more technical certifications just to install and support them. However, functionality, user-friendliness and cost-effectiveness come at a price, which includes risk. Developing sound OR assessment models today will become ever more critical as these systems continue to evolve and impact more and more business processes.
- *Integration*: Every year more and more processes become automated, saving time and money and improving operational efficiency. While these gains are good for business, and theoretically improve shareholder value, that assumption can quickly turn if the risks associated with those embedded technologies are not understood and anticipated. The assumption "it worked yesterday, why shouldn't it work tomorrow?" could prove devastatingly wrong at a cost that could be more than the business can bear. As technology is used in more deeply integrated ways, spanning multiple business boundaries and processes, it is becoming imperative that the FI have a clear understanding of the risks associated with those technologies, not just the isolated processes that depend on them.

- *Emerging threats*: Today we are seeing the evidence of things to come in the form of computer viruses, spam, system hacking, denial of service attacks, phishing, pharming, Trojan horses and on and on. Although the financial-services industry has certainly recognised losses associated with these threats, a certain percentage of it ends up in the category called nuisance. This trend can only get worse as criminals get smarter and electronic crime tools become more sophisticated. As an example, presently well-managed institutions utilise state-of-the-art antivirus programs that are updated as frequently as possible. But those protections are only as good as the tools provided by the antivirus vendors and things such as zero-day exploits (viruses released before protective updates can be made available) could prove to be a significant challenge to security officers trying to protect external facing systems. The need for a clear business-level understanding of the impact of these ever more sophisticated threats is more critical than ever.

## SUMMARY

To wrap up this discussion, there are a few points worth making, the most important being, "Do it, and do it now." As was discussed throughout this chapter, the need for a clear understanding of the operational risks of technology is only going to increase. The methodology and approach laid out in this chapter will not be right for every institution but may be perfect for another. But hopefully the broad concepts and general principles discussed will give some insight into how to approach this type of modelling. Start small if necessary, perhaps with a subset of technology that is assumed to be the highest risk, and build from there.

As was stated, the beauty of this type of analysis is that it does not have to cover every single piece of technology to bring value. Build awareness around the goals and objectives of the assessment of these operational risks, and make sure that any models that are developed are very closely integrated with assessment models focused on processes, so that work is never duplicated. Utilise the expertise that exists within the organisation. This is one type of analysis that, simply put, just embodies a lot of common sense.

"What would happen if ...?" How you choose to fill in the blank is up to you.

1 The correct term would actually be "loss" of the technology because loss considers not only component failure, but also obsolescence, cost increase beyond economical viability, vendor failure, or any other scenario that ultimately translates to "here today, gone tomorrow". However, I caution using the word "loss" in this context because that term is typically reserved for a monetary loss and could create confusion.

2 Which in and of itself represents an operational risk. The vast majority of all projects are underestimated in terms of implementation cost, particularly soft dollar costs (which are typically as much as 10 times the hard-dollar cost) and the operational impact of dedicating staff resources when projects go beyond the planned implementation period.

# Section Five

# Comparative Views of Implementation

The last section contains three very special chapters designed to help readers gain a broader understanding of how their colleagues around the world are implementing their approaches to operational risk.

The first chapter, by Vandana Rao and Ashish Dev, talks about implementation issues that are specific to the US, using KeyCorp's own programme as a model. While it covers some of the basics of an OR framework, it does so from a distinctly US point of view.

The second chapter provides the results of an industry survey conducted in Germany by the Bundesanstalt für Finanzdienstleistungsaufsicht (BaFin) and the Bundesbank into how firms are implementing their operational risk programmes. This chapter outlines the "real-world" practices in financial services firms in this European country, including the strengths and shortcomings of firms' approaches to solving key OR challenges.

The third chapter is based on a study conducted among Spanish banks on their own implementation of operational risk. It looks at such subjects as how firms are defining OR, what kinds of data they are collecting and what modelled data are being used for within firms.

I included these chapters not just because they make for interesting reading, but also because they provide executives with an idea of what general practices are evolving in both Europe and the US in OR implementation. I hope that readers will find them to be both illuminating and the basis for debate and discussion.

# 12

# *Operational Risk: Some Issues in Basel II AMA Implementation in US Financial Institutions*

**Vandana Rao; Ashish Dev***

Indiana University East; KeyCorp

As recently as in 1999, *Derivatives Strategy* ran an article (Webb, 1999) saying that there was no consensus in the industry on a precise definition of operational risk (OR) and concluded that such a consensus was unlikely to emerge in the near future. This would probably have been the case but for Basel II placing due emphasis on OR. As a result, in the last five years, Basel II has been the catalyst that has forced a consensus. It was not uncommon, five years ago, to consider OR as a residual; everything other than credit risk or market risk was, by default, OR. Today, in keeping with semantics, we can call the residual concept "other risk" in contrast to the concrete definition of OR that has emerged. An industry consensus defines OR as "the risk of direct or indirect loss resulting from inadequate or failed processes or systems, human factors, or external events". Basel II adopted this definition but eliminated the reference to indirect losses. By now most financial institutions have adopted the above definition of OR with relatively minor modifications.

An industry working group that has had significant influence, as the Basel II formulation of OR progressed, is the Working Group on Operational Risk (WGOR) of the Institute of International Finance.

*Special acknowledgement is due to Anupam Sahay of KeyCorp who, jointly with Ashish Dev, developed some of the concepts and schematics explained in this chapter. Any errors, however, are the authors' responsibility. The views expressed are those of the authors and not necessarily those of KeyCorp or Indiana University.

This group's work on the definition of OR and its focus on events (categorisation of events, in particular) and data as well as possible methodologies (the advanced approaches) for computation of adequate regulatory capital were incorporated significantly in the Basel II consultative paper of 2001 (CP2). This group also persevered to restrict the definition of OR (in contrast to "other risk") as far as possible to concepts and items that are quantifiable[1] or potentially quantifiable in the near future and the belief that robust methodologies will emerge for OR just as they did for market risk in the early and mid-1990s. The group's deliberation coupled with the weight of BIS as an international bank regulatory body may be credited with catalysing the immense change in banks' attitude and their methodology and approach to OR. Over time, Basel II moved towards incorporating more qualitative elements and permissible approaches based primarily on qualitative score cards, the most important arguments being (i) historical data are backward-looking and (ii) much more so than market or credit risk, OR in an organisation depends strongly on the culture of the business units towards risks and controls and also such controls can change in short order with the introduction of new technology. This culminated in what has come to be known as *advanced measurement approaches*[2] (AMA) of Basel II. Three characteristics of AMA are worth noting here. One is that there is no prescribed formula or calculation except that the horizon and confidence level are specified; and a bank can choose its own methodology and come up with its own capital charge, subject to regulatory approval of the soundness of the methodology. The second is that a combination of quantitative and qualitative elements (described later in the chapter) is a requirement. The third is that AMA is as much about managing OR as of measuring and calculating regulatory capital for OR. More generally, Basel II has gone well beyond minimum regulatory capital. It has defined OR in somewhat unambiguous terms. It has also dwelt considerably on policy, oversight and management of OR. The first and third characteristics together prompted, during high-level discussions, the coinage of the phrase that AMA is in effect "Pillar 1.8" – it has the characteristics of both Pillar 1 and Pillar 2, but is perhaps closer to Pillar 2. Nonetheless an explicit charge for OR under Pillar 1, as decided by Basel II, perhaps had a faster catalytic effect than if it were to be captured under Pillar 2.

While the above definition of OR by Basel II clearly delineates the scope of OR by highlighting the major causative factors, it is still at a high level and serves only as a guiding principle. Note that the definition is fundamentally focused on operational events. It is pertinent to contrast this event-centric concept with process-centric "operations risk" or dollar-centric "operational expenses (cost of doing business)". A more practical definition is in terms of a systematic categorisation and enumeration of operational events. Basel II has proposed three levels of "event type" categories with numerous categories under each level. The first level has seven event categories. A review of the event categories at all three levels leaves little doubt as to what constitutes OR in a bank. Thus, in Basel II, the categories complement the high-level definition of OR. Tables 1 and 1A provide an illustration of OR event-type categories at all the three levels.

Having granular subcategories helps in understanding what OR is and facilitates easier management and oversight. On the other hand, the more granular we get, the fewer data points are available, making a statistically robust estimate of loss distribution and computation of capital more difficult. That is why Basel II has mandated only categorisation of events at Level 1. Further granularity is a choice of the bank depending on availability of data.

The Basel II definition explicitly includes legal risk or the risk of loss due to litigation, and compliance risk or the risk of loss due to failure to comply with laws and regulations. It is coincidental that, right around the time of Basel II, the regulatory environment in the US has considerably heightened the focus on compliance issues. Managing this one component of OR alone has required many banks to create a large number of positions and make significant investments in systems for day-to-day compliance with regulations. Specific examples of compliance issues are the Anti-Money-Laundering (AML) and Bank Secrecy Act (BSA).

In recent years, some banks (both large and medium-sized) in the US have suffered very high-severity operational events in the area of compliance alone. Compliance has always been a traditional function in a bank and is often viewed as separate and distinct from operational risk management (ORM). However, tools and methodologies being developed by banks in OR can be applied to management of compliance risk with considerable benefit. This goes well beyond just the inclusion of compliance losses for calculation of capital.

**Table 1** Basel II major event types

| Event type (Level 1) | Examples |
|---|---|
| Internal fraud | Unauthorised trading, embezzlement |
| External fraud | Forgery, robbery |
| Employment practices and workplace safety | Workers' compensation, harassment |
| Clients, products and business practices | Noncompliance of regulations, breaches of trust |
| Damage to physical assets | Natural disasters, terrorism |
| Business disruption and systems failure | Software/hardware failure, utility outage |
| Execution, delivery and process management | Data entry, missed deadline, vendor disputes |

**Table 1A** Illustration of Levels 1, 2 and 3

| Level 1 | Level 2 | Level 3 |
|---|---|---|
| External fraud | Theft and fraud | Theft/robbery<br>Forgery<br>Check kiting |
| | System security | Hacking damage<br>Theft of information (with monetary loss) |
| Employment practices and workplace safety | Employee relations | Compensation, benefit, termination issues<br>Organised labour activity |
| | Safe environment | General liability (slip and fall, etc)<br>Employee health and safety rules events<br>Workers' compensation |
| | Diversity and discrimination | All discrimination types |

The Basel II definition of OR does *not* include business risk or strategic risk. Sometimes, at senior decision-making levels, an argument is made that Basel II operational risk capital is expected to be less than 20% of total minimum regulatory capital for most financial institutions. This is much less than the difference between well-capitalised (which is where most banks in the US are – mostly voluntarily and some through rating-agency constraints) and adequately capitalised financial institutions under Basel I. In contrast, strategic and business risks are much higher and Basel II does not address those risks. It appears that, on average, mergers and acquisitions have eroded[3] (rather than created) more shareholder value in the long run than there has been erosion of value from operational loss events. Thus almost the whole premium paid in a merger or acquisition is liable to be lost when held to a high level of confidence.[4] Therefore, capital for strategic risk can be significantly higher than capital for operational risk. But the emphasis of Basel II in this case has not been one of magnitude but rather one of covering what can be measured (at least in the near future). It is generally accepted that capital for strategic risk will be subject to more judgement on the part of executive management and also the regulators. The same is true of reputational risk.

## ADVANCED MEASUREMENT APPROACHES

As the use of the plural suggests, "advanced measurement approach*es*" does not refer to a single approach or formulation. Each bank can choose its own model and methodology. But certain guiding principles have been specified. Four distinct components (in addition to 99.9% level of confidence and one-year horizon) constitute the fundamentals of AMA:

(1) *Internal loss-event data*: Banks are required to collect internal loss-event data for a period of at least five years, with provision for a shorter period (three years) during the early implementation stages. Data must be collected at the Category 1 level, but banks are free to collect data at Category 2 or Category 3 levels or even finer levels.
(2) *External loss data*: Operational events of the rare kind happen only to the unfortunate few. Therefore, it is necessary to include events that have happened to similarly placed institutions in the industry since the event has not occurred in the internal history of the bank.
(3) *Scenario analysis*: Operational-loss data are currently rather sparse in most financial institutions. In the foreseeable future, therefore, there is a need for the use of "soft" data – estimates of losses based on what-if scenario evaluations of business (both line management and risk management) experts.
(4) *Internal control and business environmental factors*: Much more so than credit or market risk losses, operational risk losses depend

strongly on internal controls and business environment factors. The latter change over time, sometimes at short notice. Therefore, the historical loss data (both internal and external) are required to be adjusted to reflect changes that internal controls and business environment factors have undergone. This provides a forward-looking component to the otherwise backward-looking historical data.

## LOSS DISTRIBUTION APPROACH

Before going into more details about each of the four components above, we introduce the basic features of a methodology for calculating capital called the *loss distribution approach* (LDA).[5] Versions of LDA have been used by actuaries in the insurance industry for some time. Several banks involved in Basel II AMA have adopted one variant or other of an essentially loss distribution approach. It is by no means the only broad approach but seems to be emerging as the most common one. Within the broad approach, there can be many variations depending on the exact implementation.

LDA conceptually separates (i) *frequency* per unit of time (week, month) of occurrence of a particular type of operational event irrespective of the size of the loss and (ii) *severity*, that is, the net dollar loss given that an event has occurred. Most commonly, a frequency distribution is posited as a Poisson distribution, which has a single parameter. With sufficient data, the mean can easily be estimated in a robust manner, yielding the particular Poisson frequency distribution. The severity distribution is clearly long-tailed. But there is no consensus as to what distribution is most suitable (at least under certain conditions). The two most commonly used are lognormal and Weibull distributions. Both lack adequate data points at the right tail of the severity distribution and the fact that both these distributions are long but thin tailed, have led many to use extreme-value theory (EVT). Recently, empirical evidence provided by De Koker (2005), showing that (large) operational losses follow a power curve, provides a solid basis for using EVT and, in particular, generalised Pareto distribution in the tail and a lognormal or Weibull distribution in the body. Generation of the loss distribution from the estimated frequency and severity distributions is necessarily done by a "convolution" of one random variable on another, which has to be done by simulation.

**Figure 1** Developing OpRisk capital – basic LDA

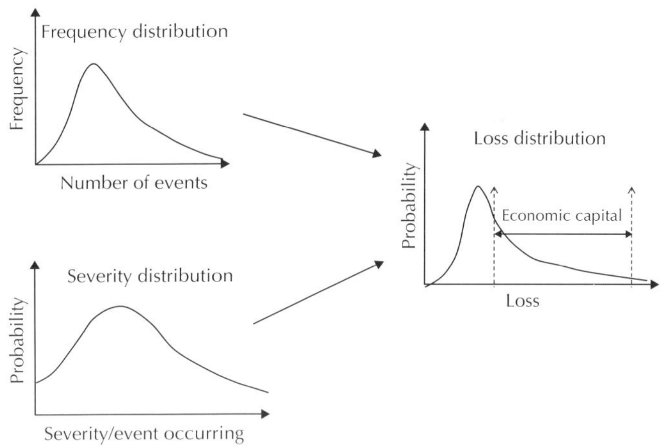


Figure 1 depicts a schematic diagram of how the loss distribution approach works.

## Internal loss-event data

Basel II AMA requires a bank to have five years of internal loss-event data. Just three years ago few banks could claim to have been collecting operational-loss data systematically in all areas of the institution. Data on fraud events and cases leading to litigation were generally available and an occasional business unit would be collecting information of errors and losses with the purpose of reducing such occurrences. A typical senior manager would not have a clue as to the average and variance of losses incurred due to operational events in their area, except for some very large loss event. Yet for a traditional commercial or retail bank, in almost all quarters it loses more from numerous low-severity events than from any high-severity event. While capital is more sensitive to low-frequency, high-severity data points (or scenarios), in order to improve operational efficiency and reduce operational losses on a sustained basis, a bank needs to tackle the high-frequency, low-severity events. This is the major reason for collecting information on internal loss events; not just the losses but enough information to do root cause analyses, which enables one to take sensible corrective actions and "stop the bleeding" (see Nakada, 2004). The secondary reason is to obtain enough data to derive a loss distribution and economic capital. Many banks have already started collecting internal loss-event data enterprise-wide.[6] The typical threshold used by most is US$10,000, except perhaps for branch banking, which may justify a lower threshold. Below are some desirable practical features of an internal loss-event database:

- multi-source interfaces:
  - automated: general ledger, litigation database, security database;
  - manual: direct loading by reporter;
  - ability to track back to source record;
- dynamic online reports:
  - real-time data can be exported in order to create dashboards, pie and bar charts;
- automated data extraction for providing data to industry consortiums;
- ability to incorporate changes in organisational hierarchy:
  - synchronised with current organisational hierarchy;
  - closed and merged cost centres maintained for auditability;
- fine control on data access security:
  - access defined by role;
  - views defined by profile (organisational hierarchy);
- maintaining revision history.

Data-collection scope may include elements that are over and above Basel II AMA requirements. Basel II AMA excludes OR events that end up as credit losses. Some banks include significant portion of credit–OR boundary events (eg, credit losses owing to operational mistakes) as part of operational risk.[7] In fact, in a normal year the total loss from such credit–OR boundary events may exceed total loss from Basel II OR events in a commercial bank. For purposes of managing OR, information on such credit–OR boundary events can be very useful. Basel II AMA does not require information content from "near-miss" events. However, a persistent positive trend in number of "near-miss" events is a sure sign of loss events likely to occur (increase) in the near future. Basel II AMA does not refer to "indirect losses" but some banks have chosen to include "indirect losses" as a separate component of internal data. Indeed for some operational-loss events, the indirect cost may well

**Figure 2** Internal data capture

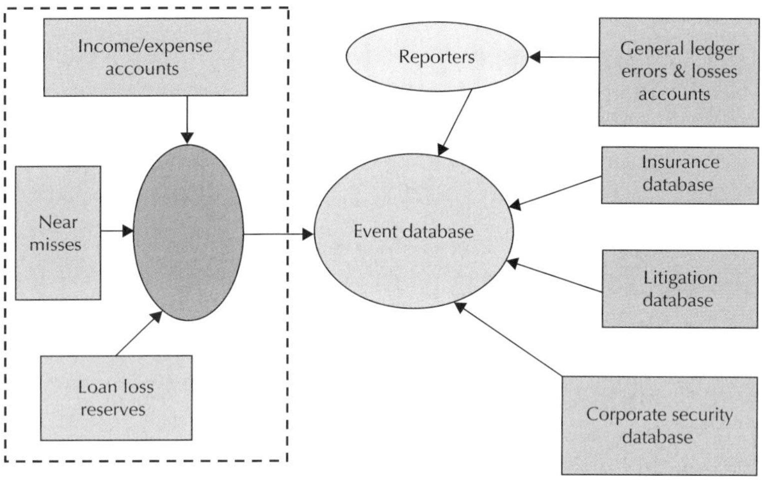


exceed a low-severity direct loss. For example, to rectify an inadvertent mistake essentially by one person at one place in a fiduciary business may require sending of documentation (legally required) to millions of customers. Traditionally, most business units of a bank do not even keep track of indirect costs, and such costs get posted as expenses in general ledger accounts that have many other (usually larger) entries.

## EXTERNAL LOSS-EVENT DATA

Capital (economic or regulatory) for operational risk is driven by events in the (long) tail – the so-called low-frequency, high-severity events. Such events happen to only the occasional bank. Therefore, even if a bank collects internal loss data for several years it is by no means certain that it has captured the tail events adequately. That is why external data can help a bank to understand the tails of OR loss distribution, where internal data are insufficient (as in most cases) to adequately quantify the unexpected risk of loss.

There are two distinct types of external data. One is the result of the formation of consortiums of banks that contribute data to an independent third party in an agreed-upon format and definitions.

The first such consortium in the US was the Multinational Operational Risk Exchange (MORE), with Net Risk as the independent third party. But before consensus could be reached on several issues, particularly the issue of scaling, the initiative died out when Net Risk was acquired by Fitch. More than 20 large and medium-sized banks from the US and Canada participated in the deliberations.

An international consortium called Operational Risk exchange (ORX), mainly consisting of large banks, has been collecting loss-event data for the last few years. At present about 15 very large European and North American banks contribute loss-event data and the number is likely to grow as the cost of participation comes down considerably. Recently, the Risk Management Association (RMA) entered into collaboration with ORX and will be the independent third party acting as a repository for data and ensuring data integrity. In the US, another consortium,[8] with the American Bankers' Association (ABA) as the independent third party, has started collecting data contributed by several medium-sized banks. In the UK the British bankers' Association (BBA) started such a consortium almost around the time the MORE initiative began. However, it is generally believed that the BBA and ABA data consortiums are inadequately funded and contain data contributed by only a handful of participants.

The second type of external data is compiled from publicly available operational-loss events – typically ones that are low-frequency, high-severity events. The two well-known external loss-event databases are provided by Fitch Risk (now encompassing Algorithmics) and SAS.

The two most important issues with any consortium are (a) scaling of data derived from institutions of all different sizes of operation and (b) a common minimum threshold for loss per event below which no data will be collected and the impact of consequent truncation. The same issues are present with public loss-event databases.

## RISK AND CONTROL SELF-ASSESSMENT

The incorporation of *internal control and business environmental factors* in Basel II has come to be known in the industry as *risk-and-control self-assessment* or RCSA. RCSA has been defined in KeyCorp as "a qualitative but highly structured assessment of the various operational risks associated with day-to-day conduct of business and the degree and quality of internal controls in place to keep such risks within tolerable limits by the business units themselves in a consistent and periodic manner across the institution providing useful management information about the operational risk the institution as a whole is bearing". RCSA is a subject in itself and will not be examined in detail in this chapter.

Implementing the same platform for Sarbanes–Oxley (SOX) 404 certification, self-testing for compliance with laws and regulations (non-compliance is part of operational risk under Basel II definition), as well as all other operational risk and control self-assessment, enables considerable savings in cost and manpower. In order to satisfy all these objectives, the system needs to be flexible to begin with and a careful three-way mapping of processes, organisation points and significant accounts needs to be worked out. Furthermore, if the same platform can be used for internal loss-event data collection and economic capital computation module, it allows an automatic internal consistency between quantitative loss data and qualitative self-assessment, which is often not the case (see Peccia, 2004). This is feasible as long as the loss-event categories can be mapped to one of the foci of the three-way mapping referred to above. The leading vendors of OR systems seem to be leaning towards this concept.[9]

The result of an RCSA exercise can provide a "score" for each loss-event type and business unit. The qualitative assessments may be subjective but they need to be highly structured so that they can be scored in a Likert-type scale. Yet often it is the *evidence* of effectiveness rather than an *assertion* of being effective that drives the rating. The score is determined by the "degree of existence" of a condition of effective control rather then the mere existence or non-existence of the condition. Hence a "fuzzy" judgement is called for (see Peccia, 2004). Since a vast majority of business-unit managers and even risk managers are not quite used to scoring of assessments (in contrast to subjectively rating an assertion), it is helpful for clarity and consistency if a library is created of the characteristics that must be present in order to give a risk or a control a particular score. The Internal Control Framework of COSO also provides sufficient guidance on rating of control environments. Both the extent of inherent operational risk and the quality and effectiveness of controls need to be assessed and their scores combined to get a composite score. This is not an easy task but qualitative scoring and creating composites have been done in the social sciences for many years.

The more difficult concept is how to incorporate the effect of the qualitative scores on calculated capital or on the frequency and severity distributions in a LDA. What is becoming progressively clear is that there is no valid means of directly adjusting capital for better or worse scores of RCSA, except in an ad hoc manner. Combining qualitative and quantitative measures by assigning ad hoc weights after calculation of economic capital numbers (weighting economic capital) does not have a solid theoretical foundation. Adjusting the frequency and severity distributions themselves for better or worse scores of RCSA is more defensible. One approach is to create Bayesian posterior distributions (see Alexander, 2003) and another is the approach of "thinning" of distributions (see Sahay and Dev, 2005). Neither of these is well established in the industry but they are mathematically valid approaches.

Figures 3a, 3b and 3c depict the elements of appropriate adjustments for qualitative scores in order to compute capital.

**Figure 3a** Developing OpRisk capital – adjustments

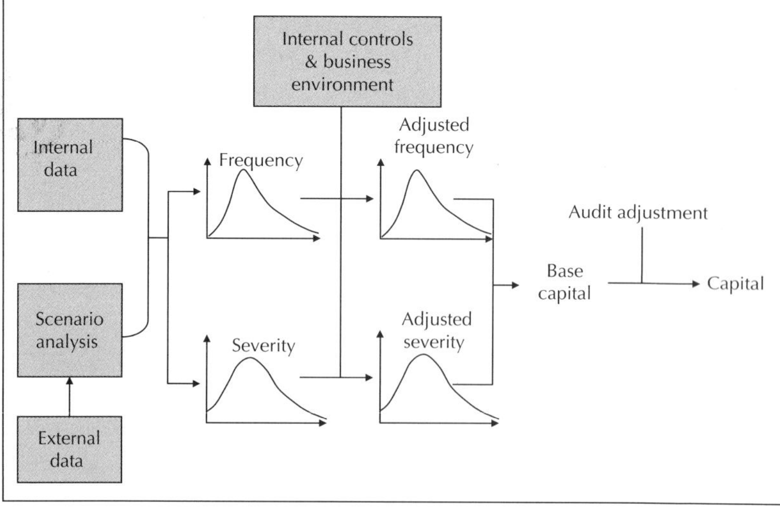

**Figure 3b** Adjustment to frequency

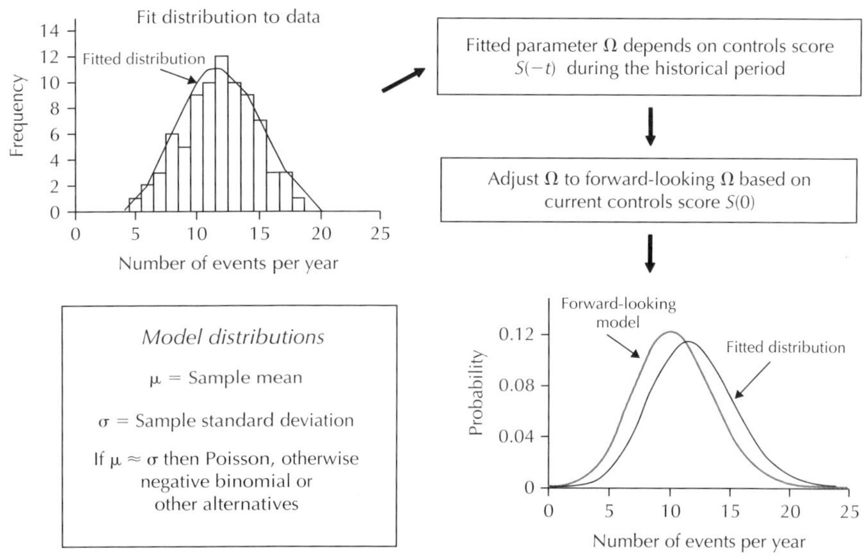


**Figure 3c** Adjustment to severity

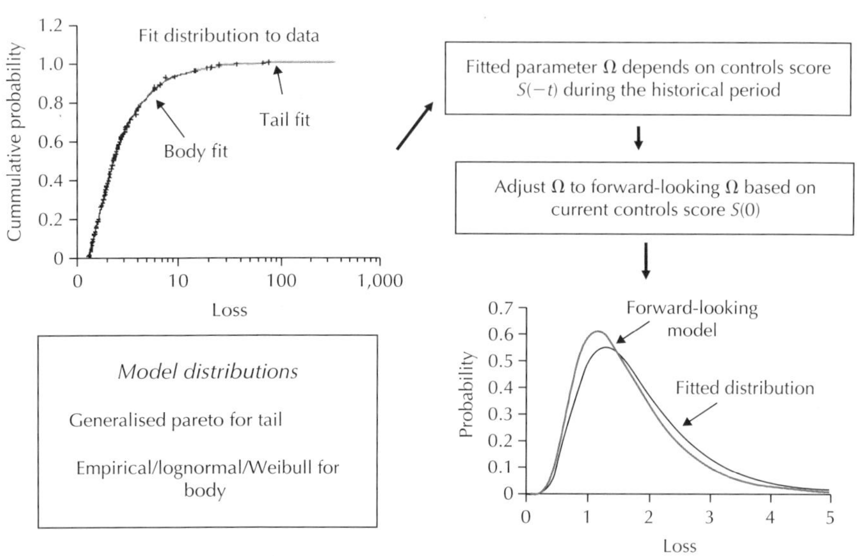

## SCENARIO ANALYSIS

The status of data on operational losses is at best nascent. It is highly unlikely that any data source can be expected to cover all probable events for a particular bank. Hence, there is a need for creating plausible scenarios and their incorporation in the computation of capital. In a way, it parallels the requirement of stress-testing in market and credit risk. Scenario analysis can be used as the predominant method of the quantitative computation of capital (see Anders and Van Den Brink, 2004). Alternatively, it can be used to supplement data points, particularly in the severity distribution in LDA. Basel II AMA permits both but requires that scenario analysis form part of the calculation. However, most banks seem to be leaning towards the latter approach.

A lot of debate has gone on (in the context of MORE and ORX and elsewhere) about whether a particular data point from a publicly available data source or from a pooled data consortium is relevant to a particular financial institution. The first issue is one of scaling, since sizes of business vary between banks by orders of magnitude. The second issue is one of appropriateness. If a bank does not have a certain type of business at all, it is straightforward to eliminate those data points before incorporation. But the more difficult question is appropriateness from the perspective of culture, risk appetite and controls that may differ considerably between the bank and the source bank (perhaps unknown) from which the data point was created. One way of getting around the scaling and appropriateness issues is to create virtual events based on expert knowledge. A detailed root-cause analysis of an external event is prepared and then discussed in focus groups of experienced persons knowledgeable about the business. Each step of what happened in the external event is analysed and a consensus arrived at as to what would have transpired (both quantitative numbers and qualitative description) if that step happened in the bank in question. Every step is sequentially analysed in this way. This creates a scenario that can then be used as a data point. From this perspective, descriptive elements of an external data source are more important than the quantitative data point.

## KEY RISK INDICATORS

The genesis of key risk indicators (KRIs) in operational risk arises from the more commonly known key risk factors for heart attack in a human being. Resulting from studies in Long Island, New York, in the 1970s, followed by further refinements, a small number of easily definable and observable key risk factors were identified by the medical profession that can predict the propensity of heart attack in a human being, eg, high cholesterol, smoking, obesity. It may be difficult but not impossible to lower the levels of one or more key risk factors that are beyond the normal range, through medication or exercise. Physicians routinely check for a few such risk factors in patients beyond a particular age, even if they do not have a heart problem. The causal relationship between the risk factors and chances of heart attack has been estimated by medical researchers through the collection of data and by performing controlled experiments over a long period of years. From this analogy, four characteristics of KRIs of operational risk emerge that are not only desirable but perhaps also critical: (1) a KRI has to be measurable quantitatively; (2) a KRI has to be a statistically robust predictor (ie, to say a leading indicator) of the probability of the occurrence, if not the severity, of an operational risk event; (3) KRIs for each major operational event category have to be limited in number; and (4) it has to be possible for an OR manager in a financial institution, through expensive or inexpensive changes and controls, to affect the value of a KRI over time.

There are two rationales for limiting the number of KRIs to 20 or fewer. One argument is pragmatic. With the emphasis placed by Basel II on board and management oversight of OR, it is necessary to create a dashboard of a limited number of important indicators of the health of OR and its management in the institution that can be presented to the board and executive management. Once an institution has implemented an enterprise-wide RCSA system, the information contained is too vast and needs to be encapsulated in the shape of a dashboard for senior decision makers. A limited number of KRIs can form a constant part of the enterprise risk management (ERM) dashboard (Lam, 2003). The second argument is statistical. It derives from the principle of parsimony, which requires that an econometric specification – estimating the significant indicators that explain the variation in probability of an operational risk event happening – limit the number of explanatory variables used for predictive purposes.

While loss-event data can be considered backward-looking (realised events and losses), periodic RCSA can be considered contemporaneous-looking, KRIs can be considered forward-looking. That is, they are leading or predictive indicators of potential future operational events and losses. However, which KRIs have the most predictive power is yet to be determined even heuristically, let alone econometrically. In mid-2003, the RMA, in consultation with RiskBusiness, started a KRI study with seven banks as founding members.[10] The original idea, apart from the conceptual framework, was to start with a very large number of potential KRIs and, through focus group discussions, whittle them down to a manageable number.

Many other banks have since become interested in the KRI study but the consensus number of KRIs is still over a hundred. The remaining task is not only to narrow down the number but also to show econometrically (and not just from commonsense and experience) that they are indeed statistically significant predictive indicators. There are other industry initiatives to build a library of KRIs. In the meantime, several financial institutions have developed their own heuristic KRIs and have started measuring and reporting them. Whether or not they stand the test of rigorous statistical predictive power, these KRIs are a good qualitative start for operational risk management and reporting. These internal KRIs, however, have two drawbacks: they are simply too many in number and they are not comparable across institutions.

The concept of KRIs (for that matter the RCSA system, in general) has similarities with statistical process control (SPC) in industrial firms, variously known as *total quality management* propagated by Edward Deming and the Six Sigma initiative, introduced by Motorola and popularised by General Electric. If the RCSA system is built with operational processes as the lowest building block, then the information collected from such an enterprise-wide system can be used for process improvement and process re-engineering (as well as management of operational risk), thus improving efficiency. These concepts have been known and applied in enlightened manufacturing companies for decades (see Shepard-Walwyn, 2004). A unified conceptual treatment of KRIs and key performance indicators can be found in Vinella (2004). However, for an average reader, just as in the case of OR events, the best way to present KRIs is to list unambiguously examples of KRIs that have a significant effect on the frequency of OR events and severity of losses.

## GOVERNANCE ISSUES IN OPERATIONAL RISK

Basel II has gone well beyond minimum regulatory capital for OR. It has dwelt considerably on policy, oversight and management of OR. The "Sound Practices" document from the Basel Committee on Banking Supervision (2003) enumerates 10 high-level basic principles of OR management. The establishment of a central OR function independent of business units is a requirement of governance under Basel II. Under AMA, this "governance rule" becomes even more critical. First, it is necessary to ensure consistency in subjective ratings of RCSA by a large number of personnel. Second, "self"-assessment inherently has moral hazard, which only an independent unit can guard against.[11] Third, in OR it is almost a necessity for any one bank to participate in industry-pooled initiatives, which generally span across all businesses. The central OR management function itself must be subject to periodic validation by internal audit as well as the business-unit OR management. The emphasis by Basel II on the independent OR function has created considerable tensions in some institutions between internal audit, risk management and finance (see Howitt, Mainelli and Taylor, 2004, dealing with human factor in operational risk in general; and Leighton, 2004, on this topic specifically).

Three of the principles in the Basel "Sound Practices" document deal with oversight by the board of directors and executive management. In the US, this has been followed by an interagency "Advanced Notice on Proposed Rulemaking for Basel II Operational Risk" (only AMA is applicable in the US). This has led banks to create enterprise-wide operational risk policy, independence statements and a mechanism for reporting and escalating operational risk issues and reports to the board. Compliance with laws and regulations that are part of OR and the heightened regulatory compliance regime (including SOX) have increased the workload of the audit committee of the board considerably, so much so that compliance and OR now take up almost all the attention of the audit committee in many financial institutions, to the near exclusion of strategic discussions appropriate to board level.

**Figure 4** An illustrative governance structure

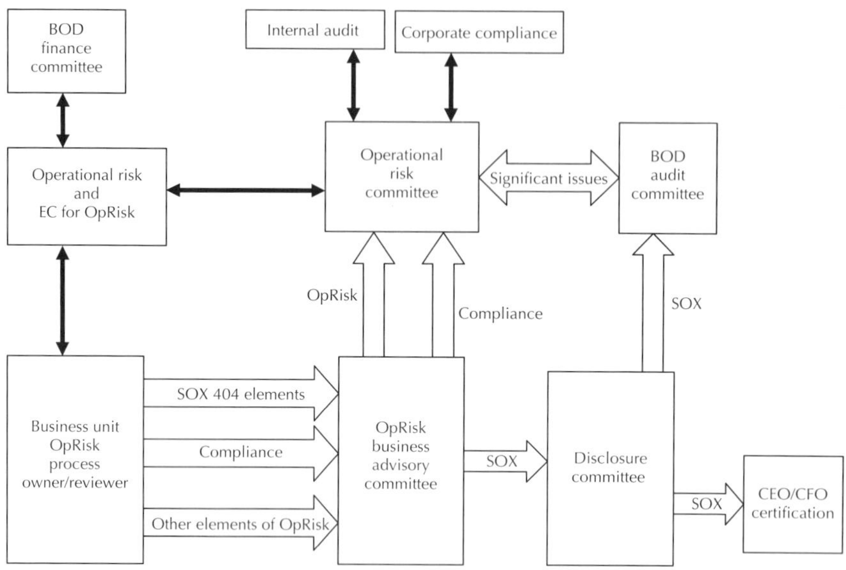


Figure 4 is a schematic diagram of an illustrative governance structure for operational risk. The structure is primarily in the context of RCSA (SOX 404, compliance self-testing and internal control and business-environmental factors for OR at large).

## CONCLUSION

Business managers in financial institutions have been dealing with day-to-day operational risks for a long time. There is a certain level of understanding, and a realisation that such risks must be kept under control and even "managed". But, till recently, this understanding has often been based on common sense and has been designated as something to be dealt with in the course of business as usual.

The deliberations of Basel II international banking regulation rules started around 1999 and ended in the shape of an Accord in April 2003 (CP3). One of the remarkable features of Basel II is the inclusion of OR in the deliberations and formulation, particularly, of the advanced approach (known as AMA). Basel II focused much-needed attention on operational risk among regulators and practitioners (and among some academics) including definition, quantification, measurement and management of OR. Basel II has thus catalysed a great deal of original and pragmatic work in the area of OR in the last few years. It also necessarily catalysed some convergence in the industry, certainly in terms of definition and, to a larger extent, in terms of methodology and even systems. The changes in the last few years have been as significant as if an entirely new discipline has come to be created (Davis, 2005).

In placing focus on OR management in financial institutions, Basel II has elevated OR reporting and management to frequent board oversight. Perhaps not coincidentally, this has come at around the same time as enhanced focus on corporate governance in the US on the heels of corporate scandals such as Enron, Tyco and WorldCom. Taken together, these have helped garner the attention of executive management in almost all institutions towards operational risk. In all the publicity, an important message may have been lost, namely that operational events in a financial institution are often preventable (not necessarily at exorbitant cost) and that efficiency squarely depends on the individual institution's culture, people and systems. Thus, both an emphasis on and investment in operational risk are good risk-management strategies in the long run. It should not require Basel II or corporate scandals to endorse that conclusion.

It is quite possible that such attention and oversight are merely temporary. Sooner or later, board oversight of operational risk will become less urgent and more formal, if not routine. By that time, it is hoped that enterprise-wide systems for control and measurement will have been put in place, a somewhat informative and consistent reporting process instituted and, most importantly, significant improvements in measurement, quantification and methodology related to operational risk would have evolved and standardised. For the financial-services industry, ultimately it is the measurement, analysis and methodology that will have a lasting effect – perhaps a quantum improvement in efficiency towards preventing operational losses in the financial industry across the board, as has been the case with statistical process control in the manufacturing industry.

**Figure 5** OpRisk overall framework

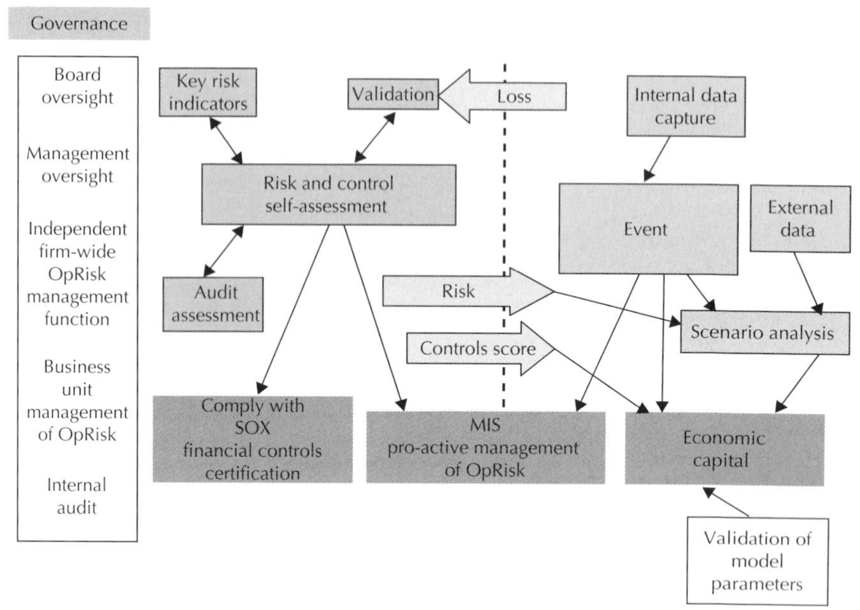


We conclude the chapter with Figure 5, which is a schematic diagram of the OR (AMA) overall framework, bringing together all the items discussed so far in this chapter. As with any schematic, all aspects are needed in the way they synthesise into the overall framework, but not all are equally difficult or significant. The ones in the critical path are the most important. At this point in time, it appears that measurement and methodology (be it highly quantitative or loosely structured) are in the critical path of development of operational risk as a major discipline.

1 Perhaps inadvertently it resulted from the fact that quite a few members of WGOR, including the chair and one of the authors of this chapter, were of a quantitative bent of mind.

2 Basel II has three broad approaches to operational risk: *basic indicator approach*, *standardised approach* and *advanced measurement approaches* (AMA). In this chapter we shall be concerned only with AMA for two reasons: (a) the book is about AMA implementation and (b) in the US only AMA is permitted by the US regulators.

3 Robust econometric analysis of such shareholder value creation or erosion resulting from mergers and acquisitions, on average, can be done only when the dust settles, which is often precluded by a second merger following on the heels of the first one.

4 The answer to the question of whether there is more than a 0.1% (or one-in-a-thousand) chance that the whole premium will have to be written off in the future seems to be yes if history is anything to go by.
5 In this chapter we will not go into detailed conceptual and mathematical underpinnings of LDA. However, since we go into details about incorporation of qualitative scores in quantitative LDA distribution(s) later in the chapter, a brief introduction to LDA is being provided here. A non-mathematical introduction can be found in Dev and Sahay (2004). A practical application of the LDA approach to calculation of economic capital for operational risk in a bank can be found in Frachot, Moundoulaud and Roncalli (2004). A good summary of advantages and limitations of the LDA can be found in Haubenstock and Hardin (2003).
6 KeyCorp started collecting internal loss event data on a pilot basis in the second half of 2002 and rolled it out throughout the organisation in mid-2003.
7 Obviously such events as well as indirect loss data have to be excluded when computing regulatory capital under AMA.
8 KeyCorp was one of the active initial members of the MORE consortium. It is a founding member of the ABA consortium.
9 KeyCorp was one of the first banks to implement (customise) a system by adopting this integrated approach in 2003–4, in consultation with Protivity. Perhaps this was the main reason why KeyCorp won the OpRisk Award in 2005 for the best medium-sized (under US$125 billion in assets) bank in operational risk AMA implementation.
10 See Taylor and Davies (2003) for a detailed insight into the KRI Framework Study, in which Citi Group, Deutsche Bank, Dresner Bank, JP Morgan Chase, KeyCorp, Royal Bank of Canada and State Street were the founding members.
11 The best way to guard against moral hazard is through innovative capital attribution methodology. For example, suppose audit of a particular business unit's self-assessment results in systematic downward revision of self-assessment scores, the new economic capital can be several times the economic capital that would have been attributed if the business unit had self-assessed correctly (ie, assigned lower scores – appropriately) in the first place.

## REFERENCES

**Alexander, C.,** 2003, *Operational Risk, Regulation, Analysis and Management* (London: Prentice Hall Financial Times, Pearson Education), pp 129–68.

**Anders, U. and Gerrit Jan Van Den Brink,** 2004, "Implementing a Base II Scenario-Based AMA for Operational Risk", in Michael K. Ong (ed), *The Basel Handbook* (London: Risk Books), pp 343–68.

**Basel Committee on Banking Supervision,** 2003, "Sound Practices for the Management and Supervision of Operational Risk", BIS, February.

**Basel Committee on Banking Supervision,** 2003, "The New Basel Capital Accord", Consultative Document (CP3), BIS, April.

**Davis, E.,** 2005, *Operational Risk: Practical Approaches to Implementation* (London: Risk Books), p xvii.

**De Koker, R.,** 2005, "Allocating Capital for Operational Risk", Presentation at GARP Workshop on Applying Economic Capital Within a Financial Institution, Zurich, April.

**Dev, A. and A. Sahay,** 2004, "Measuring and Calculating Capital for Operational Risk: Achieving AMA Compliance", *RMA Journal*, March, pp 2–7.

**Frachot, A., O. Moundoulaud, and T. Roncalli,** 2004, "Loss Distribution Approach in Practice", in Michael K. Ong (ed), *The Basel Handbook* (London: Risk Books), pp 369–96.

**Haubenstock, M. and L. Hardin,** 2003, "The Loss Distribution Approach", in C. Alexander (ed). *Operational Risk, Regulation, Analysis and Management* (London: Prentice Hall Financial Times, Pearson Education), pp 171–92.

**Howitt, J., M. Mainelli, and C. Taylor,** 2004, "Marionettes, or Masters of the Universe? The Human Factor in Operational Risk", *RMA Journal*, special edition, May, pp 52–7.

**Lam, J.,** 2003, *Enterprise Risk Management* (Hoboken, NJ: John Wiley & Sons), pp 207–28.

**Leighton, O.,** 2004, "The Organisational Turf War", *Operational Risk* **5(11)**, November, pp 18–21.

**Nakada, P.,** 2004, "Taking the Pulse of Your Op Risk Strategy", ERISK Commentary, November/December, p 4.

**Peccia, A.,** 2004, "Measuring and Calculating Economic Operational Risk Capital", in A. Dev (ed), *Economic Capital: A Practitioner Guide* (London: Risk Books), pp 183–207.

**Sahay, A. and A. Dev,** 2005, "Operational Risk Quantification: Forward Looking Adjustments", *Risk*, April.

**Shephard-Walwyn, T.,** 2004, "KRI VAR, Lessons from Manufacturing for the Financial Services Industry", *RMA Journal*, special edition, May, pp 48–51.

**Taylor, C. and J. Davies,** 2003, "Getting Traction with KRIs: Laying the Groundwork", *RMA J*ournal, November.

**Thirwell, J.,** 2004, "Insurance and Operational Risk", in Michael K. Ong (ed), *The Basel Handbook* (London: Risk Books), pp 467–90.

**Vinella, P.,** 2004, "A foundation for KPI and KRI", *Operational Risk* **5(11)**, November, pp 38–42.

**Webb, A.,** 1999, "Controlling Operational Risk", *Derivatives Strategy* **4(1)**, January, pp 17–21.

# 13

# AMA Implementation in Germany: Results of BaFin's and Bundesbank's Industry Survey

**Patrik Buchmüller; Marcus Haas; Bernd Rummel; Karsten Stickelmann***

Tübingen University; Deutsche Bundesbank; BaFin; Deutsche Bundesbank

This chapter gives an overview of the implementation of advanced measurement approaches (AMA) in Germany from the supervisors' point of view. It summarises and in some aspects comments on the pictures German supervisors have recently drawn from the AMA implementation efforts they have seen from their banks so far.

Regarding the approval of the AMA, the Federal Financial Supervisory Authority (BaFin) and the Deutsche Bundesbank issued an application package and a press release in October 2005, announcing that applications for the approval of the AMA are possible now. This application package will soon also be available in English on BaFin's and Bundesbank's Web sites (BaFin (www.bafin.de) and Bundesbank (www.bundesbank.de)). Banks and other interested practitioners should carefully read those documents as well as the draft new solvency ordinance (proposed implementation of the EU guidelines into German law), which will be enacted in 2006.

To get a better idea of how German supervisors will implement the operational risk (OpRisk) part of the new European directive and Basel II before the enactment of the solvency ordinance, it is

*The authors express their personal views. This chapter does not contain any official statement either from BaFin or from Deutsche Bundesbank.

helpful to read the recommendations of the Fachgremium OpRisk (Industry Working Group on Operational Risk), which also have been published on BaFin's and Bundesbank's web sites, albeit only in German. In this committee, experts from BaFin and Bundesbank, together with experts from German banks and industry associations, have agreed on recommendations on how to implement some crucial requirements in the area of operational risk.

Besides working on national rulemaking, BaFin and Bundesbank, naturally, also show interest in how German banks implement the new requirements on operational risk. In August 2004, German supervisors asked the banks under their supervision what approaches they plan to use for the calculation of OpRisk capital requirements. According to the results of that survey, 58 credit institutions in Germany wanted to introduce an AMA in 2008 and 134 a standardised approach for operational risk in 2007 (see also BaFin, 2005, p 96). Especially, the high number of potential AMA candidates was surprising and raised some concerns about the application process. The high number of potential AMA candidates reflects the fact that, in Germany, smaller banks regard the implementation of an AMA at least in the medium term as realistic. Still, after further discussions with the banks, German supervisors believe that the actual number of applications for AMA use in 2008 will be far lower than 58.

To collect information on the status of implementation and related work in progress as of year end 2004, German supervisors have developed a structured questionnaire for an industry survey. This questionnaire with 59 short questions on implementation issues and references to the Basel framework text is available on BaFin's and Bundesbank's web sites in a German version. Banks were asked to briefly answer the questions in the questionnaire and to provide additional information and documentation, for example, their OpRisk framework, their roll-out plans concerning operational risk and details concerning their OpRisk model. This industry survey was based on the requirements from the new Basle Accord, not the European directive, because of some uncertainties with the details of the European directive at that time. Altogether, 15 banks (from all three pillars of the German banking system) have participated in the survey on a voluntary basis. The results of the survey have been put together by a supervisory working group with members from BaFin and Bundesbank, and are based on the written answers of the above-mentioned 15 banks as of year end 2004. To keep the survey consistent, additional information from conversations with individual banks in 2005 has been added only for the purpose of clarification, not for the purpose of updating the results.

The results of the industry survey itself (in German) can be found on the web sites of BaFin and Bundesbank. The following chapters follow in principle and with some abridgement and additional comments the structure and content of the industry survey. It should be noted again that views expressed in this chapter represent personal views of the authors and not necessarily those of BaFin and Bundesbank.

## TOPIC OVERVIEW AND STATE OF IMPLEMENTATION

Banks may receive supervisory approval to use internally developed AMA to calculate their regulatory capital requirements for operational risk if these approaches are used for managing operational risks within the bank and if regulatory requirements are fulfilled. These requirements refer to the scope of application of an AMA, including partial use in combination with another approach (standardised or basic indicator approach) as well as qualitative and quantitative requirements. The latter include methods and procedures for the identification, measurement, monitoring, reporting and management of operational risk and how these are embedded in the organisational structure. Special requirements exist regarding the four elements (internal data, external data, scenario analysis, and business-environment and internal-control factors) that have to be included in the AMA. Altogether the AMA must adequately cover the operational risk of the individual bank.

The state of AMA implementation varies among the different banks that have participated in the survey. Especially large private banks, but also the Landesbanken, have made significant progress in developing methods and implementing the AMA.

The basic concepts for managing operational risk are largely outlined and already implemented in most banks. Only few banks are just starting their implementation efforts. However, there is still need for further development concerning the modelling of operational risk, especially regarding model validation and taking into account business environment and internal control factors.

Implementation projects for the latter are sometimes less prioritised or stopped because of lower business relevance. For some areas of the regulatory framework, such as approval of the use of correlation and insurance within the model or the use of business environment and internal control factors, the industry is awaiting supervisory regulation to be finalised or additional regulatory guidance, for example, additional explanatory notes, to be published. BaFin and Bundesbank are working within the Expert Group on Operational Risk (Fachgremium OpRisk) together with industry experts on solving these issues.

## AMA – SCOPE OF APPLICATION

With supervisory approval, banks can use an AMA for calculating the regulatory capital charge for operational risk on an individual and a consolidated basis. A bank will be permitted to use an AMA for some parts of its operations and the basic indicator approach or standardised approach for the remaining parts ("partial use") if certain conditions are met. It is necessary that already, with the application for AMA, a significant part of the operational risk be included in the model and that, within an adequate time period after approval, all major activities will be included in the AMA.

If a bank applies for the AMA on a consolidated basis, the group-wide application also includes the use of the AMA by individual subsidiaries on a solo level. The capital requirements on the solo level can be calculated using an allocation method or an individual AMA. Especially for significant subsidiaries outside of the European Union, the latter might be necessary, subject to requirements of the host supervisor. A bank that uses the AMA on a group-wide level may also use the standardised or basic indicator approach for its subsidiaries on a solo level. In Germany banks will not have to apply for the use of those simpler approaches but will have to notify BaFin in advance about the use of the standardised approach. More details concerning the use of the standardised approach can be found on the web sites of BaFin and Bundesbank.

### Partial use

Almost half of the banks surveyed plan a partial use; only a few have not yet decided. The remaining part state that they will not use the partial use.

According to a recommendation of the German Industry Working Group on Operational Risk, the inclusion of a significant part of the OpRisk activities should be verified using the relevant indicator from the Standardised and Basic Indicator Approach (gross income) or another suitable indicator. According to this recommendation, German supervisors should regard 50% of the chosen indicator as a rough benchmark to decide whether a significant part of all OpRisk activities is covered by the AMA.

BaFin and Bundesbank give the impression in their survey that banks have already developed their own measures to determine significance. These include measures based on (administration) costs, headcount, internal capital figures and gross income as well as combinations of these measures.

**Roll-out plan**

If a bank applies for the AMA starting in 2008, German supervisors will allow it to calculate the regulatory capital requirement until 2008 using the BIA, if an adequate risk management is established. Based on the requirements in the Basel framework, a permanent partial use is not allowed under normal circumstances. The bank must provide its supervisor with a plan specifying a timetable on how to roll out the AMA across all but an immaterial part of its operations. Based on the above-mentioned working group recommendation, an AMA bank must show in their implementation plan that after five years at least roughly 80% and after ten years at least roughly 95% of their business activities and all major areas will be included in the AMA. Within the partial-use period the bank must ensure that an adequate risk management is available also for those parts not included in the AMA. If all but an immaterial part is included in the AMA, German supervisors will probably allow AMA banks to calculate the capital charge for the remaining immaterial part by scaling up the model results and if necessary using add-ons.

Most of the banks have not yet given detailed information regarding their implementation time schedule. Some banks wait for more regulatory guidance. Most banks state that they will implement the standardised approach as of 1 January 2007 and will move to the AMA afterwards, but a final decision for the implementation of the AMA starting 2008 or later has not yet been made by all banks. Few banks mention how they define the immaterial parts, which will not be included in their AMA.

For those parts not covered by the AMA, most banks want to apply the standardised approach. Some consider using a combination with the basic indicator approach in exceptional cases.

#### Definition of areas to be included in the AMA

For the partial use, banks have to define areas for which an AMA or a simpler approach will be used. These areas can be determined based on business line, legal entity, geographical aspect or suitable internal delimitation.

The question regarding the definition of areas included in the AMA was not relevant for seven banks answering the questionnaire, since they do not intend a partial use. The other banks mostly indicate the use of a delimitation based on internal business lines; only one bank wants to implement a partial use based on legal entities.

#### Mapping of gross income

To calculate regulatory capital requirements with a simpler approach within the partial use, it is necessary to determine the relevant indicator. On a consolidated basis this might be problematic if (non-banking) subsidiaries are taken into account that do not file a financial statement in line with the bank accounts directive. Moreover, the relevant indicator on a consolidated basis is often less than the sum of the relevant indicators of the subsidiaries due to consolidation effects. In principle, banks use the consolidated financial statement to determine the relevant indicator and allocate this indicator to the business lines afterwards.

Banks mostly state that they use IAS (International Accounting Standards) segment accounting to derive the indicator for the corresponding business line. Two banks want to allocate the relevant indicator derived from a consolidated basis to the different business lines using certain parameters (eg, legal entities' gross income, total assets, costs, headcount).

#### Significant subsidiaries with an AMA on a standalone basis

Based on the Basel framework, the host supervisor may require significant subsidiaries to calculate regulatory capital requirements on a standalone basis. The rules within the European Union are less strict. The directive suggests a joint group-wide approval process.

Under normal circumstances within this approval process, a joint decision of home and host supervisors about the feasibility of the AMA for calculating regulatory capital charges on a consolidated and on an individual basis should be achieved. This includes methods for the allocation of capital determined on a consolidated basis to the individual subsidiaries.

Only a few banks explicitly mention that they will calculate a standalone AMA for individual subsidiaries. Some banks expect large problems with this approach because of the limited availability of data. Others think there is no benefit for calculating capital requirements for individual subsidiaries, because the management of operational risk is done on a business-line not a legal-entity basis.

### Allocation mechanism

In principle, supervisors prefer risk-sensitive methods for allocating capital, but it might be interpreted from the CEBS's (Committee of European Banking Supervisors) consultation paper that simpler approaches could under certain circumstances be used as well (see CEBS, 2005, p 464) if an adequate allocation of capital for individual subsidiaries can be achieved. As there is no standard for such an allocation method in the directive or in CEBS's guidelines so far, the validity of an allocation can be verified only within the approval process.

The allocation of regulatory capital is relevant only for banks that operate on a consolidated basis (groups). Two groups already plan to use a risk measure for allocating capital. Others want to use the relevant indicator (gross income), headcount or costs.

## OPRISK FRAMEWORK

The OpRisk framework contains organisational guidance that includes rules for the identification, assessment, monitoring (including reporting) and management (control/mitigation) of operational risk. Strategic commitments and a bank-specific definition of operational risk, which can be extended beyond the regulatory definition, are part of this as well.

### OpRisk strategy

The new Basel Accord demands the installation of a framework, where banks determine their operational risk appetite, the organisational guidance and the essential features of the risk-management process (see Basel Committee, 2004, para 737). Directive 2000/12 EC includes such requirements in Appendix V. Not all banks taking part in the survey have already developed a risk strategy in line with the above-mentioned requirements.

Operational risk is immanent in the banking business. It is therefore elementary to determine which risks should be taken by the bank and which should be mitigated using management action, should be avoided or transferred to a third party. These decisions should be used in the internal management. To do so, methods for the identification, assessment, monitoring (including reporting) and management (control/mitigation) of operational risk have to be developed and put into practice. Moreover, the parties responsible for the above have to be determined.

### Determination of risk appetite

From the banks included in this survey only a few made explicit statements concerning their risk appetite, but some give a broad indication. Some banks have not yet determined a risk appetite for operational risk. In some cases this is envisaged in line with the determination of an overall risk appetite. The answers of half of the banks indicate a risk-averse position regarding operational risk. These banks state their willingness to largely avoid large operational risks or to use mitigation techniques. Some banks say they want to judge their operational risk looking at their risk/return situation.

There are no statements regarding limitation (it should be noted that the idea of limitation for operational risk can be interpreted in a rather broad way) of operational risk from a third of the banks. This was partly justified by stating that an effective limitation of operational risk in a systematic way is not possible. Nevertheless, banks check limit utilisation and use this indicator in their management process. Despite these systematic problems, approximately half of the banks strive to implement a limitation for operational risk that is linked to the overall risk capacity of the bank.

### Transfer of operational risk to third parties

The majority of the banks pursue concepts that allow transferring parts of the operational risk to third parties. More than half of the banks indicate that they use insurance to transfer risk. Some banks state that insurance is of significant importance, especially for low-frequency, high-severity areas of operational risk.

Further methods to transfer risk mentioned by banks are the securitisation of risks (catastrophe bonds) and, with some restrictions, outsourcing. From a regulatory standpoint, the use of other risk mitigants is still problematic, although a last-minute change in the text of the directive now allows this in principle within the European Union. The consequences of outsourcing certain areas to third parties for the OpRisk exposure of a bank must be analysed on a case-by-case basis and included in the model in a risk-sensitive manner.

### The definition of operational risk

The measurement system of a bank must comprise at least the regulatory definition of operational risk. This definition includes legal risk but does not include reputational and strategic risk. For internal use, extensions to this regulatory definition are permitted.

Seven banks use the Basel definition for operational risk for internal purposes as well. Six banks use a somewhat tighter wording in their definition of operational risk as they explicitly use the word "employee" instead of the more general category "people". Losses caused by external people are sometimes explicitly defined as external events, which results in an overall consistency with the regulatory definition.

Most banks include legal risk explicitly in the definition of operational risk. Sometimes, individual risks (such as legal risk, crime risk) are excluded from the internal definition. If such risks included in the regulatory definition are excluded in the bank's definition, this should not be acceptable for regulatory purposes.

Few banks enlarged their internal definition by including reputational risk. They included qualitative judgements of related potential effects in their OpRisk database but they do not include them in the modelling.

## OPRISK CONTROL AND MANAGEMENT FUNCTION

The OpRisk control and management function (ORCMF) develops and implements as well as executes methods for identification, assessment, monitoring (including reporting) and management (control/mitigation) of operational risk. ORCMF, as well as the business divisions and internal audit, must have enough resources available. Conflicts of interest between ORCMF and the business must be avoided.

Regarding the above-mentioned topic, the "Sound Practices for the Management and Supervision of Operational Risk" are often used as a basis for the implementation. All in all, the implementation is well advanced in this area.

### Tasks and responsibilities in the ORCMF

The implementation of the organisational structure for OpRisk control and management is largely completed in most banks. All concepts include centralised and decentralised functions for the management and control of operational risk. The centralised functions must be sufficiently independent from the business to avoid conflicts of interest. Only a few banks have not yet completed the underlying concepts.

Nearly all banks divide their ORCMF mainly into the steps identification, assessment, monitoring (including reporting) and management (control/mitigation).

### Senior management responsibility

All banks know that the ultimate responsibility for operational risk remains with senior management. Banks mention the following topics as the most important tasks of senior management:

- adoption of a risk strategy;
- establishing an OpRisk culture;
- approval of an OpRisk framework (eg, policy, guideline, handbook) and changes to the framework if necessary;
- establishing the necessary organisational structure;
- budgeting process;
- determining limits for operational risk;
- decisions if OpRisk topics are escalated (for instance, losses, risk-assessment results) as well as decisions necessary for steering the business; and
- responsibility for the overall risk capacity of the bank.

Only few banks state that the centralised OpRisk function directly reports to its responsible board member. In one rather small bank the centralised OpRisk function is assigned to the head of controlling, who directly reports to the board member responsible for controlling.

### Tasks and organisational structure of the ORCMF

All banks delegate OpRisk control and management tasks to a centralised function and decentralise some responsibilities to the business lines. In some cases an additional OpRisk committee takes on more general OpRisk management tasks.

According to the survey the major tasks of the centralised OpRisk function are:

- development of an OpRisk strategy;
- definition, updating and control of implementation regarding the OpRisk framework;
- developing guidelines and concepts that are related to the OpRisk framework;
- developing (including validation and optimisation) of qualitative and quantitative methods and tools to identify, assess, analyse, report, control and manage operational risk;
- systematic OpRisk control within the bank;
- leading the yearly qualitative risk assessment (such as self-assessment);
- consolidation of all relevant risk information for the OpRisk reporting;
- escalation and control of escalation done by other functions regarding important OpRisk facts as well as making suggestions for possible (re-)action to the board and if available to the OpRisk committee;
- calculation of the OpRisk capital and the regulatory capital requirements (including allocation); and
- centralised point of contact for questions regarding operational risk, to coordinate activities and to support the business.

Additionally, banks list among the tasks a backtesting and benchmarking of the model results as well as the contact to supervisory bodies to explain the so-called *use test* and to show that the regulatory requirements can be fulfilled.

Partly, the above-mentioned tasks are performed by decentralised functions that are assigned to the centralised OpRisk function.

According to the survey, senior management of the relevant organisational units, business divisions and corporate centres are in principle responsible for the operational risk in their area as well as for proactive risk management. Moreover they are responsible for ensuring that the delegated tasks of the OpRisk management and control process are adequately performed in their area (eg, reporting of loss events).

The banks taking part in the survey assign the following tasks to senior management:

- proactive risk management in their respective area of responsibility, which includes decisions about taking, avoiding and transferring risks. Furthermore, initiation, escalation and implementation of decisions regarding risk mitigation;
- making sure that the OpRisk framework as well as rules, standards and methods of the centralised OpRisk function are met;
- making sure that the relating requirements regarding the organisational structure are met;
- development of rules, processes and methods for their area that are in line with the OpRisk framework;
- playing their part in the risk assessment;
- monitoring developments in Operational risk relating to their area of responsibility;
- creation and support for risk awareness and risk culture; and
- providing all the relevant OpRisk data, especially for the centralised OpRisk function.

Besides the centralised and decentralised functions, about half of the banks have OpRisk committees in place with members from different areas of the bank to support senior management. Sometimes there are different committees for the different regional parts of the group. Some banks have committees for other risk areas in addition to the OpRisk committee, which all report to an overall risk committee with members from senior management.

The tasks of the OpRisk committee include:

- definition of a risk strategy;
- monitoring of the implementation;

- discussion of the overall risk situation;
- decision regarding actions in the escalation procedure;
- improving the quality of risk management;
- supporting the management of risk that is spread to different business lines;
- sometimes developing standards and procedures as well as suggestions on how to solve fundamental OpRisk questions; and
- sometimes presenting suggestions to the risk committee or senior management.

A particular task of internal audit is the independent assessment of the implementation and the functioning of the OpRisk control and management processes. This includes the examination of the processes in the centralised OpRisk function. Only few banks state that an audit of the OpRisk data quality or the OpRisk measurement systems has already taken place.

Sometimes information from internal audit is considered in the scenario analysis and audit reports are used to check the loss data and risk records. From a supervisory point of view, it is necessary to make sure that an independent examination by internal audit for these areas can still be ensured.

### Independence of the ORCMF

The ORCMF is usually split between a centralised and a decentralised function. The centralised function is in charge of developing the methods and taking on coordination tasks in risk management, such as the creation of OpRisk reports. This function must be independent from the business lines, which bear the major operational risks. Decentralised OpRisk functions are often embedded in the business-line hierarchy and execute operative tasks within the business line. In these cases it is necessary from a supervisor's point of view to make sure that the guidelines of the centralised OpRisk function are paid attention to.

### Staff resources of the ORCMF

Given the available information regarding staff resources, a judgement if the resources are sufficient was not always possible. For some banks the staff resources seem to be rather tight.

The available data from 13 banks lead to the result that the ratio of headcount of the centralised OpRisk function to headcount of the parent bank lies between 0.03% and 0.38% (mean 0.14%). Data concerning the OpRisk headcount in internal audit and the business lines was often not available. If available, the data were not comparable because headcount was not given in terms of full-time equivalents. Therefore, no additional ratios were calculated. Furthermore, the appropriateness of staff resources must be viewed in relation to the size and complexity of the individual bank and not only in relation to headcount.

Staff working in the centralised OpRisk function mostly have several years of experience in different areas of the banking business, mostly in risk control and management with an economic or scientific/mathematical background.

### OpRisk culture and staff awareness

Besides implementation of the framework and related training programmes, most banks surveyed provide additional information regarding operational risk, for instance, by intranet publishing, staff magazines and telephone or email service via the centralised OpRisk function.

### Reporting and management information system

Roughly half of the banks use a partly automated link to incorporate OpRisk information in the reporting and management information system (MIS). In all banks the centralised OpRisk function is responsible for processing the risk information for the OpRisk reporting. In most banks the centralised OpRisk function is also responsible for checking the quality of the data that are used in the reports.

The reports are sent mainly to the board, senior management, operational risk or risk committees, as well as senior management of business lines or subsidiaries. Only in some cases does the supervisory board receive these reports regularly. However, this is a necessity for the supervisory board to fulfil its duties properly.

The reporting frequency varies depending on addressee and content between weekly and yearly. A yearly reporting is sufficient only for certain parts of the information. For others, a higher reporting frequency seems necessary. Senior management should decide about reporting frequency and the basic content of the reports, but this task can also be delegated to an OpRisk committee or the addressees of the reports.

Senior management and people responsible for the different business lines mainly receive complete OpRisk reports quarterly or semi-annually, whereas loss data are submitted on a monthly basis.

The reports mainly contain:

- occurred losses, which are grouped regarding region, organisational units, risk category and date of occurrence;
- reporting regarding course and reason for large losses or losses which occur frequently;
- peer-group comparisons using consortium data;
- OpVAR;
- risk indicators and risk profiles;
- usage of loss limits;
- new developments regarding methods and concepts; and
- management action intended, suggested or already in place.

Only about half of the banks explicitly state that they have an ad hoc reporting for large losses in place. In these reports, information on large losses is given or major changes of the risk situation are noted. In principle, an ad hoc reporting is necessary for an adequate risk management. The supervisory board should receive reports at least semi-annually or annually.

### Loss reaction processes

Half of the banks have an ad hoc escalation procedure in place, triggering action at a given loss amount, which ranges between €10,000 and €500,000. Only three banks use more sophisticated loss thresholds. Sometimes the kind of loss reported is defined qualitatively, for example, a requirement to report all fraud losses or all losses that are known to the public.

Eight banks state that it is the responsibility of the business divisions to react to losses. In four banks, the ORCMF is involved in this process. In most banks, the OpRisk function is informed about new processes already in place or suggestions regarding future risk mitigation action. Two banks also give this information to internal audit, which can start further examinations.

### Interfaces between the OpRisk function and other functions

Besides collecting loss data in their own area and playing their part in scenario analysis, some functions adopt more tasks regarding the management of operational risk. These tasks refer mainly to an exchange of available information or an involvement in the development of disaster recovery plans. Interfaces sometimes exist between internal audit and the OpRisk function for the examination of processes as well as for the use of information and experience from internal audit in the OpRisk management. This overlap is acceptable only if the independence of internal audit can be maintained. Further interfaces and the respective delimitation of areas are quite heterogeneous and determined by the individual organisation of the bank. Therefore, a more detailed comparison is not possible.

## OPRISK MODELLING

If the regulatory requirements for a measurement system are fulfilled, the model used for internal control may also be used for the determination of regulatory capital. Besides the requirements regarding the input factors, there are also requirements to the measurement system.

Advanced measurement approaches have to adequately incorporate internal and external loss data and scenario analyses, as well as individual business-environment and internal-control factors for capital calculation. Detailed requirements exist for the adequacy of the model, recognition of correlation effects, consideration of expected losses and insurance, and the process of model validation. Key for the approval of the model is the so-called use test, in which the bank must show that it adequately uses the results of the risk-measurement system for internal controls.

### Model approach

Six of the participating banks have already created and implemented a concept for modelling. Other banks have done first studies and are now creating concepts or have not yet done significant work in this area at all. Concerning the type of approach, most banks use a loss-distribution-based approach (LDA). Only a few banks plan a scenario-based approach (sbAMA).

For the LDA, mostly internal loss data have been used so far. The importance of external data varies among banks. Several banks do not comment on the use of external data. Few banks use expert estimates or scenario analyses to alter the model parameters. Some banks, however, do not possess a significant number of internal losses, especially low-frequency, high-severity losses. Thus, appropriate techniques for complementing internal data with external data in order to compensate for the lack of low-frequency, high-severity events are needed.

Scenario-based approaches use external losses for creating scenarios. Further, internal and external loss data have to be used for a validation of the scenarios.

Most banks do not comment on the type of external data that will be used. External data may be drawn from public sources or bought from external vendors. Some banks are members of a data consortium. The external data used must be relevant to the bank using it. It may thus be necessary to adjust the loss frequency and loss severity distribution of the external loss data. Only a few banks have decided on such a scaling mechanism, which is usually implemented via size variables such as number of employees, gross income and number of transactions.

Few banks already use explicit correlation estimates and insurance within the AMA. Most banks, however, do not comment on this topic in the survey and are still in the planning phase.

Value-at-risk (VAR) is mostly calculated using a Monte Carlo simulation. Sometimes, extreme-value theory is used. A challenge for such a separate modelling is the treatment of the discontinuity when combining the two parts of the distribution.

The data used for modelling are grouped by risk category (event category or risk cause) and business lines in most banks. The categorisation is mostly based on the Basel guidelines. Some banks however use a less granular categorisation, due to poor data availability or deviant internal categories.

Almost all banks use the Poisson or (negative) binomial distribution for estimating the loss frequency. The loss severity is modelled mostly with the lognormal, sometimes with the Pareto or Weibull distribution. Parameters for distributions in scenario-based approaches are mostly guessed by experts. Maximum-likelihood and GMM methods are mostly used as analytical tools.

Qualitative adjustments to the modelling results are made at different levels. Sometimes, the qualitative aspects of the measurement system, such as self-assessments, are used in the overall model as a weighting factor. In very few cases, distributions for different data areas are given different factors. The qualitative weighting factors mostly represent a degree of freedom in the model, which was often hard to comprehend on the basis of the banks' documentation and which was mostly justified through qualitative means.

For model validation the banks were still awaiting regulatory guidance, since the number of internal losses is often not sufficient to justify a statistical validation. The parameter estimates and the choice of distribution are usually judged qualitatively. A quantitative validation is sometimes done via a chi-square test. BaFin and Bundesbank have extensively covered the validation issue with the industry in the Industry Working Group on Operational Risk.

*Main drivers of operational risk*

The primary goal when deriving risk drivers should be to minimise the number of unknown events that might lead to major operational losses. This is done implicitly in most banks through the analysis of internal and external data and scenarios.

Even though not explicitly mentioned, nine of the participating banks understand scenarios of single or combined major loss events as the main drivers of operational risk and incorporate said scenarios into the model. Two banks evaluate the risks for individual business lines through qualitative expert estimates or the backward-looking analysis of historical data and incorporate the results into the model.

The question concerning the main risk drivers seems to have caused some controversy. Half of the banks do not derive main risk drivers with regard to their individual firm. Often, only those risk cells are identified that reflect the largest operational risks according to the model used. Many banks define extreme loss events (sometimes defined by size) as their main risk drivers. A description of the risk content in the sense of a driver or loss event, however, is not given through quantification.

*Severe loss events*

Severe loss events are defined differently among the banks. Seven banks have not yet explicitly defined severe losses. Four banks use an absolute value (between €25,000 and €500,000) for the definition of severe losses. Other banks use relative values that are derived from the VAR or the operating profit. Two of these banks define reputational losses as severe losses, independent of their size.

Seven banks do not treat severe losses separately in the model. In other cases these losses are modelled via the peaks-over-threshold (PoT) method or extreme value theory.

*Calculation and consideration of the expected loss*

The capital calculated with the AMA must incorporate the unexpected as well as the expected loss. If a part of the expected loss is adequately captured in a bank's business practice, BaFin will allow this part of the expected loss to serve for a reduction of OpRisk capital requirement. For this it is necessary to describe how the size of the expected loss is determined and how it is covered in business practices, such that banks' own funds remain untouched. To determine the expected loss, statistical as well as other objective methods may be used.

Some banks determine the expected loss as the expected value of the loss distribution. According to the current regulatory debate, a statistical calculation based on the loss distribution is allowed in principle, while it is not yet clear which statistical value is to be used as a cap. The Operational Risk subgroup of the Accord Implementation Group (AIGOR) already published further guidelines on this issue (see Basel Committee, 2005) and CEBS will presumably publish further guidelines on this issue soon.

Most banks consider expected losses from operational events in their business practices, or plan to do so. Two banks have decided so far to cover expected losses with capital. Five banks include these losses, sometimes based on their experience, into their pricing calculation, or plan to do so. Another five banks provision for expected losses in their business planning, or plan to do so.

Proving that expected losses are adequately treated in business practice has been very difficult for banks so far. One way to do this might be a crosscheck of occurred losses with the funds provided/pocketed for those losses via pricing.

*Correlation assumptions in AMA models*

Dependencies between loss events and diversification effects can be considered in the model via correlation assumptions, including the aggregation of risk figures for the calculation of the capital figure. However, those assumptions must be sound and well founded.

Almost half of the banks do not give precise statements on how they plan to quantify or consider correlations within the AMA. The other banks model loss events using a frequency and a severity distribution, where data are grouped in the cells of a business line/risk category matrix. None of the banks explicitly mentions that it models dependencies between loss frequencies and loss severities or between loss severities within individual cells.

To aggregate risk estimates, sometimes simple dependency structures (Gaussian copula) are used for the frequency distributions between cells, while the severity distributions are assumed to be independent.

According to the provided documentation, some banks model directly on a top-down basis or use methods similar to a top-down approach, such that no aggregation of risk numbers is required. It remains open as to whether, in these cases, the risk-measurement system is granular enough for an adequate internal management of risks.

Four banks aggregate the risk figures on a cell basis to a VAR for the entire bank. The methods used differ from a simple sum (perfect correlation between cells) to a correlation of zero for some cells in combination with a correlation of one on a higher level (for instance, across certain event types).

BaFin and Bundesbank have discussed correlations intensively within the Industry Working Group on Operational Risk and are confident that CEBS will issue guidance on this issue soon.

*Enhancement and expansion of the model*

Most banks are currently focusing on the development or completion of missing components and are only partially concerned with refinements or enhancements to the model. Thus, processes towards model expansion do not yet play a significant role.

Overall, the model development team is also responsible for the expansion of the model. Usually this is done within the centralised OpRisk function. The development and enhancement of the model is sometimes done in cooperation with external partners, such as software developers, universities and other banks. Refinements to the quality of the data are essential for the expansion of a mathematical model. They will then allow one to draw new conclusions with respect to model parameters and assumptions. Some banks refer to expert knowledge from the market and credit risk areas and from internal audit for the enhancement of the OpRisk model.

### *Validation of the model*

The EU directive suggests that supervisors examine the satisfactory operation of the validation processes, whereas Basel II demands the validation via an independent function. Specialised knowledge is required for validating the model, which is sometimes present only in the centralised OpRisk function. Therefore, part of the validation process may temporarily be done by the centralised OpRisk function if internal audit is adequately involved in monitoring the validation process.

Due to the low number of loss data, a validation with statistical means is not possible in all cases. Therefore, quantitative and qualitative methods may be used for validation. A comparison with the capital requirements for simpler approaches is not sufficient to validate the model.

Only a few banks make general remarks on validation within the industry survey. Specific regulatory requirements are not included in the current guidelines and an industry standard on validation has not yet been established. Most banks are still in the development phase of validation.

Some banks envision a check of the model by internal audit. It remains open, however, whether model details (such as parameter estimates) are incorporated or whether only the processes of modelling and risk control are examined. Only a few banks establish a unit for model validation within their organisation that accesses independent resources such as credit risk management within the risk management unit.

Furthermore, some banks contemplate the use of expert estimates or benchmarking for model validation. This may be supported by data consortiums, which possess a larger number of loss data.

### *Relevance of the four elements within the model*

All four elements (internal data, external data, scenario analysis, and business-environment and internal-control factors) must be adequately combined within the AMA. How this combination is done and what importance is given to each element is not defined in the regulatory guidelines. Therefore, external data may be used to create scenarios and derive loss distributions from scenario analyses within the AMA. It must be assured, though, that there is no double-counting of risk-mitigating effects within the model.

For eight banks, internal loss data play a dominant or at least an important role in the model. For one-third of the banks, the concepts are already advanced enough to display the increased importance of internal loss data within the model. Most banks also use external data directly within the model to capture extreme losses or use a mixed approach with two different loss distributions. Scenario analyses are often used as a complement to the loss distributions, especially where data are sparse or in the area of extreme losses. Few banks will use scenario analysis as a predominant tool in the long run.

Few banks consider the results of scenario analyses as the most important model input factor. The other three elements are seen by those banks mostly as a support for expert estimates on loss figures within the scenarios. In some cases, a validation of scenarios or model results with internal and external loss data is considered.

The incorporation of business-environment and internal-control factors is still in the conceptual phase in most banks. Only a few banks consider them in the quantification phase of the model so far.

*Consideration of insurance in the model*

Insurance may be incorporated into the AMA model if regulatory requirements are fulfilled. The maximal reduction for OpRisk capital, however, is limited to 20%.

Nine banks do not yet incorporate insurance in the model. Some banks consider mostly property and liability insurance. These banks use insurance within the model to derive the overall loss distribution. Sometimes insurance is modelled separately and tied to loss events using an allocation table. The modelled compensation payments, including haircuts, are deducted from possible gross losses to determine possible net losses. The potential insurance cover included considers deductibles, liability caps and payment possibilities. Some banks use insurance payments directly to generate net losses and model with those losses. In these cases, actual insurance payments are considered. Banks would then have to demonstrate how capital-reducing effects will still be available in the future and how the regulatory requirements, especially the haircuts and the 20% cap, will be fulfilled. Sometimes, insurance is used within scenarios to alter the loss distributions that enter the model.

Some banks have the technical means to use insurance within the model. However, they are not yet doing so, since the regulatory requirements for a capital reduction cannot be completely met.

So far, only some banks calculate the capital-reducing effect of insurance. Sometimes, banks state that insurance will not have a strong influence on the VAR; sometimes a reduction of the VAR of up to 35% is expected, which would far exceed the regulatory acceptance level.

*Consideration of outsourcing*

Outsourcing of business activities plays a major role for some banks; for others it is utterly insignificant. The operational risk (eg, legal risk) arising from outsourcing must be considered within the model and within risk management, especially if OpRisk events that occur in outsourced activities will affect the bank itself. The EU directive explicitly requires business continuity plans to be available for all major business functions. This also includes functions provided from third-party members via outsourcing.

Some banks have detailed outsourcing guidelines that incorporate decision processes for outsourcing. In addition, these banks have documentation on outsourced processes and business activities and pose implicit organisational and conduct rules to the service providers.

Operational risk related to outsourcing is mostly captured using qualitative self-assessments. Some banks use a so-called *risk stocktaking*, which includes the evaluation of outsourcing contracts concerning risk exposure and the implemented and required emergency plans. Furthermore, the quality of service-level agreements and the possibility of switching to other service providers in case of a default are evaluated. These evaluations are sometimes divided into major and non-major outsourcing providers. The risks arising from non-major outsourcing providers are sometimes modelled with risk indicators, while the major risks are incorporated in the model via scenarios or explicit loss events.

Some banks consider the risks arising from outsourced functions with methods that are also used for the modelling of insurance. Occurred risks are incorporated into the modelling, taking into account contract clauses on the liability of the service provider.

*Relevance of the AMA for risk management*

According to the EU directive, the AMA will be closely integrated into day-to-day risk management of the bank. The measurement system must factually be used for risk control and mitigation. Furthermore, methods should exist that allocate regulatory capital to business units. This requirement, known as the use test, is key for the approval of an AMA and needs to be implemented at the time of the examination. CEBS has already published guidelines on the requirements of the use test.

The degree of maturity of the AMA and its incorporation into risk management varies. Only a few banks already use advanced controlling methods.

All banks use the standardised risk measure value-at-risk (VAR) to display their OpRisk loss potential. The economic capital for operational risk is calculated with confidence levels that sometimes exceed regulatory demands. The economic capital is usually calculated as a quantile of the loss distribution minus the expected loss, depending on the desired external rating. The economic capital calculated is sometimes already used as a control element through its allocation to the business lines. This is done to generate incentives for improved risk management. Some banks also use the risk measures to calculate return on capital. Different ratios are used that reflect the overall performance measurement concept of the bank, such as return on equity, economic value-added and return on risk-adjusted capital.

Most banks add that they are communicating information relevant to management via management reports. Almost all banks, for example, use qualitative surveys, which do not enter the model, to generate actions that affect operational risk management.

### Internal data

Internal loss data are an important foundation for the modelling and management of operational risk. The quality of the data and its homogeneous allocation to risk categories and business lines, as well as the separation from other fields of risk, is very important for the goodness of the measurement system and for the validation of models based mostly on scenario analyses. The relatively low number of data compared with other risk categories causes problems. A data history of five years or three years for the initial use is a regulatory requirement if the bank intends to use the AMA to calculate regulatory capital requirements.

The work on internal data is complete in almost all banks. In some cases, remaining tasks such as belated data capture or quality-assurance methods (eg, concerning the allocation to risk categories) still have to be completed. Clear internal guidelines on the allocation of loss data and methods for the clarification of boundary issues, and therefore for the improvement of allocation criteria, are a must to ensure the homogeneity of the data. A check of the data gathered in the business lines is usually done within the central OpRisk unit.

The data are processed using IT-based databases. Besides well-known products, some banks also use self-developed tools or still have to implement IT-systems that guarantee the availability and integrity of the data. The required data history will be present in all banks until 2008. Whether the quality of the data will be sufficient in all cases, and thus allow for the generation of objective risk measures with the AMA, is especially dependent on the further efforts to improve the data basis regarding the amount and homogeneity of internal and external loss data. Furthermore, detailed statements on loss causes must be available for external data in order to generate scenarios or to validate scenarios generated, especially in the area of extreme loss events.

*Allocation of internal loss data*

Two types of allocation should be distinguished:

- The categorisation of loss data for the allocation to the regulatory categories, where it is sufficient to allocate to the Tier 1 categories of Basel II.
- The categorisation of loss data to internal categories used for modelling, which may differ across banks depending on their business activities and risk situation.

A refinement of the regulatory loss and business line definitions for internal use may be reasonable and helpful for risk management. The development of an industry standard in this area will be especially useful to share loss data via data consortiums. Nevertheless, the regulatory categories are a common source for modelling and especially for a standardised exchange of loss data across banking groups. Therefore, banks must be able to sufficiently allocate their loss data to these event categories and business lines.

*Event categories*

The Basel event categories and the allocation examples presented in the appendix of the Basel framework do not present a complete and consistent loss event categorisation, since the examples are not final and not concise.

To improve the allocation quality, banks often use decision trees, central contacts and training with example events.

Almost half of the participating banks use the internal loss categories according to the Tier 1 and Tier 2 categories of Basel II. Some banks adapt their internal categories to the Tier 2 categories of Basel II. If Tier 3 event categories are used also, then banks usually supplement the Basel guidelines with their own allocation criteria. Sometimes, however, methods for a complete and consistent allocation are still missing.

Most banks have already defined internal Tier 1 and Tier 2 loss categories – for instance, based on data standards of existing data consortiums. An allocation to the regulatory categories is in these cases guaranteed via allocation methods, while the model is based on the internal categories.

*Business lines*

The principles and criteria for the allocation of loss data to the business lines must be consistent and coincide with the allocation principles of the relevant indicator in the standardised approach.

Business activities and internal organisation among banks is heterogeneous. Some banks closely follow the regulatory business lines; others are organised more granularly. Some banks are active in only very few business lines.

Some banks directly associate internal business lines with the regulatory Tier 1 business lines. Most banks have a more detailed structure and associate loss data with internal profit centres or processes, which are then associated with the business lines, sometimes at Tier 2. Few banks distribute loss data associated with internal categories proportionally to different regulatory categories via an allocation key. This is allowed for regulatory reporting only if the allocation is plausible, concise and sufficiently documented. For modelling purposes the total loss of a single event may not be divided into single losses unless a perfectly positive correlation is assumed.

*Losses in centralised functions*

For management purposes, it seems appropriate to separately collect and model losses in centralised functions. For regulatory purposes, however, it is necessary to allocate these losses to the regulatory business lines.

In some cases, it could not be derived from the provided documentation if that is always the case. In principle, the proportional allocation will blur information necessary for the modelling and management of the risks, which should be taken into account in the loss database – for example, via the grouping of single, connected losses with associated loss data points. Some banks see the need for further regulatory guidance on this subject and suggest the creation of a ninth business line for losses in centralised functions. Such a business line is already used by several banks. This is allowed for internal purposes; for regulatory reporting, the introduction of a ninth business line is not expected in medium-term.

Losses in centralised functions are mostly allocated to the regulatory business lines according to the cost unit principle or, in some cases, causal analysis and assigned to the regulatory business lines via allocation keys. These allocations keys must be chosen objectively. The derivation of the allocation keys is not always sufficiently documented.

*Loss events in several business lines*

Loss events may touch several business lines. In most cases, these losses are collected separately per business line (cost carrier) and combined using associated loss numbers. This seems adequate, since the loss amount is easiest to determine in the affected unit. When doing so, however, it should be guaranteed that loss events that exceed the loss threshold cumulatively are also considered in cases in which the single losses per business line lie below the threshold. In principle, the associated loss numbers are given by the centralised OpRisk function. In some cases, connected losses are grouped into a single, common loss and the loss amount is distributed to the business units with an allocation key. In such cases perfectly positive correlation is assumed in the model.

In a few cases, the loss is allocated entirely to a single business line, usually the one that is affected the most. In some cases, the loss may be associated with a superordinated business line. This might, depending on the portion of these losses on the total dataset, lead to a bias in the results of the model and have negative effects on risk management.

*Associated losses*

Grouping losses that occur separately but have a common cause is necessary to receive an aggregated sum of losses. This is essential for making informed decisions on necessary measures. Most banks group losses using an associated loss number. Sometimes, the possibility of successive losses is explicitly mentioned in the database. Other databases allow for an indication on whether the collection of a specific loss event is completed.

Some banks collect such losses as single loss events if they affect only a single business line or have a common cause. A belated grouping of losses is sometimes possible. The creation of associated loss events and *ex post* supplementing of individual loss events with additional connected losses are in principle adequate data-collection practices.

*Boundary regarding credit risk*

Losses caused by operational risk related to credit risk must be identified, collected in the loss database and marked separately. These risks, however, are still considered only for credit risk capital requirements.

All banks examine credit losses for operational risk. In general they register credit losses in the OpRisk database and mark these losses.

The thresholds for the examination of credit losses for operational risk are very diverse and lie between specific provisions of €1,000 and €500,000, in a single case even €2,000,000. Even though the principle of proportionality needs to be applied here, the thresholds used by some banks seem to be too high to uncover the operational risk connected with the overall credit exposure. In some banks, an adjustment of the thresholds is being discussed.

*Boundary regarding market risk*

There are no special requirements on how to deal with operational risk within the market risk area. Such risk has to be considered for OpRisk capital calculation.

Most banks treat and collect operational losses in market risk according to the overall company guidelines for operational risk. In some cases, a marking of operational losses in the area of market risk is planned.

In practice, losses from operational risk may not always be differentiated from losses resulting from market risk. To ensure an adequately complete data collection, special measures are required. However, hardly any usable pieces of information on this topic are provided in the banks' documentation. Processes that are based on the existing front-office/back-office structure should be sufficient to ensure an adequate capturing of losses due to systematic double checks.

To ensure a complete collection of losses from market risk, in some cases reconciliation of the front-office trades with accounting is done. In the event of severe losses, principles for an ad hoc reporting are in place in some banks. A plausibility check for completion of the data collection can also be performed in the back-office areas.

*Relevance of internal data*

The continuing relevance of the internal data used needs to be ensured to avoid biases in risk measurement and management. One-third of the banks already have methods for ensuring the ongoing relevance of their internal data. Some further banks are fine-tuning their concepts on this subject. Partially, the type and extent of the adjustment is checked on a case-by-case basis. Documented guidelines for such procedures will be required.

From the point of view of some banks, the short time horizon of the data collection and the scarcity of the data are seen as obstacles for the development of methods. The necessity for the definition of such methods is not yet understood by all banks.

The basis for the evaluation of the relevance was the current organisational structure/business units, activities/products/processes, risk-mitigating effects in place and the time between the occurrence of a loss event and the time of modelling. All banks that present concepts use qualitative factors for adjusting the loss data.

Some banks also adjust for the current organisational structure/business units, activities/products/processes. Methodically, the historical loss data are attributed to the new structure or, if an activity is abandoned, removed from the modelling process. However, banks still keep the available data. Partially, loss events that can no longer occur due to risk-mitigating measures are exempted from the modelling as well. Some banks consider the timeframe between the occurrence of a loss and its inclusion in the model when judging the relevance of their data. In these cases, a lower weight is given to older data compared with newer data. In some occasions, it is planned to abandon losses that are older than five years. In any case, low-frequency, high-severity losses are still considered via respective scenarios or are still used for modelling.

An adjustment of the loss severities and frequencies of collected loss data with qualitative factors (scaling) has not been performed by any of the participating banks so far.

When judging the quantitative relevance of loss data, some banks state that they are scaling losses to current price levels and exchange rates before modelling. An inflation adjustment for historical loss severities was performed with the German consumer price index.

The allocation of responsibilities for the assessment and adjustment of the data is apparent in only few banks. The responsibility in these banks is with the centralised OpRisk function. Sometimes, reconciliation with the business is planned. In one bank, the relevant business lines, corporate centres or subsidiaries perform the assessment on a yearly basis. If the relevance of internal loss data is assessed by the business lines, conflicts of interest must be avoided by adequate regulations.

*Loss history*

A sufficient number of losses and the timeframe of their occurrence are an essential basis for loss-data-based models. It is apparent from the documentation of the banks, that all participating banks will reach the required three-year loss history with the introduction of the AMA in 2008. Some banks have entered losses into the loss data collection belatedly.

One-third of the banks have submitted a viable assembly of the captured loss events, categorised by business lines and risk categories. Some banks also have submitted an overview of the captured losses. However these overviews could not be evaluated further due to the low number of data.

The comparability of the presentations is restricted due to the bank-specific categorisation. Nonetheless, it is obvious from the loss data that, with the exception of one bank, most losses occur in the risk categories execution, delivery and process management. The fewest loss events are found in the risk categories employment practices and workplace safety, business disruption and system failures as well as internal fraud.

Almost half of the banks began collecting losses between 2000 and 2001; the others started between 2002 and 2004. Most banks currently hold between 100 and 500 datasets for operational losses. Only a few banks possess 1,000 or more datasets.

*Data thresholds*

Suitable thresholds must be defined for capturing loss data in a database. The spectrum of these thresholds varies from €100 to €10,000 and thus does not exceed the example in the Basel guidelines. For the collection of operational losses from credit risks, the thresholds were sometimes much higher.

For some banks losses from criminal activities have a special status and are collected in any case independent of the size of loss amount. Two banks differentiate the thresholds by business lines. These banks have defined a lower threshold for the areas of private banking and the subsidiary business. Furthermore, some banks allow their subsidiaries to define lower loss thresholds.

Banks will have to deal with the subject of loss thresholds in the future as well, by considering how higher thresholds will increase model risk by creating biases or errors in the estimated parameters. Furthermore, it should be examined how different loss thresholds will affect the parameter estimations. The statistical methods used in the AMA model have to be examined concerning their capability to treat truncated loss data.

*Loss datasets*

All banks use databases for the collection of internal loss data, in which a large number of data fields (between 40 and 100) is used for the capturing of a loss event. The datasets of all banks contain at least the required fields of gross loss, time of loss, risk mitigation and description of loss trigger and cause.

Concerning the time dimension, the databases of all banks require the capturing of the time of occurrence of a loss or a loss event. All banks also capture the time of recognition of the loss event or loss.

Almost all banks assign a status (open or complete) to the datasets/loss events. Most banks also capture the time of accounting or further accounting information. Sometimes, multiple data fields are reserved for a description of the loss event. For a better assignment of the losses, most banks capture the product, process or project involved.

Some banks determine the loss severity using the amount of payments made or the recovery value and incorporate also the cost of internal services used and occasionally also lost revenue. Most banks however capture the gross amount of a loss directly and consider only in few cases, internal costs or opportunity costs. If the amount of a loss can not be determined directly, most banks capture a potential loss amount. All banks also capture loss mitigating effects, in some cases the mitigation effects are separated by type.

About half of the banks state, that they capture the loss amount in the currency of the country in which it occurred. This seems to be plausible.

All banks also structure their data in a way that they can also capture gains connected with OpRisk events. Only few banks state however, that they do so. For the administration of the loss data captured within the bank, most banks define technical datasets within the system. These usually comprise the date of capturing and the person entering the data. Some banks also include an editing history (such as changes or checks) into their datasets.

Most banks plan to use the loss data collection as the basis for management action. These banks have reserved some data fields for suggested management action and their realisation.

## External data

Relevant external data must be considered in the measurement system. This includes data on loss events from loss databases of third-party vendors, consortia and association databases, and public sources.

External data are especially relevant for the measurement of risk events with potentially high losses and for the development of scenarios. For the latter, datasets containing a precise description of the losses are required. This is often not the case for anonymised consortium datasets.

Some of the banks are members of the data consortiums ORX (Operational Risk data eXchange association), VÖB (Association of German Public Sector Banks), BVI (Bundesverband Investment and Asset Management eV) or Gold (Global Operational Risk Loss Database). The quality of the external datasets and its homogeneous allocation to event categories and business lines is very important for the quality of the measurement system and for model validation. This is especially true for loss data from data consortiums. Therefore it is necessary that, not only within banks but also within data consortiums, the quality of the datasets is guaranteed through adequate processes.

### *Choice of external data sources*

Some banks have already made concrete choices on external datasets and created relevant concepts, for example, how external data should be used in the model. One-third of the banks has at least made a decision on the data sources and outlined concepts on how to use external data.

Some banks have not yet made a decision on the use of external data; some are awaiting the creation of a solution from their respective banking association.

External data are gained from publications, via public providers and the participation in data consortiums. Public data sources used include OpVantage, Fitch First and SAS Global Data. External data providers extract information mostly from public sources and usually collect only data exceeding a high threshold, for instance, US$1 million. The thresholds of data consortiums are usually much lower.

Almost half of the participating banks are involved in the exchange of loss data via the data consortiums ORX, VÖB, Gold and BVI. The thresholds are much lower than with public external data providers. Almost all banks get external data from more than one source and use the datasets for different purposes within the model. It was not always possible to determine whether the number of external loss data are sufficient to adequately capture potentially severe loss events.

When choosing external data providers, the business activities should be considered. For example, banks with worldwide business activities should select data providers with worldwide loss data and similar business and geographical focuses. For banks that are active only in Germany, the participation in a national data consortium may be sufficient.

For banks that get external data exclusively from data consortiums, a lack of low-frequency, high-severity losses might be problematic when modelling the tails of the loss distribution.

To adjust the external datasets to internal standards, adequate scaling mechanisms should be installed.

### *Scaling methods*

No homogeneous use of scaling methods is established so far. A scaling of external data to adjust them to the individual institution seems necessary whenever banks are incorporating data from other banks that differ in terms of size, business activities and complexity.

Sometimes, external data are entered into the model without scaling. This is adequate if losses have occurred in similar size, business activity and complexity. Partially, the loss severities are scaled due to expert estimates or gross income, headcount or total assets. Some banks assess the relevance of external datasets before scaling and exclude datasets irrelevant to their business activities. Few banks consider all external datasets as relevant. Most banks have not yet made precise commitments on this subject.

### *Independent validation of the use of external data*

If external data are used, banks have determined an independent function for validating the conditions and processes concerning their use. Usually, this is internal audit; sometimes it is delegated to a trustee of the data consortium. In principle, the latter is possible only for consortium data, not for public data.

### *Purpose of external data*

The following purposes for external data use are stated by a third of the participating banks.

- *Use of external data within the model*: External data are used by the majority for the modelling of sparsely filled risk cells and for the modelling of high-impact areas (tails). Partially, these datasets are used for an adjustment of the internal loss distribution or for the validation of the results of scenario analyses.
- *Use of external data in scenario generation*: The majority of the banks use external data for this purpose.
- *Use of external data for validation*: Partly external data are used for this purpose.
- *Use of external data for other purposes*: Partly external data are used as information sources for OpRisk management and for benchmarking within the business lines.

### *Datasets for external events*

The submitted data must contain all regulatory required and other significant information on OpRisk losses (such as date of occurrence, date of capturing, gross loss, net loss, insurance payment). Whether the creation of the datasets and the processing of external data will meet the regulatory requirements can be judged only in the overall context of the model. Aside from the number and the structure of the data, a homogeneous understanding of the recorded values is essential.

The following conclusions can be drawn:

- a consistent definition of OpRisk terms is currently not always provided in practice; the loss definition may vary across different data sources;
- the consistent collection practice for losses (such description of a loss event including cause) is not always given;
- the consistent categorisation by event categories and business lines leaves room for improvement; and

- the anonymisation of the datasets provided by data consortiums leads to a lack of important information.

### Scenario analysis

Scenario analyses are methods in which experts estimate the probability and potential severity of risk events. Scenarios are understood as assumed causes of events and their effects on the bank and its business. Scenarios can be derived from, for instance, external datasets. Scenarios must be validated using actual loss experience, which is mostly reflected in internal data and in external data in the case of high-severity events.

*Use of scenario analysis*

All banks plan to use scenario analysis within the AMA. In most cases, the implementation of these methods was planned to start in 2005. Half of the banks say they will use scenario analysis for business reasons as well, such as the qualitative identification of process and control weaknesses.

*Validation and adjustment of scenario analyses*

Most banks are still in the conceptual phase of validating their scenario analyses. This is also the case for some of the banks that have already implemented their concepts for scenario analyses. In principle, scenario analysis should be performed at least annually. This includes the creation of new scenarios and the abandoning of obsolete ones. The results of the analyses are sometimes checked for plausibility with internal or external data. Only a few banks have developed methods for determining and reducing the inaccuracies of expert estimates.

### Business environment and internal control factors

Operational risk is influenced by the business-environment and internal-control factors, such as a change in the complexity of the business activities, the business volume or in internal controls. These changes must be captured adequately. Business-environment and control factors may be included in the measurement system, for example, through the use of objective indicators or by expert opinion determined in a systematic process. The influence of these factors on the model must be validated over time with internal and external data.

Concerning the use of business-environment and internal-control factors within the model, most banks have not yet developed advanced concepts. Only in few cases are the factors identified and raised periodically as risk indicators. The methods for incorporating these factors as a model component are mostly still in the development phase. Internal control factors are already used for risk management, though. However, only a few banks have implemented corresponding methods in the model as well.

Some banks do not see the necessity to define and raise indicators for these factors on a regular basis. Instead, these banks state that they survey and judge the quality of their processes and their internal controls within their scenario analysis or other tools for self-evaluation. Business-environment factors should be considered in theses methods as well. In some cases, it is planned that internal audit validates the estimation results and methods with the help of available loss data. However, these estimates do not necessarily enter the measurement system. This is problematic, especially if the factors suggest an increase in the VAR.

## OPRISK MANAGEMENT

OpRisk management is fundamentally different from market and credit risk management. Operational risk is usually not taken to create a profit and is not restricted to certain portfolios. Operational risk is implicitly generated with each activity and is intrinsically present in the entire bank. The management of operational risk is closely tied to modelling and the use test. In addition to the results of the model, further indicators on significant risks (for instance, key risk indicators) are often used for managing operational risks. In principle, the term *OpRisk management* comprises the reduction, avoidance, transfer and acceptance of operational risks.

### Methods for OpRisk management

In about half of the banks, the business lines are responsible for the management of operational risk. Some banks differ between the decentral responsibility of the business lines and the measures taken by the central OpRisk function, the OpRisk committee and senior management. In only a few banks, the responsibility of the

OpRisk function is restricted and allows only recommendations on risk-mitigating measures to the business lines.

Expected losses from operational risks are considered, for instance, in pricing calculations. A reduction of the risk may be achieved, through, say, process improvements. Some risk events, however, may not be completely avoided, such as natural catastrophes, terrorist attacks and external fraud. A business continuity plan and the use of insurance may reduce or transfer the results of such events.

Risk management is often based on reports, which also include measures on how to avoid future losses. About half of the banks have tied a self-assessment to OpRisk management, which is supposed to evaluate the effectiveness of the measures.

Only a third of the banks use AMA model results for management purposes. Partly, in this area room for improvement has already been identified. The other banks are still working on concepts or began the work on concepts in 2005.

Aside from specific management methods, banks also use traditional control elements such as double checks, internal audit and organisational guidelines.

### Risk indicators

Risk indicators are principally planned within the framework of OpRisk management or are already implemented. The indicators should be as forward-looking as possible. From the viewpoint of the banks, sufficient accuracy of the prediction could be confirmed in only a few cases.

Some banks use global risk indicators for all business areas and additionally other, more specific, indicators for single business units. The latter are chosen by the OpRisk unit in accordance with the business lines involved.

Risk indicators from the personnel or IT department as well as process-oriented indicators are used mostly. Popular indicators include staff turnover and indicators regarding complaints. In some cases, a large number of indicators are used. The indicators are often raised monthly, or occasionally more or less frequently. The adequacy of the used frequency can be judged only individually for each indicator.

Risk indicators are often part of the reporting system. Sometimes, indicators are raised monthly but reported only in longer time intervals. Sometimes, the risk indicators are translated into a traffic light scheme with predefined thresholds. Other banks will define thresholds only if a sufficient number of relevant data are available. Besides the thresholds, the change of the indicators over time permits the extraction of relevant information for management and the drawing of conclusions on the effectiveness of the measure implemented.

Some banks check the adequacy of the indicators on a regular basis, for instance, through the connection between indicator and loss events. Sometimes, the relevance of the indicators is judged with self-assessments or changes to the VAR.

Most banks state that they use risk indicators as early-warning systems. Partly, banks have rules in place that require further analysis or development of appropriate measures if thresholds are exceeded. Some banks use risk indicators for risk quantification as well. In these cases, the OpVAR values are adjusted within a certain framework.

### Insurance

All banks use at least basic insurance to cover their operational risk within the risk-management framework. Occasionally, insurance effects are already considered in the loss database. The use of insurance in the model, however, is tied to regulatory requirements, especially regarding the future availability of the insurance coverage. So far, only few banks state that they use insurance within the model according to the regulatory guidelines.

### Outsourcing

When outsourcing relevant activities with respect to the banking business in Germany, it is necessary to consider BaFin's circular No 11/2001. According to the European directive, emergency and business continuity plans should be in place for all major activities. This includes activities that have been outsourced.

Only a few banks consider outsourcing as a risk-management tool and regard it as a risk-transfer method. The risks arising from outsourcing (including legal risks) should be considered within the model.

Major outsourced activities are systematically captured and considered in scenario analyses by some banks. Risks from minor activities are sometimes evaluated with key risk indicators. Losses from outsourced activities are collected by the banks if they affect the bank itself.

New outsourcing activities are evaluated in advance with respect to their operational risks. Half of the banks say that they use service-level agreements for the management of outsourced activities.

### Other risk management tools

Currently, no bank states that it uses other tools, such as derivatives, for risk management within the OpRisk framework. Very few banks plan to actively use such tools in the future, depending on industry development and supervisory requirements.

### Incentives for the improvement of OpRisk management

The creation of incentives for the improvement of OpRisk management within the AMA – for example, through capital allocation – is a requirement from the Basel guidelines that is not implicitly mentioned in the EU directive. Still in this context, a validation and improvement of the AMA is required since the models are not yet fully developed.

Some banks name different methods as part of their incentive systems for the improvement of OpRisk management:

- lower regulatory capital for business lines that successfully reduce their operational risk;
- capital allocation also for economic capital;
- target agreements based on risk indicators; and
- partial deduction of known and booked losses for bonus calculations.

Some banks also refer to training measures, OpRisk workshops and the tasks of internal audit.

## OUTLOOK

Since the beginning of the industry survey, a major proportion of the participating banks have made further progress regarding concepts and implementation of their AMAs. Especially the increasing number of available loss data allow banks to refine and improve their measurement methods and their methods for validation in a dynamic process. As a consequence, the risk-management processes, which are in parts based on the results of the measurement system, could be improved.

The partially low data availability, which often poses a challenge for AMA model development, is improving noticeably. This is especially due to the work of data consortiums, in which the participating banks are exchanging data according to uniform standards. For risk measurement it is essential that the data used within the AMA model be collected and categorised in a consistent manner. Therefore, the anonymised consortium data must, aside from relevant information on the loss events, contain specifications that make the integration of these data into the bank-specific AMA models possible. The data consortiums as well as the banks should perform adequate quality checks to ensure the required data quality.

As a general conclusion, the authors have the impression that the survey among German AMA candidates was very helpful for the supervisors. With this input from the industry supervisors and other interested parties were able to get a deeper insight into the limitations and the potential of the different advanced measurement approaches in banks. This information should help to increase the quality of the rules and guidance on operational risk in Germany as well as within CEBS and AIGOR.

Still, the debate between supervisors and banks about acceptable and unacceptable AMA variants has to increase to ensure a level playing field throughout the AMA application process. A major instrument for achieving this in our view is the organised contact among supervisory experts in the international working groups, but also with industry experts, for instance, via our national Industry Working Group on Operational Risk. We hope that also with publications such as this, the dialogue will be stimulated.

## REFERENCES

**BaFin,** 2005, "Annual Report 2004", Bonn, May (available at www.bafin.de).

**BaFin and Deutsche Bundesbank,** 2005, "Abschlussbericht zur Industrieaktion AMA operationelles Risiko", Bonn and Frankfurt am Main, September (available, in German only, at www.bafin.de and www.bundesbank.de).

**Basel Committee on Banking Supervision,** 2004, "International Convergence of Capital Measurement and Capital Standards. A Revised Framework", June (available at www.bis.org).

**Basel Committee on Banking Supervision,** 2005, "The Treatment of Expected Losses by Banks Using the AMA Under the Basel II Framework", Basel Committee Newsletter, 7, November (available at www.bis.org).

**CEBS (Committee of European Banking Supervisors),** 2005, "Guidelines on the Implementation, Validation and Assessment of Advanced Measurement (AMA) and Internal Ratings Based (IRB) Approaches", Consultation Paper, 10, July (available at www.c-ebs.org).

# 14

# *Operational Risk Management in Financial Institutions: Some Empirical Evidence from Spain**

**Ana Fernández Laviada; Francisco Javier Martínez García**

University of Cantabria; Financial Accounting and Auditing Group

Operational risk (OR) – *the risk of losses resulting from inadequate or failed internal processes, people and systems, and external events* – is not new. This is a fact that everybody knows. However, its control and management have acquired increased importance for financial institutions to remain competitive. A new vision for operational risk management (ORM) is emerging due to new regulatory and management requirements.

Basel II, the New Capital Accord, finally approved by the Basel Committee on Banking Supervision on June 26, 2004, includes a regulatory capital charge for OR. The accord offers different management-oriented alternative methodologies to quantify capital. In theory, the more sophisticated the methodology, the lower the capital charge. This means that OR should be adequately managed in order to assume lower levels of capital.

In this context, banks try to develop an effective ORM framework that allows them to identify, assess, monitor and control or mitigate their OR.

Currently, our research focuses on the definition of the elements that constitute an effective ORM framework in financial institutions. With this end in view, we take as a theoretical and conceptual model the one proposed by the AS/NZS 4360 Australian standard,

*Support from Marcelino Botin Foundation is gratefully acknowledged.

which was updated in 2004. We apply this model to ORM by reviewing and analysing worldwide best practices, regulations and proposals published by regulators and experts on the subject.

To analyse the current situation of the Spanish financial sector and check the adapted model, we surveyed the leading institutions in the industry. This chapter presents the main results obtained from the questionnaire and shows the Spanish financial system has made great efforts in ORM in recent years. As a result, important progress has been achieved in very little time and it can be said, in general terms, to be on a par with the top leading international systems.

ORM is part of the financial-services industry because OR is a fundamental part of doing business and, as such, cannot be fully eliminated. As Power (2005, p 578) points out, suggest that OR has been "invented" is not merely figurative but fanciful because neither OR nor ORM is a new idea. However, a new vision of both is emerging.

Deregulation and globalisation of financial services along with the growing sophistication of financial technology and the emergence of new businesses and channels have created a great variety of operational risks for financial institutions, making the activities of banks and thus their risk profiles more complex. Scandals and collapses primarily associated with some of these risks are numerous.

In spite of its being a practice as old as business itself, it was only recently, at least in this industry, that a consensus was reached on its definition. Traditionally defined as "everything other than credit, market or liquidity risk", it was not managed from a proactive point of view, but from a merely reactive perspective, as institutions approached those risks without any method, instead of elaborating specific contingency plans for them (see Hübner, Laycock and Peemöller, 2001).

OR is often difficult to perceive, quantify and manage and thus it represents one of the greatest challenges that institutions face nowadays. Some of the most experienced leading firms in the industry have seen their institutions suffer huge loss due to OR, since it has been neglected or misunderstood by many institutions for a very long time. Others thought they were adequately managing operational risks, for they had taken some steps to protect against fraud and other contingencies. However, they lacked the day-to-day management that in the long run lays profits to waste entirely and can adversely tarnish the reputation of the institution (see Fernández, 2003a).

Therefore, although ORM is not a new commitment for institutions, it has now acquired a new credibility, becoming a growing concern for regulators and institutions as it can help to add business value.

Such changes in OR perception and interest are mainly due to two important developments. On the one hand, institutions are now aware that complete and efficient ORM can help them to achieve the objectives of their organisation. The traditional approaches to risk management do not provide the board of directors with enough information about how much OR their organisation may face. That is the reason why prevention of great loss is often flawed. These approaches consider operational risks as independent facts, but do not look at the relationships existing among them. Such inconsistency means these perspectives cannot be completely efficient.

On the other hand, the New Basel Capital Accord[1] (NBCA), known as Basel II, of the Basel Committee on Banking Supervision[2] (BCBS) has been very instrumental. The collapse of Barings and derivatives blowups in the mid-1990s were, among others, the factors that led to a revision of the original Basel Capital Accord of 1988. The NBCA put forward an allowance model, which is more risk-sensitive and, further, distinguishes OR, which hitherto was implicitly included in credit risk management. It also requires banks to allow regulatory capital to OR as an independent category for the first time ever.

Thus, in response to regulatory and management requirements, institutions that have not done that yet are expected to begin to allocate a part of their resources to ORM. This means they must endeavour to establish a ORM framework to lay the foundations for its management, by incorporating the strategic, organisational and technical principles of ORM.

Much remains to be done in spite of recently achieved progress, as indicated in the research work recently published by SAS (2004), which pointed out that nearly one-fifth of respondents do not have an OR programme according to Basel II requirements, in spite of the average total of expected losses per year is US$18.8 million.

Currently, our research focuses on the definition of the elements that constitute an effective ORM framework in financial institutions. With this end in view, we take as a theoretical and conceptual model the one proposed by the AS/NZS 4360 Australian standard, which was updated in 2004 (see Frost *et al*, 2001). We apply this model to ORM by reviewing and analysing worldwide best practices, regulations and proposals published by regulators and experts on the subject (see Fernández, 2004).

We thus surveyed industry leaders to analyse the current situation of the Spanish financial sector and to check the adapted model. This chapter presents the main results obtained from this questionnaire.

The questionnaire was sent and personally delivered in January 2004 to the highest people responsible[3] for OR of eight representative institutions of the Spanish financial sector, three savings banks and five banks. They were selected according to their pioneering role, their special concern and interest for OR and their participation in some national or international consortiums[4] or exchange of operational data, allowing them to upgrade their databases and to get access to more information in order to reorganise and improve ORM in their institutions.

The remainder of the chapter is structured as follows. The next section briefly presents the key aspects for implementation of the framework of ORM, as this is not our main objective here. The following section reviews similar works, which allow us a comparison with the Spanish financial situation. Then, we present the results obtained from the survey and the final section summarises and concludes the chapter.

## FRAMEWORK FOR OPERATIONAL RISK MANAGEMENT

Institutions, especially financial ones, consider risk as a source of competitive advantage that ought to be managed, because business success relies on excellence in risk management.

Various institutions are more and more obligated to go "intelligent" in their risk management. If we agree that risk is an essential part of the value generated by companies, then management excellence implies identification, assessment, monitoring, mitigation and control, and it decides how, when and how much one is ready to bear under a previously planned strategy.

Risk management ought to be applied to all levels of the organisation and affects all products, operations, activities, procedures and systems.

Basel II establishes that "A bank should develop a framework for managing operational risk and evaluate the adequacy of capital given this framework. The framework should cover the bank's appetite and tolerance for operational risk, as specified through the policies for managing this risk, including the extent and manner in which operational risk is transferred outside the bank. It should also include policies outlining the bank's approach to identifying, assessing, monitoring and controlling/mitigating the risk" (paragraph 737).

Two methods can be applied to ORM:

- *Quantitative methods*: These consist of creating events databases, similar to those of non-performing loans by credit risk, which are used for organising and calculating the capital at risk.
- *Qualitative methods*: These are based on the use of tools for identification, quantification and follow-up of OR, which permit the detection of exposure to risk and its mitigation before some adverse event takes place.

Through the appropriate combination of both, institutions are expected to set up a framework that adequately measures and quantifies OR in order to meet the requirements of regulatory capital. To do so, they will need a systematic procedure to record operational loss data as well as to evaluate the risks within the institutions and to adopt a framework to analyse data and risk evaluations and to translate them into exposure to OR.

However, although this regulatory framework aims at measuring such exposure in terms of capital figures, the validity of these estimations will depend on both the suitability of the model and the risk-management methods being used in the institution.

Important progress has been achieved, but too many efforts aim at a quantification of OR as a solution to the problem. However, ORM is more a question of *improving* managerial practices than of measuring them. The actual role of supervisors ought not be excessive demand for some minimum capital figures but that of promoting efficient ORM by requiring institutions to prove they are taking all the necessary steps to control operational risks.

An appropriate framework for ORM will provide a strategic ORM system and will ensure that both an efficient management and a suitable method of measurement have been established within the organisation. In practice, the framework adopted by the institution must show the extent and complexity of business lines as well as its organisation chart. The unique nature of every institution means it is impossible to define a single framework that is suitable for all institutions. However, some key aspects must be considered in any ORM framework:

- to establish adequate policies and procedures;
- to endeavour to identify and assess operational risks;
- to carry out monitoring and effective feedback;
- to establish a good internal control system; and
- to implement sound controls and verifications for the ORM framework itself.

Basel II recommendations are one of the main foundations for ORM. As a consequence, they must be introduced within the theoretical principles of the management framework, together with other best industry practices not included within the BCBS recommendations that are proposed by other regulators.

The framework must consider the ORM process, including all its phases, as well as its relation to business strategy and the institution's risk appetite. The process is optimised by using an adequate infrastructure, which in most cases is an important differentiating element for the market and regulators.

The implementation of a complete management framework includes:

- defining clearly what OR is;
- defining an appropriate organisational structure for its correct implementation;
- developing an adequate risk culture;
- identifying and evaluating the main risks for the institution;
- collecting the data, both from internal and external sources, that will permit adequate future projections;
- establishing the most appropriate quantification method; and
- establishing the best management approach.

As remarked in the introduction, we applied the risk-management model, proposed by the AS/NZS 4360[5] Australian standard of 2004, to ORM, thus highlighting the main elements of management procedure, in this case for ORM.

## PRELIMINARY RESEARCH

In 1998 and 1999, three organisations – the International Securities Dealers Association[6] (ISDA), the British Bankers' Association (BBA) and Robert Morris Associates (RMA) – sponsored research on ORM. These three associations, together with the multinational PricewaterhouseCoopers (PwC), carried out research that culminated in December 1999 with the report entitled "Operational risk: the next frontier", in which the OR situation was comprehensively analysed in 55 worldwide financial institutions. Their analysis was subsequently used as a reference for other research works.

Since the first NBCA draft was issued in June 1999, the BCBS has carried out various impact surveys with the aim of knowing more about the incidence of its measures on the concerned institutions. Specifically, two studies involving OR have been carried out since then.

The first one was issued as a part of QIS2 by the Risk Management Group (RMG) of the BCBS in May 2001. The results from the 30 collaborating institutions were published in January 2002 (see Basel Committee on Banking Supervision, 2002a). Then, in March 2003, a tabulated abstract of individual operational risk loss data compiled by the RMG among 89 institutions, which answered the questionnaire "Operational risk loss data collection exercise", was published in June 2002 as a part of QIS3 (see Basel Committee on Banking Supervision, 2002b).

On the other hand, a division of PwC, which specialises in fully comprehensive risk management and has a unit providing risk solutions to the financial sector,[7] carried out research on the position of the Spanish financial sector in relation to the NBCA recommendations. It analysed ORM in the major Spanish financial institutions, considering the best practices of the sector in each case and their relative position in relation to the new requirements of the NBCA. Sixteen financial institutions, among banks and savings banks[8] participated in this study and results were presented in July 2002 (see PwC, 2002).

During the last quarter of 2002 in the Spanish financial sector we undertook a preliminary research to approach OR (which we designate UC 2003), this time focusing on savings banks. The questionnaire was sent to the 46 savings banks that form this sector.

Thirty-six of them answered the questionnaire and their results were compiled in Fernández (2003b).

Also in the same period (October 2003), this time for the US market, the Risk Management Association (RMA) published the results of its research (see Risk Management Association, 2003). It was sent to 479 institutions by mail and 46 complete questionnaires were obtained.

The following year FitchRatings (2004a) published a report that looked at the progress achieved by the banking industry in the development of ORM methodologies. As a continuation to this report FitchRatings surveyed 50 of the major financial institutions in the world. Answers from 42 institutions from Australia, Canada, Europe, Japan, South Africa and the United States were obtained. The results of this survey were summed up (see FitchRatings, 2004b), and the key aspects of ORM and the implementation of Basel II were identified.

Finally, in June 2004, SAS, a business-intelligence-oriented company, in collaboration with Incisive Media Financial Publishing, published research (see SAS, 2004) in which they collected OR data from more that 250 worldwide companies.

## THE QUESTIONNAIRE: ANALYSIS OF THE RESULTS

The main results obtained from the questionnaire are described below according to its original structure, which was divided into eight parts, as follows.

### Definition of operational risk

Of course, we first asked them to define OR. As expected, given the rapid evolution that institutions in this sector are going through, all those surveyed adopted, by the time our research took place, the Basel definition, at least for capital requirements.

Basel II constitutes an essential starting point for a standardisation of criteria and a reference framework that permits analysis of the progress that financial institutions have achieved for ORM.

The adoption of this definition is also to be found internationally,[9] and, if we compare it with the results from the PwC research for the whole Spanish financial sector in 2002 or with our research on the savings banks in 2003, we find that Spanish leaders in the sector show the same tendencies as their international counterparts.

Furthermore, as remarked in the case of savings banks, institutions not only adopt this definition but also agree on it, and only one of them still considers it somehow nebulous.

## Operational risk classification

In spite of the efforts made by the BCBS or by associations such as the Operational Risk Exchange (ORX),[10] this cataloguing process is not easy, as illustrated by the results from the surveys. Most institutions showed their discontent with risk classification: 87% think categories are not clearly defined and 62% do believe that, in addition, these categories do not consider all the possibilities. Although opinions about their adequacy are mostly favourable at Level 1, all institutions except one consider they are not well defined at Level 2.

In depth analysis of the problems that arise in practice and the lack of detailed definitions imply that usually the same event can be classified into different categories. This in turn implies duplicity problems and thus the institutions surveyed remarked on the need for more elucidating examples.

As far as these risk categories are concerned, we wished to know which were the most important ones for the institutions surveyed, considering both their frequency and their severity, in order to compare them with the data published by the BCBS in its impact studies (see Basel Committee on Banking Supervision, 2002a; 2002b).

With regard to loss frequency (see Figure 1), the most relevant risk categories are, first, "execution, delivery and process management", which was also found to be the most important category for 75% of the institutions surveyed; and, second, "external fraud" for 50%. On the other hand, it is important to note that none of the institutions surveyed considered "employee practices and workplace safety" or "damage to physical assets" to be among the three most outstanding categories.

Regarding loss severity (see Figure 2), the most important risks are again "execution, delivery and process management", followed by "external fraud". In this case, "internal fraud" is remarkable since it not only shows a similar level to "external fraud", but also constitutes the third most relevant risk for 50% of the institutions surveyed. As in the previous case, some categories are not considered to be among the three most relevant ones by institutions, and

**Figure 1** Which categories have been the most relevant in your entity with reference to their frequency?

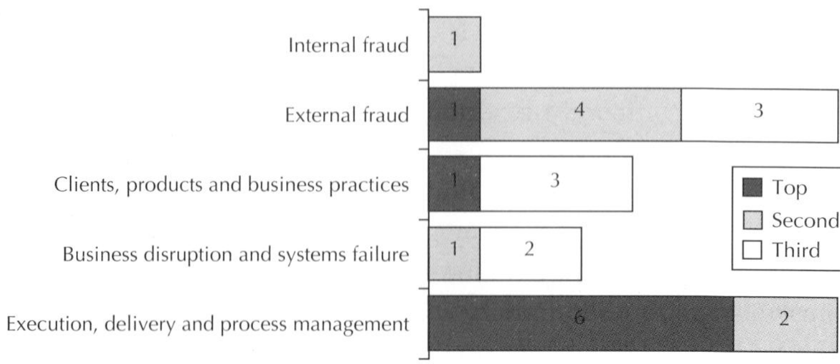


**Figure 2** Which categories have been the most relevant in your entity with reference to their severity?

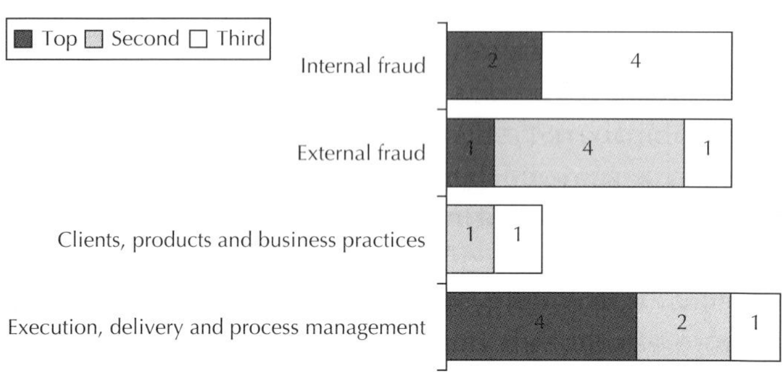


"business disruptions and system failures" are not found to constitute an outstanding risk.

It is important to assess the progress of these indicators according to risk categories, since institutions continue to develop their internal databases, as we shall see later.

By comparing the results from our research with the data published by the BCBS in the two above-mentioned documents (see Table 1), and by considering that their differences can be due to the different typology of the participant institutions, the following conclusions can be drawn.

**Table 1** Number of individual loss events and total gross amounts by event type

| Event type | Frequency | | Severity | |
|---|---|---|---|---|
| | 2002 (%) | 2001 (%) | 2002 (%) | 2001 (%) |
| Internal fraud | 3.3 | 2.7 | 7.2 | 10.7 |
| External fraud | 42.4 | 36.4 | 15.5 | 20.3 |
| Employment practices and workplace safety | 8.5 | 2.7 | 6.8 | 2.9 |
| Clients, products and business practices | 7.2 | 6.4 | 13.1 | 27.5 |
| Damage to physical assets | 1.4 | 4.5 | 24.3 | 3.0 |
| Business disruption and systems failure | 1.1 | 5.3 | 2.7 | 0.8 |
| Execution, delivery and process management | 35.1 | 42.0 | 29.4 | 34.8 |

*Source*: BIS

- As far as frequency is concerned, the main difference lies in the great importance that Spanish institutions attach to the category "clients, products and business practices". Both research works show that "external fraud" and "execution, delivery and process management" are the two most outstanding categories, even though the impact studies indicate an increasing tendency to "external fraud" risks.
- Although the two main categories are the same in both studies as far as severity is concerned, important differences appear with regard to the third most outstanding risk. While Spanish institutions do not attach importance to the category of "physical damages" (no institution considers this one to be among the first three categories), an exponential growth of this category to the detriment of "clients, products and business" has been found in the studies carried out by the BCBS (24.3%). We shall look at this remarkable difference later.

## Business lines

An additional problem that institutions face is that of the business lines, or units, where operational loss must be allocated. Most institutions surveyed consider these lines to be vague and, in addition, a quarter of them think they do not adequately fit into the Spanish

**Figure 3** Which lines are most affected by OR in your business?

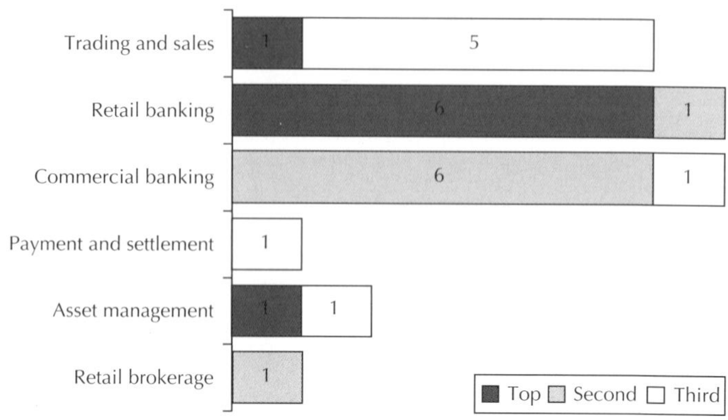


financial system. On the other hand, the most outstanding solutions refer to a clear definition of their content and even the creation of other new ones to fit the Spanish banking model.

Afterwards, an analysis of the global effects that OR has on the different business lines in terms of frequency and severity shows that the most affected sectors are, in order of importance, "retail banking", "commercial banking" and "trading and sales" (see Figure 3).

A comparison of our results with the data provided by Basel confirms they are in consonance with the two works published, since these are exactly the three lines being exposed to the highest quantity and impact of operational loss (see Table 2). "Retail banking" can be especially highlighted due to the high loss registered (61.1%) in relation to the rest of the units, while, considering its severity, they are almost on a par with "commercial banking", with 29.3% and 28.9% respectively.

As for the rest of the lines, "corporate finance" and "agency services", not even indicated by the Spanish institutions surveyed, were also the least affected according to the Basel studies. Indeed, what surprises us and is therefore worth highlighting is the differences found between the two consecutive Basel studies, which prove quite significant in some cases. For example, consider loss frequency. While in the case of "retail banking" the number of events has practically doubled in one year, in "commercial banking" it has fallen to almost a third. If we consider loss severity, different and

**Table 2** Number of individual loss events and total gross amounts by business line

| Business line | Spain | Basel | | | |
|---|---|---|---|---|---|
| | Freq/Sev | Frequency | | Severity | |
| | 2004 (%) | 2002 (%) | 2001 (%) | 2002 (%) | 2001 (%) |
| Corporate finance | 0.0 | 0.9 | 7.4 | 3.5 | 0.3 |
| Trading and sales | 75.0 | 10.9 | 19.1 | 14.9 | 4.9 |
| Retail banking | 87.5 | 61.1 | 39.4 | 29.3 | 67.4 |
| Commercial banking | 87.5 | 7.2 | 22.9 | 28.9 | 13.2 |
| Payment and settlement | 12.5 | 3.9 | 4.8 | 3.25 | 7.0 |
| Agency services and custody | 0.0 | 1.5 | 2.2 | 4.25 | 1.8 |
| Asset management | 25.0 | 2.3 | 2.1 | 2.70 | 1.6 |
| Retail brokerage | 12.5 | 6.9 | 2.1 | 11.70 | 3.9 |

*Source*: BIS and Fernández (2004)

significant tendencies can be found, even though they are not so pronounced. In "retail banking" it has decreased a little less than 50%, while commercial banks experienced a similar increase.

We consider these differences are to a large extent due to two factors. First, there was the lack of a clear definition of the lines themselves, as occurred in the events classification, which has brought about some changes in these lines as they became more concrete. Secondly, due to the number of collaborating institutions, QIS2 collects the data of 30 banks while in QIS3, 89 institutions participated, thus significantly modifying in some cases the results obtained.

## Organisation

The organisational structure is the bank-wide foundation for all ORM activities. The internal audit department has traditionally been responsible for verifying the existence of adequate controls in order to mitigate operational loss. The big challenge institutions face is that of creating an organisation structure that boosts the homogeneous processing of OR information within the entire institution, which clearly assigns responsibilities for management, control and monitoring, and which relies on a centralised ORM unit, which is independent of the internal audit department, as BCBS recommends.

To start with, we must highlight the fact that all the institutions surveyed have incorporated ORM, although half of them are still at the implementation stage. Aware of the importance of this risk, all have allocated specific resources to OR-related issues. This is especially evidenced by verifying the personnel who are partly or totally assigned to this risk. However, some big differences can be found among these institutions, since we can find some with only two part-time employees and one with as many as 35 employees entirely committed to different tasks concerning OR. Of course, this fact has a very positive impact on the considerable progress this latter institution has achieved.

A first step in this framework is to appoint someone to be responsible for OR. As a result, the creation of a specific OR department has been the option adopted by most institutions surveyed.

BCBS requirements call for the creation of an independent unit to be responsible for ORM, and 88% of the institutions surveyed have already done or are planning to do this. These results show the progress achieved within the sector, since only 38% of the institutions had created an independent unit hardly one year ago according to PwC research.

Institutions continued to centralise OR-related functions in this unit, according to the best practices of the sector and the model proposed by Basel II. However, 87.5% also count on specialised staff members within their different business and support units. Furthermore, in 50% of the institutions, this unit reports risk management, since it is equivalent to credit and marketing units.

The functions assigned to this unit are the definition of policies and procedures for OR management and control, the designation and implementation of evaluation methodology and OR reporting system, as well as the identification, assessment and monitoring of OR (see Figure 4).

Less progress was achieved on matters concerning an OR committee, despite the fact that the percentage of institutions that have already created or planned to create this committee has doubled, compared with the PwC survey. Nevertheless, only two institutions have implemented this committee within their management system, although two others are working on such implementation.

Although the functions of this committee have not yet been determined in those institutions that are still working on it, it has

**Figure 4** Which functions has this independent OR area?

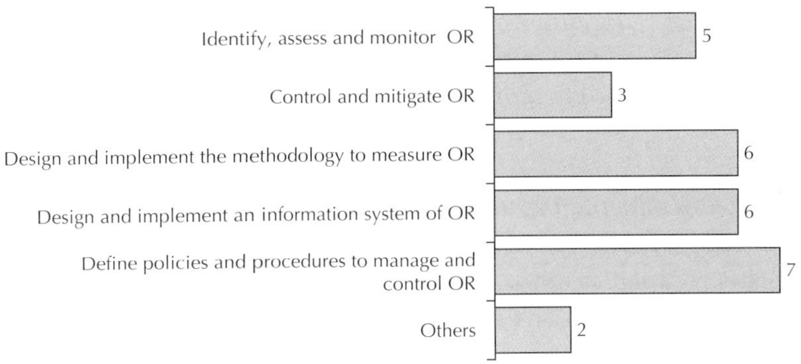


been assigned a number of functions in the two institutions that have fulfilled the implementation step:

- ❑ identify essential matters in the organisation and corrective actions to mitigate risk;
- ❑ report to the board of directors;
- ❑ solve essential issues in the business units; and
- ❑ determine the level of risk appetite and the risk profile of the institution.

In some cases other objectives have also been included, for instance, determination of the best practices for ORM or promotion of OR reporting within the organisation.

On the other hand, this committee normally includes the person responsible for OR, the director of risk, internal audit, the people responsible for business lines and in some cases staff committed to systems, human resources or top management tasks. This composition reinforces the idea that this risk covers and affects the whole organisation, and therefore all its members must be aware of and must participate in its management.

Finally, regarding the organisational model of the institution we wished to know which other parties were involved in the management procedure, since it affects the whole institution, as we pointed out in the previous paragraph. Although we can see that almost all of them were mentioned, logically the OR sector and the internal audit department are the two parties that are mainly concerned, since they are directly related to the entire procedure.

Concerning the internal audit department, the NBCA admits it can be the person responsible for initially developing ORM, especially in the case of institutions with few resources, although this department must be confined to supervisory tasks and to the subsequent follow-up of the process. In fact, the institutions surveyed confirm this statement since their audit department has adopted this new function, even though it remains a key unit for OR issues within entities.

All institutions will have to assume this new function of internal audit, not as a directly responsible unit, which is now the function of the new OR independent unit, but that of supervision, monitoring and reporting the necessary information for the ORM process as the ORM framework becomes more and more stable.

To sum up the elements implied or involved in the ORM process, we would like to highlight the fact that 100% of the institutions surveyed report OR information to senior management, sometimes even on a monthly basis, while only 50% report this sort of information to the board of directors. These results are similar to those obtained by PwC in 2003.

### Tools

The creation of a framework for ORM relies on the use of a set of tools allowing the identification and assessment of operational loss as well as measurement, monitoring, control and mitigation of the different risks.

That is why we wished to know what tools were in use or whether their use was planned in the various Spanish institutions (see Figure 5). Thus, we found that, in the first place, all of them use at least three different types of tools for management and, in particular, 62.5% of the institutions surveyed use five out of the six tools included in the survey. Secondly, loss databases, self-assessments and risk indicators are the three most important tools since they are being used – or their use is planned – by 100% of the institutions. Besides, regarding the future use of other tools, triggers that hitherto were used by only one institution are in the limelight. Thirdly, only one institution admitted it never used and was not planning to use triggers or risk maps.

**Figure 5** Which tools are used or are planned for use for the future?

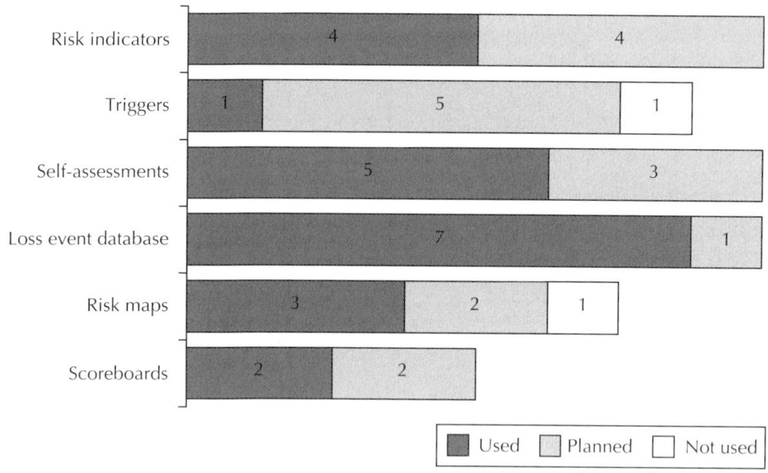


Some conclusions can be reached by comparing these results with those obtained from the PwC study.

- ❑ Use of all the tools as a whole has increased.
- ❑ Loss databases, which represent an essential element for global management, both quantitatively and qualitatively, have attained the expected level of acceptance and development, being used by almost 100% of the institutions surveyed.
- ❑ Likewise, self-assessments have been used by 62.5%, while the rest already plan to use them.
- ❑ Risk maps and process flows are the only tools that have not yet gained wide acceptance among institutions, perhaps because they do not completely fit this risk.

The results of a survey carried out in 1999 (see British Bankers Association, PwC, International Swaps and Derivatives Association and Robert Morris Associates, 1999) showed that 71% of the participants used or planned to use the five tools and almost 30% did not yet use the loss databases. These results put us not only in the forefront of but above leading international institutions – not surprising given the moment when both surveys were carried out (see Figure 6).

Regarding those who promoted their creation and use, OR areas were responsible for 50% of cases, although the internal audit

**Figure 6** Tools used or planned

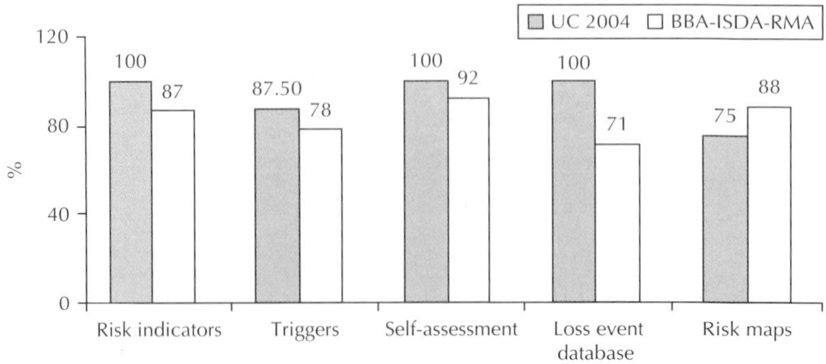


department, the risks departments and even top managers are also considered to be responsible for 37.5% of cases.

Likewise, an analysis of information users shows that all of them use it, even though the OR area is again its main user. At this point, it is important to highlight the progress of institutions since, in the case of the PwC survey, the main user of the information generated by these tools was the internal audit department, which is now relegated to a secondary position.

Regarding its purpose, this kind of information is mainly used, as might be expected, for day-to-day management; second, as a mechanism of control; and, third, for capital allocation, although it is also used to manage and support other operations. We found that, although capital allocation was the main reason originally, which led to study and work on OR, it is no longer the prime objective of information sources. Now day-to-day management and the achievement of the objectives of the institution are two important reasons underwriting the need for an adequate management of this risk.

An in depth analysis of the most useful tools could provide us with detailed information about who makes use of them, for what purpose, how they are created and what their advantages and disadvantages are.

### *Indicators and triggers*

As we saw at the beginning, 100% of the institutions surveyed use or plan to use these tools for predicting, assessing and determining OR levels in their institutions. Thus, to sum up we could state:

- OR-related staff areas are those that use indicators to the largest extent, followed by business areas and the internal audit department, whereas only related areas and audit departments have triggers on them;
- the frequency of following them up can be variable according to the specific indicator or triggers used, although it is generally carried out on a quarterly or monthly basis; and
- these indicators are mainly used to identify operational problems, to decide and to analyse different tendencies, even though they are also used for other purposes.

*Self-assessments*

The business units of five institutions surveyed continue to use this tool to identify risks associated with their operations, to evaluate their control and to determine what points need to be improved. The remaining institutions planned to do so in the short term.

In order to create these self-assessments, institutions depend on different sources of information. However, their input is mainly obtained from the compilation of operational loss, especially now that these become more and more complete and reliable. However, workshops, questionnaires or risk maps, and research on mitigating measures are also important sources of information since information from operational loss is sometimes not enough.

If we compare these results with those from the PwC survey, we can see how workshops and meetings were the main information source in those days, while compiled loss came in the fifth position. It is a normal situation, in any case, since information on the operational losses of institutions was hardly available, a fact that led institutions to use other information sources.

*Databases*

As pointed out earlier, loss data is one of the most important elements for ORM and quantification. Internal loss data are not sufficient, and at present the way of increasing the range of loss is by using external databases of losses or by joining a consortium.

In this sense, it is worth remarking that all institutions already have an operational loss database, although one of them is still at the implementation stage. The differences found with the results from the PwC imply a growing awareness of the need to compile loss data and highlight the emphasis that the BCBS puts on their creation.

All these databases are efficiently collecting data, and their collection – both manual and automatic – takes place within the institution's own systems. In the collection of data, and for a better qualitative and quantitative ORM, all institutions classify their losses in relation to the different business units and to the type of event, something that was done by only 36% of the institutions in 2003 according to PwC. By January 1 2007, most institutions will have longer than four-year records of historical data.

The advantages of having an internal OR database are the possibility of analysing errors, both for their frequency and impact, knowing the causes of the errors and taking remedial or palliative measures against loss. For this reason, all institutions produce regular statistics with the data collected.

The NBCA emphasises the use of external data as a means of complementing those provided by internal databanks. It is precisely the need for those data that is the motive for all institutions to consider creating a database of external loss for the entire financial sector.

Among the most glaring obstacles to this objective are the great heterogeneity of the participants and the high cost involved in its creation. These two factors, which have always been decisive because they are not published – though it would be more appropriate to say that they have been intentionally hidden – are of greater concern than the public declaration of internal flaws and weakness of management.

And, among the advantages that will accrue to them by having this databank, they point out that not only would they acquire a benchmark orientation for their management but also that it would enable them to complete their internal databases, and, by so doing, improve their models, in addition to identifying sectors of risk that had perhaps not yet been considered by the institution. All these advantages led 43% of our institutions to join a consortium, while the remaining 57% plan to do so in the near future.

Of utmost importance when joining a consortium are geographic and activity/business proximity of the participants. That is why national consortiums are very much in vogue. However, we cannot overlook the impacts of globalisation on institutions and the resultant interest for consortiums at international level.

## Reporting

The reporting function must be included within the ORM framework. In order to be efficient, it is important that information be transmitted with a varying degree of detail according to the need of the receiver. Logically, the business and risk areas, together with the internal audit department, will receive more detailed information than the top management and the board of directors, but all must receive reports on the situation of OR in the institution.

This is very important. In surveyed institutions almost all the areas and related parties received some OR information. However, since they are still at the development stage, let us for the moment use the results merely for guidance.

Although many areas are involved and different types of information are reported, we will give prominence to some of the results that we consider more important (see Figure 7).

- *Board of directors*: At least half the respondents indicated that they regularly sent OR information to their board of directors, especially summaries of the statistics of loss and at least the capital allocated by OR.
- *Senior management*: All the institutions provide senior management with OR information, some only with information about the allocated capital or about loss statistics; but the majority also inform them about major losses incurred and the tendencies of indicators.

**Figure 7** What information do they receive?

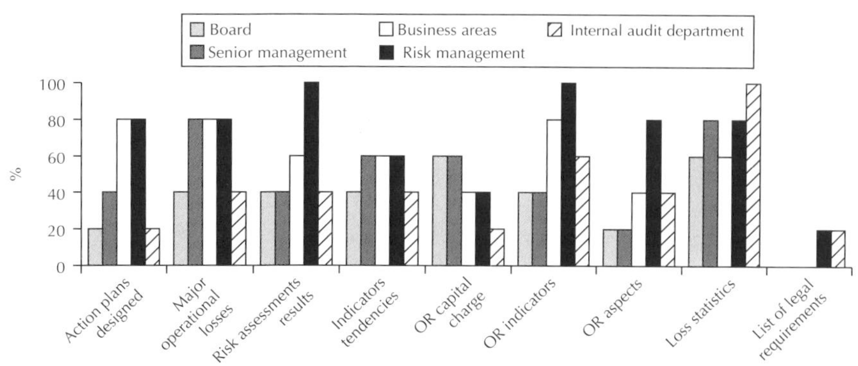

- *Business lines*: In contrast to the previous two, they do not often receive the capital level assigned to this risk, but they do receive information about OR indicators, major loss and action plans designed for the best management of this risk.
- *Risk managers*: These are the major recipients of information and, together with the internal audit department, the only ones who receive, in at least one of the cases, a list of legal requirements about OR. All institutions provide them with information about OR and about self-assessments.
- *Audit department*: In all institutions the audit department receives information about statistics of loss, but after taking on the role of supervision it does not receive much information directly, unless it asks for it in the course of its work.

As for who writes up these reports and the frequency with which they are submitted, we would say many departments are involved, although it mainly behoves three to do so. OR area, staff and business areas are those who primarily write them up on quarterly or monthly basis according to what the information is about and for whom it is destined.

However, the fact that they are still at the development stage let us to consider the results merely for the purposes of orientation.

Finally, we wanted to know how well trained the institutions are in order to undertake the requirements of Pilar III, "disclosure and market discipline". Even though only 25% do have the training to be able to meet those demands, all confirm that they will be well prepared by 2007. The frequency with which it will be provided is yet to be determined by the majority, but those who have already decided it confirm they will be doing that quarterly.

When it comes to evaluating the level of development attained regarding the information process by OR, 50% consider that, despite the fact that they are developing it, it is only partially implemented.

### Capital requirements

One of the NBCA's innovations is the inclusion of OR, for the first time, among the requirements of regulatory capital, as market and credit risk. There has been and still is controversy, however. For this reason, we wanted to know the opinion of leading Spanish financial institutions. Most of them agree with this inclusion, even though half of them still consider the requirements planned to be excessive. Just one institution does not believe that these losses should be treated in terms of provisions and not in capital terms.

In April 2004, FitchRatings indicated in a survey carried out among the major international institutions, which did not take into consideration smaller companies, showed that 75% of them would endeavour to implement the advanced approach proposed by Basel, as expected.

Likewise, in our case, from the three approaches that Basel offers to calculate OR regulatory capital, none will opt for the basic, and the majority turn to an advanced approach, primarily through the loss-distribution approach (LDA). Implementation will be complete among those already decided. These data tally with the desire expressed by more than half of the institutions studied in the PwC survey of 2002.

However, it is possible that, by the time the final text was published, some change might have taken place or the institution that had not yet decided which method follow, at the time the survey was undertaken, will have already opted for one.

The NBCA also demands that a series of qualitative criteria be followed so that different methods can be applied. Most of them fulfil the 10 principles of the "sound practices" document but just one confirms that it has fulfilled all the qualitative requirements established by Basel. While two others have almost fulfilled most, one of the institutions admitted not having any cover at the moment.

Therefore, this is something to which most institutions should pay more attention in the future in case they want to apply the selected advanced method.

*Economic capital methodologies*

Once institutions have adopted the most appropriate methodology for their purposes, the quantification results from OR will be used to fulfil the demands of Basel, which is a priority application for three of the respondents. Also, all institutions plan to make use of this information as a cost and profit analysis before taking certain measures, in order to identify critical issues for their board of directors and to review their insurance policies (see Figure 8).

Although calculation methodologies prove more complex, OR measurement and determination of the subsequent problems for

**Figure 8** Once OR is quantified, for what purpose is this information used?

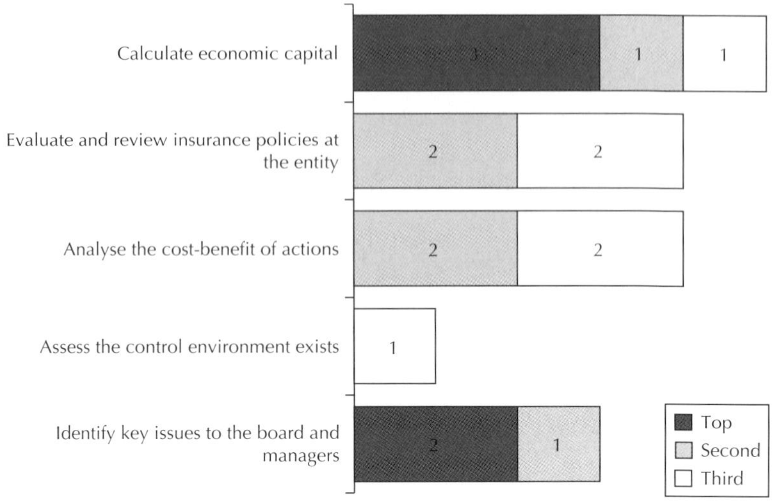


institutions are difficult to solve due to the lack of both internal and external data. This fact currently constitutes the main obstacle for OR quantification. This situation implies again the need to create an internal loss database and to complement this information with external loss data, which exactly corresponds to the situation shown by PwC two years ago.

*Insurance*

Finally, regarding the possibility that institutions have to reduce capital requirements by OR through mitigating the effect of insurance risk, two issues should be considered: first, acceptability or non-acceptability of consideration of this possibility for capital allocation; second, the determination of the relationship existing between the insurance and ORM areas of their institutions.

Concerning the first one, it is remarkable that all institutions agree on this possibility even though half of them consider they could still be more flexible.

As for the degree of integration between both sectors and their policies, the fact that such integration does not already exist in most cases must be remarked, although institutions plan to achieve this point in subsequent phases. This means the current situation is quite similar to that described two years ago.

### Respondents' conclusions

First, we should point out that all institutions declared that they would keep working on this, although Basel finally would have decided not to require capital for this risk, since this management has been found to be necessary for the good functioning of any institution.

Secondly, the reduction of loss through operational errors (which is indeed the main advantage for half of the institutions surveyed), the fulfilment of regulatory requirements, the reduction of control risks and the improvement of the quality of their services are some of the advantages that institutions expect to obtain from a comprehensive ORM (see Figure 9).

**Figure 9** What advantages do you expect to receive by managing OR?

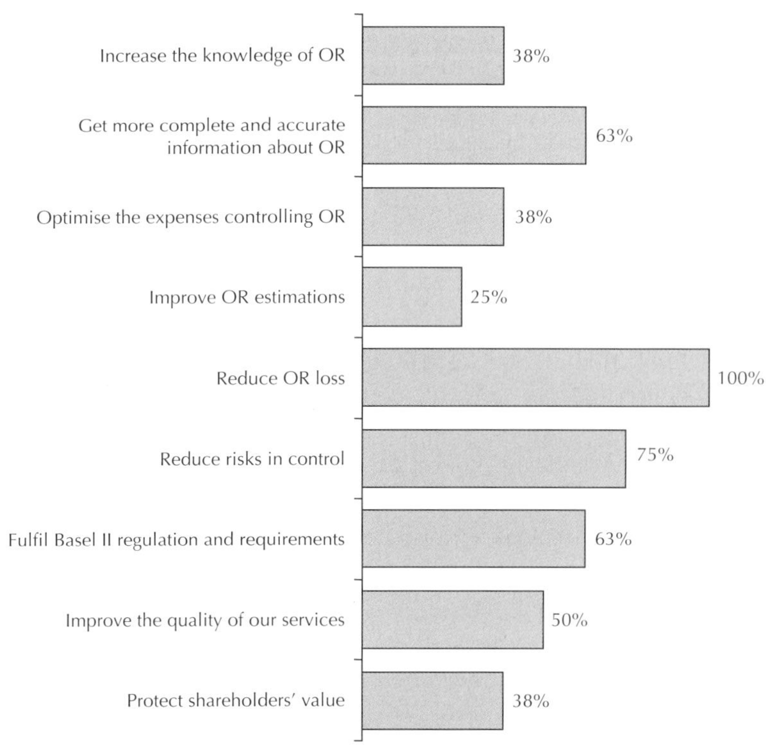

**Figure 10** Which do you believe is the main goal in your organisation?

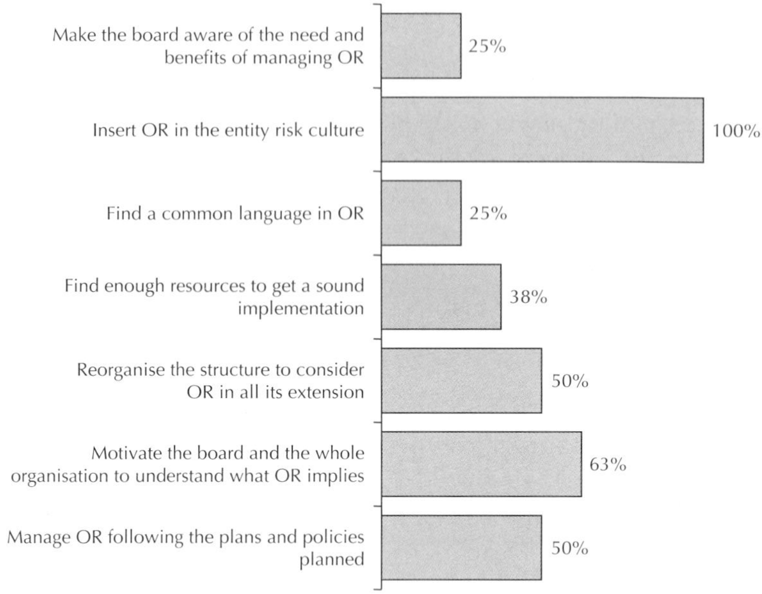


Thirdly, the main challenge that the surveyed institutions face is that of introducing OR in the institutional risk culture, which proves to be an essential element for the success of the ORM framework. Encouragement of management proceedings and staff members and reorganisation of the institution's structure and ORM according to the policies and plans instituted for this purpose are also difficult tasks to tackle, although they must be considered (see Figure 10) as essential elements to guarantee the entire process.

As a consequence, institutions usually train their staff members and provide in depth manuals to establish the main measures to be adopted.

Finally, we asked them to make an exercise of self-assessment. The average, from 1 to 10, was 5.25 but the grades are really divergent and needed of a final thought.

We can distinguish three different groups: those that fall within the outstanding brackets, being sure of their development and progress; those that are acceptable but not prominent; and those that are not even on average.

If we look again at each of them, we are not surprised that precisely, those who consider themselves more prepared are the ones who have devoted more efforts and have taken more seriously the need for progress in this risk, as they already did with other risks.

It is our hope that in the future they continue working with the same zeal, and those who in the beginning perhaps merely looked for the fulfilment of legal requirements will surely discover that the advantages accruing from ORM are of benefit to their institutions.

## CONCLUSIONS

Finally, we sum up the main results from the research in the following points.

(1) In recent years the Spanish financial system has made great effort in ORM and, as a result, important progress has been made in very little time. It can be said in general terms that it is on a par with the leading international systems. However, among Spanish leaders some differences can be observed. While some of them have readily appreciated the advantages, through assigning sufficient resources and means, others are still merely obligated by legal requirements and they do not devote all the necessary attention to it.

(2) We cannot deny that the origin of the growing interest shown in this risk is in the Basel II capital requirements, which the majority of institutions have accepted, though still consider excessive. However, all would continue with their procedures, even if Basel were withdrawn, for it has been demonstrated that it is necessary and contributes to optimum value for institutions.

(3) To instil OR into the culture of organisations will be the major challenge that confronts institutions that wish to implement successfully a complete ORM policy. However, the comprehensive management of this risk will not only help them to fulfil the standards and regulations in force, but also enables them to reduce loss due to operational errors and risk control, and to improve on the quality of services, which in the final analysis will provide great protection for the shareholder.

(4) All institutions have currently adopted the OR definition as proposed by Basel, despite the fact that events classification and business lines mapping have some problems for their

practical implementation. Operational loss due to "execution, delivery and process management" and "external and internal fraud" are the most frequent categories and of major impact for the majority of the institutions surveyed, while "retail banking", "commercial banking" and "trading and sales" are the three business lines that prove most affected by operational loss.

(5) At least half the institutions have already introduced reforms in order to incorporate ORM into their structure. The majority already have or are creating independent units entrusted with policies and procedures for ORM, in addition to designing reporting systems and the most appropriate technology.

(6) Despite the fact that all units and departments within the institution are somehow involved in this framework for comprehensive ORM, the internal audit department still occupies a prominent position, although it has adopted a secondary supervisory role as stipulated in the principles of Basel, for in most cases the process was initiated by and promoted from this department.

(7) All institutions use various tools, especially risk indicators, self-assessments and internal loss databases, the last of these being essential for correct OR measurement. Generally, the information they provide is used not only for quantifying the capital, but also for helping in the day-to-day management of institutions, since they allow an analysis of the reasons for loss through the statistics obtained. This in turn implies the elaboration of corrective measures and a review of stipulated policies.

(8) The need for internal and external data to complement databases so as to correctly quantify OR has led institutions to collaborate or to join consortiums, both national and international, given the fact that financial institutions are increasingly developing within a context of globalisation.

(9) The role of reporting is essential for the correct functioning of the entire framework and, consequently, all institutions have indeed begun submitting OR information to the senior management and to the board of directors. They also provide more comprehensive information to the rest of business, staff and risk areas.

(10) At the time of this research, pending the final publication of the Capital Accord, most institutions have decided to follow some of the advanced approaches, and most of them will fully implement these measures, even though some institutions must still evaluate them. However, given the scant implementation of the qualitative requirements, which only one institution totally fulfilled, institutions will have to devote more time and resources to this if they wish to implement the advanced approaches.

Substantial progress has been achieved but there is still more to be done and we hope this research helps the reader to understand the situation a little better.

1 After five years of research, the final text was approved on June 26, 2004, and was published under the title "International Convergence of Capital Measures and Regulations", available on the BIS web site. The new agreement will come into force by the end of 2006 in those institutions that adopt the standard and basic IRB methods of measuring their credit risk, or by the end of 2007 in those institutions that use advanced methods to measure credit risk or OR.

2 The main international forum for banking supervisors. Its primary objective is the improvement and integration of supervising operations worldwide. Even though it has no legal authority, its recommendations are generally accepted at an international level, given their high technical quality and the support the forum obtains from prior discussion with the interested parties.

3 To whom we would like to express our gratitude for their collaboration, for without their participation this research would not have been successfully completed.

4 For example, the Operational Risk Exchange Association (ORX), which was founded in 2002. It initially regrouped 12 leading firms of international reputation. It started operations in 2003 and anonymously facilitates exchange of data among its members, who can adopt, for in-house purposes, convenient definitions and methodologies in order to record their in-house loss. They must in turn send the ORX data according to the definitions and regulations of the consortium every four months, as published in the Web site in February 2004.

5 This standard, jointly issued by Standards Australia and Standards New Zealand, is considered as a possible starting point for future international standards (see Frost *et al*, p 26).

6 The International Swap and Dealers Association was created in 1985. Everything related to this activity can be found in the web site: www.isda.org

7 The Financial Risk Management (FRM) unit within the Global Risk Management Solutions (GRMS) division focuses on the financial sector.

8 The average profile of the participating institutions is that of an organisation with an average number of 1,125 offices and 8,330 employees. They were selected according to their leadership in the sector and their special concern for the new context defined in the draft Accord published by the Basel Committee in January 2001 (see PwC, 2002, p 6).

9 See Risk Management Association (2003), where 82% of the institutions surveyed declared use of the Basel definition.

10 URL: www.orx.org

## REFERENCES

**Basel Committee on Banking Supervision,** 2002a, "The Quantitative Impact Study for Operational Risk: Overview of Individual Loss Data and Lessons Learned", BIS, January.

**Basel Committee on Banking Supervision,** 2002b, "Operational Risk Data Collection Exercise", BIS, June.

**Basel Committee on Banking Supervision,** 2003, "The 2002 Loss Data Collection Exercise for Operational Risk: Summary of the Data Collected", BIS, March.

**British Bankers Association, PwC, International Swaps and Derivatives Association and Robert Morris Associates,** 1999, "Operational Risk: the Next Frontier", United States.

**Fernández, L. A.,** 2003a, "Control del riesgo operacional en las entidades financieras: análisis conceptual y contrastación empírica desde la perspectiva de los derivados", doctoral thesis.

**Fernández, L. A.,** 2003b, "Análisis conceptual del riesgo operacional desde la perspectiva de los derivados", Research Final Report, Fundación Marcelino Botin.

**Fernández, L. A.,** 2004, "Avances en el riesgo operacional en las entidades financieras", Research Final Report, Fundación Marcelino Botin.

**Fernández, L. A. and F. J. Martínez Garcia,** 2006, "El Riesgo Operacional en las Entidades Financieras: Una Aproximación Empírica a las Cajas de Ahorro Españolas", Revista Española de Financiación y Contabilidad, Forthcoming.

**FitchRatings,** 2004a, "The Oldest Tale But the Newest Story: Operational Risk and the Evolution of its Measurement Under Basel II", special report, January.

**FitchRatings,** 2004b, "Operational Risk Management & Basel II Implementation: Survey Results", special report, April.

**Frost, C., D. Allen, J. Porter, and P. Bloodworth,** 2001, Operational Risk and Resilience, Understanding and Minimising Operational Risk to Secure Shareholder Value, Butterworth Heinemann, Oxford.

**Hübner, R., M. Laycock, F. Peemöller,** 2001, "Managing Operational Risk", in *Advances in Operational Risk: Firm-wide issues for financial institutions* (London: Risks Books).

**ORX,** 2004, "ORX Reporting Standards", ORX, February.

**Power, M.,** 2005, "The Invention of Operational Risk", Review of International Political Economy, **12(4)**, October, pp 577–99.

**PricewaterhouseCoopers,** 2002, "Gestión del riesgo operacional en las entidades financieras españolas", Report.

**Risk Management Association,** 2003, "Progress in Operational Risk Management in the US Banking Industry", October.

**SAS,** 2004, "Operational Risk Management in the Financial Services Industry", Conducted by SAS and *Risk* Magazine.

# Index